T0300791

talkin'
greenwich
village

Also by David Browne

Crosby, Stills, Nash and Young: The Wild, Definitive Saga of Rock's Greatest Supergroup

So Many Roads: The Life and Times of the Grateful Dead

Fire and Rain: The Beatles, Simon & Garfunkel, James Taylor, CSNY, and the Lost Story of 1970

Dream Brother: The Lives and Music of Jeff and Tim Buckley

Goodbye 20th Century: A Biography of Sonic Youth

Amped: How Big Air, Big Dollars, and a New Generation Took Sports to the Extreme

The Spirit of '76: From Politics to Technology, the Year America Went Rock & Roll

Jeff Buckley: His Own Voice (coedited with Mary Guibert)

talkin' greenwich village

The Heady Rise and Slow Fall of America's Bohemian Music Capital

DAVID BROWNE

Hachette
BOOKS

New York

Hachette Books
Hachette Book Group
1290 Avenue of the Americas
New York, NY 10104
HachetteBooks.com
Twitter.com/HachetteBooks
Instagram.com/HachetteBooks

First Edition: September 2024

Published by Hachette Books, an imprint of Hachette Book Group, Inc. The Hachette Books name and logo is a trademark of the Hachette Book Group.

The Hachette Speakers Bureau provides a wide range of authors for speaking events. To find out more, go to hachettespeakersbureau.com or email HachetteSpeakers@hbgusa.com.

Books by Hachette Books may be purchased in bulk for business, educational, or promotional use. For information, please contact your local bookseller or Hachette Book Group Special Markets Department at: special.markets@hbgusa.com.

The publisher is not responsible for websites (or their content) that are not owned by the publisher.

Print book interior design by Amy Quinn

Library of Congress Control Number: 2024940402

ISBNs: 9780306827631 (hardcover); 9780306827655 (ebook)

Printed in Canada

MRQ

Printing 1, 2024

To anyone who's ever entered one of the clubs in this book,
walked onto its stage, tuned up, and changed lives

contents

introduction
Come Gather 'Round

To draw on music terminology, this book emerged from an intro and a coda. Its genesis was the fall of 1978, when I arrived in Greenwich Village to start my freshman year at New York University. Growing up in northern New Jersey, in a house with a view of the Manhattan skyline some twenty-five miles away, it was impossible not to think about the city. Bus rides into New York, to attend a concert at Radio City Music Hall or Carnegie Hall or see a movie that hadn't made it to the suburbs or hunt down the plethora of used-record stores, only reinforced its allure. Even as we read about the city's downward economic spiral, it still felt like the place to be, alive with arts and thrills.

Settling into my college dorm—on East Tenth Street and Broadway, down the block from the renovated Hotel Albert, a onetime way station for musicians—I sensed that the heyday of the Village music world had peaked. The giants from the previous decade were rarely if ever listed in the *Village Voice* club ads, and some had even passed away.

But starting on my first night in the city—which included a pilgrimage to the area's leading and most eclectic venue, the Bottom Line—music clearly remained woven into the fabric of the neighborhood, even if the material was frayed. Other landmark clubs I'd heard about, like Folk City and the Village Vanguard, were still open for business and presenting acts whose names were familiar to me. One could easily spend infinite hours, as I did, flipping through bins of used and rare vinyl in the seemingly countless record stores south of Fourteenth Street. There I found copies of out-of-print LPs by Phil Ochs, Tim Hardin, the Blues Project, and other Village-connected legends I'd read about but rarely heard, even on the FM radio of the time. My roommates and I could walk along Bleecker Street and hear music drifting out of the Bitter End, the Village Gate, or the recently opened Kenny's Castaways. Each week's edition of the *Voice* devoted page after page to ads for those and other venues. NYU offered classes in folk music and guitar, both of which I took. The newsstands that seemed to inhabit every street corner had racks stuffed with magazines devoted entirely to music, even to specific genres.

In the fall of 1981, as part of my journalism degree, I enrolled in a class on magazine writing. Pitching my professor on a story about an apparent folk revival in the Village, I found myself embedded in the scene as much as an outsider could have been. That season, a new club, Speak Easy, had opened in the back of a falafel restaurant on MacDougal Street. Drifting between that space and the long-standing, Bob Dylan–associated Folk City around the corner, I heard what amounted to the next generation of songwriters by way of early performances by Shawn Colvin, Suzanne Vega, and others. To my shock and awe, I found myself standing next to or even talking with new and vintage musicians and hearing tales of Ochs, Hardin, Odetta, and, of course, Dylan, still its most famous graduate. At Folk City or Speak Easy, I would glance at the bar and see Dave Van Ronk, Danny Kalb, or a relative newcomer like Steve Forbert hanging out there. Sometimes I summoned up a degree of courage to speak with one of them, but I was just as often intimidated. I observed a few sessions of a songwriters' workshop, the Songwriters Exchange, at the Cornelia Street Café and caught a weekend afternoon set at the Village Vanguard. Sixties legends like Tom Paxton and Eric Andersen would periodically return to town and play one of those clubs, and I was fortunate to catch some of those as well.

As I began my career as a music journalist, I continued to pop into all those clubs over the decades that followed, and I remained in the Village for almost twenty years. Cut to many, many years later, shortly before the coronavirus made the Village, and nearly every other place, shut down temporarily. When I was working on a profile of Ramblin' Jack Elliott for *Rolling Stone* in the summer of 2019, he and I wandered the streets he still knew well, even as he approached the age of ninety. Strolling along MacDougal Street, he paused and reminded me that a particular set of stairs led to what was once the Gaslight Cafe. As we entered what was now one of the stylish wine bars and restaurants in the area, Elliott started talking up the maître d' about the night Johnny Cash stopped by and also vividly recalled its long-ago wall decor. The employee had no idea what Elliott was talking about, and we soon left. A few months later, I made my way to what used to be the Village Gate and was now another music venue, Le Poisson Rouge. But as I zigzagged my way through streets once teeming with live-music venues, all I found were banks, drugstore chains, head shops, and more upscale restaurants.

Of the landmark venues that had embodied the musical spirit of the neighborhood, the Village Vanguard, the Bitter End, and the Cafe Wha? were still alive and holding down the musical fort (and, as of this writing, still are). The space once home to Village Gate has continued as a live-music venue, LPR (now short for Le Poisson Rouge). In late 2023 the Cafe Wha?, under new management, presented a historically minded tribute to Dylan, Van Ronk, and Joni Mitchell to salute an era gone by.

In recent years the scene has also been immortalized in other media. Ethan and Joel Coen's *Inside Llewyn Davis* used Van Ronk's posthumous memoir, *The Mayor of MacDougal Street*, written with Elijah Wald, as its starting point and even integrated artwork from his apartment in one of its sets. It wasn't remotely a strict biopic and infuriated many who knew Van Ronk, who saw the film as too bleak and depressing. But it drew attention to that era, especially among those born decades later. As much of a fairy tale as it could be, *The Marvelous Mrs. Maisel* also re-created the Gaslight Cafe, a historic gathering spot and workplace, and reminded at least some who watched the series that that venue had existed in the first place.

Still, my return trips to the neighborhood only reinforced the sense of a music community that was, at best, on life support. The action was now in

Brooklyn or other parts of town. What happened? Why had such a vibrant
and vital music center been reduced to this? The time to tell that story had
arrived, at least for me.

First, a few explanations. Adhering to age-old maps of the city, I limited this
book to the area from Fourth Avenue to the Hudson River, east to west, and
Fourteenth Street to Houston Street, north to south. One could quibble about
such designations: does Greenwich Village extend to Canal Street, as designated by Local Community Board 2? For my purposes, I stuck with the heart
of the Village. Hence you won't find much here about the East Village scene
and particularly CBGB, which has been chronicled in many other books. The
West Village was a saga all its own.

As I was pulling together a time line of music-related events in the Village
dating back more than a century, the year 1957 announced itself as a pivotal
moment when the scene as we knew it began to coalesce. It also became apparent that it all began to crumble in the mid-eighties, starting with the shuttering of Folk City. One of the few legends who was there at the beginning and
stayed right through to the bitter end, no club-reference pun intended, was Dave
Van Ronk, that bear-like titan of Village vernacular music. As I was reminded
during my research, his many guitar students and protégés included Maggie and
Terre Roche of the Roches and Danny Kalb and Steve Katz of the Blues Project.
Each act embodied a particular period in Village music history: Van Ronk its
early, formative days; the Blues Project the amplified Village of the mid-sixties,
when many musicians electrified a once largely acoustic scene; and the Roches
(with their sister Suzzy later) the renewed jolt in the scene the following decade.
A million musicians came in and out of the Village, or so it seemed, but the interconnected stories of Van Ronk, the Blues Project, and the Roches provided the
narrative thread I sought. It would be impossible to include every musician who
played there, and an entire book could be devoted to each genre and era that
made its way in and out of the Village over the decades. My goal was to trace the
arc of the larger story and give the reader a sense of the flavor of each period, with
venues, club owners, and accompanying interconnected musicians to match.

Those talents, their peers, and the many who preceded and came after were connected in other ways. Starting with its storied contributions to literature, Greenwich Village clearly attracted bohemians, misfits, and outsiders. In modern parlance, it was a safe space for those who didn't fit in elsewhere or sought to reinvent themselves. It also seemed to attract those who, like the neighborhood itself, stuck with their convictions, refused to be compromised, and would only begrudgingly consider the marketplace beyond the Village. Even when they did, the results could be unnatural or unsatisfying. The collapse of the Village music world, that oasis of nonconformity, also spoke to the rise and fall of bohemia itself around the country—its many venues now symbolically occupied by banks or chain drugstores.

During my many reporting and research trips to the neighborhood—to see live music, to unearth documents in libraries and in private collections, to meet with local icons in the apartments in which they still lived—the mythic Village still announced itself. I saw Christine Lavin and David Massengill at the Bitter End (part of the annual, multi-arts Village Trip festival), guitarists John Scofield at the Blue Note and Kurt Rosenwinkel at the Village Vanguard, and an afternoon jam at Smalls, the basement jazz club that was a later and vibrant addition to the area. I saw the aftermath of a post-pandemic rave in Washington Square Park that, like the infamous 1961 "beatnik riot," involved ugly skirmishes with police. I could still observe singers or musicians in the park, sometimes even near the fountain that had once helped birth the scene. All were welcome reminders that the Village as we'd known it still hovered—and with any luck, could possibly rise up in song once more.

talkin'
greenwich
village

Chapter 1
the rising sun
1957

The night the new kid showed up, David Amram thought he'd already met his share of Greenwich Village characters and eccentrics. Born in Pennsylvania, a trumpet player who'd switched to the more mellifluous French horn, Amram had performed in army bands before moving to Manhattan in 1955. There, the curious and loquacious musician found a neighborhood equally taken with Beat poets and writers. By the first month of 1957, he'd left his apartment on the Lower East Side and moved into a fifth-floor walkup on Christopher Street, which put him squarely in the West Village and the new center of the action downtown.

That year, twenty-seven million people owned homes across the country—more than twice as many as a decade before, and many in newly created suburbs. For them, the so-called postwar American Dream was a fantasy come true. But Amram, along with a mounting number of musicians who began migrating to New York City, had a different type of dream in mind. Following on the heels of writers and painters, they longed for a world where they could live idiosyncratic, artistic lives and reject the mounting conformity around them. And nothing embodied that appeal more than Greenwich Village.

Since the beginning of the century, jazz had been among the soundtracks of the area that extended from the Hudson River to Broadway (or close to it) going west to east, and from Fourteenth Street to Houston Street north to

1

south. Many of those Village bars and nightspots were gone or sported new names, but as Amram learned as he began poking his head into any club or hole-in-the-wall that welcomed the music, the options again seemed plentiful. At 15 Barrow Street, just off Sixth Avenue, a narrow staircase took him down into Cafe Bohemia, a former strip club about the size of a suburban rec room. As legend had it, Charlie Parker had run up a thirty-dollar tab at the bar and offered to play there to work off his debt. He didn't show, but a sign announcing his appearance led other bop players to show up. Before long, Cafe Bohemia, around the bend from the triangle-shaped Sheridan Square, was reborn as a jazz club, the likes of Charles Mingus and Miles Davis occupying its small, slightly elevated stage.

As Amram recalled, the regulars were "a total spectrum of American society—street people, college professors, weirdos." Still, he knew he'd found something of a home when, walking past the club another night, he came upon John Coltrane sitting on the sidewalk, wolfing down a piece of berry pie. Seeing the French horn tucked under Amram's arm, Coltrane launched into a spellbinding riff on black holes in the universe, ancient Egypt, and the pyramids. Amram also met the formidable Mingus, a small mountain of a man known both for his volcanic bass playing and equally explosive personality. Sitting in with him one evening, Amram felt a sharp jab to his ribs. "Listen to the bass, motherfucker!" Mingus barked. Another night, Amram heard, "No more than two choruses, motherfucker!" After Mingus had been needling him far too much another evening, Amram summoned up the courage to confront him: "You can't treat me like this. Man, I'll see you outside!" Mingus was so taken aback that he put his arm around Amram and bought him a drink. "If I had said, 'I love playing with you,' he would have hit me in the mouth," Amram said. "He was much more comfortable being in that [confrontational] kind of situation."

Those were just a few of the lessons Amram learned at the Cafe Bohemia and its environs. The Village was, in his view, "a gigantic 12-step program of people considered total losers and failures and disgraces because they were pursuing something unrealistic and more or less deemed worthless by society. But they were doing it with a vengeance."

Cafe Bohemia itself barely held more than fifty customers, but as Mingus told Amram, every night for him was akin to playing Carnegie Hall. "Man, if everyone's stoned or looking to score dope or wants to borrow money from you," Mingus told him, "just find one person who's listening and then play for them all night." To Amram, such encounters made clear how the Village performance spaces differed from the ritzier jazz spots uptown: a freedom to make mistakes, to learn and stretch out without fear of losing an audience or botching a possible record deal. He also felt that the impermanence of Village jazz—the way it was never the same twice and had its own spirit and values— held a magical allure for audiences and musicians alike.

The first month of 1957, Amram, with his French horn and a small combo, started an eleven-week residency at the Five Spot, the increasingly fashionable jazz bar on the eastern border of Greenwich Village, just off Third Avenue in Cooper Square. The club had once been the Bowery Cafe, the last stop of the night for winos and the working class. In 1946, after they'd returned home from serving in World War II, brothers Joe and Iggy Termini had inherited the space from their father, renaming it the No. 5 bar after its address, 5 Cooper Square. Unexpectedly, urban planning, normally never a friend to music venues in Manhattan, came to the bar's rescue. When the city began tearing down the Third Avenue overhead El train in the summer of 1955, the neighborhood grew airier, sunnier, and more appealing to those who wouldn't normally venture into it. As the *Daily News* described it, "Gone are the shadows that covered the dingy flats tracing some of their soot to the steam locomotives that ran above the street."

Eager to remake the place, the Terminis hired a jazz quartet that had caught the attention of painter Herman Cherry, who lived across the street and who began bringing in his artist friends. The renamed Five Spot wasn't as posh as uptown jazz joints or Harlem's Cotton Club: sawdust covered the floors, and musicians attempting to jam on its stage could smell urine from the restrooms on the other side of the wall. Its capacity was limited to 75 people. But the beer was 75 cents a bottle, the chicken in a basket only $1.75, and the Terminis were open to the progressive jazz starting to bust out around them. Cherry adorned the walls with his art and flyers and with posters for jazz shows around town, and it wasn't long before anyone who wedged into the Five Spot could spy Jack Kerouac, Frank O'Hara, or Willem de Kooning at one of its little wooden tables. Pianist Cecil Taylor became the first jazz name to play there; Thelonious Monk would be booked later in the summer.

Even in that context of artistic dissidents, Amram didn't fully know what to make of the six-foot-two twenty-year-old who approached him one night. Although he still bore hints of baby fat on his face, Dave Van Ronk already had the rumpled magnetism of a hardened sailor, down to his grainy voice and the strands of dark hair that would fall over his face. During a break, Van Ronk approached Amram: "French horn—I don't hear that much in jazz," he said. Amram then listened as the kid launched into a discourse on German composer Richard Wagner's complicated politics, followed by an analysis of Aleksandr Kerensky, the socialist revolutionary who'd been cast aside and denigrated after the Bolshevik revolution. "I don't think he got credit for his ideals," Amram agreed, but Van Ronk continued. "His ideals are what sank him!" When Van Ronk went on at length about Leon Trotsky, Amram received a crash course on the Russian Revolution.

Amram didn't know it at the time, but as with so many musicians who gravitated to the area, Van Ronk had a troubled backstory and a yearning to leave it all behind. His parents, Charles Van Ronk and Grace Alice Ritz, had broken up not long after the birth of their son David Kenneth Ritz Van Ronk in June 1936. Van Ronk would never meet his birth father and never expressed any interest in doing so. He and his mother wound up in Richmond Hill, Queens, a neighborhood of, he would say, "working stiffs" and "paralyzing boredom." At fifteen he was essentially kicked out of school by a principal who called him "a filthy ineducable little beast," a phrase he would remember for decades. A stab at what he called "continuing education" didn't last too long. Soon after, he was arrested for juvenile delinquency and petit larceny.

Van Ronk's mother had pushed him into piano lessons, which gave way to ukulele. Van Ronk first heard "St. James Infirmary," already recorded by Louis Armstrong, Artie Shaw, Jimmie Rodgers, and Cab Calloway, while listening to a jazz band in the early fifties, and it became one of the earliest, if not *the* first, blues songs he would learn on the ukulele. Soon Van Ronk started singing with a local vocal group. He'd been introduced to jazz by way of radio and the piano-playing grandmother who helped raise him. He'd also learned about blues thanks to economics: during a visit to Chelsea's renowned Jazz Record Center in search of a disc by Armstrong's Hot Five, he'd instead found a less expensive record by Blind Lemon Jefferson. "If the Hot Five cost a dollar and a half and the Blind Lemon Jefferson cost 35 cents," he recalled in his posthumously published memoir, "if you're a 14-year-old kid, what are you going to do?" In grade school he learned to play guitar, taking lessons from a local jazz guitar player and worshipping Charlie Christian, the Black swing and jazz guitarist. Van Ronk later told his friend Christine Lavin that he would tape sheet music to the ceiling of his bedroom and practice while lying in bed.

Van Ronk also learned tenor banjo, considered a more acceptable instrument for jazz at the time, and became enamored of trad jazz, which harked back to the genre's New Orleans roots in the early twentieth century. For a moment he imagined he had a career playing that music and joined a few combos in and around the city while working at a printing company in downtown Manhattan; he also toiled as a messenger for the Commercial Bank and Trust. Another rising genre at the time held little appeal. "God, I hated folk music when I was a kid," he said onstage later in life. "I wanted to play jazz in the worst way. And I did." But jazz gigs didn't translate at the time to earning a decent living, and he would long joke that he went into playing jazz weighing 240 pounds and was down to 170 by the time he gave up on it as his main focus.

Van Ronk would later place his first visit to the Village at around 1951. The area wasn't as romantic as he'd envisioned: exiting the train, he was surprised, he wrote, to see that it looked "just like fucking Brooklyn," all apartment buildings and narrow streets. He still needed income, and the merchant marine, the organization of civilian seamen that helped transport goods by sea in and out of the States (and would serve as a second line of defense in wartime), became a solution. On January 22, 1957, just before the start of Amram's Five Spot shows, Van Ronk had his fingerprints registered with the merchant marine. Before he shipped out, he yearned to hear jazz and dropped by the Five Spot. As he would later write, he knew the venue well; he lived in an apartment across the street with friends, and they would often listen to musicians warm up in the afternoon and snap up the players' leftover joints in the phone booth inside.

That night he introduced himself, Van Ronk told Amram he remained invested in jazz but that he'd become discouraged by the amount of technique involved in mastering it. Despite his misgivings about folk, he'd begun to realize it would be comparatively easy to master. Thanks to the *Anthology of American Folk Music*, an assortment of reissued 78s by collector Harry Smith released in 1952, Van Ronk had heard recordings by Dock Boggs, Mississippi John Hurt, and other mysterious denizens of a world of American music largely unknown to him and his friends. The music was raw and rambunctious, eerie and spooky, and it couldn't help but pull him in.

Van Ronk realized that acoustic music like folk wasn't considered as sophisticated as jazz. "You may not like *my* music," he told Amram. Jazz had its place, he continued, but folk was "different." Both the songs and stories in folk, and the music's place in American history, spoke to him. It may have also better suited his range. His grandmother sang Irish ballads with a voice so loud that, he later wrote, she "drove the neighbors nuts." Van Ronk's delivery, a scratchy and primal bark that also had a sweet, lilting side to it, was more at home in folk than in jazz.

Amram came away from the encounter thinking of Van Ronk as "a great guru philosopher, crazy and wonderful." But Van Ronk wouldn't be able to take in much more of Amram's residency. On March 31, the day after Amram's last show, Van Ronk would be officially endorsed for service as a merchant mariner, toiling as a seaman, mess-hall worker, and "wiper," a worker who cleaned the components of a ship engine; his first tour of duty was scheduled to start April 11. By the time he returned in mid-summer, the Village would be an even more welcoming place for him, his friends, and their music. A new era was on their horizon, and everything from the number of musicians on the scene to the authorities and landlords keeping an eye on it all would soon ramp up.

Music and Greenwich Village had been inseparable for decades, but as Max Gordon sensed early on, the relationship wasn't always congenial or supportive. Gordon wasn't the first entrepreneur to open a club in the Village, but he was among the earliest to find himself face-to-face with its hurdles. An elfin-looking man born in Lithuania but raised in Portland, Oregon, Gordon had opened the first incarnation of what he called the Village Vanguard on Charles Street in early 1934. But police hassles, local laws, and the fact that the space contained only one restroom soon drove him to find a new home for his business. Looking elsewhere, he came across an oddly shaped room not far away: a basement with a wide bandstand area that narrowed as it moved toward the bar in the back.

True to its neighborhood and its reputation for attracting political and cultural iconoclasts, the space had its own idiosyncratic origin story. To serve the city's west side, a new subway line had been constructed in the 1920s. Because it would snake through the Village, a slew of buildings were torn down or sliced in half to make room for tunnels and stations. As a result, one of those structures, at 178 Seventh Avenue South, now resembled a pie cutter; Gordon soon learned why its previous incarnation—a speakeasy, the name for burrowed-away joints and spaces illegally selling alcohol—had been called the Golden Triangle. Retaining the Village Vanguard name, he rented the space— with a cash infusion from someone he later called a "shylock who liked the idea of a club because he thought he could pick up women there"—and moved whatever was inside the first space to the new one. As he was preparing for its grand opening on February 22, 1935, a cop walked in, saw that Gordon was using beer cases for seats, and asked, ominously, if he was selling alcohol, which required a liquor license. "Let me sell the beer," Gordon replied. "Then I'll have the money to pay for a license." He was off the hook, at least for a while.

Since its inception, Greenwich Village had functioned as both sanctuary and battleground. Galleries, small presses, and enough writers with enough works to line the shelves of a small library were drawn to its narrow, crooked, often confusing streets and ambience. At various points, Mark Twain, Edgar Allan Poe, Edith Wharton, O. Henry, and Henry James had called the Village their home; Herman Melville worked at the US Customs Office there. Willa Cather, Eugene

O'Neill, Theodore Dreiser, and Stephen Crane all bunked at one time or another at the so-called House of Genius on Washington Square South. Even the geography of the area played into that image: as historian and onetime *Village Voice* editor-in-chief Ross Wetzsteon would later write, the sheer bewildering layout of the Village—especially the new grid laid out in 1811 that overlapped with the meandering streets of the Village—had "metaphoric resonance as well: rejecting orderliness, refusing conformity, repelling the grid."

The ethnic groups and factions that came in and out of the area had periods of cooperation and intermingling. They could also clash, as when the Lenape indigenous people who had called it home eventually battled with Dutch settlers in the middle of the seventeenth century. In time, the Village's developing music community would prove to be equally turbulent, if not as violent. Although it would be difficult to determine the first or earliest venues in Greenwich Village, music clubs began appearing in the early twentieth century. In 1919, weeks after the US Senate overrode President Woodrow Wilson's veto of the Volstead Act, which prohibited the sale of alcohol, police raided the Greenwich Village Inn, a speakeasy on Sheridan Square. The spot was managed by Bernard "Barney" Gallant, a restaurateur and member of the New York Liberal Club, a prominent debate and discussion group. Gallant became a local hero when six staff members at the inn were arrested for selling hard liquor to undercover police; to spare his staff, Gallant himself spent several weeks in the Tombs, the city's notorious jail.

That notoriety extended to the Greenwich Village Inn Orchestra, such a sensation that an uptown radio station ran wires down to the club to broadcast its melodies on the air. Thomas Edison's phonograph company soon issued Greenwich Village Inn Orchestra recordings, such as the peppy foxtrots "Somebody's Crazy About You" and "Keep on Dancing." Meanwhile, customers at nearby bistros might have heard the district satirized in song by Bobby (or Robert) Edwards, the so-called "Bard of Bohemia" who'd graduated from Harvard and moved to the Village in 1904. In his lengthy ballad "The Greenwich Village Epic," he eagerly skewered the area as "the field for culture's tillage / There they have artistic ravings / Tea and other awful cravings."

In the middle of Prohibition, the cocktail of the Jazz Age, speakeasies, illegal alcohol, public dancing, and white and Black crowds commingled in bars and clubs was too much for the wealthier and more politically connected part of New York eager to control that type of conduct. When it was first put into effect on January 1, 1927, Local Law 12, otherwise known as the "Cabaret Law," was a reaction to illegal bars and sought to put constraints on what it called a "public dance hall" or a "cabaret." The latter was defined as "any room, place, or space within the city where any musical entertainment, singing, dancing, etc., is permitted as part of the restaurant business or the business of selling food or drink." To obtain a cabaret license, which cost $50 a year, owners had to pass through a gauntlet of inspections from the building, licensing, and health departments, and businesses would have to close between 3 a.m. and 8 a.m. (Decades later, it would be alleged that the interracial dancing in clubs, especially in Harlem, may have also given rise to the law.) When the law was amended in 1931, another layer of bureaucracy was included: the issuing of licenses was transferred to the police commissioner, who was also tasked with inspecting each venue.

Even before he allowed his first customers into the Village Vanguard, Gordon learned how the new law worked. After he'd graduated from Portland's Reed College in 1924, Gordon moved to New York to attend Columbia Law School but was stranded in the city without a job after he decided not to pursue a law career. Encouraged by a friend, he borrowed some money and opened a coffeehouse, the Village Fair, on Sullivan Street, in 1932. There he hosted poets and writers and learned firsthand about the tricky and sticky relationship between the neighborhood and the police, even during the waning days of Prohibition. Since clubs weren't allowed to sell booze, Gordon, as he later wrote, would always see "a guy in a doorway hanging outside Village joints" who could supply a bottle of some libation, which could then be taken inside. Gordon ended up under arrest after an undercover cop convinced a waitress to buy some alcohol, then bring his bottle of booze *to* him while he was inside the Village Fair. The charges against Gordon were eventually dismissed, but it was too late to salvage his business.

As a columnist of the time put it, Gordon's new Village Vanguard on Seventh Avenue South lay "at the foot of a gloomy flight of stairs," but the murk lifted once customers looked around. Its light-blue walls were festooned with murals depicting horses playing a piano and women floating through space, and the entertainment Gordon served up was equally lively. Early on, poets, including Harry Kemp and Maxwell Bodenheim, dominated the lineups. By 1937, Walter Winchell, the syndicated columnist, snarkily commented that Saturday nights at the Vanguard were filled with "'bohemians' from Brooklyn and the Bronx squinting through the soupy smoke."

Reflecting the Village's nonconformist inclinations, the Vanguard also became headquarters for some of the city's most insubordinate art. At the end of the thirties, the Revuers, a comedy posse that included Judy Holliday and Adolph Green, began working up satirical songs and skits. As with its parody of the upscale *Cue* magazine and its listings, the sketches often took aim at the uptown crowd. Also at the Vanguard, a group that called itself the Calypso Singers mocked Wendell Willkie, the presidential candidate who'd switched from the Democratic Party to the Republican (he paid "an income tax that's not too alarming," they sang). Meanwhile, their version of "Netty Netty," a naughty slice of calypso meets swing, included bedroom-frolic lyrics that, Winchell wrote, "will make you blush."

Folk music also settled into the Vanguard, which booked Lead Belly, the stately, white-haired folk and blues singer who had served time in prison and was discovered by folklorist John Lomax and his son Alan during a visit to one of those prisons. During World War II, soldiers on leave were spotted at the club listening intently to Richard Dyer-Bennet, a British-born, California-raised singer and guitarist who performed in a suit and bow tie. His pristine, starchy style treated folk as if it were classical music, but the traditional songs he'd collected, ones about returning soldiers and dead knights, made him one of the Vanguard's regular bookings. The South Carolina–born Josh White was a quadruple threat as a singer, guitarist, actor, and occasional bandleader. Crashing through racial barriers, White became a genuine crossover star of his time, starring on Broadway, selling a million copies of "One Meatball," and appearing occasionally at the Vanguard (where he would appear on the same bill as Lead Belly).

In the audience at one of White's shows in 1949 was Elliott Adnopoz, a Brooklyn kid who would eventually be better known as Ramblin' Jack Elliott. As Elliott and his friend Peter LaFarge, a cowboy singer and balladeer, sat a few rows back from the stage, LaFarge chuckled at something White said. White recognized the voice and invited them both backstage, where Elliott caught sight of a bottle of Cutty Sark whiskey and "three beautiful blonde women," he recalled. "Never seen anything like it. And he played beautifully." The Vanguard was so crowded for White's sets that Gordon once had to haul out beer cases for added seating. In 1951 Harry Belafonte made his public transition from jazz to folksinger, singing work songs at the Vanguard.

Just a few years after it opened, the Vanguard had plucky company. A short walk down Seventh Avenue South and then east on Sheridan Square, Cafe Society was the brainchild of Barney Josephson, a shoe salesman of Latvian descent then living in Trenton, New Jersey. After a trip into the city, Josephson became obsessed with the idea of opening a club there and found his own basement, this one at Two Sheridan Square. At one time a speakeasy, the space had been vacant for a number of years. Playing off the Depression era in which the country was mired in the late thirties, Josephson gave his club both an ironic name and setting. To gently satirize doormen at upscale apartment buildings, club greeters wore gloves with the fingertips torn off, and the walls were decorated with pointed drawings of the obscenely wealthy (like an old, balding rich man leering at a young blonde, his arm around her). Behind the bar was a mural of animals, including an elephant nursing a hangover with an ice pack on its head. Large pillars obscured some of the views, particularly from the back, but Cafe Society still felt, in the words of the club's motto, like "The Wrong Place for the Right People."

Josephson made it clear who the right people were. As a young man, he'd picketed a Jim Crow theater in New Jersey and seen Duke Ellington play the Cotton Club. As one report at the time described it, he wanted a home for "reputable Negro artists," and Cafe Society would be that place—less stuffy and more racially integrated than the fancier joints. Josephson also insisted that Black entertainers wear suits and banned references to "crap shooting" and other pastimes. The move struck some as smoothing down Black culture, but to Josephson, changes like those would dignify the performers even more.

When Cafe Society opened in January 1939, Josephson had a liquor license but not a cabaret one, and construction was so rushed that he was forced to resort to a nearby hot-dog stand to feed customers. But from the start, the club was a sensation. Producer and record scout John Hammond, a friend of Josephson's, suggested he hire Billie Holiday as one of its first acts, and it was there, that same year, that Holiday debuted "Strange Fruit," an eerie, almost cinematic song written by Abel Meeropol, a Jewish schoolteacher from the Bronx who was inspired by a magazine photo of a southern lynching. Reports would vary regarding how much Holiday initially liked the song, but at Cafe Society it became one of the first and most prominent written-about performances in the Village. The song would be saved until the end of her set, at which point the wait staff would ask customers to neither eat nor drink in order to ensure as much quiet as possible. Some in the crowd, who simply wanted entertainment as opposed to a chilling social commentary, walked out. Holiday would end up singing at the club for eight months straight, and more importantly the Village began developing a reputation for music as provocative as the literature that had preceded it.

Although little else offered up at Cafe Society downtown would match "Strange Fruit" in terms of headlines, Josephson was relentless in pursuing a diverse lineup and crowd. The club hosted a rare racially mixed band in 1939. Pianists Pete Johnson, Meade Lux Lewis, and Albert Ammons made it a destination to hear New York boogie-woogie, the caffeinated form of blues piano that had started in Texas earlier in the century before migrating north to cities like St. Louis and Chicago. When writer Damon Runyon took young friends down to see those pianists at Cafe Society in 1939, he wrote that they "almost went into convulsions when the music started." Ivan Black, a publicist who worked to ensure that the club received good press, went into overdrive, feeding an item to a gossip column about a "Cafe Society Cocktail" made with rum and lime.

In October 1940, Josephson opened an uptown sibling of Cafe Society on East Fifty-Eighth Street, but the downtown joint continued to take artistic risks. A folk and blues scene, which was also taking hold at the Vanguard, filtered over to Cafe Society, which booked Josh White, Sonny Terry, and Susan Reed, an eighteen-year-old redhead who crooned folk songs. As on Easter Sunday in 1941, where else would one go in New York City to see the Golden

Gate Quartet singing "John the Revelator" and pianist Art Tatum playing composer Jules Massenet's *Élégie*? The landmark "From Spirituals to Swing" concert at Carnegie Hall in 1938, produced by Hammond, traced the history of Black music for both white and Black audiences. For its part in the series, the Cafe Society hosted its own events of the same name, one in 1940 bringing together—for $1.50 a ticket—Holiday, Tatum, Lewis, and Sister Rosetta Tharpe, the sexually fluid Black singer and guitar player who propelled gospel music into the mainstream.

Not far away, first in a loft in the East Village and later at 130 West Tenth Street, a three-story brownstone, what amounted to a Village folk-music commune was hatched. The Almanac Singers, a loose-knit group centered around Pete Seeger, Lee Hays, and Millard Lampell, had already been around for a few years, singing antiwar and pro-labor songs. Soon after their friend Woody Guthrie joined up with them in the middle of 1941, the group had moved to the Tenth Street digs, dubbed "Almanac House," where they continued the Sunday-afternoon music-making jams that had started in previous dwellings. If visitors timed it well, they'd encounter Lead Belly, White, or Dyer-Bennet sitting. With Guthrie part of the group, the Almanac Singers helped pay their rent with hootenannies in the basement.

Left-centric and sympathetic to Communism, the Almanac Singers had already recorded two albums before Guthrie joined up, and they were soon featured on radio shows and courted by agents. But their views made them a natural target for the FBI, which had already begun monitoring them. The press, once on the group's side, began turning on them, calling them "the favorite balladeers of the Communists." Thanks to the fragile relationships within the group—Seeger as the hardworking organizer, Hays as the alcohol-inclined wild card and grump—the Almanacs already had a nitroglycerin quality to them, and they crumbled in the early forties.

The spirit of the Almanac Singers carried on, albeit without Guthrie. Seeger started what looked to be a promising career of his own, but before long he was singing with Hays, Ronnie Gilbert, and Fred Hellerman. By 1948, the group, eventually called the Weavers, had already played publicly before Max Gordon hired them at the Village Vanguard starting in the last month of 1949. With their penchant for formal wear and a repertoire that included more than a few apolitical songs, like Lead Belly's lullaby "Goodnight, Irene," the Weavers subversively blended folk, traditional songs from around the planet, and a soupçon of Village politics. During their run at the Vanguard—which the *Daily News* dubbed part of the "cellar circuit"—they were signed to Decca Records.

But as with the Almanac Singers, forces began bearing down on the musicians and the world they were creating in the Village, and the music scene south of Fourteenth Street was slowly being crushed in the second half of the fifties. Cafe Society crumbled first. In 1947 Barney Josephson's brother Leon, who had Communist inclinations, was found guilty of contempt after he declined to answer questions from the House Committee on Un-American Activities. The brothers were soon pegged as Communist sympathizers by columnists like Winchell. With Leon Josephson in jail, business at both clubs plunged. The uptown club closed in 1947; a year and a half later, the downtown space was put up for sale. New owners retained the name and tried to adapt to changing musical times, hiring musicians who played bebop as well as more traditional Dixieland. One teenager who managed to sneak into Cafe Society and hear Holiday during her later days was Van Ronk, who would recall her ravaged but still alluring intonation.

Even if the downtown or uptown Cafe Society had continued to flourish, neither may have been able to book some of the artists it wanted. In 1940 the city had expanded on its Cabaret Law with the issuing of cabaret cards, which musicians would need to play nightclubs or other venues where liquor was sold. As part of the application process, they had to be photographed, fingerprinted, and interviewed as if they were criminals; they could easily lose their card if they had ever been arrested or had a prior record. As a result, Holiday and Thelonious Monk were among those who lost out on Village club work; Monk even resorted to using a fake name, Ernie Washington, to get gigs.

When Seeger and Hays were also targeted as either members of the Communist Party or sympathetic to it, the Weavers imploded nearly overnight; their record deal and live shows abruptly came to an end. On November 15, 1954, two FBI agents zeroed in on Hellerman, who, in the words of one report, had "entertained at various other Communist Party rallies from 1947 to 1953."

That day, Hellerman was approached by two agents at his home at 7 Morton Street in the West Village. After the agents introduced themselves, Hellerman resisted any interaction, insisting that his personal and private activities were none of the Bureau's business and refusing to speak with them. He also argued that the Bureau had no right to maintain files or keep track of anyone unless that person had broken the law. In their report the agents wrote that Hellerman was told "in no uncertain terms" that the Bureau had the right to "pursue its responsibilities."

Hellerman was neither arrested nor jailed, and a few of the other venues in the area, like the Village Vanguard, survived. But the arrival of rock and roll, with the first records by Chuck Berry and Elvis Presley right around the corner, was one of several signs that the Village was being left behind or scorned.

As the Village music community of the first half of the century was crumbling or under siege, a fresh one was ascending, and few witnessed it more up close than Lionel Kilberg. On March 10, 1957, the twenty-seven-year-old salesman for the Air Express freight company dutifully filled out the same application for New York's Department of Parks, as it was then known, that he'd been using for two years. Once again, he was requesting permission for "folk singing with instruments" around the fountain in the middle of Washington Square Park, from 2 p.m. to 6 p.m., each Sunday in April. In phrasing he duplicated for each monthly application, he typed, "Only purpose [is] to gather for the playing and singing of folk music," adding, as he always did, that the sessions had been taking place for roughly a decade and that an estimated three hundred people would participate. Again, he typed "no" in the spaces that asked if the gatherings would involve a parade or speeches, or if buses and trucks would be needed.

The application was approved by two city officials nine days later, and starting Sunday, April 7, the weekly gatherings once again resumed in the park. By subway, foot, or car, a parade of youthful and very earnest musicians began filtering into the park, lugging cases or bags filled with acoustic guitars, banjos, fiddles, autoharps, or mandolins. A new season of music making in the ten acres of the park would begin and, in this year's case, with a newly added level of scrutiny.

For more than three hundred years, Washington Square Park had lived several different lives: marshland, a burial ground for impoverished yellow-fever victims, a site for public executions, and a drilling-practice area for New York's militia, by which time it had been renamed the Washington Parade Ground in honor of the first president. In 1827 the area was proclaimed a public park, with accompanying winding paths and additional trees. But a structure completed in 1895—a seventy-three-foot-high marble arch—not only distinguished Washington Square Park but also served as a portal into another world increasingly set to music. That same decade, bandleader Luciano Conterno's famous 9th Regiment Band played the "Star-Spangled Banner" in the park; within a few years, other ensembles performed the "William Tell Overture," French composer Charles Gounod's *Faust*, and the act-three quartet from Verdi's *Rigoletto*. The classical-music tradition would continue right through 1957; that summer, conductor Fritz Rikko was scheduled to conduct works by Vivaldi, Bach, and Haydn.

Folk sing-alongs and strum-alongs also found a place in the park. According to musician Barry Kornfeld, a local couple, Hank Lifson and Jean Silverstein, had started singing and playing guitars together in the park each Thursday. In the summer of 1945 a local printer, George Margolin, was reportedly walking through the public space, guitar in hand, when someone called out, "How 'bout a song?" He obliged, gathering a small crowd around him. The following year, he was back, singing, as he told historian Timothy Josiah Morris Pertz, "Jimmy Crack Corn," "I've Been Working on the Railroad," and other all-chime-in favorites as well as pro-labor songs that reflected his leftist orientation.

Be it musicians, would-be players eager to learn a technique or two, or those who just wanted to watch, the preferred destination was the fountain with the recessed bowl that sat just south of the Washington Arch. The fountain was actually the second such structure in the park. Built in 1851, the first had been called "very nice" in the inaugural issue of the *New York Times* that September. But it lasted only about twenty years. In the 1870s a new fountain was needed—in part to make sure that the carriage horses clomping through

Washington Square could have more water—and the original was demolished and replaced with one made of graywacke stone and relocated from the southeastern entrance of Central. Roughly seventy feet in diameter, it featured a recessed basin that, from above, looked like a giant eyeball in the middle of the park. With the advent of the folksingers, it had become a makeshift performance area, musicians taking up spots along the concrete rim. Around the perimeters of the park, painters sitting on fold-up canvas chairs sold their art—or had the pieces scrutinized by young women and men in sandals, some with black-rimmed glasses and books on existentialism (or what the *Times* called "high-class paperbacks") jammed into their back pockets.

As the crowds began building, the Department of Parks, along with the wealthy neighbors who lived in the string of row houses and apartment buildings that encircled portions of the park, took notice. In what constituted the first conflict over music in the park, officials determined that such gatherings would require official authorization.

Everyone knew that risks were involved in not obtaining the proper approvals for any similar gatherings. When organizers of a pro-Bolshevik march in the park earlier in the century hadn't filled out the necessary paperwork, the protesters ended up clashing with police. Unwilling to make such a mistake, the folk musicians took the Department of Parks up on its threat and began requesting permits. As Kornfeld would later write, "They were repeatedly refused until, as legend has it, a certain young lady had to sit in the lap of a Park [*sic*] Department official in order to secure that first permit."

The first permit may, in fact, have been firmed up by a woman—none other than Jean Silverstein. In the spring of 1949, Silverstein, then living on Park Avenue, completed the one-page application to have a "group assemble for folk singing" from 3 to 7 p.m., "every Sunday that the sun shines (April through Sept.)." To justify the request, she typed, "We are a group that likes to sing. Many children come down to sing with us and on Sunday afternoons in the summer it's pleasant to sing outdoors." (Curiously, the application was originally made out for Union Square Park, but that name and address were xx'ed out and replaced with Washington Square Park.) Along with another bass player, Irwin Lutzky, Kilberg took over the permit paperwork a few years later, by which time the city had already curtailed the sessions, which now had to wrap up at 6 p.m.

As the fifties progressed, the fountain jams made local heroes of some of the pickers who frequented them. Kilberg was known for his so-called Brownie bass, a homemade washtub bass made from a West Virginia metal tub and a pole used for window washing. A bass-fiddle string (or sometimes a piece of clothesline) ran from the bottom of the tub to the top of the pole, where he placed a miniature fire hydrant toy in honor of his late dog, Brownie. By lengthening the pole and playing with gloved fingers, Kilberg could hit several different notes. With guitarist Mike Cohen and banjoist Roger Sprung—a TV repairman by day at his home in Lake Mohegan, New York—Kilberg played in a trio, the Shanty Boys. Sprung, a masterful musician who'd been alerted to the park sessions by his brother (and early permit holder) George in 1947, had such a loud, sparkling style that it sounded as if he had an amplifier, which he didn't.

The lineups would also include skilled banjo players such as Eric Weissberg, Marshall Brickman, and Erik Darling, who would later take Seeger's role in a reconstituted Weavers. Although bluegrass and old-timey music dominated the outdoor hoots, it was also possible in 1957 to venture into the park and hear a blues singer or a mandolinist playing the Italian folk songs he'd learned from his family. A bearded, bedraggled-looking Woody Guthrie suddenly appeared one day; his wife, Marjorie, would also sometimes drop off their son, Arlo, and let him wander around with his guitar until he found a group he could join.

Even when the designated permit holder was carrying a copy of the paperwork in his or her pocket on those Sundays, the city seemed intent on hampering the proceedings as much as possible. One afternoon, police allowed only one musician to play because the original wording on the permits referred to a singular "stringed instrument." If more than the number of people specified on the application showed up, some would be chased off. To add extra hardship to the proceedings, the permits—which, starting with Silverstein's first, allowed for the sessions to go on for months, until the start of fall—eventually had to be renewed each month.

Along with the increasing scrutiny of the city and the denser groups of tourists and onlookers who began to gather around the singers and players, the media were starting to take notice. The *New York Times* had run a short article on Kilberg and his Brownie bass in 1955, but two years on, other outlets were getting in on the act. The same year of the *Times* story, Dan Wolf, Edwin Fancher, and Norman Mailer had launched the *Village Voice* to compete with the comparatively old-school *Villager*. Priced at five cents, the *Voice* ran all of eight pages weekly, filled with local news, observations, and crammed restaurant and store advertisements. Its first edition included a front-page story about the fountain jams, and in April 1957 it published a photo of the first spring session of the season.

The *Daily News* soon after ran a Sunday feature story, which reached five million readers, on what it called "The Circle"—the name for the performers who gathered in and around the fountain. In it, Kilberg recalled the sight of an introverted kid who watched a group of players, was pulled in for a sing-along, and eventually asked one of the musicians for banjo lessons. "This kid has found himself new friends," Kilberg said. "Most of the tourists look on the folk at the Circle as bohemians, but actually these kids come from the five boroughs. They come down here to play some music and let off some steam. I believe there's nothing better for a person than singing and yelling in a crowd." They were also kids who felt disconnected from pop culture and the Eisenhower era, looking for common ground and a place where they could congregate and meet fellow outsiders who'd discovered folk music. Some didn't care much for rock and roll, and if they had liked it, they wouldn't have necessarily told anyone.

At promptly 6 p.m., the music in the park would have to stop. "The cops would come in like a phalanx—'put away that thing,'" recalled Peter Stampfel, a beatific, genial fiddler and banjo player who'd grown up in Wisconsin and arrived in New York City a few years later. "They hated that people were playing music." To some, like Kornfeld, the curfew was tolerable; after four hours, everyone was worn out from all the strumming, harmonizing, and fingerpicking. Some would break into smaller groups and head out for a meal or resume the playing at the local American Youth Hostel on Eighth Street. Jane Jacobs, an associate editor of *Architectural Forum* and Village resident who became caught up in the battle for the park, would call it "the incubation ground for the revival of folk singing, literally it was." But the time restrictions placed on the musicians were another reminder that the nascent scene was being monitored; the musicians were literally playing on borrowed time.

███

On April 25, 1957, just over two weeks after the Sunday afternoon hoots resumed, Gerdes Restaurant formally reopened in its new location at 11 West Fourth Street, at the corner of Mercer. Much like at its previous nearby location, Gerdes would still be a working-people's bar. In its first advertisement in the *Villager*, the prominent community newspaper, the new Gerdes promised "giant sized cocktails served daily." For the moment, there was no mention of music.

That same day, residents of the Village would awake to the news many had heard about and dreaded: a proposal for a four-lane roadway that would slice through Washington Square Park had been endorsed by T. T. Wiley, the city's traffic commissioner. The plan to connect Fifth Avenue, on the north side of the park, to West Broadway, on the south, dated back nearly a century. In the 1870s, Boss Tweed, the Tammany Hall powerhouse, had wanted to provide those living on what would eventually be renamed West Broadway with ritzier "South Fifth Avenue" addresses, a potential boon for the real estate market. A roadbed was built, but the plan stalled. In 1952, Robert Moses, the parks commissioner who had earlier introduced plans to close off the park, announced he would be picking up where Tweed left off. Because the roadbed built in the Tweed era still existed, Moses wanted it to connect to "Fifth Avenue South" as well as to a proposed Lower Manhattan Expressway. Wiley and others, including Manhattan Borough president Hulan Jack, insisted that the plan was necessary to relieve the traffic congestion that would begin in midtown and work its way down to the Village; after all, they maintained, Fifth Avenue hit a dead end. Over the next few years, numerous proposals were discussed for the highway, some involving a partially sunken road and a footbridge for pedestrians.

In its first issue of 1957, the *Village Voice* warned, in an alarming editorial, "The Square is certain to be an issue" that year. But the plans for remaking the Village weren't limited to the park, as Gerdes co-owner Mike Porco was learning all too well. By the time he was eight, Porco had been trained in his native Italy to be a carpenter and cabinetmaker. His father and grandfather had already moved to America, and his father summoned young Mike to work with him. In February 1933 Mike landed in America from his home country, expecting to be met by his father; instead, his uncle Angelo greeted him at the dock, informing him that his father had died while Mike was en route. Mike was eighteen and didn't yet know a word of English, and his uncle Angelo became his surrogate father.

The Porcos lived in the Bronx, where they soon opened a family restaurant, but the Village, and its buildings tightly packed with blue-collar workers and diverse families, beckoned. Porco found a job at Gerdes, part of a five-story warehouse at 11 West Third Street, at the southwest corner of Mercer. Herman Gerdes had first leased the space in 1911, eventually opening a liquor store that became a sandwich shop and then a family restaurant. Eventually, his grandson William Gerdes took it over. In 1952 Gerdes sold it to Porco, along with his brother John and a cousin, Joe Bastone, and the three men planned to continue pulling in the working-class Italians who were its reliable customers.

The timing was not on Porco's side. The following year, the city announced a "Committee on Slum Clearance," headed by Parks Commissioner Moses. A formidable city makeover artist, Moses had made his name on large-scale projects like Jones Beach State Park and the Northern and Southern State highways, which connected Manhattan with parts of Long Island but also demolished long-standing communities in the process. His latest proposal, called Washington Square Southeast, was of a piece with his previous works, such as bulldozing parts of the South Bronx for the Cross Bronx Expressway. The white population of the Village was starting to flee to uptown or the suburbs. To reverse that trend, Moses turned to the recently instituted Title 1 of the 1949 Federal Housing Act, which would allocate federal funds to demolish so-called slums to make way for private housing. Starting in 1955, the land south of the park, which included 16 residential buildings and 132 families— what the New York Times called a "blighted area"—was condemned by the city. That October, the city turned the area over to Moses, who envisioned selling the land to private developers for a proposed massive apartment complex and to New York University, which offered $25,000 as a show of interest in the project and would pay a mere $5.50 per square foot.

For Villagers, the thought was unsettling. Washington Square Southeast, wrote former New York State assemblyman Nicholas A. Rossi in a letter to the *Times*, "would begin the destruction of our Village." Slowly, though, the plans took shape. In a move that enraged locals who didn't consider their homes to be slums, the board of estimates voted unanimously in the first month of 1956 to raze buildings from Mercer Street in the east over to West Broadway, then from Washington Square North to Houston Street. In the end, more than a thousand mom-and-pop businesses, along with 650 industrial and commercial buildings, came down. An estimated one hundred families were moved out to make way for Washington Square Village, three monolithic buildings with more than 2,000 apartments that sat between West Third, Mercer, West Houston, and West Broadway.

Few felt the impact of those plans more than the owners of Gerdes, which, by the summer of 1957, would be on the wrecking-ball list as part of NYU's expansion plans. Forced to move to a new site, Porco and his partners lucked out when they found a two-thousand-square-foot, high-ceilinged space on West Fourth Street. The restaurant was separated from the bar area by a waist-high dividing wall, which could draw two different crowds and two different sources of income. When it opened in April, Gerdes dubbed itself, on its matchboxes, a "restaurant and cocktail lounge" with "party facilities" and "excellent food." Since the new Gerdes would remain a restaurant, Porco was able to obtain a new liquor license, and the plan called for the spot to be open twelve straight hours, from 8 a.m. to 8 p.m.

Even though it was a mere one block north of the first location, the new Gerdes faced challenges from the start. Many of its regulars were now gone from the neighborhood; even worse, the corner of Mercer and West Fourth was more desolate than it had been before the demolitions. NYU's more aggressive push into the area meant an influx of students, some of whom were tapping into the revived interest in folk music. No one at Gerdes thought to lure them in with ballads or musicians, but that would change soon enough.

During one of his return trips to the city in 1957, likely in the summer, Dave Van Ronk was taking in the sights along MacDougal Street. In decades past, the block had been home to speakeasies and so-called tearooms that were gathering places for gay women. Now the one-way strip was lined with butcher and sandwich shops and cafés like the San Remo, the Italian restaurant that transformed at night, in the words of the *Daily News*, into "a hangout for the youngsters who like to consider themselves bohemians."

But as Van Ronk noticed, a new and curious business had opened its doors in the storefront at 110 MacDougal, on the east side of the block. Flapping out front was a flag, complete with a logo depicting a fan-like wheel. Hand-painted lettering on the front door announced the space was now the "Folk-Lore Center," home to "Books Old and New on Folklore Folk Dance." Inside were shelves of LPs, stringed instruments, and guitar strings, and the owner was Israel Young, a Village character all his own.

The son of Jewish immigrants from Poland, Young—Izzy, as everyone called him—had been born in Manhattan in 1928. When he was barely two years old, his family moved to the Bronx so that his father could open a bakery. After Young was enrolled in the High School of Science in 1945, a fellow member of the Astronomy Club introduced him to square dancing, which became an unexpected passion. Although he would never consider himself a performer of any type, Young joined the American Square Dance Group, which he would later call the city's first major folk group. Before long, he was sporting blue jeans and a red bandanna, and square dancing with them. "It would be like, you know, masturbation," he told folklorist and writer Richard Reuss. "After you do it, you say you'll never do it again, and then another." The folk songs that accompanied the dancing were secondary, but Young was nonetheless lured into the melodies and stories of traditional music. "It was pure, it was simple, it was direct, it was honest and sincere," he told Reuss. "It was a light to me. And I said, 'This is the way life should be.' In the way of the folk songs, even if someone got killed, it was a direct relationship."

At Brooklyn College, Young was initially a premed student, then switched his major to English, and eventually stopped attending classes altogether. By then, the early fifties, he'd begun collecting rare books and soon had the idea of publishing a catalog selling folk-music books—and, in turn, opening a store to carry them. As many would eventually observe, business did not come naturally to Israel Young, but the last week of February 1957, he signed a lease for 110 MacDougal.

Young sported the short hair, button-down shirts, and horn-rimmed glasses of a book-loving nerd. But while he may have been a bookworm, he was far from a pushover. He had the brusque, rough-hewn accent of the Bronx kid he was, and his chest was so stocky that it always looked as if he were ready to butt heads (or bodies) with someone. He wasn't fond of the hardy-voiced commercial folk groups that were starting to spring up, and if any customers were to disagree with him, he wasn't afraid to kick them out. In the Greenwich Village of 1957, folk music couldn't have found a more perfect bodyguard.

The idea of a folk store wasn't as harebrained as it sounded. In what were the makings of another boom—or "folk scare," as many, including Van Ronk, would joke—the music was again storming into the mainstream. In late 1955 the Weavers had re-formed, and the recording of that show, *The Weavers at Carnegie Hall*, showed up in record stores in April 1957. *Cashbox*, the prominent music-business magazine, called it "a must for any folk record collection." The same month, Harry Belafonte, now a folk and calypso singer, had not one but three albums in the Top 10; Elvis Presley had only one. Out in San Francisco, the Kingston Trio, a trio who looked as if they were students in the most clean-cut college in the country, took over a residence at the Purple Onion. With their striped shirts, carefully rehearsed harmonies and stage patter, and generally go-down-easy sound, they were even more polished than the Weavers, never mind the scraggly Almanac Singers. Within months, they would be signed to a major record label, Capitol.

In terms of its square footage, the Folklore Center (the hyphen was dropped after the sign was made) couldn't compete with the more expansive record stores uptown, but that wasn't Young's goal. He wanted to sell not just music books but also sheet music, and as he would write in his journals, he began selling ten-inch LPs, some to libraries and some to dealers of rare books. "This should be a tremendous beginning offer that will make me many friends and also see who is on my side in Folk Music," he wrote in a journal. He had doubts that folksingers would buy books, "and if they do, they expect discounts, etc." But he also hoped his store would be a gathering place for the community and the authentic style of music he championed.

On April 5, 1957, two days before the Sunday jamborees in the park would resume, the Folklore Center opened with a party starting at 9 p.m., and the folkies and old-timey music fans stayed until 4 a.m. The following week, a photo in the *Village Voice* of the tightly packed store was captioned "The Mob Scene"; Young was described as "an adventurous book dealer." The use of *mob* would take on an entirely new meaning in the years to come, both in the Village and within the Folklore Center. But for now, the idea that anyone could flock to such a singular storefront was satisfying enough. As Young had written in his journal in February, when he signed the lease, "I love the future."

August 18, 1957, brought its usual barrage of news in the city and its boroughs. Two cars collided in the East Village, injuring nine, including a sixty-eight-year-old woman pedestrian; a milk strike loomed; the Yankees trounced the Baltimore Orioles, seven-nothing, in the first game of the day's doubleheader. Beyond Manhattan, two guided-missile facilities had been discovered in the Soviet Union, and Sir Winston Churchill's son-in-law died from an overdose of sleeping pills. But in a community of musicians eager for more professional places to make something approaching a living, the opening of the Village's first venue for something other than jazz made for a blazing headline all its own.

Starting that month, stashed among the books and periodicals on display at the Folklore Center was the first magazine devoted to the community in and around the park. Dubbed a "non-profit, great-cost amateur publication," the first issue of *Caravan* was sixteen pages of mimeographed folk-music news, gossip, and reviews edited by Lee Shaw, a twenty-five-year-old equally taken with science fiction and vernacular music. Her sci-fi fanzine *Quandry* had a following, as did the similar-subject magazines she worked on with her husband of the time, fellow fantasy writer Larry Shaw. After witnessing the Sunday park jamborees, she decided to participate by way of a publication that would document the scene.

Initially, Shaw called her collection of folk lyrics and folklore *Chooog 2-5*, but after one issue she scrapped it and began again with *Caravan*. Based out of the couple's apartment at 78 Greenwich Street, the first edition featured a column devoted to "The New York City Scene," which updated readers on a Washington Square Park session that had been rained out a few weeks earlier; as a result, *Caravan* reported, a television talent scout missed out on the action. When Young asked if he could carry *Caravan* in the Folklore Center, Shaw increased the printing—to two hundred copies—and gave half to Young in exchange for free records.

In its news-tidbits section, *Caravan* also announced "Dave Van Ronk is back." Van Ronk's merchant marine duty—what he would call "the most regular work I ever did"—had taken him to New Orleans and California and introduced him to parts of the country he'd never seen before. The work also exposed him to the racism that acutely existed outside the five boroughs of Manhattan. "Even in a city like New Orleans," he would later tell the *Village Voice*, "you'd make some Negro friends and then you couldn't even find a place to sit down and talk to them."

Upon his final return to New York, Van Ronk crashed at the Shaw apartment and started attending the Sunday-afternoon jams in Washington Square Park, which he may have discovered around the time he first visited the Village. But Van Ronk had returned in more ways than one. *Caravan*'s inaugural issue included a critique of new releases from Elektra Records, an indie label devoted to folk and world music that had its offices on Bleecker Street. According to the critic, bylined "Blind Rafferty," one collection of Haitian music "sounds like a chic nightclub act," and an Elektra blues record suffered from a "sickening glibness." As many would soon find out, Rafferty was, in fact, Van Ronk, and the column and subsequent pieces made it bracingly clear that he had his opinions on what was, and wasn't, authentic.

Caravan also heralded the arrival of a new "coffee-shop-what-have-you." Revealing how compact the Village community was compared to those in other cities, the new music venue, at 106 West Third Street, was around the corner and just a few minutes' walk from the Folklore Center. The long, dank space was said to have been a livery stable for former vice president Aaron Burr and later a garage, but a Village landlord named Rick Allmen sensed a different future for the building. The son of a pharmacist who'd hoped Rick would follow him into the family business, Allmen instead pulled together two hundred dollars, half from his savings and half from a friend, to open a music club. Renting three trucks to excavate the remnants of the former garage, Allmen borrowed tables and chairs from friends; his father offered to help paint the walls, and Allmen's grandfather would pitch in on the dishwashing. To ensure that the place was warm when the weather turned cold, Allmen had to bring hot charcoals to emit added heat. But he also realized that candles would work better: they'd lend the space, he said, "the image everyone has of the Village."

Allmen named the place the Cafe Bizarre, for good reason. Desperate for any decor whatsoever for his venue, he didn't know what to say when friends came by with a few discarded mannequins they'd found, but he strung them up from the ceiling with wires and at odd angles. The creepy fixtures, he told the *Brooklyn Daily*, lent the space "the most fantastic and eerie look you could imagine." To Van Ronk, it felt like a "cut-rate Charles Addams haunted house," but anything that called attention to a Village club at the time wasn't necessarily a bad thing.

On opening night, August 18, 1957, the stage amounted to wooden platforms, a ghoulish MC made weak attempts at scary jokes, and the sound system periodically emitted feedback squeals. But the lineup brought together a certified star on the scene, Odetta, the Alabama-born actress who had switched over to folk and already had several albums to her credit; her deep voice and persona were regal and imposing. Also on the bill were Logan English, a Kentucky-raised folksinger and guitarist—and, in one of his first professional gigs, if not *the* first, Van Ronk.

Now twenty-one, Van Ronk was still finding his way as a singer and fingerpicker, and he could never recall what songs he performed that night. But *Caravan* reported that at the beginning of his second set, Van Ronk sang "blues with an intensity and vitality, and sometimes violence, that comes across powerfully to an audience." Others on the scene were more musically pure, both in terms of their delivery and instrumental skills, but few were as uncompromising as Van Ronk. Here was a roughhouse kid from Queens who loved the blues (and ragtime and jazz) but merged it with his own voice rather than imitate his sources. He didn't gently harmonize or croon, instead riding roughshod over the melodies. When needed, he could also veer into a softer, singsongy voice. But as fresh as he was, he sounded prematurely grizzled, like someone singing around a campfire during an expedition to the Old West a century before.

Though skeptical of the Cafe Bizarre, starting with its furnishings, Van Ronk later had to admit that the experience of playing on a stage, a single spotlight on him, was transformative. The experience both shocked and elated him. Afterward, Odetta complimented him. Maybe he, along with some of his friends on the scene, had a future in all of this.

█ █ █ █ █

When he showed up at the Village Vanguard in the middle of October 1957 to prep for his first shows as a bandleader, Sonny Rollins sensed that the club hadn't fully made the transition from its past life to its new incarnation. Walking down the stairs to the basement, he took note of the wooden floor that had once welcomed dancers. In another vestige of its previous life of hosting poets, folksingers, and cabaret acts, the club still had a maître d'. At some point Rollins also spied Mo Howard, the bangs-haired member of the Three Stooges comedy group, another holdover from a former era.

Earlier that year, Rollins had been approached at a different venue by Max Gordon about playing at his club in the Village. The name "Village Vanguard" rang a vague bell for Rollins; he thought he might have played there as a sideman with someone or other, maybe Miles Davis. Gordon never said it explicitly to Rollins, but change was coming to the Vanguard. In June 1957 he'd placed an ad in the *Village Voice* announcing his club's revised menu—creole shrimp, chili, and ribs—but more importantly its "new jazz-room policy." The Vanguard had featured the music before, but jazz would now dominate the bookings.

Dating back to the early decades of the twentieth century, jazz was hardly foreign to the Village. On West Third Street, Eddie Condon's Place, named after the guitarist and bandleader, offered traditional fare; David Amram first went there when he was all of fourteen, and in later years two Village musicians, Terre and Suzzy Roche, would be so inspired by a set they saw at Condon's that they would write a song about one of its players. Jazz had also been on the menu periodically at the Vanguard. In the forties, Gordon booked jazz pianist Mary Lou Williams and trumpeter Hot Lips Page, with Monday-night jam sessions starting in 1942. In 1948, Gordon's future wife Lorraine, then in a relationship with the head of Blue Note Records, suggested that Gordon book Monk. The dates were famously ill-attended, but Gordon didn't completely ditch the idea of sticking with jazz.

By the time Gordon approached Rollins about a booking, the music was undergoing one of its cyclical reinventions. The big-band era that had begun just before World War II was winding down, and the music was growing more daring with the arrival of bebop, then cool jazz and hard bop. The progress coincided with the Vanguard's own business issues. By 1957, according to Lorraine Gordon, her husband was encountering problems booking the nightclub acts and comedians who'd once brought audiences into the club. Thanks to the television revolution, audiences seemed more inclined to stay home and watch those entertainers on the new technology. (The club had also experienced a few earlier hassles: in 1944 it was cited by the Office of Price Administration for a violation after Gordon started charging $1.50 for ham and eggs, a 30-cent increase; he had to pay a fine.) Even though he was far from an expert on jazz— in time, he would turn to Davis to suggest new acts, according to Lorraine— Gordon sensed that the music was entering a new phase, and in mid-1957 he made the decision to concentrate on it.

With his short fade and goatee, Rollins was physically the man for the job; he resembled an elegant beatnik, someone born to be in the Village at that time. Walter Theodore Rollins had hailed from Harlem, where he had started as a piano student but switched to alto and then tenor sax as a teenager. As evidence of his gift, he was all of eighteen when he first started recording with other musicians; by the time he was twenty, he had already gigged with Monk, Davis, and Art Blakey. During the early fifties, Rollins was on fire, recording with Davis and Monk and on his own.

But thanks to a heroin habit, his life was starting to go off the rails. His addiction led him to lose out on a gig with Charlie Parker, and Rollins was arrested for drugs and spent time in a federal narcotics rehab hospital in Kentucky in 1955. Moving to Chicago after he was released, Rollins toiled at menial day jobs to avoid falling into old habits. "I was trying to stay away from the nightclubs where I would know people and it would be an enticement to get back into drugs," he recalled. "Guys would say, 'Hey, Sonny, I got some good stuff—let's go get high.' But I resisted the temptation."

After practicing alone in the basement of a YMCA where he worked as a janitor, Rollins was invited to fill a vacant slot in the Clifford Brown and Max Roach Quintet. Brown's death in a 1956 car accident put an end to that promise, but Rollins, who had temporarily returned to New York between tours with that band, stayed in town and began making even greater strides. In 1956 alone he rolled out an astounding six albums; one of them, *Saxophone Colossus*, was his definitive statement up to that point. By then, critic Leonard Feather was calling Rollins "a tenor sax force in jazz."

For Rollins, the Village didn't necessarily encourage such mad-scientist experimentation. "If I got a gig in Birdland, I would be playing my ass off trying to play," he said, referring to the midtown jazz spot. "And if I played at the Vanguard I did the same thing, so that didn't apply to me. I was just trying to make the gig." But he noticed the difference in the clientele: in his mind, the Vanguard audience was more racially diverse than the crowds at Birdland and other uptown venues. He was also drawn to the Vanguard by its ambience: "small and friendly, and one of the best sounds in New York," he said. Although he always applied pressure to himself and musicians, the Vanguard itself felt stress-free to him. He could feel free to creatively wander, even if it meant firing one of his first lineups at the club. "I was a hard task master," he said. "I was firing guys left and right if they didn't live up to my standards. I'm not sorry about it. I was trying to get the music right. I was young and reckless."

In October, Rollins started a two-month residency at the Vanguard, and with a splash. His new label, Blue Note, decided to record one of his performances for a live record, which would not only be Rollins's first such LP but also the first taped at the club. Here, at least, the pressure was on; Rollins would now be leading his own band, and the venerated recording engineer Rudy Van Gelder would be taping the shows. Chaos and upheaval were also in the mix. By the time of the recording date, November 3, Rollins had opted for a trio—himself, drummer Pete "La Roca" Sims, and bassist Donald Bailey. The combo played an afternoon set, but for the second, Rollins replaced them with his first choices, drummer Elvin Jones and bassist Wilbur Ware. As author Aidan Levy wrote, Jones appeared at the club "half in the bag and still seething" over being fired from another gig.

No matter the state of the rhythm section, Rollins walked on a tightrope wire: there was no set list or any other accompanist, such as a pianist, who could ground the music or take solos when Rollins needed a break. But all those potential distractions only freed him up further. Throughout the sets, he would hold long notes, grunt and squawk on his instrument, and play everything from Dizzy Gillespie's "A Night in Tunisia" to the more relaxed and sensual "Softly, as in a Morning Sunrise" (from the 1927 operetta *The New Moon* and cowritten by Oscar Hammerstein). He played one of his own songs, "Sonnymoon for Two," a twelve-bar blues inspired by his marriage that year to Dawn Noreen Finney. Unlike his former boss Davis, Rollins didn't enjoy listening to tapes of his shows and didn't bother to do it this time. But Blue Note edited down the two sets to the length of one LP and began prepping the album for release early the following year.

For the time being, Rollins and Gordon were getting along, and Rollins would remember Gordon's fascination with jazz musicians, as well as the softness of his hands. "You know he never did any hard work," Rollins said. "His hands were like a baby's hands." Rollins still steered clear of drugs, even as he saw with increasing and disturbing frequency the way that pot and heroin were affecting some of his friends and colleagues. For him, and a parade of players to follow, the Village had a new habitat for their music.

The voice emanated from somewhere in the park, although Happy Traum couldn't determine the precise spot at first. Growing up in the Bronx, the kid born Harry Traum—but nicknamed "Happy" by a household helper and then his parents—was one of many teenagers starting to flock to Washington Square Park. At summer camp, a few older counselors invited him to a late-night drive into the Village, where Traum had seen something magical: two musicians playing nylon-stringed guitars at the fountain. Learning of the Sunday-afternoon join-along sessions, he began taking the subway there, gravitating toward musicians he could accompany and learn from.

Traum followed the sound of that thunderous, raucous singing, which led him to a bench east of the fountain. There sat a roustabout with a wave of dark hair, huddled over his Gibson, singing and playing "St. James Infirmary." Also known as "Gambler's Blues," the song was dark—the narrator, drinking at a bar, telling the tragic tale of finding his lady friend in a morgue—and Van Ronk's prematurely wizened delivery made it sound as if he'd witnessed that sad sight for himself. Traum went over and introduced himself. Even though Van Ronk was sitting and playing alone—unusual in and of itself because all the other musicians playing in his vicinity seemed to prefer groups—Traum perceived the power of Van Ronk's personality and his role as, he said, "a figurehead of sorts."

Van Ronk hadn't returned to the park and music of his own accord. In hopes of auditioning at the Chicago club Gate of Horn for its owner, Albert Grossman, Van Ronk had hitchhiked to Illinois in the fall of 1957, but Grossman was unimpressed when Van Ronk sang a few songs, and the musician retreated to New York. Along the way, he'd lost his wallet, which contained his seaman's papers. The thought of meeting with officials to replace them was, he wrote, "asking for trouble" given his political views. Back to Manhattan it was, where Van Ronk struggled to put money into the pockets of his peacoat. Since the Cafe Bizarre wasn't offering regular work, he began working at a bookstore on University Place while continuing to crash with the Shaws. One of his regular haunts was the Cafe Figaro, a coffeehouse at 186 Bleecker, at the corner of MacDougal Street, where anyone could linger all day over a coffee and a game or two of chess, and it was there, on a fall 1957 day, that he recognized a woman he'd met months before and wanted to know a little better.

Even before they'd been introduced, Van Ronk and Terri Thal were kindred spirits in their political and musical interests. Raised in Brooklyn, the child of Jewish immigrants from Russia and Austria-Hungary, Thal was already politically engaged: she attended meetings of the Young Socialist League and had been inducted into the world of folk by way of Pete Seeger records. Tall, strapping, often bluntly opinionated, and fond of cat's-eye-frame glasses, Thal radiated independence and robustness. She and Van Ronk had first crossed paths at a party on the Upper West Side in either late 1956 or early the following year. "A guy named Shel was driving me crazy, saying he wanted me to go into the bedroom with him," Thal recalled. "It had nothing to do with sex. He wanted to turn me on. I was still a kid from Brooklyn. Marijuana was that evil stuff that grew in the fields outside Lafayette High School." A scruffy guy who turned out to be Van Ronk approached them. "Shel, leave her alone," he said. As Thal would recall, "We spent the rest of the evening together. He said he didn't want to see somebody drive away an attractive woman."

Now, months later, Thal and some of her friends from Brooklyn College were at the Fig, as the locals called it, and there was Van Ronk again. Recognizing her, he wandered over to their table, struck up another conversation, and offered to escort her back to Brooklyn, a ride that took him an hour each way. Very soon after, they were a couple. She knew he was a folksinger, but, she said, "Being a folksinger was not that big a deal then. There was no work in New York, and no way to earn a living as a folk singer."

Soon after Thal and Van Ronk's reconnection at the Fig, the fall temperatures became too chilly for Sunday-afternoon hootenannies in Washington Square Park; permits to play outside were rarely filled out after October. The November issue of *Caravan* confirmed that the gatherings would wrap for the season. In the spirit of good-natured folk ribbing, the magazine added, "This means dozens of folksingers searching for backrooms (preferably with heat) wherein to gather and sing. Be warned!"

But on the heels of a year that saw the music community expand in ways few would have predicted, the end of the park jams no longer had an air of finality about them. Thal was right in the sense that, at that time, making a living as a folksinger (or jazz player) seemed as unimaginable as hearing that music on the radio. But maybe it would be possible in the future. The opening of the Cafe Bizarre and the revamped policy at the Village Vanguard offered more

opportunities for exposure and, perhaps, pay. Ads for the Vanguard, the Five
Spot, and Cafe Bohemia were beginning to appear in the back of the *Village
Voice*.

In October, the same month Rollins had settled into his run at the Vanguard, a new jazz club, the Half Note, opened at Hudson and Spring Streets
in what was still known as the South Village. With pianist Randy Weston as
its initial booking, the Half Note demonstrated its dedication to jazz even in
the way its menu included hero sandwiches named after different styles, like
a New Orleans (sausage and parmesan cheese) and a Cool (a combo of cheese
and cold cuts). By December, the club was playing host to Charles Mingus—a
match that felt right to *Daily News* jazz critic Don Nelsen, who called the Half
Note "a snuggery where [Mingus] could develop his special brand of jazz for
the public ear." Meanwhile, the Five Spot's profile had been further enhanced
in mid-summer, when *Esquire* had included a photograph of a puffy-cheeked
Amram playing his French horn to a huddled-together, multiracial crowd at
the club.

Thanks to exposure like that article, along with the attention the park had
received in the New York press, the world above and far beyond Fourteenth
Street began taking notice of the Village's artistic panorama. The *Village Voice*
itself was about to be immortalized by Hollywood; early in 1957 the movie
Stage Struck, starring Henry Fonda and Susan Strasberg, had been filmed
partly along MacDougal Street and included a fake coffeehouse that shared
a name with the paper. Joe Gould, the highly eccentric Village fixture who
claimed to be writing a huge tome about the lives of ordinary people, died that
summer. But his passing felt less like the end of an era than the beginning of a
new one.

Even the battle for Washington Square Park was looking a little less dire by
year's end. At a town hall meeting, local Villagers vehemently argued against
the plans to build the proposed roadway, and internal city conflicts were also
bubbling up. At one public meeting that fall, Moses and Manhattan Borough president Hulan Jack argued over whether the proposed roads should
be thirty-six or forty-eight feet wide; Moses called the former "ridiculously
narrow." Activist Shirley Hayes submitted the signatures of sixteen thousand

residents who supported the novel idea of closing the park to traffic entirely. For the moment, the area makeover was delayed.

Consciously or not, the culture overall was shifting in favor of the nonconformists who were increasingly making their way to the Village. Early in the year, the US Customs Office had seized copies of Allen Ginsberg's *Howl and Other Poems*, published by San Francisco's City Lights Books in 1956. For selling the work, Lawrence Ferlinghetti, the owner of the City Lights bookstore and publishing house, had been arrested, along with one of his clerks, on obscenity charges. In early October 1957, both were acquitted of "willfully and lewdly" selling supposedly indecent literature. In what felt like a vindication of the counterculture, the judge in the case decreed that despite language that was "coarse and vulgar," the paperback had "redeeming social importance." The cathartic release that was rock and roll couldn't be denied, but an ominous roadblock loomed when Elvis Presley, whose walloping "Jailhouse Rock" dominated the radio that fall and early winter, received his army draft notice on December 20 while on Christmas break at his Graceland home.

The Village and its musicians were far from in the clear. In the spring of 1957, Joseph McCarthy, the Wisconsin senator whose investigations of alleged Communists in the government had made him a national scourge, died of complications connected to alcoholism. But that same year, Pete Seeger was indicted for refusing to answer questions about his political affiliations before the House Un-American Activities Committee (he would eventually be convicted, but an appeals court would shoot down the indictment), and the FBI now had Van Ronk in its sights. In late 1956 he'd attended a meeting of what the Bureau called the Young Socialists League on West Fourteenth Street (it may have actually been the Socialist Youth League, a Trotskyite group), and the FBI, which was tracking the organization, had included his name in a report. On December 4, 1957, an FBI informant called the Bureau with some information—"in which the Bureau would probably be interested"—about Van Ronk possibly working with what the report called "a 'New Anarchist Youth Group,' which would be similar in principals [*sic*] to the Industrial Worker [*sic*] of the World." The Bureau responded that it appreciated the tip but that the caller "should not actively seek information on behalf of the FBI." The Bureau itself, though, would actively resume keeping an eye on Van Ronk.

Despite the protests from the community and the petition that appeared to hit the brakes on his plans, Moses remained committed to the idea of connecting the areas above and below Washington Square Park. Shortly before Christmas, a major rainstorm engulfed the city in 40-mile-per-hour winds, toppling the Christmas tree erected in Washington Square Park. But more unsettling news was to come. The actual day prior to Christmas, Moses reiterated his plan to alter Washington Square Park. In a seething statement issued by the Department of Parks, he deemed the idea of closing off the park "completely unworkable," claiming it would "endanger lives and destroy the value of abutting property." The developers of the apartment complexes south of the park were, he said, "formally, officially and reliably promised under the Slum Clearance Act a Fifth Avenue address." By New Year's Eve, the battle lines had been drawn: the city and its agencies and real estate owners on one hand, the reborn music community on the other.

Chapter 2

green, green rocky road

1958–1960

A s his slowly expanding FBI file bore out, Dave Van Ronk continued to be a person of interest for more than just other musicians in Washington Square Park. His name, along with those of countless others deemed Communist sympathizers, remained on the Bureau's surveillance list. By 1958, a roundup of his activities noted that on May 10, he'd played at a "YSL [Young Socialist League]–sponsored function at 100 Seventh Avenue South," around the corner from the former home of Cafe Society.

A few days later, Van Ronk made his way to another address, one that held far more promise for his career and the Village music community. Arriving at the corner of Thompson and Bleecker Streets, he pushed open a steel gate on the Thompson side, walked down a flight of metal stairs, and found himself in a small courtyard. A press statement would later describe that entrance as resembling "the back stairs of an old boiler room." But the Village Gate was further proof that, one square foot at a time, a new world was materializing before the eyes of Van Ronk and anyone else who saw the Village as a sanctuary and refuge.

For the earliest signs of that momentum—a slowly interconnecting web of clubs and coffeehouses—Van Ronk didn't have to look far beyond the Mac-Dougal Street apartment he'd begun sharing with his friend Samuel Charters, a musician and scholar of jazz and blues. On the ground floor of his five-story tenement at 116 MacDougal sat the Caricature, a cozy gathering spot where bridge players met in the front room while Van Ronk and his friends congregated in the back to play music, generally for no pay. Next door, at 114 Mac-Dougal, was the Kettle of Fish, a restaurant and bar whose ads boasted it was home to "an assortment of Village characters," thirsty musicians and writers among them. Across the street, at 105 MacDougal (otherwise known as 13 Minetta Street) lay the Commons, a sizable space that served as one of the new "basket houses" in the area—venues where singers and musicians weren't paid, but waitresses would pass around a basket or a similar container after the performances to collect cash. "They were very aggressive," said Dick Weissman, a banjo player from Philadelphia who went straight to Washington Square Park when he reached the city. "They'd throw it in their faces and say, 'What do you got for the musicians?' Which was great for us, because we didn't have to do anything."

On a good weekend, a performer like Weissman could bring home five to ten dollars, which more than helped toward his thirty-five-dollar monthly rent. And as Van Ronk learned when he was walking down his block and approached by Jimmy Gavin, one of a group of actors who had also taken to folksinging in the neighborhood, the Commons wanted to cram in as many entertainers as it could on any given night. As Van Ronk recalled, the work could be grueling: several sets starting at eight p.m. and lasting until roughly midnight, a slowdown just before dawn, then a few more sets for the after-hours crowd. "One of the things I remember most was walking out at eight in the morning, after being in a dark coffeehouse all night, and stepping out into the sunlight," he told writer Jack McGavin. "Boy, would that hurt when it hit your eyes."

At the Folklore Center, also on MacDougal, Izzy Young began hosting concerts, if one could use such a formal name for shows in such a cramped business. In the early months of 1958, two of them featured Van Ronk, both on his own and with a jug band that included John Cohen, a kid from Queens who, along with his friends Tom Paley on banjo and Pete Seeger's half brother Mike on fiddle, had started the New Lost City Ramblers. Paley was already a seminal figure in the burgeoning folk community, having cut an album in 1953 and also introduced the older two-finger banjo technique to the folk scene. "That was the gold standard," said Peter Stampfel. "Everyone wanted to be a hot-shit picker like Tom Paley." But the Ramblers weren't just another folk group; they insisted on playing old-timey music as close to the source as possible, dubbed "country music for city people," and their unbending approach found a natural home in the Village. Their slightly nasal voices and repertoire ("Roving Gambler," "Don't Let Your Deal Go Down") seemed to transport Washington Square Park to a patch of Appalachian hillside.

When the trio made its first album, in 1958, *The New Lost City Ramblers*, it was only natural that it would be available on Folkways, the decade-old label that had helped introduce Woody Guthrie to the world; it had also released Harry Smith's influential *Anthology of American Folk Music* collection. Folkways soon had competition from another outsider who'd escaped to the Village in the interest of reinvention. Raised on the Upper East Side, Jac Holzman was so unhappy, thanks to an emotionally distant father, that he ran away from home several times before he was a teenager. His grandmother, a part-time political commentator, introduced him to radio, which led the young Holzman into a fascination with recording technology. In 1948, around the time the Washington Square Park jams were starting, he was initiated into folk by way of a classmate at St. John's College in Maryland, and his discoveries included many Village regulars, including Guthrie, Lead Belly, Richard Dyer-Bennet, and Susan Reed. His own label, Elektra, started inauspiciously in 1950, when he recorded a campus recital by a soprano during his senior year.

Taking a year off from school, to which he never returned, Holzman moved to an apartment on Grove Street, lured by the Village's image as, he would write, "the symbol of free living and free loving." He eventually took over a sheet-music store on West Tenth Street and turned it into a full-time record emporium that specialized in international folk music—all the while recording local artists, from Reed to actor turned part-time folksinger Theodore Bikel, for Elektra. To make sure that his records made it into nearby stores, Holzman would sometimes deliver them by way of his Vespa. In 1954 he moved Elektra to 361 Bleecker and eventually an office on West Fourteenth Street. By 1958, Elektra had released more than 130 records: albums by Bikel; a set of Kentucky mountain music by Jean Ritchie; collections of folk songs from Italy, England, and Nova Scotia; blues records from Sonny Terry and Brownie McGhee, among others. Holzman also rescued Josh White from his banishment from the record business and signed the Shanty Boys, the Washington Square Park bluegrass trio featuring bass player and permit-holder Lionel Kilberg.

Clubs, coffeehouses, and now a local record company: the Village was becoming a self-contained, if geographically limited, industry. To the annoyance of anyone who lived and worked there, it was also attracting beatniks both real and fake. New York wasn't the original home of the beats, but it would soon host several hubs, including the basement of 116 MacDougal underneath the Caricature.

That location had had several different lives—a speakeasy in the pre-Prohibition years, a lamp store, and a carpentry shop before it closed during World War II. Thanks to a Pittsburgh car salesman, the space would soon be reinvented for the community sprouting up around it. John Mitchell, an army veteran who'd gone into the used-auto business, was visiting the city when his car broke down in the Village. Intrigued by the area, he moved to New York in search of a new life and business. By all descriptions a charismatic player, the wiry, gaunt-faced Mitchell already had a wife and child in California, would soon have another child (Christina) with Alene Lee (whose relationship with Jack Kerouac fueled his novel *The Subterraneans*), and reportedly had a new wife, Royce Mitchell, in the city. In 1956, a few years after he'd been in town, he and Royce opened the Cafe Figaro, the coffeehouse at Bleecker and MacDougal. When the couple broke up, Mitchell lost the Figaro; according to Van Ronk, Mitchell may have put his wife's name on the ownership papers for tax reasons.

For Mitchell, a business rebirth was hundreds of yards away. The subterranean part of 116 MacDougal met his goal of what the menu would eventually describe as "a meeting place, a focal center where this new generation of American youth, products of the Atomic Age, could openly and comfortably, intelligently discuss their existence and display their art, read their writings and poetry, and enjoy their music—be it folk or jazz." Since the space had been vacant for so long, it was strewn with trash, discarded furniture, and coal soot from the shaft that ran up to the building above. As he would later tell his son John, Mitchell cleaned the place out himself, jamming piles of dirt into his pockets and dumping them onto the street until the basement was ready for business.

Once the cleanup was done, Mitchell's new business had room for eight small round tables in the middle, flanked by four booths on either side. The restrooms would be across the room from the stage, which was itself only eight by ten feet. Because he hadn't applied for a liquor license (and didn't have a cabaret one, either), the food offerings would have to be confined to coffee, pastries, and, in time, ninety-cent hamburgers and basic sandwiches and omelets. But it would all suffice. Tapping into the influx of writers, poets, and tourists now infiltrating the neighborhood, Mitchell named his undertaking the Gaslight Poetry Cafe, with hours—from seven in the evening to six in the morning—suitable for creative types who kept irregular hours.

Around the same time Mitchell was scoping for a new business, an up-and-coming concert producer and impresario born Arthur Joshua Dlugoff was considering a club of his own in the Village. Art D'Lugoff (the apostrophe was added later, to make it easier to pronounce) came from a Jewish family that had moved from Harlem to Brighton Beach in Brooklyn. Maybe it was his background—his mother from Palestine, his father from a town in Russia, his grandparents liberal orthodox—but D'Lugoff, who had the look of a hungover rabbi, was drawn to underdogs. While busing tables in the Catskills, he not only heard Latin music but also saw how it appealed to the Jewish families who rented rooms there. Like Max Gordon at the Village Vanguard, he'd given law school a try but dropped out and tried a little bit of everything, from selling encyclopedias to working as a copyboy at the *Daily Compass* newspaper.

During his time in the US Air Force, when he was stationed in New Zealand and Australia, D'Lugoff helped put on shows for soldiers aboard his ship. Ultimately, he parlayed that aspect of his military life into a career in entertainment. He began managing a folk group, the Tarriers, landing them a prestigious slot on *The Ed Sullivan Show*. He started promoting concerts in the city, including at the Circle in the Square theater (formerly the Greenwich Village Inn) on Sheridan Square. By the mid-fifties, D'Lugoff had also taken note of the blacklisted or barely working folksingers who needed a place to perform. As he would recall, "I liked to go to some of the hootenannies—the Weavers and Pete Seeger—and I said, 'Maybe I can make a living putting these people on. Maybe it's a commercial business.'" With that, he found his calling.

Tired of renting other people's spaces, D'Lugoff was determined to open a place of his own—"a coffeehouse with a liquor license," he would later say—to avoid the high rents that prestige spots like Carnegie Hall would charge. Initially, he had a piano bar in mind, but a real estate agent directed him to the basement of the Mills Hotel at 156 Bleecker, the intersection of Bleecker and Thompson Streets. Writing about the transient business in 1937, gossip columnist Walter Winchell described its "acrid smell of antiseptic in the lobby of the Mills Hotel—for down-and-outers"; D'Lugoff himself called it "the largest bums' hotel in the city." The surrounding area consisted largely of strip clubs, shoe stores, and bars, and Bleecker Street came to an end just a block away, where it slammed into LaGuardia Place. But the basement of the Mills, which had been a laundromat, was 8,500 square feet for a reasonable $400 a month, and D'Lugoff and his brother Burt grabbed it. To transform it, they had to rip up the tile floor, build a stage, and add dressing rooms and air-conditioning. D'Lugoff began working so many long hours, with so little time to shave, that he grew a beard not unlike that of Cuban guerrilla leader Fidel Castro. In the end, he named the club the Village Gate, both a nod to its street-level entrance and to the Gate of Horn, the must-play Chicago folk club.

In the Village, the fluttering of flamenco guitars could often be heard emanating from coffeehouses and restaurants, and the Village Gate's opening night, on May 15, 1958, presented one of the stars of that genre, Spain's Carlos Montoya. But leading up to that evening, D'Lugoff hosted several soft openers, even before a stage was mounted. One featured the Clancy Brothers and Tommy Makem, among the unlikeliest of the Village's first folk-music stars. The Clancys hailed from County Tipperary in Ireland and had engaged in their share of wandering before Pat, or "Paddy," and Tom arrived in New York in 1951. The two brothers had served in Britain's Royal Air Force and had come to the States by way of Canada, looking to pursue their first passion, act-ing. Like most struggling actors, they took what work they could, including in a Cleveland auto-repair shop. But when they got to New York, they rented out the Cherry Lane Theatre, a 189-seat space on Commerce Street in the West Village, where they were joined by their younger brother Liam and by Makem, whose family also had roots in Ireland's County Armagh.

To raise money for their theater productions, the brothers and Makem had taken to singing in that theater and wherever else anyone would have them. That included the White Horse Tavern, the West Village bar that had become a well-stocked home away from home for Dylan Thomas, Jack Kerouac, and other writers. Soon after came an album of rebel songs, *The Rising of the Moon*, released in 1956 on Paddy Clancy's own Tradition Records. By 1958, the group and its repertoire of hearty drinking and folk songs, combined with the musi-cians' thick Irish sweaters and their own prodigious boozing habits, made them feel authentic. Hearing the Clancys became a rite of passage for Amer-ican "folkniks," a term conceived by Izzy Young to describe city types who'd taken to the music.

Everyone in the Village seemed to adore the Clancy Brothers and Tommy Makem, so it was only natural for Van Ronk to check them out at an early night at the Village Gate. He came with his friend Barry Kornfeld, the bespectacled, crew-cutted banjo player and guitarist and contributor to *Caravan*. Originally from Queens, Kornfeld had heard Pete Seeger's *My Darling Corey* album, had learned to play the banjo from instrumental manuals, and had begun head-ing down to the park as soon as he could. Embedding himself with one of the small bluegrass bands, he'd yell out the name of one of the three hoedowns he knew and begin playing along, waiting for everyone to join in. In the park he'd also met Van Ronk, who came over to him one afternoon, asked to borrow his guitar, and played a few ragtime tunes.

When the Clancys and Makem's set at the Gate wrapped up, everyone, including Van Ronk and Kornfeld, stayed and joined in on a version of the tra-ditional Scottish ballad "Wild Mountain Thyme." Many of them were blitzed out of their minds on the free beer that D'Lugoff offered up for the occasion, and now there was even more reason to celebrate.

In February 1958, just before the metal entrance to the Village Gate creaked open for the first time, Blue Note Records unveiled Sonny Rollins's *A Night at the Village Vanguard*, largely culled from his second set that night the previous fall. The album wasn't instantly embraced, but it would amount to Rollins's breakout statement as a bandleader. Starting with the words on its cover, *A Night at the Village Vanguard* would play an equally important role in the part of town where it was cut. After two decades in business, the Vanguard didn't need to be legitimized, but both it and the Village scene could benefit from a dose of national attention, and the Rollins album, the first of many to be recorded at the Vanguard, proclaimed the existence and legitimacy of the venue to anyone who walked into a record store. For Max Gordon, it was the type of advertising that money or public relations couldn't buy.

Acoustic music was still struggling to find its footing and its venues in the Village. As Van Ronk saw for himself during his visits to the Five Spot, jazz was having a far easier time settling into the district. In terms of performance spaces that actually paid and welcomed musicians who had LPs to their credit, it was becoming the dominant genre in the neighborhood. By early 1958, the *Daily News* reported on a jazz community consisting of the Vanguard, Cafe Bohemia, the Five Spot, and the Half Note. The music rattling those spaces knew few bounds. In July 1958, Miles Davis and John Coltrane teamed up at the Vanguard, the same month that Thelonious Monk, who finally had a cabaret card, took over the Five Spot with saxophonist Johnny Griffin, bassist Ahmed Abdul-Malik, and drummer Roy Haynes. Released by Riverside mere months after Rollins's Vanguard album, *Thelonious in Action: Recorded at the Five Spot Cafe* captured the short-lived lineup; "Evidence" was a showcase for Griffin's ability to wail around Monk's chord voicings. Tying the community together, Rollins succeeded Griffin in Monk's band in the fall of 1958.

The connection between jazz and the beats—both based in improvisation, both linked to drug culture—was undeniable and only becoming more prevalent. The Five Spot itself became ground zero for the worlds' intermingling. Early in 1958 the club began hosting evenings of what it called "jazz-poetry" every Monday; one paired Charles Mingus with Langston Hughes. Meanwhile, over at the Vanguard, Kerouac started reading over jazz accompaniment on Sunday afternoons at the Vanguard, although the stint lasted only a week once Kerouac tired of the live accompaniment.

The media picked up on the bond between the two art forms and largely treated it as a novelty. "Now don't think that we don't dig Beethoven-oorini," a "youngish-looking cat in blue jeans and T-shirt" told the *Daily News* early in 1958. "We dig everything, man. It's just that jazz is it. It has it, it means it, it says it." His girlfriend, clad in a black sweater and sitting next to him, added, "Jazz is cool and it has a beat and it makes us move. That's what we've got to do—move and go."

But there was nothing funny or fleeting about what also happened at the Five Spot starting in mid-November 1959, when Ornette Coleman, a twenty-nine-year-old, Texas-born saxophonist, began a run of shows there. Coleman had shown up in the city from Los Angeles with a heady reputation and enormous mystique—a kid who'd played in Texas juke joints and worked as an elevator operator in California but was now seen as one of the future giants of his music. It wasn't just that Coleman played a white plastic alto sax; it was his entire approach, abandoning chording instruments and the chordal approach for what came to be known as free jazz.

Coleman was hardly the only musician in his field who was dynamiting known boundaries. But starting with reporters who were invited down to the Five Spot to hear a preview of his sets, he made arguably the most explosive impression. "Some walked in and out before they could finish a drink, some sat mesmerized by the sound, others talked constantly to their neighbors at the table or argued with drink in hand at the bar," wrote George Hoefer in *DownBeat*, the prominent jazz magazine. Once the shows began, the critical reaction was mixed, with Coleman viewed alternately as an innovator and a menace. Some writers, like John S. Wilson of the *Times*, grappled with Coleman's music's inventiveness and challenges (what Wilson called "simply elusive staccato riffs"), whereas another *DownBeat* critic wrote that each of Coleman's performances should have been covered by insurance in the event of ill health.

Coleman didn't seem to care one way or another. But his music—and the way it would affect other musicians around him—was also emblematic of the patience the Village had for such experimentation. Once more, the neighborhood had become home to a musical art form that may not have incubated anywhere else.

■ ■ ■ ■

At first, Sheila Jordan thought the Page Three was much like the Village Vanguard a block north. Arriving for her first gig at the club at 147 Seventh Avenue South, she ventured down a series of steps, past restrooms and through swinging doors; a kitchen was on the left, and a small performance space with a tiny bandstand lay straight ahead. But once her eyes adjusted to the darkness, she realized the men were in fact women in suits, and there may have also been a few men dolled up as women. As pianist Dave Frishberg would later write, the Page Three was "a museum of sexual lifestyles."

In the Village, such a sight was not necessarily new; gay men and women had been gravitating to the neighborhood for half a century, and illegal bars that attracted gays had begun popping up on Bleecker and other area streets in the 1920s. "Tearoom" became a euphemism for lesbians' meeting spots, among them Eve's Hangout at 129 MacDougal. Run by Eve Adams, formerly known as Chawa Zloczower before she emigrated to the United States from Poland, it soon became a gathering space for gay women. After a neighbor tipped off the police to what was taking place, an undercover policewoman, posing as a lesbian, helped bust Adams. Called "one of Greenwich Village's most famous and ultra-modern maids" by the *Daily News*, she was arrested for disorderly conduct and soon deported for writing an allegedly obscene book (a collection of poems, *Lesbian Love*), and Eve's Hangout was shut down. (Perhaps coincidentally, its progressive spirit lived on when the top floor of the building was eventually occupied by Pete Seeger and his wife, Toshi.)

The demise of Eve's Hangout didn't dissuade anyone in the Village from presenting entertainment steeped in gay and drag culture. As early as 1931, the Nut Club, at 99 Seventh Avenue South, presented a revue that included men dressed as female dancers. Starting in the mid-thirties, the Howdy Club, at 47 West Third Street, pulled in a gay female clientele and presented male impersonators. Lesbians also found a safe space at Tony Pastor's Downtown, also on West

Third Street, which billed itself as "New York's Most Colorful Nite Club" on its matchbox covers. Before John Mitchell had reconfigured the space first known as the Gaslight Poetry Cafe, that location had been home to Louis' Luncheon, a gay hangout in the 1920s. Writing about the rise in prostitutes in the city in 1954, the *Daily News* chastised the Village as "a concentrating point for sexual deviates." Ramblin' Jack Elliott, the Brooklyn cowboy known for his ranch-hand looks and rakish charm, would recall playing a gay bar in the Village in 1953: "They were an excellent audience. I think they liked my *jeans*."

By the time the Page Three opened in 1956, those joints had endured their share of rough times. The Mob may have supported them—a prominent member of the Genovese crime family co-owned Tony Pastor's, and, according to historian C. Alexander Hortis, a Genovese associate ran the Howdy Club—but the crackdowns continued. On the same day, November 15, 1944, both the Howdy Club and Tony Pastor's were found guilty of allegations tied to what were called "moral charges." According to the filings, the Howdy Club was cited for presenting Leon La Verdi, a male dancer who "exhibited feminine characteristics which would appeal to any male homosexual." The owners of Tony Pastor's were found guilty of welcoming lesbians. Neither club was closed for good, but both had their licenses suspended through the first week of December, and the Howdy Club didn't make it to the end of the year.

Although she was unaware of most of that history, Sheila Jordan was at home with dark horses and long shots. In the hardscrabble coal-mining town of Summerhill, Pennsylvania, Jordan, born Sheila Dawson, was raised by her grandparents; her mother, who'd given birth when she was seventeen, considered herself too young for the task. As a teenager, Jordan left home and moved to Detroit; by then, her mother had developed a drinking problem and, Jordan said, "married creepy guys who beat her up and came on to me." (Later, when producer George Russell came to see her at the Page Three and asked where she was from, Jordan replied, "Hell—I came from hell.") In Detroit she began frequenting jazz clubs with Black audiences and met Frank Foster, a rising sax and flute player who would later work with Count Basie. The two wound up living together.

After Foster was drafted during the Korean War in the early fifties, Jordan moved to New York, partly owing to the prejudice she encountered in Detroit;

she and Foster, who was Black, were harassed by police. Her move to Manhattan was also inspired by her musical hero, Charlie Parker, who lived there. In the city, she landed a job as a typist at the advertising agency Doyle Dane Bernbach (DDB), met Parker, and fell into a relationship with pianist and frequent Parker accompanist Duke Jordan, whom she married in 1953. Tragedy ensued when Duke became addicted to heroin.

Throughout her unsettled life, singing had long been one of the few things that brought Jordan joy. When an executive at DDB learned she had a developing talent as a vocalist, Jordan was soon heard in the company's ads for watches and refrigerators. But Jordan longed to tackle the jazz ballads she loved, and in front of an audience. When a friend told her about "this place in the Village" that featured "different kinds of music," Jordan, looking to reboot her life as she neared thirty, investigated.

Jordan hadn't heard of the Page Three at all, but neither had most of Manhattan. No ads or listings could be found for it in the local press, and newspaper music writers and gossip columnists hardly mentioned it. To make a reservation, one had to scour the Manhattan phone book for a number. Unlike Trude Heller's Versailles, a club on Sixth Avenue and Ninth Street that also attracted a gay clientele, the Page Three wasn't known for luring out-of-town tourists, who may well have been freaked out by what they saw once they descended its stairs. The alternative world it welcomed started with its hostess, Jackie Howe, who was often seen wearing a man's business suit. Her partner in club management, Kiki Hall, often served as the emcee, singing proudly racy lyrics as he welcomed the talent onto the Page Three's stage. Jazz players like Frishberg would back random vocalists, and it was also the place to encounter strippers or a male singer who made himself up to resemble a woman. Esther Sutherland, who went on to an acting career, tackled blues and ballads; Carol MacDonald, who would later become the guitarist in one of the first all-women rock bands, Goldie and the Gingerbreads, was also working out her skills at the Page Three, years before she came out.

Impressed with Jordan's first performance there, Howe offered her a regular spot—two, in fact, a Monday jazz night and a second that was more of a free-for-all. "It wasn't like the Vanguard," Jordan said. "It was a variety show: a

jazz singer and a blues singer and a comedian and a dancer. It had to be mixed."
The dressing room was in the kitchen, and the pay was six dollars a night—four
of which went to a babysitter for her and Jordan's daughter, Tracey, and two for
a cab home to the family apartment on East Twelfth Street.

But as a place to work up a repertoire and start fine-tuning the vocalese that
became her trademark, the Page Three suited Jordan just fine. For the singer,
who was diminutive and often wore her dark hair in strict bangs that lent her
the aura of a somber chanteuse, the customers who frequented the Page Three
were not a distraction but an accepting crowd who loved jazz. Those gigs often
teamed her with estimable pianists like Frishberg, Herbie Nichols, and Johnny
Knapp, as well as drummer Ziggy Willman, and Jordan could lose herself in
"If You Could See Me Now," one of Sarah Vaughan's signature songs, and
Frank Sinatra's "I'm a Fool to Want You."

As the months and years went on, Jordan would often be accompanied by
bass player Steve Swallow, who'd quit Yale halfway through his sophomore
year and moved to New York to work on his craft. He'd had a taste of the Village in the fifties, when he took the train from New Haven, Connecticut, to
the city, bought a ticket to a production of *The Iceman Cometh*, and caught
Miles Davis at Cafe Bohemia. Then, after Allen Ginsberg gave a reading at
Yale, Swallow followed the poet and his crew to a New Haven bar, where he
picked Ginsberg's brain about what it was like to live in New York City. Ginsberg suggested certain parts of town and the cheap one-dollar steaks at Tad's
Steakhouse in Times Square, and Swallow soon relocated there.

From the folk coffeehouses that were starting to pop up to the Page Three,
Swallow began grabbing whatever work he could as an accompaniment.
Barely twenty, he was, he recalled, "this frightened little kid hoping to make
it in the city," and the Page Three felt like an especially foreign world to Swallow, who was straight. "It was a vehemently gay scene," he said. "You went
down the steps into this very dark club, and as soon as you were in there, you
had a license to be yourself. There was a remarkably forgiving atmosphere
down there. Anything was acceptable. And that was something I'd never
experienced." He and Jordan clicked musically, often performing voice and
bass duets.

Both were particularly taken with Herbert Khaury, a stringy-haired, one-man freak show from the Bronx who played a ukulele, sang in an eerie quaver, and had a deep reservoir of knowledge of pre–rock-and-roll history and songs. Known by various stage names, including Larry Love and eventually Tiny Tim, he made the Page Three one of his rounds in the Village, sitting in with the band or hanging out with the crowd, which accepted him as one of their own. Swallow didn't initially know what to make of him, but he grew to respect his skills and the way he was a fully formed persona. "He wasn't alone in the Village," Swallow said. "People were constructing characters for themselves and becoming them. And Tiny was fully invested in his character."

Perhaps too much so: worried that Tiny's eccentric look could make him a target for those who viewed him as a weirdo, Jordan cornered him one day in the Page Three. "He had long hair and, at the time, guys did not have that," she recalled. "And I told him, 'Tiny, do me a favor, or do *yourself* a favor. Your hair is great, but when you leave this club and ride the subway, put it up under your hat, because if you don't, you're going to get attacked.'" She wasn't sure he ever listened, but she hoped he would take her advice.

In June 1958, one bit of good news reached Van Ronk. Although he'd had to register for the Selective Service a few years earlier, he was now designated 4F—"unacceptable" for military service "for physical and mental (psychiatric) reasons." According to his evaluation, his tendency toward being "very tense and jittery" was one reason, along with his "moist, clammy hands" and halting, stammering speech. The Korean War had ended five years prior, and now, at least, he wouldn't have to fight in any future conflict.

That designation was a relief, but it didn't help answer questions about how Van Ronk *could* support himself in the years ahead. At the time he and Terri Thal had met, Van Ronk "considered himself an anarchist," Thal said, but even anarchists needed some sort of paycheck. At the end of one park session, as the police had begun signaling to the musicians to scatter, he approached Dick Weissman and asked him, "Can you make a *living* doing this?" Weissman replied that, yes, it was possible if one jumped back and forth between recording, performing, and teaching.

Whether the inspiration came from Weissman or not, *Caravan* announced that Van Ronk had begun giving lessons in his home, and anyone interested should reach him by leaving a message at the Folklore Center, which had become one of Van Ronk's haunts. Being paid for live gigs, though, was still not a viable option. The Cafe Bizarre was not going to work out as a permanent home for folkies; as Van Ronk would later write, Rick Allmen (whom Van Ronk called "an unprincipled man") would pay for name acts like Odetta but not for upstarts like him. The club would soon claim to be making an impressive $75,000 a year, but its ads in the *Village Voice* listed only "folk singing" with no names attached. That slight only added to its reputation as, Van Ronk wrote, "a tourist trap, selling the clydes [customers] a Greenwich Village that never existed except in the film *Bell, Book and Candle*."

In order to protect themselves and not be exploited by any current or future club owners, a bunch of musicians, including Van Ronk, formed the Folksingers Guild. For a short period, the loose-knit group thrived, producing multiple-act shows at the Folklore Center and the Sullivan Street Playhouse, a former speakeasy converted into an intimate theater space. Thal handled what amounted to the publicity, notifying local press about the shows. "The only expenses were the cost of an auditorium, which was very low," Thal said. "The rest of the money was divided among the performers. At the worst-attended concert we produced, the performers each were paid $1." The guild was always a little precarious—its biggest draw, folksinger and guitarist Paul Clayton, declared he was a professional and shouldn't adhere to its rules. "They were trying to establish a union for folk singers because the [Musicians Union] had no interest in this," said Weissman, who was a member. "But it fell apart when it came to setting a minimum. The same old story—you're barely making it and somebody offers you a gig and, in solidarity, you shouldn't take it. But you needed the $25. People started scabbing, so to speak." According to Thal, the final chord was struck when the treasurer grabbed the little bit of money they'd saved, around $50, and disappeared; the Folksingers Guild soon dissolved.

Unbeknownst to Van Ronk, the FBI was keeping track of that and his other activity. By the beginning of 1959, he was still being monitored by the Bureau, which took note of his attendance at Young People's Socialist League (YPSL) "business meetings" between October 1958 and January 1959. Unrelated to that surveillance, Van Ronk had fled New York yet again, this time not for the merchant marine but for more work in his chosen profession. California, he heard, had plenty of work for musicians. Leaving Thal temporarily behind, he hitched a ride to Chicago for a YPSL conference, then continued out west, where friends told him he could make money in coffeehouses.

First in San Francisco and then in Los Angeles, Van Ronk saw the "folk boom" up close and realized how separate he felt from it. But he used the work he landed in clubs and coffeehouses to refine his repertoire and performance chops. Returning to New York in June 1959, just in time for Thal's graduation from Brooklyn College, he found he was still enough of a name in the community that his homecoming was announced in the pages of *Gardyloo*, a new folkzine launched by Lee Shaw shortly before Van Ronk's return. (*Caravan* had become too overwhelming a proposition for her, so she handed it over to banjo player Billy Faier to run.) Soon after, Van Ronk and Thal moved into a fifth-floor walk-up at 219 West Fifteenth Street, five streets north of the Village Vanguard.

Van Ronk had begun venturing back into the park on Sunday afternoons; one day in late July, he played alongside the New Lost City Ramblers' Mike Seeger and John Cohen. That same day, someone even spotted Woody Guthrie, supposedly his first appearance in the park in five years. But money was still a debilitating issue. "Dave wasn't going to earn a penny as a folksinger in New York," Thal said. "It was a problem, because Dave couldn't do anything else. He was pretty incapable of holding down a nine-to-five job. He tried occasionally, but it never worked. He tried the job that many young socialist men worked at, in a print shop run by comrades. But even there, he couldn't handle it." To help pay the rent, Thal took a job teaching world and American history at a high school in the area. Her pay, $70 a week, more than covered their $70-a-month rent.

Van Ronk also returned to a world that had ramped up slightly. He actively disliked the fake beats—with their goatees, berets, and bongos—who were suddenly popping up in the Village, calling it "horseshit." But he admired actual poets, and the Gaslight Cafe had begun hosting poetry readings shortly before Van Ronk had taken his side trip to California. Ginsberg, Kerouac, and Gregory Corso would read occasionally, as did Black poet Amiri Baraka, then an expelled Howard University student named LeRoi Jones. The Gaslight would also be a creative base for Hugh Romney, a winsome-faced twentysomething poet from in and around the Northeast (prone to reciting lines like "the eggs of jazz grew ripe in Dixie"), and John Brent, a poet, writer, and fledgling actor. Romney (who would later be reborn as Wavy Gravy, West Coast peace activist) soon became the venue's poetry and entertainment director.

Edna Walker-Malcoskey, an established novelist and poet, once asked John Mitchell how much he paid the poets, to which he reportedly replied, "Oh, we don't charge poets anything." But Mitchell was happy to take money from the tourists who, as Romney would later recall to Van Ronk, "would line up five deep around the block to look at beatniks, an intellectual freak show." The out of towners who came to gawk—amusingly dubbed "stare-niks" by the *Daily News*—also loved to take jabs at the locals: "Hey, Castro, get a shave!" they'd yell to some of the poets on their way to the Gaslight. To ensure that the applause in the club didn't irk the apartment dwellers living above it—the sound would travel up the coal chutes—Mitchell told the audiences to snap their fingers instead.

As Weissman had also suggested, Van Ronk became determined to put his music on record. He'd made his recording debut, along with Paul Clayton, Peggy Seeger (Pete's half sister), and others, on *Our Singing Heritage Volume 1,* a collection of traditional songs on Elektra in the fall of 1958. The *New York Times'* new folk-music chronicler, Robert Shelton, cited Van Ronk's "two visceral, rocking Negro songs," one a cover of the 1920s blues lament "Nobody Knows You When You're Down and Out." Folk music was becoming a commodity: that same year, the Kingston Trio, with their robust harmonies and striped shirts, had actually scored a number-one hit with "Tom Dooley," a traditional murder ballad that sounded unlike anything else on pop radio—and benefited mightily from that distinction.

Van Ronk didn't consider himself a folksinger, but he began badgering a few record labels, including Elektra and Folkways, to record him. Folkways' Moses

Asch decided to take a chance and recruited folk authority Kenny Goldstein, a frequent visitor to the Folklore Center, to produce Van Ronk's debut. Goldstein already had a slew of production credits to his name, including records by folksinger and radio host Oscar Brand and Ed McCurdy, the former crooner and radio host who had reinvented himself as a folksinger and written "Last Night I Had the Strangest Dream," a gentle antiwar ballad regularly covered in coffeehouses and basket houses.

Now it was Van Ronk's turn. In a day, maybe two, the record was cut at Goldstein's basement studio on Long Island. When it was released in 1959, *Dave Van Ronk Sings Ballads, Blues and a Spiritual* was described in the *Times* as "an uncommonly interesting young white singer's excursion into Southern Negro folk song," adding, "There is a lot of vigor and 'low-down' simulation of style by a performer with a voice from the gravel pits and a neatly articulated guitar." Van Ronk would come to see the record as a halting first step. "My singing sounds high and forced," he would later write, and his guitar playing "made me want to crawl under a rug." Upon receiving a copy of the album while he was in California, Van Ronk also instantly despised the cover, a photo of an espresso machine rather than the person who was singing and playing.

But as an indication of his capabilities and of the music emerging from the Village, the album made for a valid carrying card. Accompanying himself on guitar, Van Ronk galloped from "Duncan and Brady," the real-life tale of a cop killed during a barroom fight, to an interpretation of Jelly Roll Morton's "Winin' Boy" that revealed the charming winsomeness Van Ronk could also summon up. On a version of the Reverend Gary Davis's "Twelve Gates to the City," he showed how he and his guitar could evoke gospel spirituals without a church in sight, and he delivered a slow, haunted take on the traditional "In the Pines," which he'd learned from a recording by Irene and Ellen Kossoy, twin sisters from Manhattan who came across like a female and even folksier version of the Everly Brothers. Unlike the Kossoy Sisters' take, Van Ronk's rendition of "In the Pines" felt like a walk down a darkened woods path. The album also featured one of his earliest attempts at songwriting, a straight, spare blues called "If You Leave Me Pretty Momma."

Dave Van Ronk Sings Ballads, Blues and a Spiritual didn't make much of a dent in the world outside of the Village; the Kingston Trio had little to worry about. But the record made it clear that Van Ronk was a presence all his own. One day that year, Izzy Young played the album for Alan Lomax, the folklorist who'd traveled around the country interviewing and recording Guthrie, Lead Belly, Muddy Waters, and nearly every important vernacular performer or songwriter of the time. Lomax had just returned to the States after close to a decade in London, where he'd moved after the House Un-American Activities Committee had begun poking around into his friendship with Communists. (Lomax would always deny that he left the States for that reason.) After *Ballads, Blues and a Spiritual* had finished, "Izzy said, 'Where is he from?' and Alan said, 'Alabama—he's a Black man from Alabama,'" Thal recalled. "Izzy told him how wrong he was. Our theory was that Alan never forgave Dave for Alan's mistake." However, the mere fact that Van Ronk had convinced an expert like Lomax that he wasn't white was compensation enough.

At his home in Mount Vernon, roughly twenty miles northeast of New York City, seventeen-year-old Danny Kalb was engaged in one of his regular pastimes, listening to a folk radio show hosted by George Lorrie, a folksinger and pro-union activist. Worried that a trip to Eastern Europe would have him pegged as a Communist sympathizer, Lorrie had changed his last name from Levine. Whether he knew that backstory or not, Kalb was more focused on music that night. A neophyte guitarist, he'd played rock and roll in a high school band, but thanks in part to his parents' record collection, he was now more attracted to the blues. Kalb was especially struck by a new recording that Lorrie played—what Kalb assumed was a Black blues singer who, Lorrie told his listeners, taught guitar and could be found in Washington Square Park on Sundays. "I said, 'Fuck all, I'm going to go there and get this Black blues singer to teach *me*,'" Kalb recalled. He had no idea how much money he needed to raise for the lessons, but he knew he needed to meet that singer, who Lorrie said was named Dave Van Ronk.

Teenagers like Kalb were still drawn to the park, scoping out players they'd heard about or whose styles they wanted to learn. But no one was sure how long they'd be able to keep doing so. Plans to construct a roadway through Washington Square Park continued to move apace. In a letter to *Caravan* in February 1958, Lionel Kilberg, still the keeper of the permits for those jamborees, expressed his concern about the park's fate. "From appearances," he wrote, "the area may be wiped out to make way for a highway. I don't resent the highway, but I would appreciate the aid of other folksingers in New York City in locating a new site." He added that he was open to suggestions for replacement areas, which included a public space near the East River. *Gardyloo*, meanwhile, took note of the "antagonism of the police and the press" toward the folksingers in the park.

Thankfully for the families and musicians in the area, opposition to Moses's proposals was accelerating, led by the awkwardly named but efficient Joint Emergency Committee to Close Washington Square Park. Alongside Carmine DeSapio, the sharply dressed Village district leader and Tammany Hall boss, the committee also included Shirley Hayes and Jane Jacobs. At a hearing in September 1958, dozens of speakers advocated for an alternate plan: closing off the park entirely to traffic. Joined by former first lady and Village resident Eleanor Roosevelt and an ambitious US congressman, John Lindsay, DeSapio put his support behind the idea of cordoning off the park. Roosevelt even led a delegation to city hall to protest the highway proposal. Facing that combined clout, the board of estimates signed off on a plan to close the park for thirty to sixty days to allow both sides to monitor the results. In December 1958 a *New York Times* editorial applauded the city for backing the idea: "The Square was a place of 'repose,' crying out to be saved from 'progress.'"

Two months later, in a triumphant victory for the Village, its residents, and the music, traffic was permanently vanquished from the park. The fountain remained in place, and the Sunday-afternoon hootenannies—like the all-star bluegrass jam that June, which brought together banjo player Eric Weissberg, mandolinist Ralph Rinzler, and the Greenbriar Boys, featuring singer and guitarist John Herald—had a future. Decca Records, which had canceled the Weavers' recording contract a few years before, cashed in on the folk resurgence by releasing *The Best of the Weavers*, the first compilation of the group's career.

As for Kalb, folk may have only been a portion of his musical interests, but the intersection of music and politics was built into him. His father, Fred, had been a trade-union organizer before working at a law firm that specialized in workers-compensation law. Danny was born in Brooklyn in September 1942; around 1950, Fred, his wife, Gertrude, and the family, including Danny's younger brother, Jonathan, moved to the suburb of Mount Vernon. Disillusioned with the Democratic Party, Fred and Gertrude supported Henry Wallace, the former vice president to Franklin Delano Roosevelt and now third-party candidate for the Progessive Party, in his ill-fated bid for the presidency in 1948. Their musical tastes were equally liberal: the Kalbs's record collection housed discs by Josh White, Nina Simone, and Paul Robeson, along with classical records. Gertrude played piano, and Fred had a deep bass voice when he sang.

By his own admission, Danny was a terrible student, with a sarcastic streak that could infuriate some and endear him to others. But his self-assuredness and occasionally goofy side, the way he could burst into giggles when he found something funny, set him apart; already smoking by his teen years, he seemed prematurely bohemian. "Danny was pretty formidable," said his cousin Peter Kogan. "He was a really confident, good-looking guy. The kind of guy you would look up to." Like many kids his age, he'd become enamored of rock and roll when it erupted in the mid-fifties. But when his high school band fell apart during his senior year, "I gravitated straight away to the blues," he later told archivist Mitch Blank. "So Lead Belly, Josh White, and Brownie McGhee were my natural form of things once I got immersed in it."

Likely the same summer that traffic was banned in Washington Square Park, Kalb went in search of the mysterious blues singer he'd heard on the radio. Kalb had first taken lessons from Jerry Silverman, who worked for *Sing Out!*, the politically minded folk magazine, but Kalb was more intrigued by that voice from the airwaves. Venturing into the park one Sunday, he started at the fountain. "I asked someone, 'Excuse me, can you direct me to the Black blues singer Dave Van Ronk?'" he recalled. "They looked at me a little funny, but someone said, 'Van Ronk is over there.'"

Kalb walked over a far-off spot in the park, where a disheveled-looking guy sat with a guitar, singing and playing in the same style Kalb had heard on the airwaves. "I go over and there's no Black guy there," Kalb said. "He's not Black!" Although Van Ronk was immediately imposing, Kalb asked if he gave lessons. "Yeah, kid, I charge money!" Van Ronk shot back. He told Kalb he charged $15 a lesson, gave him his address on Fifteenth Street, and instructed him to be there in a week.

On the appointed day, Kalb arrived, rang up to Van Ronk, made his way up the five flights to the apartment, knocked on the door, and heard nothing. Walking back down, he sat on the small stoop, waited fifteen minutes, rang up again, and went back upstairs. This time, the door flung open, and there stood Thal, clad, as she sometimes was at home, in just a bra and panties. "Come in, kid!" she barked. Van Ronk was lying in bed, shirtless but with his pants on and cradling a guitar. "All right, kid—sit down!" he said. "Let's hear some blues."

For the next half hour or so, the two traded blues parts. Van Ronk admired Kalb's speed and quick-study dexterity—the bits of stinging-bee notes he would slip into his playing—and Kalb realized that Van Ronk could be a mentor to him. At the end of the session, he handed over his fifteen dollars and made the decision to continue with the lessons as long as Van Ronk would have him. With Van Ronk's supervision, Kalb began shifting from what he called the "sweet blues" into the heavier, duskier Mississippi Delta style. But the appeal wasn't merely musical. From the songs to Van Ronk's lifestyle in the Village, Kalb had found his calling. "I knew this was better than anything I'd ever known in my life before," he told Blank. "I wanted to do this life!" He would be neither the first nor last person to knock on that door and find a portal into a more liberating world.

▌▌▐▌▌

For a thirty-five-cent café au lait and as much time as one needed to relax and enjoy it, it was still hard to beat the Cafe Figaro, once co-owned by the Gaslight's John Mitchell. Its round tables and dim lighting lent it the feel of a hang for locals more than tourists; Van Ronk would later write about the large tab he accumulated during afternoons there. The Fig was now owned by Charles T.

(or Tommy) Ziegler and John Mitchell's ex-wife Royce, who, in a bit of Village gossip everyone chewed over, were now a couple themselves.

As a result of the corner of Bleecker and MacDougal getting busier by the day, it was only a matter of time before someone noticed that espresso wasn't the only thing being served at the Fig. October 4, 1959, marked the twelfth straight Sunday afternoon that live music was presented inside, this time by way of the Silvermine String Trio. Fifteen minutes into their performance—a piece by Bach or Schubert, depending on the source—Ziegler was startled when two uniformed cops entered and asked to see his cabaret license. He wasn't serving liquor, so Ziegler didn't have such paperwork to show them, and the music came to a quick halt. Tellingly, the concert went on—but in a private apartment on East Twentieth Street, six blocks north of the Village boundary.

The more people streamed into the area to see live music, the more the violations seemed to increase. The first jarring wave of crackdowns had slammed into the area in the spring of 1959, when police started making examples of coffeehouses that featured poetry readings but didn't have cabaret licenses. That June, a truce of sorts was declared: after a degree of blowback by the community, Bob Lubin, another Gaslight poetry director, argued in the press that poetry was art, not entertainment, and Deputy Police Commissioner Walter Arm decided the summonses weren't worth the court time they ate up. Invited by Mitchell to appear at the Gaslight, Arm stood before a group of reporters and recited his own verse: "Technically, a beatnik spouting poetry is an entertainer under law / But, though in violation, to the cops he's just a bore / He can talk throughout the night if he doesn't incite to riot / We hope he keeps talking till his audience yells for quiet."

The moment was amusingly surreal; Arm said afterward that his department would rather "laugh it off" with such a gag than issue summonses. But the October bust at the Cafe Figaro was among the first signs that the nascent music scene, and the people it was bringing into the area, were setting off alarm bells. Nine months after the Figaro bust, Ziegler was handed another summons during yet another free afternoon show, even though a judge had ruled that the performances were classical entertainment, not barroom music.

That charge was dismissed a month later, but the cleanup operation would continue into the new year. The Village Gate's Art D'Lugoff would call the cabaret law "nasty," but few doubted that it was profitable for the city. The annual license for club owners had climbed to $150, and cabaret cards for musicians were $2 a year. In 1958 the city's License Department, whose sixty inspectors would make periodic surprise visits to venues and bars to ensure they were abiding by the law, reportedly raked in $1.5 million in cumulative licenses from everything from nightclubs to street painters and soapbox orators. Of that windfall, $231,000 came from nightclubs.

Reflecting D'Lugoff's varied tastes, the Gate presented an eclectic range of music: within its first year, it featured jazz acts (Art Blakey, Nina Simone, Herbie Mann, Randy Weston), avant-garde composers (Edgard Varèse, John Cage), and Israeli and African dance troupes. Still, the Gate nearly had to close after being cited three times for "dimming its lights during entertainment," which was prohibited in the cabaret law. Appearing on WNYC radio, D'Lugoff argued that he had complied with the lighting request but had still received fifteen violations since opening. Meanwhile, on a June weekend in 1960, the Cafe Bizarre was cited for a fire violation. After Allmen and his co-owner, Sadie Rickoff, sued the city and the city's fire commissioner for keeping the club closed, it finally reopened in October 1960. The Cafe Rafio, a coffeehouse at 165 Bleecker, just a few streets down from the Figaro, opened in the spring of 1960; a skilled guitarist, Dick Rosmini, was often heard there. But even though it was a basket house, not a cabaret, it had already received several summonses by year's end.

The pushback wasn't limited to police and fire-marshal ordinances; the clubs and coffeehouses were also beginning to feel the wrath of people who lived in the adjoining buildings and were taken aback by the incursion. Blacks, many of them formerly enslaved people, were among the first nonnatives to settle in the Village. By the time of the Civil War, that group constituted a quarter of the neighborhood, and the streets where they lived, such as Bleecker and Minetta Lane, were referred to as Little Africa. But by the end of the 1800s, the Italians who'd fled their native country for better economic conditions came to dominate the Village's immigrant population. After some families began leaving the Village for more well-to-do parts of the city, the ethnically Italian portion of the area also began to diminish. By the time the coffeehouses and cafés were settling into the area in the mid-fifties, the percentage of Village residents who were Italian, according to the US Census, had dropped from 67 to 51; that number would fall to 41 percent by 1960.

Yet the antagonism between the locals and those they saw as invaders— the beats, the fake beatniks, and the Black kids who were drawn back into the neighborhood—was not going anywhere. As the *New York Times* noted in the fall of 1959, "The Village, particularly on Friday and Saturday nights, harbors a sinister quality of hatred just under the carnival atmosphere." Uptown Blacks who ventured into the neighborhood were disparaged by those in the neighborhood as "A-trainers," after the subway line they were most likely to have taken from their homes, and the white women who accompanied them were slagged as "Bronx bagel babies." The *Times* reported on the sight of a Black man walking by the Kettle of Fish and being called a "spade" by an Italian kid, who added, "Come back this way one more time and we'll split your head open."

A few times, taunts burst into actions. In the summer of 1960, a racial brawl broke out in Washington Square Park after young Italians used screwdrivers and can openers to menace what they saw as outsiders, and during that same summer, a group of young Blacks—one saying, "We've been pushed around long enough"—chased Italians out of the park. One Black artist referred to the Italian social clubs as "medieval torture chambers."

According to Thal, she and Van Ronk were keenly aware of what was transpiring around them. "It was an Italian neighborhood," said Thal. "People lived there. And we came in and we destroyed it, and they hated us. We brought tourists, noise, and garbage. It wasn't just the folk singers and the coffeehouses that did that. By the early sixties, streets that had been reasonably quiet—both residential and commercial streets—were full of tourists. At night, there were throngs of noisy, screaming hordes. We invaded somebody's neighborhood. It's something Dave and I were acutely aware of. If you came in after the music scene had started, and that world was all you knew, it never would have occurred to you that people lived there."

The friction extended to the clubs. What was called the "Minor Mafia," a group of young Italians, began shaking down coffeehouse owners for 25 percent of their profit for protection fees. One fall 1959 morning, windows of four businesses known to attract both Black and white audiences, including the Village Gate, were smashed. The Cafe Bizarre installed Plexiglas after its front window was obliterated. Whether the reason was unpaid protection fees or simply anger, no one could say, and the Italian community in the South Village, still grappling with the changes on its streets, was not pleased with the *Times'* coverage of the confrontations. But one community leader, speaking anonymously to the *Voice* about the clubs, admitted that he and others were going to "enforce the laws and make it difficult for them to operate."

With the opening of the Cafe Wha?, whoever was conducting the enforcement would soon have another potential target. The space, down yet another flight of stairs, had been a garage and, before that, a horse stable. (A dip in the middle of its tiled floor, directly in front of the stage, was intentional—that was where horse manure would collect.) Its owner, Manny Roth, hailed from the Midwest and had opened the Cock and Bull bar on Bleecker Street. But the basement of 115 MacDougal seemed like the perfect spot for the beatnik crowd. It could cram in three hundred, three times the size of the nearby Commons, and Roth even painted the walls black for added beat-era atmosphere.

Among those who began entertaining there was Noel Stookey, a tall, laconic type who'd honed his skills as an emcee and comic at Michigan State University. Stookey had also developed a singing voice by serenading women on campus as part of a campaign to help a friend get elected to student government. With money he'd made by way of a winning a photo-caption contest—he was awarded a batch of camera flashbulbs, which a friend bought from him—he came to New York from Pittsburgh, took a job at a photographic chemical company, and started visiting the Village to play chess at the Commons. One day, a few chess tables were replaced with a stage. "We're gonna have entertainment now," Stookey heard someone say.

Starting at the Commons, then at the Cafe Wha?, and ultimately at the Gaslight, Stookey began working as an emcee, singing or telling jokes, or getting laughs for his imitations of a flushing toilet, all between the scheduled acts. On a smoke break from the Wha? one night, he was standing at the corner of MacDougal and Minetta Lane when he was approached by a group of "local hoods," he recalled. He said hello—in what he called "an affable Midwestern way"—but the next thing he knew, he was punched in the nose; two held him while another hit him in the face.

Luckily, a patrol car was parked down Minetta Lane, and the toughs ran off without inflicting further damage on him. "This was their home," he recalled. "All these hippie-dippies were bringing in people." But the message was clear to him and everyone else. Along with the cops in the park and the city inspectors, it was a reminder that another community was keeping watch on the fledgling scene.

By the dawn of 1960, something wasn't clicking at Gerdes Restaurant on West Fourth Street. The tables with their red-checkered cloths were inviting but often empty. Because jazz clubs were doing well, Mike Porco had decided to roll a few dice on the music. Starting with a trio featuring pianist Don Friedman, clarinetist Jay Cameron, and bassist Eddie de Haas, he'd introduced a weekly Sunday-afternoon jazz show in the summer of 1959. But as capable as the musicians were, the crowds still weren't showing up, and Porco had to consider other possibilities—one of which dropped into his lap thanks to the Folklore Center's Izzy Young.

At his store, which continued to pull in folk musicians and somehow make the rent, Young had met Tom Prendergast, a Madison Avenue advertising exec who dreamed of opening a folk club—and had enough disposable income to make his wish a reality. The two men entertained the idea of turning the Folklore Center into more of a professional performance space than it had been, but it simply wasn't big enough. One day they ventured into Gerdes, which was, as Young told writer Richard Reuss, "just a bar with drunks in it . . . a completely empty place."

Young and Prendergast "looked like investigators," Porco later told author Robbie Woliver, as he observed them ordering beer and scoping out the place. But they could tell that something about Gerdes—the separation between the bar and dining room, the proximity to New York University and its students—had potential. Approaching Porco, they asked if he presented music there and had a license, then suggested hosting folk performances in the restaurant. Although Washington Square Park was just a few minutes' walk away, Porco didn't know much about the types of players congregating there. Young and Prendergast filled him in on the popularity of the Kingston Trio, Burl Ives, and Joan Baez. A nineteen-year-old with a penetrating, siren-song soprano, Baez had become a barefooted star on the Boston and Cambridge circuit, had already wowed the crowd at the 1959 Newport Folk Festival, and was about to release her first album on Vanguard. Young and Prendergast proposed paying the acts; handling promotion, lighting and advertising; and taking home the cash from ticket sales. Porco would retain the food and bar earnings.

Porco went along with their plan. As he told Woliver, "If he [Young] could bring in some people, that's all I was looking for at the time." In its first music ad in the *Village Voice*, Gerdes was now "New York's First Folk Music Cabaret," and in late January 1960, with folksinger Ed McCurdy headlining, the rebranding continued. At the suggestion of Erik Darling of the Weavers, the restaurant had an additional name—the Fifth Peg, in honor of the fifth tuning peg of a banjo, which wasn't on the headstock.

At first, Young and Prendergast's idea appeared to be validated. Largely thanks to Young's profile in the Village, the early nights pulled in respectable crowds, although the locals who congregated at the bar still tended to be too boisterous. Fairly soon, Young and Prendergast had lured in two of the Clancy Brothers ("We only had enough money to pay for two, but every night we would get four anyway," Young told Reuss), bluesmen Sonny Terry and Brownie McGhee (who played a set that included "Midnight Special" and "Mean Old Southern"), and Brother John Sellers, a delicately featured gospel and folksinger who'd grown up in Clarksdale, Mississippi, mentored with gospel giant Mahalia Jackson, and moved to New York in 1959. "The Bizarre was there and a couple of coffeehouses, but this was the first actual venue for folk with a stage and a professional setup," said Peter Stampfel. "That was a game changer."

To his friends, Young was never known as a particularly savvy businessman; at least once, at the Folklore Center, he had to run to the bank and asked one of his customers to mind the store while he was out. He was also combustible. Even so, the Fifth Peg was testing Young's acumen: it was costing too much to advertise and pay the talent. "In other words," he told Reuss a few years later, "we were subsidizing Gerdes," adding "we were schmucks, because there was no possible way that we could make money out of it. 'Cause paying the singers as much as we did, we could barely break even."

Issues began mounting between Porco and his new partners. When Young went to Porco to tweak their deal—asking for part of the bar tab—Porco ended the arrangement. As he told author David Hajdu, "I had nothing against the man. But I didn't need him anymore." On his last night hosting at the Fifth Peg, in May, Young clambered on stage and, he said, "really gave it to everybody." About two weeks later, he placed an ad in the *Village Voice* that read, in part, "I feel bad. Everything I do turns out to be successful—artistically only. Now the Fifth Peg is added to the list." He promised a return to the "active folk scene" soon.

By way of Tommy Makem, Porco enlisted a new partner for the shows, twenty-one-year-old Charlie Rothschild, and the club name changed once more, to Gerdes Folk City—or, as it became known in its ads, Gerde's Folk City, although no one seemed to know the origins of that apostrophe. The split between Young and Porco shook the scene. As Van Ronk told Hajdu, "If you bought a guitar pick in the Folklore Center, you couldn't be seen in Gerde's." Young expressed his own displeasure by placing a sign in the front window of his store cursing Rothschild out, until Rothschild's lawyer sent a cease-and-desist letter, and the notice came down. Folk-music gentility didn't always translate to the people backing or making the music.

The new Folk City went in search of a second wind—and, to Young's irritation, found it thanks to the *New York Times* and Robert Shelton. Born Robert Shelton Shapiro (he dropped his surname to downplay his ethnicity), Shelton had grown up in Chicago and, after a stint in the army, moved to New York to work as a copyboy for the *Times*. He also began writing on the side, and folk music, especially shows in clubs and concert halls, became one of his beats. More so than anyone at the *Village Voice*, which barely covered the burgeoning folk scene, Shelton was a regular visitor (and lingerer) at the Gaslight and elsewhere. Although he hadn't covered any of the bookings at the Fifth Peg, he was now embedded at Folk City to such a degree that he helped Porco devise a way to fill the normally quiet Monday nights at the space. Settling on what amounted to an amateur night, Porco first called it "Monday Night Guest Nite." But after brainstorming with Rothschild and Shelton, he settled on "hootenanny," a word with roots in union folk songs. Fifteen people, then fifty, would show up, and the number rose a bit more with each passing week.

Carolyn Hester, the first headliner at the new Gerde's Folk City (hereafter simply called Folk City), embodied the new breed that was starting to hear about the Village and move there with heightened expectations. Born in Waco, Texas, in 1937 and possessing a pure contralto voice, Hester first ventured into New York twenty years later, when she and a friend had driven from their home state. Hester's mother told her that people in the subway were friendly and that she should ask any of them for directions should she get lost. Hester first wanted to be an actress, taking classes at the American Theatre Wing and working temp jobs; after returning home, she returned to New York in 1958. This time, she discovered the Folklore Center, marveling at the collection of stringed instruments on its walls and all the records smushed into that space. Through Young, she heard about the new Monday-night sessions at Folk City.

Showing up at the club for an audition, Hester brought along a copy of an album of folk songs (such as "Danny Boy") and recent material she'd cut in Texas for producer Norman Petty's Coral label. "It was pretty dingy-looking," she said of Folk City. "I'd never heard of a hoot before." When she showed Porco her LP, he didn't ask her to sing anything but informed her that NYU students were coming in and that he was building an audience with them. "I did this thing with Izzy," he told her, "but I want to step it up a bit."

With her alluring persona and hint of a Texas drawl in her voice, Hester became the first major female artist on the scene, and she and Van Ronk crossed paths early on. Van Ronk, who later came to praise her, wasn't taken with bel canto—a style of singing that emphasized flawless perfection and vocal beauty—and lumped Hester in with Baez, its most popular practitioner.

Likewise, she didn't know quite what to make of him. "Sometimes you thought he was your buddy and sometimes you weren't sure," she said. "I don't know if he drank or was moody." Later, after she'd been away from the circuit for a while, she ran into him again, and he surprised her with an upbeat greeting that could have also been a warning. "He said, 'Glad you're back, it's about time. You left us for a while, too long. Don't do that,'" she recalled. "I thought, 'Either, don't do that you're naughty, or don't do that, we missed you.'"

For a while, the poets who gave readings at the Gaslight remained, as Van Ronk would say, the "big-ticket items." But as he saw when he returned from his trip to California, they were soon pushed out by the very people who were supposed to help them keep their gigs. When a name poet like Ginsberg would read at the Gaslight, lines would slither all down MacDougal Street. The only way for John Mitchell to clear the house for new customers would be to ask folksingers, particularly those who didn't quite have the same melodious harmonies as the Kingston Trio, to take the stage and warble away. "At the end of three songs, if anyone was still seated, we could get fired," Van Ronk later informed one of his audiences. "We turned the house over like *that*." Gradually, though, that situation began to reverse itself. Thanks to the folk movement taking hold around the country, Village clubs and their schedules began leaning more in a musical direction.

After returning from California, Van Ronk had likely done his first post–Cafe Bizarre performances at the Commons, but he soon shifted over to the Gaslight, where his friend, guitarist and singer Roy Berkeley, was among the first musicians to be booked. The pay was still minimal, and in the early months of 1960, Van Ronk still toiled at day jobs, working at a typographer's office on West Fourth Street and then the Lafayette Radio Electronic Corporation on Sixth Avenue.

But in good news for Van Ronk and his friends, the opportunities to play music seemed to be multiplying by the week. As displayed in the pages of *Caravan*, most folk shows had once taken place in theaters or clubs like Town Hall or Carnegie Hall. In 1959 the *Daily News* noted an uptick in coffeehouses in the Village. By the fall of 1960, at least forty were circling the Bleecker and MacDougal area. In his column "Frets and Frails" in the December 1960-January 1961 issue of *Sing Out!*, Izzy Young took note: "Just one year ago, there was hardly a place in NYC for a folksinger—now he can sing at some 50 places, mostly coffee houses."

As Ramblin' Jack Elliott saw when he made his Folk City debut in December 1960, the people drawn to those venues could be unpredictable. The former Elliott Adnopoz, son of a Brooklyn doctor and surgeon, had been exposed to rodeo shows and cowboys in New York, had fled his home at least once, and had renamed himself several times, eventually settling on Ramblin' Jack Elliott. (The adjective, which reflected the long and winding tales that would spill out in conversation, came to him by way of Odetta: visiting her one day, he heard Odetta's mother remark, "That ramblin' Jack is here!") Elliott met and became a sidekick of Woody Guthrie; after the two had a falling-out involving Guthrie's new wife, which Elliott didn't understand, he made England his home in the mid-fifties. Weary from traveling around Europe, he grew curious about what was happening in his home country.

To his surprise, Elliott encountered a Greenwich Village hosting his type of music far more than it ever had before. Even so, Folk City wasn't quite what he expected. "Most of the patrons were local drunks who had drunk there before it was a folk club," he said. "They'd come in and they weren't a very good audience. Drunk and talking. You really had to start learning the craft of how to be a performer in front of a non-sympathetic audience that didn't know who you were. There were a few devoted folk fans trickling in, but it seemed like at least half the people in there were very noisy." But he, like others, welcomed it as a place to practice what they yearned to do.

Over at the Gaslight, the situation remained dingy. "Van Ronk once said, 'You don't want to go in there when the lights are on,'" his friend and fellow musician Tom Paxton said. "They swept, but not all that much." But it was also becoming more professional and sticking to stricter schedules, as well as $1 cover charges, and Mitchell was even starting to pay the talent. Club workers were now seen standing on the sidewalks outside their business, handing out flyers and beseeching people to walk in. As John Brent told the *New York*

Times, "Now it's all organized. We don't just let anyone stand up and shout 25 lines of obscenity." In the same week, anyone wandering into the Village now could see Cisco Houston or the Shanty Boys at Folk City, Hester at One Sheridan Square (a new venue that had previously housed Cafe Society), or, at the Village Gate, a "Washington Square Indoors" series of Sunday-afternoon folk shows.

The challenges of presenting live music in the Village continued: in October 1960, four coffeehouses—the Cafe Wha?, the Commons, Cafe Bizarre, and a new addition, Phase Two—were sentenced for operating without cabaret licenses. But in each case the fine—only $5 or $10—was suspended, and a newly formed group, the Coffee House Trade and Civic Association, rose up to contest the cases in court.

The owners were undeterred. Just before Thanksgiving 1960, Van Ronk was gifted with his first full-performance write-up in the *New York Times*. In a roundup headlined "Folk Music Makes Mark on City's Night Life," Shelton described the new energy emanating from Folk City (which he called an "inhospitable-looking saloon"), the Cafe Bizarre, and the Commons. At the Gaslight, Shelton also caught Van Ronk, whom he aptly described as a "24-year-old droopy-mustached city boy" with "a great fluency with Negro folk song," a "distinctive, rough-hewn voice," and a "rhythmic, rock-of-Gibraltar rhythmic sense on guitar." Shelton also cited Van Ronk's "natural yet dynamic" stage presence.

Although Shelton didn't specifically say it, Van Ronk, now bearded or goateed, depending on the time of year, had grown into his music as much as he had into his look. Not as chaste-looking as young folksingers were wont to be, he instead exuded a roughhouse masculinity that was undeniably sexy and spellbinding. Fewer poets may have been appearing at the Gaslight and elsewhere in the area, leading the *Times* to announce, "Voice of the Beatnik Is Being Stilled in the 'Village.'" But a bevy of new voices were preparing to take their place.

in the wind

1961–1962

Although he'd absorbed much during his lessons with Dave Van Ronk, Danny Kalb wasn't able to take advantage of the coffeehouse and club boom. In the fall of 1960 he left Mount Vernon, and the Village, to enroll in the University of Wisconsin at Madison, where some of his friends were matriculating. Either in late 1960 or likely early January 1961, he heard a knock on the door at a rooming house where he was living with a high school friend and fellow student, Jeff Chase. Standing before them was a kid with a pudgy face and a mop of hair (and, Kalb would tell Mitch Blank, "marijuana in his mittens," although it's unclear if that was true). "He says, 'I'm a folksinger—I need a place to stay for a couple of weeks,'" Kalb said. Then eighteen, Kalb didn't have much familiarity with "traveling folksingers," as he later told Blank, but Chase, who was a bit more experienced in that regard, suggested they let him crash.

At the time, where Bob Dylan was from and where he'd been were never fully clear. In the months ahead, he would tell people he'd run away from home at thirteen or fourteen, played at a strip-club joint in Colorado, and mowed lawns for a living around the country, some of which may have been true. What was undeniable is that his birth name was Robert Allen Zimmerman; he'd been born in Duluth, Minnesota, in May 1941; he could play guitar and piano; and he'd already ventured into playing rock and roll with high

school friends before immersing himself in country and R&B. Enamored of
Woody Guthrie, he decided to visit him on the East Coast, and a pit stop in
Madison—by which time he was referring to himself as Bob Dylan—was part
of his journey east from Minnesota.

Dylan had arrived in Madison with a contact for another student, Ron
Radosh, a friend of Kalb's since high school. The two had met at a SANE
(National Committee for a Sane Nuclear Policy) rally in New York City, where
Kalb, Radosh observed, was one of the kids who'd marched in from Westchester, carrying signs. Radosh didn't have room for Dylan in his own apartment but sent him to Kalb's, where Dylan stayed for about a week. Kalb then
introduced Dylan to others in the folk scene there, such as musicians Marshall Brickman and Fred Underhill, and a poet, Ann Lauterbach; Dylan also
crashed at Underhill and Lauterbach's place.

To Kalb, Dylan's fascination with folk and blues didn't immediately set
him apart. "He was nothing out of the ordinary," Kalb told Blank. "I knew
a lot of people like that." Still, they bonded over the leftist folk songs Kalb
had learned and played at summer camps during his teen years, and with
Dylan on harmonica and Kalb on guitar, they jammed on a terrace on the
campus. Dylan also joined Kalb at the Pad, a coffeehouse in Madison, where
they bashed out some blues and Guthrie songs. At the apartment of another
group of friends, Kalb taught the kid an arrangement of "Poor Lazarus,"
a blues about a Black man hunted down and shot by a presumably white
sheriff; Kalb had learned it from Van Ronk in the city before he'd left for
Wisconsin.

When Underhill announced that he and some friends would be driving his
Pontiac to New York, Dylan tagged along, entering the city the third week of
January 1961. New York had been slammed with a snowstorm, but nothing
would stop him from making a first impression. As Dylan would remember it,
he joined in on his first night at the Cafe Wha? alongside its occasional host, a
deep-voiced and sometimes stage-shy songwriter named Fred Neil. Originally
from Florida, Neil had cut his teeth writing songs in the Brill Building and
recording singles for labels like Columbia that mimicked the pop trends of
the late fifties; he'd also performed at the Cafe Wha? in a duo with another

troubadour, Dino Valenti. At the Wha?, Dylan also met Karen Dalton, a troubled Oklahoman who'd left home at fifteen, been married twice by seventeen, and moved to New York around 1960 to sing folk music. Staying with whoever would have him, Dylan was also introduced to Mark Spoelstra, a Missouri-born singer and guitarist who'd grown up in California and was yet another musician who'd found himself in the Village in search of a new home and crowd. Like Dylan, they were misfits who didn't seem to belong anywhere except downtown New York.

Other cities, such as Chicago and the Cambridge-Boston nexus, were fostering equally robust acoustic-music communities; with clubs like the Ash Grove, Los Angeles had one of its own. Dylan had logged time in the thriving Minneapolis folk community before moving to New York. But on folk or campus circuits across the country, the word of mouth about the Village painted a portrait of a scene packed with coffeehouses, beat poets, credible folk-record companies, and group hangs like the Folklore Center, along with an undeniable sense of camaraderie. Unlike most of those other cities, save Los Angeles, New York was also home to the music business—record and publishing companies, managers, agents, and the Brill Building songwriting offices. Opportunities seemed to be around each Manhattan corner.

The lure for upstarts like Dylan was irresistible, and they began making their way to the area by any means of transportation available. On a Sunday in 1960, a bus from New Jersey dropped off Tom Paxton, a short-haired, twenty-three-year-old army reservist who'd seen Elvis Presley and Little Richard perform in his home state of Oklahoma. At the University of Oklahoma, Paxton attended a campus party and heard something even more alluring and mysterious emerge from a radio: the Kingston Trio's "Tom Dooley." To listen more closely, he placed his head near the radio's small speaker. "It just didn't sound like something from Dick Clark," he said of the host of TV's pop showcase *American Bandstand*. "It sounded real. It sounded human. You could see someone actually living those words." Paxton dropped his drama studies and formed a group, the Travelers, playing frat houses and even taking his first stab at a song, a faux murder ballad. He realized that his love for this music set him apart from his college friends; he'd found his crew.

Signing up for the army reserves, where he was relegated to a clerk-typist job, Paxton was stationed in New Rochelle, New York, and then Fort Dix, New Jersey—both just a few hours, at most, from Manhattan. On his downtime, he came into the city to explore the area around Bleecker and MacDougal, glancing at the flyers for coffeehouses and clubs pasted on walls. He came across the Folklore Center and then, down the street, the Gaslight, where he heard Hugh Romney and John Brent reading. At the Commons, during another visit, he met Van Ronk, who gave him a lesson in finger-style guitar, playing a melody on the upper strings while keeping a steady bass rhythm and pattern on the lower ones. After what Paxton would call "two hours of agony," he nailed it.

That same evening, Paxton ventured into the Gaslight for its open-mic night, where he used his new technique to perform "The Golden Vanity," one of those tragic ballads involving gold, an unwed daughter, and villains. Van Ronk had made him practice for so long that his hand started to cramp up during the first verse. Somehow, he made it through the rest of the song, and more importantly, he stuck with Van Ronk, who was helping book acts at the Commons and who hired Paxton for ten dollars a night on weekends.

After Paxton completed his army obligations in the fall of 1960, John Mitchell hired him to play the late shift at the Gaslight, where the folksingers continued to gravitate from the Commons because the Gaslight actually paid. Perhaps as a result of his Oklahoma upbringing, Paxton appeared to be the most centered and normal of the Village crowd. In a voice that was gentler and more calming than his friend Van Ronk's, he filled his sets with an effortless selection of love serenades ("Every Time"), Guthrie-esque tales of the everymen who kept the country chugging along ("I'm the Man Who Built the Bridges"), and a novelty song that expressed the wonderment of childhood ("The Marvelous Toy"). With his reserve-duty haircut, Paxton didn't remotely *look* like a scruffy folkie or poet, to the point where Mitchell accused him of being an undercover cop and fired him. "I said, 'John, if I were undercover, do you think my hair would look like this? I can't wait to grow it!'" he recalled. Luckily, Romney stood up for Paxton, and he was rehired.

Around the same time Dylan came to town, so did a brunette from Colorado, with bobbed hair and piercing blue eyes, named Judy Collins. With money she'd earned selling Christmas trees in her home state, Collins had gone in search of folk records, making her way to a Denver record store. There she heard about acts like Josh White and the Clancy Brothers and Tommy Makem, and some sort of folk revival happening in New York. From what she was told, it sounded magical: a small area where people were getting work singing in clubs, writing songs, and making records.

Collins eventually played clubs in Denver and then at the Gate of Horn in Chicago, singing traditional songs in a soprano that was pure and robust. In early 1961 she and her then husband drove from Connecticut, where they were living, and into the Village. Thanks to her previous engagements, she was able to land a spot at Folk City opening for Ed McCurdy. She recalled Van Ronk and others being at her earliest Folk City show; even if they weren't, she still felt welcome. "I felt like I knew them," she said of the community. "I thought, 'I can get along with these people. They're my people and this is where I belong.'"

The crowd was dominated by men, but Collins held her own—not just vocally but by drinking anyone, male or female, under a Folk City table. One of her occasional such buddies was Dylan, who struck her as someone who was lapping up everything around him at a frenetic pace. "He was not raised literate by any means, but he was exposed to people who had incredible libraries and he started reading like a son of a gun," she said. "I don't think Rimbaud was part of his life before he got to the Village." As for his music, she had her doubts. "He was singing these old Woody songs, and I thought, 'Badly chosen and badly sung,'" she recalled. "I was *so* bored."

Dylan was apparently undeterred by any such criticism. In the spring he made a return visit to the Midwest. Sitting in the student union at the University of Wisconsin, Kalb's friend Ron Radosh heard someone call his name; it was Dylan, a grin overtaking his face. He said he'd just returned from New York and told Radosh, "I'm gonna be as big as Elvis and play the biggest arenas." Radosh was incredulous; he'd never met anyone who was so determined and who seemed to see his future before him with such clarity.

By spring of 1961, the press was zeroing in on the downtown entertainment community. On April 9 the *New York Times* published a pictorial spread, "Making the Village Scene," featuring photos of Folk City, the Gaslight, the Five Spot, and the Village Gate. A "pre-Raphaelite coif" was suggested for women who ventured into any of the clubs. Published that same month, a neighborhood guidebook, *Where to Go in Greenwich Village*, listed twenty-three coffeehouses, all within the immediate area of Bleecker and MacDougal, and thirteen music venues. Complete with a cover illustration of a goateed, sandals-clad beatnik, the guidebook also offered instructions for those who found themselves in any space hosting music or poetry. Don't be surprised, writers Rosetta Reitz and Joan Geisler advised, to walk into a coffeehouse and not be greeted: "This is the style. It is all very free and easy which is their charm." The Cafe Wha? and the Cafe Rafio were suggested for folk and jazz, and the Cafe Bizarre for beat poetry, although the authors noted that "poetry is no longer the chief entertainment."

With new surges of publicity, however, came renewed attention from the authorities. The Gaslight, along with Mitchell's behavior, was becoming a neighborhood lightning rod. As most would admit, Mitchell was innately volatile. "John was fucking crazy," said Terri Thal. "He was *incredibly* intense. He had *no* sense of humor. He was tall and lean and had big black eyes, and he drove people crazy. The word *saturnine* was written for John."

That manner started to become an issue in June 1960, when Mitchell was arrested for disorderly conduct; he reportedly shoved a deputy fire chief who'd ordered the Gaslight closed for lacking fire extinguishers and "not having exit lights over the doors," according to an employee. The Gaslight shut for several months, and Mitchell began managing the Commons, across the street, in the meantime.

Days into the new year of 1961, the Fire Department returned, claiming there had been a report of an actual blaze. After firemen wielding axes pulled up at 1 a.m., all they found were a few singers and poets, including Len Chandler, an Ohio-born Black folksinger who may have been the first musician to sing in the club, after being hired by Romney. Quick-witted, Chandler improvised new lyrics to the work song "Pay Me My Money Down," instead singing,

"Don't be alarmed, it's only the fire drill." More summonses resulted, one for overcrowding and another for the lack of a cabaret license. Even after the Fire Department taped a "fire hazard" sign on the Gaslight's entrance, Mitchell and a group of friends and customers refused to leave—resulting in what the *Times* called "an overnight sit-in and then snore-in" that carried on until dawn.

Ultimately, charges against Mitchell and the Gaslight were dropped when it was discovered an official hadn't properly signed the required paperwork. Meanwhile, the Cafe Figaro received permission to resume its Sunday-afternoon concerts without a license. A judge in Upper Manhattan Summons Court dismissed the initial charge against the café, citing a difference between a cabaret with entertainment and a "coffee, pastry and sandwiches" spot with entertainment. But the Gaslight wasn't the only coffeehouse being monitored. In April 1961, five of them, including the Cafe Bizarre and the Cafe Wha?, were busted for operating without a license, despite not serving liquor.

By then, Mitchell had had enough. For several years, it had become common and accepted knowledge that funneling money to cops was part of most every club owner's business plan. As he would later testify, Mitchell had started to pay off a local beat patrolman as little as $5 or as much as $10 a week for what he called "protection," keeping notes of it all in a journal. He claimed he had given cops $250 at Christmas 1958 but not the following year, and was now paying another price—harassment. During a Police Department investigation that followed, in April 1961, Mitchell's fellow coffeehouse owners denied allegations that they paid anyone off, or they took the Fifth Amendment. "Why should they talk?" Mitchell shot back to the *Daily News*. "They are afraid of police reprisals. They figure this whole thing will blow over and they want to do business after it is all over—with the same cops."

The skirmishes didn't end for anyone. The same month Mitchell made his public accusations, a patrolman driving down MacDougal said he had seen, from his car, a performer with a guitar in the Gaslight, which apparently struck the cop as suspicious. Mitchell—who claimed to have sixty summonses hanging over his head—had just sold the Gaslight to two businessmen, John Moyant and Harry Fry, who themselves had hired Clarence Hood, a southern Democrat and businessman (and father of Moyant's wife, Lynn), to manage it.

As the cop was writing out the summons, Mitchell burst out of the kitchen, yelling at the officer and charging out into the street. Again arrested, Mitchell was ultimately cleared of charges of interfering with police but received a suspended sentence for disorderly conduct.

In the end, Mitchell received some degree of satisfaction. In May 1961, two police officers were suspended for soliciting (and, in one case, accepting) bribes at the Gaslight and the Commons. By then, the scrawny-faced Mitchell of early years had been replaced with a bearded, disheveled man who looked more like one of the more weathered Village regulars in his café.

The venues hosting music weren't the only ones under scrutiny. So was Washington Square Park itself—and, this time, from Robert Moses's successor as parks commissioner. With Moses now committed to the 1964 World's Fair in Queens, scheduled to include exhibits on early computers and a view of the world in 2064, his job went to Newbold Morris, who stepped into the role in May 1960. Like Moses, Morris, who was approaching the age of sixty, had served in the Fiorello La Guardia administration, and he'd run two unsuccessful campaigns for mayor. In the words of the *New York Times*, he exhibited a combination of "an aristocratic background and a mild disposition."

To those who worked for him, though, Morris came across as anything but placid after he visited Washington Square Park on Sunday, March 12, 1961. As he would relay in a staff memo, he was "shocked"; "conditions were much worse" than on a trip he'd made a year before. "You can not call it a park anymore," he wrote the day after his expedition. "It is so heavily used, not by the neighborhood, but by these freaks, that there literally was not room on the walks." In a follow-up memo he asserted he had no issues with symphony concerts or chamber-music recitals in the park: "What I am against is these fellows that come from miles away to display the most terrible costumes, haircuts, etc., and who play bongo drums and other weird instruments attracting a weird public." He claimed the grass had been trampled and the park had become too crowded for women and children, and his staff was instructed to grant permits only to "bonafide artistic groups" and to issue summonses to anyone without a permit.

Amid this flurry of revised instructions, the first 1961 permit application for the seasonal fountain jams landed in the Department of Parks office. Tired of his ongoing responsibility, Lionel Kilberg had handed the task over to Izzy Young; after all, Kilberg argued, the Folklore Center was down the street from the park. Young took on the responsibility, thinking it would make for good publicity for his four-year-old business. In his first application, Young requested permission for each Sunday in April 1961, from 2 to 7 p.m. By this time, he was estimating that the Sunday sessions were drawing 300 to 400 participants, split into a half-dozen groups and including about 20 singers.

In an internal memo dated March 16, a city official flagged Young's application, noting that the office had "previously received written complaints from citizens or organizations regarding these folk singing groups." Startlingly, the memo went on to say that the department had attempted to quell the sessions by filling the fountain with water and had shortened them with an enforced 6 p.m. wrap-up time.

Although the Department of Parks was now inclined to deny Young's permission, one unnamed official added a cautionary note. "I feel certain that refusal to grant the requested permit after so many years, when they are allowed to play, will be questioned and possibly aired in the press," he wrote in a memo. "I suggest, therefore, careful consideration of the letter denying their request." His concerns were ignored. Responding to Young by mail on March 28, an official asserted that the Department of Parks had decided to restrict such gatherings to "sponsored shows."

Just over a week later, on April 4, the final word came down: the "Social Folk Singing Group" headed by Young was officially denied a permit. In a follow-up letter to Young, a department staffer wrote, "We have adopted a policy to restrict such activities to formal concerts and organized dance bands sponsored by local civic groups or the Department of Parks." Morris unveiled a plan that would push the musicians to an all-concrete, two-thousand-seat amphitheater in East River Park, way east on the FDR Drive between Twelfth and Montgomery Streets. "I am not against musicians or itinerant musicians," Morris noted. "It is just a question of a place for them."

By then, a degree of backlash was building, including from several high-profile members of the music community. Both Theodore Bikel and Oscar Brand wrote to Mayor Robert Wagner, expressing their outrage over the ban and demanding that folk singing be returned to the park. But Young, along with Art D'Lugoff and other planners, wanted a more visceral approach. In the window of the Folklore Center, Young taped a handmade sign announcing a "Protest Rally at the Fountain" on April 9 at 2 p.m. That morning, young men and women, some huddled in overcoats, began congregating in front of the store, a few clutching acoustic guitars and at least one banjo and autoharp. Others held signs: "Folk Singers Now, the Birds Next!," "Keep the Sound of Music in the Square," and "Comm. Morris 'Of Thee We Sing.'" To symbolize the death of music in the park, a few carried a cello over their heads as if they were pallbearers. By 2 p.m., the crowd would also include D'Lugoff, Pat Clancy, radio host and singer Cynthia Gooding, and Daniel Drasin, a twenty-two-year-old budding filmmaker who worked for a documentary film company run by D. A. Pennebaker, Albert Maysles, and Bob Drew.

On cue, all began their march up MacDougal Street and toward the park. The mood was as festive as it could be, under the circumstances. "We had no idea what to expect," recalled Drasin, who, along with two colleagues, was filming the rally. "We found what we found."

When the group arrived at the park, they immediately encountered about fifteen police. The captain on duty, Adrian Donohue, asked who was in charge, and one of them called out Young, who stepped forward. Compared to the kids who walked with him, Young, in his white shirt and tie, did look like the adult in the room, and he verbally pushed back, saying people had been singing in the park for more than a dozen years. With grudging permission from the police, the group was allowed to continue to the fountain as long as they didn't sing or play any instruments. Robert Easton, an eighteen-year-old biology student from the Bronx, threw caution to the wind and decided to play his autoharp anyway. Almost immediately, police yanked Easton toward a nearby restroom, pushed him into a paddy wagon, and drove him out of the park.

The sight of Easton being arrested only egged on the protesters, who sat down in the dry fountain and began singing "The Star-Spangled Banner," the Black spiritual "We Shall Not Be Moved," Woody Guthrie's "This Land Is Your Land," and other songs. "We have a right to sing here," Young told them, as police looked on. Unsure how to proceed, one police inspector told the crowd, "Look here, we're just enforcing the law."

By 3:15, the group had been singing for about an hour, and the situation was becoming as tightly wound as the strings on a guitar. "It was, 'No one's gonna tell us what to do!'" said Happy Traum, one of the marchers. "'We were not going to be pushed around! We're going to sing our songs!' It was all good natured and then before we knew it, all these cop cars and paddy wagons showed up. I was just astonished."

When the increased police presence appeared at the south end of the park, Young, along with Mitchell, led a procession of several hundred out of the area, through the arch, down MacDougal Street, and finally to Judson Memorial Church, an august building on Washington Square South. As Drasin recalled, "When the musicians got wind of the approaching cops, they didn't want their instruments to be damaged, so they left early." Reaching the church, Young later told Richard Reuss, "I looked around and there was a riot going on. . . . And then it was out of my control." A TV news crew asked Young if he could take his group back into the park and re-create their departure, but he declined. (The *Times* reported that the group attempted to reenter the park but was rebuffed by police.)

Even though most of the pickers and strummers were no longer in the park, the order came down from the NYPD to clear the fountain area. Seemingly without provocation, police pushed into the basin and began forcing anyone there—largely sightseers, locals, and a few remaining musicians, including Traum—toward the rim of the fountain. The next few minutes were a jumble of boos and catcalls from the crowd ("Police brutality!"), cops knocking a few people to the ground and dragging others off, and others in the park calling the police "fascists," complete with mocking Nazi salute signs.

In the end, ten people, including Easton and writer and *Paris Review* founder Harold Humes, were arrested for either disorderly conduct or lack of a permit to perform. Three police officers were also sent to a hospital for minor injuries, including a bitten hand. "No one was seriously hurt, but it was a show of power," said Traum. "It was the first time I'd ever experienced the power of the police like that. I grew up thinking the policeman was your friend."

The next day, a photo of police descending on the fountain made the front page of the *New York Times* ("Folk Singers Riot in Washington Sq."), while page one of *New York Newsday* was dominated by a shot of Easton and his autoharp. The Associated Press deemed the clash "a musical battleground" where "a screaming throng of several hundred pushed police against fences, trees and automobiles," although that did not appear to be the case. The *Daily News* called it a "slugfest" where "embattled beatnik musicians . . . turned peaceful Washington Square Park into a wrestling ring." (The beats and the musicians were two different worlds, but the media tended to conflate them.) In an editorial two days later, the *Times* took Morris's side: "If the attempted Washington Square Park revolution had succeeded, unregulated folk singing may have flooded all the parks in all our cities."

Five days after the confrontation, Mayor Wagner, on vacation in Florida, announced his support of Morris's revised guidelines, and hundreds of letters began arriving at his and Morris's offices. For some, Morris was a new local hero. An organization dubbing itself the Committee to Preserve the Dignity and Beauty of Washington Square Park—which included a Cub Scout pack, a local Knights of Columbus office, and the Village Business Men's Association— announced its support for Morris's actions, calling the park "overcrowded" and "unsanitary." A nearby resident wrote that she applauded the decision: "The 'folk-singing' masquerade is a cheap trick to camouflage anarchistic behavior and defiance of established mores." Another local wrote to Wagner, "As a parent I abhor the display of bad taste, such as scenes of couples lying on the grass in conditions and positions most revolting to me as an adult and certainly unfit for any child to see!!! This is a direct result of the so-called folk singing which has been getting progressively worse!" In opposition, the Greenwich Village Sponsors Association—which included D'Lugoff and the Cafe Bizarre's Rick Allmen—issued a statement calling on Wagner to erase the ban, citing Morris's "utter contempt for the universal protests of the people . . . outrageous."

The reasons for that ban depended on who was doing the responding. When word of the permit clampdown first leaked out, a Morris spokesman attempted to clarify: the Department of Parks had heard reports about supposedly unsavory characters playing music in the park and asking for money, which defied a rarely enforced ordinance banning advertising in the park. After the protest incident, Morris personally responded to a letter from a Brooklyn resident, citing what was then Section 21 of the New York City charter, which deemed that dancing, juggling, and "minstrelsy" (music played with instruments) could not be conducted in public parks without a permit—assuming, of course, it was "consistent with the proper use and protection of the park." In yet another personal response, in early May, Morris cited the permit paperwork itself as the issue: "The trouble with the system of issuing permits seems to be that one man gets a permit and 50 musicians and singers come along with him on that permit. Then each has a tremendous following in addition to curiosity seekers and visitors from out of town."

As much as the press attempted to find fault with the "beatniks," the clash, living up to the early warning of that one city official, was more polarizing than some had thought. In a letter to Wagner, the Socialist Workers Party floated the idea that the permit cancellations were intended to keep the Village "lily-white," especially in light of how "Washington Square Park and Greenwich Village represent a toehold of integration in New York City." One letter writer to Morris cited the racial tension in the area: "I guess everyone knows that the real objection to the folksingers is that some of them are Negroes. It would be moral cowardice to give in to the silly fears of some of the local residents and ban the singers."

Young believed that race played an undeniable role in the altercation. "The real estate people didn't like the so-called beatniks being assembled," he told Reuss. "The Italian community didn't like it, and one of the strongest reasons was just not liking the Negro people that came down there. That was unquestionably the primary real estate reason." The Department of Parks itself almost tipped its hand to its own biases. Responding to a letter complaining about the ban, a department spokesperson wrote to one local that it was meant to "eliminate the bohemian character" of the park and "restore it to the more proper local usage."

The following Sunday, April 16, the NYPD dispatched a gaggle of police to Washington Square Park, a move that proved unnecessary thanks to a rainstorm that kept nearly everyone away. Instead, a group of singers—including Van Ronk, Gooding, and the Clancy Brothers—played pro-hootenanny shows at Judson Memorial Church during the day. The church's head pastor, Howard Moody, was an unflagging supporter of the musicians and their community. The Sunday after, two thousand showed up to protest the ban and the arrests. The demonstration—largely contained to nearby Thompson Street, where musicians sang songs with lyrics mocking Morris—was peaceful until an NYU student was arrested after a scuffle with police. Whether he was pushed by police first or retaliated on his own was never clear, but at least the skirmish didn't incite the crowd or the police.

Morris was already sounding beleaguered. As he wrote in response to one letter in late April, "I guess I should have stayed in bed the day I decided to deny their permit—although I made up my mind last summer when watching the proceedings. Alas!" But his side also appeared to be winning. On May 1 the director of Maintenance and Operations for the city's parks announced that effective midnight that night, "all permits for use of the forum area" in the park would be denied, citing a new justification: "the involvement of the Police Department in obtaining authorization for sound equipment." Two days later, Supreme Court justice William Hecht Jr., responding to a suit brought by Young, agreed with the idea that song lyrics, clothing, "personal character," or the "social and political views" of the musicians had not played a part in Morris's edict, despite his comments to the contrary.

None of this discouraged Young, who continued his quest to return vernacular music to his local park. The day after Hecht's decision, Young applied for another permit and was again denied; this time, it was suggested to him that the gatherings move to Union Square Park, between Fourteenth and Seventeenth Streets. Young then took the audacious step of sending a telegram to the White House, "regarding suppression of freedom of expression in NYC," and requesting an "early appointment" to discuss the matter with President John F. Kennedy. A similarly worded telegram was also dispatched to New York governor Nelson Rockefeller and the US attorney general. Not surprisingly, no one bit: in a May 10 reply to Young, a spokesperson for the White House noted it would be "impossible to comply with your request," citing that the matter was "under the jurisdiction of the city officials in New York."

But to what was surely Morris's exasperation, Wagner, facing a reelection campaign and clearly thinking the park imbroglio wasn't worth the headache, blinked. On May 12 the mayor overrode his parks commissioner, announcing that the sessions could resume on a "controlled basis" from 3 to 6 p.m. each Sunday, with a rope-like barrier encircling the singers to set them apart from anything else taking place in the park. The Right to Sing Committee, an ad hoc group of club owners and others who had come together before the clash, rejoiced. "All is forgiven, come home," the group wrote in a telegram sent to Morris's Upper East Side home. Cheekily suggesting that he attend the next session, the telegram added, "We heartily invite you to lead us in song." That day, fifty-five police were on duty in the park, along with fifty singers and pickers, but Morris was not to be seen. (The following Sunday, a cop joined in with one singing group but quickly stopped when someone noticed him.) Young was happy—but also worried that any minor infraction could make it easier for the city to reinstate its ban.

For now, the area in and around the fountain was again home to banjo and guitar players, Kingston Trio–inspired sing-alongs, and a battalion of largely earnest balladeers, wanna-be field hollerers, and tourists who watched by the sidelines. Morris stewed, making few public announcements but taking out his frustration on anyone who wrote to his office. "I had a forlorn hope of relandscaping your park," he wrote back to one, adding, with more than a hint of bitterness, "Anyway, the mayor has resolved this earth-shaking problem, and on Monday morning, our people were picking up more than a thousand empty beer cans" from the area. Taking a shot at the Right to Sing Committee and the likes of Young, he replied to another, "I have an idea that they enjoy all this 'fighting for freedom,' even though the Justice of the Supreme Court has said that I am not arbitrary or unreasonable." In a sarcastic reply to Bikel on June 15, Morris deadpanned, "I am glad that you are happy and relaxed now that the folk singers are back in Washington Square Park," citing the "many telegrams" he had received from mothers already complaining about overcrowding there.

Even more snidely, he replied to a woman living at nearby Two Fifth Avenue, "You say, 'Now how about sprucing up the Square a little?' I'm sure with your exquisite taste you might have some suggestions for landscaping."

For his part, Young saw the victory as having wider ramifications, not all of them entirely positive. "As far as I'm concerned," he told Reuss four years later, "that riot was important because that was the last time that America spoke up against folk music. Then after that it was perfectly legal. Then it was okay to make money out of it." Young had a point: thanks to the likes of the Weavers, folk music had had its crossover cultural moments before. But on both an artistic and increasingly business level, something was bubbling up like never before. Young wasn't quite right, though, in thinking that the "beatnik riot" would be the last time that the music in the Village would displease almost as many people as it would enthrall.

As a result of out-of-town plans, Van Ronk and Thal had missed the skirmish in the park. But soon after, they were back in the Village and likely part of a group that made its way to Folk City. John Lee Hooker, the fifty-something blues singer, guitarist, and sharecropper's son who had literally electrified the genre, had been booked for several weeks. But as they all knew, the opening act, at least for part of Hooker's run at the club, was that upstart everyone seemed to suddenly be talking about. Either that night or at one of the basket houses, Paxton would recall, "We were sitting with our beers and this skinny kid in corduroy came up and sang three Woody Guthrie songs and we thought he was very good." Dylan came over and joined them, but Tom Paxton, for one, already sensed his mushrooming mystique. "We were very friendly but didn't really get to know him," Paxton said. "He was not to be known."

Dylan was making the most of his time in his new environs. Not long after he had pulled into town, he visited his hero Guthrie in a psychiatric hospital in New Jersey. He was crashing at various apartments, including with Village residents Eve and Mac McKenzie and musician Peter Stampfel. As Stampfel observed when Dylan briefly stayed at his MacDougal Street place, he exhibited a transplant's awe about the city. "We were on the second floor and he'd look out the window: 'Hey, dig this! Hey, dig this!'" Stampfel recalled. When someone on the street glanced up and noticed them, Dylan shouted, "Hey, that guy is digging *us*!"

Singing a few Guthrie songs and whatever else was in his bag, Dylan started turning up at the Gaslight and participated in the Monday-night hootenannies at Folk City. Owner Mike Porco was initially skeptical and worried that the kid was underage, but he finally gave Dylan money to get a cabaret card and booked him to open for Hooker. As Porco told Anthony Scaduto about seeing Dylan first perform at his bar, likely at one of the hoots, "To me it was nothing impressive, really, but look, it was good enough that he could come back." To Van Ronk, Dylan was "another middle-class Jewish kid with an identity crisis," he later told Scaduto, someone who dressed in army surplus clothes, was in need of a haircut, and was clearly concocting tall tales about his life.

But people were already starting to talk about him. At one party, Happy Traum was asked if he'd heard "Dylan," and at first he thought they meant Dylan Thomas. Many were charmed, even if they didn't quite know what to make of him. When he was still in Europe, Ramblin' Jack Elliott had heard, by postcard, that some friends of Guthrie's in New Jersey, the Gleasons, had put Dylan up and fed him. Soon after his arrival in town, Elliott took a bus to see Guthrie, and there was Dylan. The kid seemed as enamored of Elliott as he was of Guthrie, telling him he had all the albums he'd made for the British label Topic, even citing specific songs. "It was very flattering," Elliott said. "A cute guy. Peach fuzz. He hadn't gotten to the beard-growing stage, but he had round cheeks and an interesting-looking face, like a teddy bear." Traum would recall Dylan as someone who would stop by an apartment, play his latest song for people, and ask, innocently, "You *really* like that?" after he was praised for his work.

Onstage, Dylan could appear awkward or out of place one moment, assured and in command the next. Porco later said he gave Dylan some of his kids' leftover shirts and pants for one of his earliest Folk City shows; Dylan didn't seem to own much in the way of clothing or even a comb. Sam Hood, who was helping his dad, Clarence, manage the Gaslight, recalled to Van Ronk that Dylan was "pretty obnoxious—a pudgy, dirty little kid who managed to get his own way by a lot of wheedling." Hood called the early Dylan shows he saw at the Gaslight "pretty much disastrous. . . . He had his moments that could be pretty stunning, but I'm talking about before he'd written anything." He remembered more than one instance where he inserted Dylan onto the bill on a Saturday night to clear the house for another crowd.

The media wasn't immediately swept away, either. Patricia O'Haire, a *Daily News* reporter, saw one of Dylan's early Folk City sets, likely in the fall of 1961, and called it "some of the most mournful songs ever to be heard," the guitar looking "about as beat as he did." As she would later write, "'Good God!' we thought as he whined his nasal voice through the numbers. 'What are we in for?' 'Don't encourage him,' someone whispered, and he left the stage to the deafening silence of perhaps one hand clapping."

Yet the appeal of the overall package—a bit of upstart midwestern hayseed, a dose of burning ambition, and an injection of rock-and-roll sensibility into what could have been a staid folk genre—couldn't be denied. Before he'd formally met Dylan, Stampfel caught sight of him on the street with motorcycle boots, carrying a guitar case. "I thought, 'He's from New Jersey,' because you only carry your guitar case to get laid," he said. "I had his number, right?" Not long after, though, Stampfel was walking by Folk City and realized that the kid, and his harmonica holder, were making a racket inside. "It was a fucking epiphany," Stampfel said. "His phrasing was rock and roll. I realized a merger of the two was absolutely on the table. I went over to him with a fanboy crush."

When Noel Stookey was emceeing the Gaslight one night, Dylan asked to go on, and Stookey complied; he needed a music act between two poets. Dylan made his way to the stage and played a few Guthrie songs, and Stookey thought he was "passable—as good as anyone who comes into the Village doing that kind of material." He didn't see him again for another few months. When Dylan returned to the Gaslight, he played a folk song rewritten as a talking blues to reflect his own adventures. "A lot of people didn't have that background and didn't know where the song was coming from," Stookey said. "The fact that he borrowed the format and made it contemporary blew my mind."

Soon after, Stookey mentioned Dylan to Albert Grossman, a combination of Buddha and aloof bear who was spending one of many nights at the

Gaslight behind one of its small tables. Starting in Chicago, where he was born and raised, Grossman already knew what the new music needed. With a degree in economics from Chicago's Roosevelt University, he had one eye on music and the other on business. According to the *Times*'s Robert Shelton, one of Grossman's college professors was child psychologist Bruno Bettelheim, which would serve Grossman well when working with musicians and the music business. In the spring of 1956, Grossman cofounded the Gate of Horn, a fifty-seat folk club in the basement of the Rice Hotel in Chicago; the local press called it "one of the most comfortable cellars around town." After promoter George Wein brought Grossman on to help with the first Newport Folk Festival, in 1959, Grossman also branched out into management, starting with Odetta and, for a heartbeat, Joan Baez. Eventually, he moved his office to Manhattan.

In New York, Grossman slowly became an enigmatic fixture in the coffeehouses and elsewhere. Erik Jacobsen, a banjo player who had relocated to the city from Ohio, was playing in Washington Square Park with the Knob Lick Upper 10,000, his folk band, when a guy with what he recalled as an "owl-ish look" approached and told them they sounded good. "I'm a manager here," Grossman told him. With his round glasses and wave of graying hair, which would soon cover his ears, Grossman would inspire comparisons to Benjamin Franklin in a modern suit. At the Gaslight, Stookey would always remember the way Grossman sat and quietly observed, his pinky finger in his mouth. After one of Dylan's spots, Stookey put in a good word for Dylan. "You may not like his voice," he said, "but he's got it." It was unclear if the taciturn Grossman heard him or not.

In 1960 Cafe Bohemia shut down, but the following year, jazz found an expanded home base. Art D'Lugoff took out a loan for $300,000 to start the Top of the Gate, a new performance space above his original basement-level club. The timing would prove perfect: *Billboard*, surveying the downtown jazz community, would soon declare that "saxophones and good to excellent business conditions are the order of the new year" in the Village.

The music itself was changing with the scene. In 1961 Ornette Coleman unveiled *Free Jazz: A Collective Improvisation*, which sounded at times like an assortment of instruments stuck in a traffic jam and gave a name to the approach that proved so polarizing at the Five Spot. That wilder take on the music began spreading to other venues in the Village. After Sonny Rollins's 1958 Vanguard album, John Coltrane, who had left Miles Davis's group and was establishing himself on records like *Giant Steps* and *My Favorite Things*, was next in line to cut a live disc at the venue. In November 1961 he played a string of shows that were recorded with a band that included pianist McCoy Tyner and drummer Elvin Jones. With Coltrane wailing marathon solos on either soprano or tenor sax, performances like "Chasin' the Trane," which sprawled out over sixteen minutes, seemed to cut the music loose from its past and into a wilder, even more free-form zone.

As with Coleman's shows at the Five Spot, some were taken aback by what critic Gary Giddins would call "fifteen-minute solos played at a tempo so fast," whereas others saw the possibilities. Observing one of the shows, *Daily News* jazz critic Don Nelsen noted, "Coltrane can play, or at least duplicate the sound of, a complete chord on a horn that was designed to sound single notes in succession." And when he was joined by Eric Dolphy, the alto sax and flute player who wrenched unexpected sounds out of each, Nelsen wrote, Coltrane was "reinfusing jazz with the fire and meaning it has largely lost in the past few years." For his part, Rollins—who'd begun a three-year hiatus from jazz in 1959, burnt out by club life and wary of the music's increasing popularity— returned in 1962 and slowly began working his way toward free jazz as well. Once again, the gauntlet had been thrown down in the Village.

At that point, the interaction between the community's folk and jazz communities was minimal—relegated to the Electronic Workshop, a stereo and record store on bustling Eighth Street that would advertise sales for LPs in both genres. Dylan would recall sitting in with jazz pianist Cecil Taylor, whose approach to his instrument was nearly confrontational, but other such interactions were rare. The two worlds felt very much separated, with jazz shows tending to attract a more racially diverse crowd than folk ones.

But just as the poets had been crowded out of the MacDougal Street scene with the rise of folk music, the same appeared to abruptly be happening with jazz in that part of the Village. In 1961 tenor saxophonist Jimmy Giuffre, now playing clarinet, formed a new trio with pianist Paul Bley and bassist Steve Swallow, who was still also sitting in with Sheila Jordan at the Page Three. Working without a drummer, the Giuffre trio created beautiful soundscapes that didn't superficially resemble Coleman and his peers' approach to free jazz but still moved the music in new directions—delicate and interlaced lines, with the instruments gently crisscrossing in and around each other.

The Giuffre trio played around the Village, opening for Count Basie at the Jazz Gallery, a spot on St. Mark's Place in the East Village, and at Trude Heller's Versailles in the summer of 1961. As melodious as its music could be, the audience for it was proving to be small, especially in the heart of the Village. One night, the trio found itself working at a coffeehouse on Bleecker Street. Giuffre's work was either being ignored or not taken as seriously as that of the free-jazz innovators around him, which became clear at set's end, when the musicians pooled their earnings and realized they were left with all of five cents each. They took what Swallow would ironically call "our profits" and treated themselves to an after-gig bagel and orange juice at the Hip Bagel, the cool-crowd eatery at 98 MacDougal, and decided to disband. "We'd reached the end of our road," Swallow said. "It wasn't viable to keep the band together anymore."

That realization was driven home even further for Swallow one fall night in 1961 when he was working at yet another newly opened venue. The Bitter End, at 147 Bleecker, had once been the Cock and Bull, the bar owned by Manny Roth of the Cafe Wha? until Fred Weintraub, a former TV salesman who yearned to break into show business, bought it from Roth in May. The name derived from the fact that it was the last bar on the block before Bleecker Street slammed headfirst against New York University buildings. In what its manager, Paul Colby, would call "a stroke of genius," Weintraub had the plaster ripped off the walls, revealing rustic brick. Church-style pews faced the stage, which was elevated only a few feet off the floor.

As Swallow and vibes player Al Francis accompanied a reading by Hugh Romney, he saw what he would call "the worm turn before my eyes." During the second week of their run, another act was hired. The musicians grumbled, and Swallow was even less impressed when the trio, two men and a woman, seemed to know only six songs, playing the same ones every set and arguing in the kitchen between their performances about chord changes. "I was filled with contempt for them," Swallow said, "and also saw with dismay that they were the face of the future." Only later would he be told that their group name was Peter, Paul and Mary.

Running into Van Ronk on MacDougal Street one day, Albert Grossman had an idea he wanted to run by him: what if there was a folk group consisting of two men and a woman, with Van Ronk maybe as the third leg?

Along with many others in his business, Grossman had watched as folk music became increasingly profitable. Thanks to the Kingston Trio, which had seen all eight of its albums in the Top 20 of the *Billboard* album charts by the dawn of 1961, acoustic music was now a viable commodity. Joan Baez's debut had been released in the fall of 1960 and would eventually land Baez on the cover of *Time* magazine.

As disparate as the talent in the Village was—oceans of difference between Van Ronk's gruffness, Dylan's bristling wheeze, Collins's purity, and Paxton's smoothness, to cite a few—one thing bound them together. Theirs was music neither as stuffy nor as straitlaced as that of the balladeers who'd preceded them in some of those same Village spots. They were younger, looser, and funnier than the dour likes of Richard Dyer-Bennet, not content to sing woeful ballads and more open to shaking up the music. The vibrant, handsome John F. Kennedy had been inaugurated as president just a few months before the "beatnik riot," and the new-day-rising vigor of the nascent folk music felt like the ideal soundtrack for a country eager to get on with fresh business.

To tap into that energy, Grossman clearly thought that folk needed to be sexier and more poised, not as earthy as the songs played around the fountain.

Stampfel saw the differences for himself when he and a few other musicians were playing in a park just north of the Village. A group of Catholic high school students appeared, asking to hear "Tom Dooley." Ditching the Kingston Trio arrangement, Stampfel and his friends began playing the more mountain-music rendition they'd learned from the New Lost City Ramblers in Washington Square Park. The listeners were not amused. "They were incensed because we were doing it wrong," Stampfel said. "How dare we do this great song so fucked up!" The students were so outraged that Stampfel and his friend George Dawson had to flee, with Dawson hitting some of them with his banjo to avoid being smacked himself.

As Grossman told Van Ronk, he already had two members of his prospective group lined up and needed a third to sing lead and harmony and play guitar. A musical director, Milt Okun, who had worked with Harry Belafonte and the Chad Mitchell Trio, was already on board. Van Ronk thought it over, but, according to Terri Thal, the idea didn't sit well with either him or her. "Dave and I thought about it and talked about it," she said. "Dave knew the group's sound would be somewhat commercial, and that it would not be his kind of music. It wasn't something he could have done." After a day or two of pondering, he turned Grossman down.

Van Ronk wasn't the first to pass on the proposal. According to Carolyn Hester, she had been approached by Grossman for a trio involving Chicago-based folksinger Bob Gibson (a regular at Grossman's Gate of Horn) and another singer and guitarist, Ray Boguslav (the guitarist Happy Traum had first seen playing in Washington Square Park). That group convened for a few hours, but Hester had her doubts: she had already recorded two albums on her own, and the thought of putting her own solo career on hold wasn't appealing.

Grossman was undeterred; fortunately for him, other, hungrier talents in the neighborhood were happy to consider his scheme. Grossman had begun managing Peter Yarrow, the son of a Left-leaning lawyer and drama teacher who'd graduated from Cornell with a psychology degree. While still at college, Yarrow had begun singing and playing folk music, and he and Grossman met at the Cafe Wha?. Grossman took him on as a client, helping him land a slot at Folk City in May 1961. Yarrow, who had a softly yearning voice and a rabbinical look, heard a similar pitch to the one Van Ronk would receive. "Albert had a concept for a group, and Albert was right most of the time," Yarrow recalled. "He said, 'We need a woman with a strong, powerful voice, and you'll be the straight man'—since I was so square and serious at the time—'and we need someone who's a comic.'" A few names were bandied about, including Happy Traum, who ran into Yarrow on Seventh Avenue South and was invited to join. (Traum was intrigued but didn't follow up.) Grossman supposedly also reached out to Logan English, a multi-hyphenate—singer, actor, playwright—who had played with Van Ronk at the Cafe Bizarre.

Around the same time, Yarrow walked into the Folklore Center and beheld a photo of a striking blonde with bangs pinned to the store's bulletin board. "Now, you have to know—I wasn't thinking of her *voice*," Yarrow said with a laugh years later. "I said, 'Who's *that*?'" Having already heard about Grossman's trio idea, Young replied, "She'd be great if you could get her to work." Mary Travers lived almost right across the street from the store, in a walk-up apartment above the Commons. She had plenty of experience, in some cases more than the men: the daughter of labor organizers and writers, she had left her progressive Village school, the Little Red School House, to join the Song Swappers, a large-scale folk vocal group that recorded with Pete Seeger. She'd also taken a role in a short-lived Broadway revue, *The Next President*, starring comic Mort Sahl. Travers had even been one of the original waitresses at the Village Gate. But she was also a young mother with a baby at home. Grossman gave her a call and suggested she and Yarrow meet up. In her apartment, near the bathtub that doubled as a kitchen counter when a plank of wood was laid over it, the two sang a few songs together and realized that their voices, his melodious and hers a bit deeper, meshed.

According to Thal, the reasons that Van Ronk passed on completing the trio were personal as well as musical. "Mary's attitude toward me was part of Dave's decision," she said. "Mary didn't speak to me. I never knew why. We'd run into her on the street, and she'd say, 'Hi, Dave. How are you?' And Dave would say to her, 'You know Terri.' And there would be no response. I have no idea why. I never did anything to the woman. But Mary's thing about me, unless it changed, would have made the whole thing a little difficult." Little in the way of hard feelings appeared to exist, however: Van Ronk and Yarrow shared a bill at Folk City in the summer of 1961.

Both Yarrow and Grossman were familiar with Stookey from his time at the Cafe Wha? and the Gaslight. After one of those Gaslight sets, Grossman beckoned Stookey over to his preferred table in the back. Stookey assumed Grossman was going to suggest managing him; instead, Grossman asked if he wanted to be part of a group he was assembling. Stookey was instantly deflated. "I said, 'No, actually, there are things I need to do on my own,'" he recalled. "Which I thought was a pretty grown-up answer to such a fraught question."

Soon after, Stookey received a call from Travers, whom he'd gotten to know in the community; she'd introduced him to the annual Feast of San Gennaro, and he would sometimes accompany her when she stopped into the Gaslight to sing together. "She was about as gregarious a person as I ever met," he said. "She was in your face, happy, blond hair flying: 'You gotta do this, you gotta see this, you gotta hear this.'" In her call, Travers asked Stookey again about joining a group, although at the time he wasn't aware that she and Grossman were talking about the same project.

This time, Stookey went along with the idea; it was hard to say no to Travers, who soon arrived at Stookey's East Village apartment with Yarrow. Since Stookey wasn't a folk specialist, they couldn't sing Yarrow's first choice, the traditional and century-old "Cruel War," so they opted for, of all things, "Mary Had a Little Lamb." Yarrow took the lead, the others joined in, and something special ignited. "It was immediately magical for us," Yarrow said. "Our voices didn't 'match.' It wasn't like the Andrews Sisters or the Kingston Trio." Instead, their individual personalities emerged, and soon they had worked up a half-dozen songs. They also began congregating at Travers's apartment—to the relief of Stookey's roommate, Paxton, who had grown beyond tired of hearing the trio rehearse Will Holt's Brazilian-inspired serenade "Lemon Tree."

Stookey didn't hear the name Albert Grossman come up until well into those rehearsals. At that point, it all made sense, even if Stookey didn't recall specifically asking Grossman about the makeup of the group he was proposing. "At the time, it was mostly guys who were doing folk, except for [L.A. folkie] Judy Henske and Ronnie [Gilbert] in the Weavers," Stookey recalled. "But it made a lot of sense to have a good-looking woman with a great voice, a tenor with a great voice, and this affable clown in the middle. We could pick up the slack from each other."

Memories vary about whether they made their debut at the Gaslight or Folk City in the fall of 1961. In either case, the spot was an impromptu, unadvertised performance, a warm-up in front of friends. But everyone would recall Grossman's suggestions, from having the two men grow goatees to match (Yarrow was clean-shaven at the time and grew his back to match Stookey's) to asking Travers to refrain from being her usual forthright self onstage in order to build her mystique.

Grossman also asked Stookey to use his middle name, Paul, for the more pleasing-sounding Peter, Paul and Mary; the name was also a nod to the traditional "I Was Born Ten Thousand Years Ago," which references "Peter, Paul and Moses." Stookey, now known publicly as Paul, flashed on the way that Archie Leach had become Cary Grant, all in the name of show business. Perhaps he also thought he wouldn't have to worry about being called Paul for too long. As Yarrow recalled, "I had a very strong sense of purpose at that time, and Noel and Mary did not. Mary never believed this would go much farther than a year or something. Noel also was doing it on a temporary basis. But I had a different concept." So did Grossman, and it would soon pay off.

▌▌▌▌

Not long after he graduated from college, Barry Kornfeld, Van Ronk's friend and fellow traveler, moved to Boston for a year, where he taught guitar. When he returned to Manhattan in the fall of 1961, the Village seemed to have received a makeover. "The entire MacDougal Street scene exploded in front of me," he recalled. "All of a sudden there was some money to be made. You have a lot of people making a living—not a *good* living, but earning some money." Van Ronk booked him for a week or two at the Commons, where Kornfeld noticed another change—the advent of the finger-snapping applause at that venue as well.

The Folklore Center remained a gathering spot. Into 1962, Dylan would stop by or have his mail sent there. Izzy Young would take diligent notes about who popped in, what they discussed, and what deals were in the works. Judy Collins came in for dish. "'Who is having an affair with whom?'" she recalled asking. "'What march is going on next weekend?' It was the place to figure out who was around." Collins also left a note for Dylan. When one of his songs was reprinted in *Sing Out!*, she saw Dylan's name in the credits and thought it must have been a typo. But after realizing it was the same person, she wrote him a fan letter—what she recalled as a note of "sheer admiration"—and deposited it at the Folklore Center.

Whether anyone wanted it to be or not, another gathering spot became the Hotel Earle, a fleabag and junkie hangout on Waverly Place off MacDougal, near the northwest corner of Washington Square Park. Ramblin' Jack Elliott grabbed a third-floor room when he first came back to New York; next door was his friend Peter LaFarge, who would soon write "The Ballad of Ira Hayes," based on the true story of the Native American marine who helped raise the flag in Iwo Jima but suffered when he returned home to the States. A few months after Elliott settled in, three men who'd rented the top-floor suite were arrested for using the apartment (and a telescope) to scope out nearby buildings for burglaries. But the Earle was cheap, about $100 a month, and it soon become a way station for many, including Dylan, who were taking their shot at the dank, smoky coffeehouses down the block.

Few musicians seemed to have musicians' union cards: it was assumed that the union didn't care about folkies who played places that didn't serve alcohol. Because it had a liquor license, Folk City paid acts ninety dollars per week thanks to Local 802, but it was the exception. In 1961 the cabaret law was revised ever so slightly. Local Law 95 made it acceptable for coffeehouses to avoid obtaining licenses if they presented what was called "incidental music"—performances by no more than three musicians, playing keyboards, accordions, or stringed instruments. Drums, brass, and woodwinds were still not allowed. Without intending to do so, that change unintentionally helped the folk world; booking solo or duo folk acts was now more appealing and less legally risky than it had been. Simultaneously, the Monday hootenanny sessions that Mike Porco had launched at Folk City the year before were spreading elsewhere, albeit on different days. The Cafe Wha? ("NY's biggest and swingingest bomb shelter," as its ads now boasted) had started similar open-mic folk nights on Wednesdays, and Weintraub asked Porco if he could host one on Tuesdays at the Bitter End.

Meanwhile, the music industry was beginning to monitor the scene in ways it had never done before. During an engagement at the Village Gate, Collins was approached by Elektra's Jac Holzman; their mutual friend Bob Gibson had touted her as Holzman's possible answer to Joan Baez. "Dear, you're ready to make your record?" he said. In a sign of how quietly competitive the scene was becoming, John Hammond, who was now heading up Columbia's A&R Department, made the same remark to her a week later. Having already offered deals to Pete Seeger and a young Aretha Franklin, alongside his earlier championing of bandleaders and jazz musicians such as Benny Goodman, Hammond was a sizable force, but it was too late: Collins had cast her recording fate with Elektra. By then, Hester was also being managed by Grossman, who told her about Hammond's search for a Baez. Soon enough, Hester was a Columbia act as well. Somewhat embarrassed, she called the Clancys to tell them she was leaving their Topic label, but they told her not to worry—they were signing with Columbia as well.

During the early rehearsals for Hester's Columbia debut, she invited Dylan to the sessions. Hester had already met Dylan: at one of her Folk City shows, she sang the late Buddy Holly's "Lonesome Tears," introducing it as a song by Holly (they'd met during her years in Texas). As the crowd was leaving at the end of the set, this "young guy in a cap" approached Hester and asked, "Did he teach you that song or did you know Buddy Holly?" She and Dylan connected, and she invited him to play harmonica on her album sessions. At the rehearsals, Hester and Hammond decided that Dylan should play on at least one track, the 1920s gospel uplift "I'll Fly Away." Dylan himself, she said, suggested "Come Back Baby," the sauntering blues popularized by Ray Charles a few years before. Hester didn't consider herself a blues singer at all, but he told her, "You can sing this."

Even before the rehearsals, Dylan had asked Hester which label she was on; she told him Hammond had signed her to Columbia. At the session, Dylan and Hester sat across from each other at a table, Hammond next to them, and

"Dylan was doing his harmonica thing right in Hammond's ear," she said. "Hammond couldn't take his eyes off him."

In addition to helping her husband land work, Terri Thal had taken an early crack at managing Dylan, but after a few months, she had little to show for it other than a tape of his songs. Club owners and labels still considered him too raw or embryonic a talent. As timing would have it, Hester's sessions coincided with Dylan playing another set of shows at Folk City, this time with the Greenbriar Boys headlining. The *Times'* Robert Shelton, who had already seen Dylan at one of the Monday hoots, wrote it up, calling him someone "bursting at the seams with talent." Dylan was seen carting that review around during the Hester sessions. Hammond would later tell Anthony Scaduto that he had offered Dylan money for a demo. But whatever the catalyst, Dylan signed a one-album deal with Columbia about a month after the Hester sessions.

With news of those record deals, as well as the sight of Shelton regularly making the rounds and reviewing live music for the most prestigious newspaper in the country, the scene and the strategizing both accelerated. As Elliott recalled, "It was becoming more and more folk fans and not as many drunks." Happy Traum, who had lined up at some of Folk City's earlier hoots, saw the transition as well. "It changed fast," he said. "The hoots at Gerde's were sparsely attended, and then people started going hoping they'd be seen by Shelton. And suddenly you had crowds on a Monday night, along with managers and agents. There was all sorts of jockeying for position." As Traum learned, the key was not to play before the "important people"—managers and agents and label people—arrived, and yet not so late that they were gone. At the Gaslight, Paxton noticed that even after he'd signed up for a slot on open-mic night, the order could suddenly be switched so that another act could go first.

A hierarchy in the clubs soon came into view. The Gaslight and Folk City, which the *Daily News* wrote had "all the charm of an abandoned warehouse," were home to up-and-coming folkies and veteran blues acts—"on your way up or down," said Van Ronk—and the Village Gate welcomed established stars like Nina Simone. As for the Bitter End, whether because it wasn't a basement

space or because some of its employees, such as Paul Colby, had industry connections (he'd previously been a song plugger for Warner Brothers, among
other gigs), that relatively new venue quickly became what Paxton called "kind
of a launch pad for record contracts." It was the career-making spot, the one
that record-company executives were more likely to visit even if it, like the Gaslight, served only coffee and ice cream.

The opening of the Bitter End fit in with Grossman's plans for his new trio.
When he first booked Peter, Paul and Mary into the club late in 1961, nothing was guaranteed. Attendance was sparse, and the trio was still developing
their repertoire; they had so few songs prepared that they would fill out the sets
with solo spots, Stookey's comic impersonations, and a version of "Old Blue,"
the folk ode to a dead dog, that was transformed into a rock-and-roll parody.
Colby placed one, then two, ads in the *Times* encouraging people to buy tickets
as soon as possible because the house was always packed, a boast that Stookey
called "totally inflated."

But even in their embryonic stage, the trio were injecting a new vitality
into the music. Travers had a coltish energy, swooping in toward and away
from the microphone, and their image was far removed from that of their
scruffier peers: Travers wore dresses, and Yarrow and Stookey donned Brooks
Brothers suits that Stookey had bought on credit. The night of their debut
in the club that fall, Elliott scoped out the space and was impressed with the
way the Grossman team, including comanager John Court, made sure that
the sound system balanced the trio's voices in the mix. Afterward, Elliott ran
into Grossman at the Folklore Center and asked if he would manage him
as well. "He said, 'I could never manage you, Jack,' and I said, 'Why not?'"
Elliott recalled. "He said, 'You're a weird person.' I said, '*I'm* a weird person? *You're* a weird person!'" Elliott was disappointed but eventually laughed
it off.

Grossman may have sensed that Elliott was not a commercial commodity,
but he knew better about Peter, Paul and Mary. Columbia passed on the group,
but Atlantic was interested, as was a newly rising company. By year's end,
Grossman had secured the trio a hefty advance—either $15,000 or $30,000,
depending on the source—from Warner Brothers, which was still struggling to

establish itself in music, a situation that gave the group a rare degree of creative control over all aspects of their records.

By the time *Billboard* announced the contract, Peter, Paul and Mary were already moving on up, booked into the Blue Angel club uptown. But they gathered at the Bitter End for a photo for their album. Lying on a cot backstage with a 104-degree fever, Stookey had to be stirred awake to have his picture taken against the club's brick wall, alongside Travers and Yarrow. In case Stookey needed something to sit or lean on in his weakened state, album-art designer Milton Glaser and photographer Bernard Cole placed a stool among them, which Travers ended up sitting on. The Brooks Brothers suits were proudly on display, and Glaser employed a font for their name that, in another savvy business move, would become the group's logo. The Village was poised to go national.

Anyone visiting the Van Ronk and Thal apartment, especially in the summer of 1961 and periodically after, may have bumped into Dylan, who used their living-room couch as a crash pad. But one day in early 1962, Dylan himself came bursting in. Van Ronk was in the midst of a guitar tutorial with his latest student, Steve Katz, a thin, pale-faced kid from Queens who'd seen a paperback guide to beatniks in a candy store and was soon venturing into Folk City and the Gaslight. There he saw Van Ronk, who scared the hell out of him. "By the end of the songs he was slamming his guitar and yelling," Katz recalled. In need of lessons, Katz gingerly approached the musician, who, as always, said he was available for a price and invited him over.

Katz had seen Dylan at Van Ronk's a few times before, but this was different: today, the visibly excited kid was holding a cover proof of his first album. And even though the photo had been reversed by the label, showing the strings on his guitar out of order to accommodate the cover design, Dylan was clearly on his way.

One album at a time, the music being fashioned and molded in the Village was trickling out to the rest of the world. Bill Evans's *Sunday at the Village Vanguard*, taped in June 1961 (days before his bass player, Scott LaFaro, died in a car crash), was especially meditative jazz, all from a pianist described at the time as resembling "a fugitive from a library." Coltrane's *"Live" at the Village Vanguard* followed months later. Collins's *A Maid of Constant Sorrow* introduced the world to a folksinger who focused largely on traditional material, like "Wild Mountain Thyme" and "The Rising of the Moon," but sang those songs with a vigor and clarity that matched the firm, unwavering gaze of the woman of her cover portrait. Collins even worked herself up into a righteous anger on "Tim Evans," about a man wrongly accused of murder and hanged before he could be redeemed. Connecting her further with Village tradition, Collins was accompanied by the Weavers' Fred Hellerman on guitar.

For a taste of the bluegrass still loudly announcing itself in Washington Square Park, the Greenbriar Boys' self-titled album arrived by way of Vanguard. Hester's third record and first for Columbia, *Carolyn Hester*, was looser and more eclectic than her two previous albums. It opened with a fluttering version of "I'll Fly Away," featuring Dylan on harmonica. The Baez comparisons were apparent in balladry like "Los Biblicos" and the traditional "Dink's Song," a southern woman worker's lament discovered by folklorist John Lomax decades before it was regularly being played in coffeehouses. Thanks to Hester's Texas roots, the Mexican folk song "Pobre De Mi" felt unforced, as did her foray into blues, her Dylan-prompted rendition of "Come Back, Baby."

In mid-March 1962, Columbia rolled out *Bob Dylan*, recorded in a few sessions with Hammond the previous November and comprising covers and only two original songs. The flipped cover image (apparent to those familiar with guitars, at least) wasn't the only aspect that stood out. Onstage at Folk City or elsewhere, Dylan's impish side reminded some of Charlie Chaplin, and his occasional fumbling could be endearing. But the verve and audacity that Stampfel and others had witnessed at those shows tore through *Bob Dylan*. With his voice at times whooping, hollering, or growling, Dylan sounded as if he were raring to go, about to jump out of his skin, or at least the fur-lined brown jacket he sported on the cover. Whereas Collins and Hester treated traditional songs gingerly, Dylan, on his versions of "In My Time of Dyin'," "Fixin' to Die," and "Baby Let Me Follow You Down," roughed up and cavorted with them. He could be as solemn as anyone on the Gaslight stage, but he could also be mischievous.

Van Ronk was less than pleased that Dylan hijacked his arrangement of the whorehouse-visit lament "The House of the Rising Sun," recording it before Van Ronk could. As Thal would write, Van Ronk flew into a "righteous rage" when Dylan confessed what he'd done; performers weren't supposed to undercut each other like that. After a few months, the two reconnected. But *Billboard*, at least, endorsed the whole package. A month after the album dropped, the trade magazine gave *Bob Dylan* its industry seal of approval, citing it as a "Special Merit" release by "a young man (20) from Minnesota who has already made an impact among folkniks with his exciting manner with folk, blues and pop-folk tunes. . . . Dylan, when he finds his own style, could win a big following."

By the time Peter, Paul and Mary started recording their album, at an uptown studio known for advertising jingles, the country was convulsing over racial and international issues. Kennedy had begun sending so-called advisers to Vietnam, threatening to pull America into a war most people didn't remotely understand. *Peter, Paul and Mary* didn't shy away from reading the country's mood. At the suggestion of Grossman and Grossman's office mate George Wein, the trio recorded "Cruel War," a century-plus-old ballad about a woman so in love that she wants to join her partner in battle, and a robust version of "If I Had a Hammer," Pete Seeger and Lee Hays's power-to-the-people rouser from their Weavers days.

But people also needed songs that would gently take them by the hand and guide them through an increasingly fractious and confusing time. From the rousing, borderline–born-again opener "Early in the Morning" to the trio's harmonies, which were as consoling as a heart-to-heart talk, *Peter, Paul and Mary* was that chaperone. To play it safe, Warner Brothers chose their rendition of "Lemon Tree" as the album's first single in the spring of 1962. But it was the follow-up, "If I Had a Hammer," that spoke to the times, quickly becoming a Top 10 hit. Fueled by that song and Warner Brothers' savvy marketing—sending the trio out to college campuses to spread the word—the album was soon the top-selling record in the country.

Their Village peers didn't have quite the same success. Collins's *A Maid of Constant Sorrow* sold only about five thousand copies. *Billboard* was correct in wondering how many people Dylan's debut would reach. According to Hammond, the album, like Collins's, wound up selling only about five thousand copies itself, failing to make the *Billboard* album chart. Billy James, Dylan's publicist at the company, heard that Dylan had incurred the wrath of Columbia employees in the South, who took revenge by not promoting the release. Hammond's bosses began pressuring him to dispense with Dylan, whom some had dubbed "Hammond's Folly." But he stuck with his artist, and his faith suddenly began reaping rewards.

No sooner had Dylan released his first album than he was moving on, and with a grander statement all his own. In mid-spring of 1962, he emerged with "Blowin' in the Wind," a series of questions about social change that was less a rallying cry and more a thoughtful contemplation. As legend had it, Dylan's idea for the song grew out of conversations with friends, and after he had written most of it, he played the song for Gil Turner, an activist and full-throated singer who also worked as an emcee at Folk City. Starting at the club one April 1962 night, Dylan began singing it all around, impressing the likes of Van Ronk, who had been pushing him to drop his homages to Dust Bowl and folk heroes and find his own style. "I did tell him to forget the Guthrie Thirties idolization and get on with the business of the sixties," Van Ronk told Scaduto. "I mean, Guthrie's dying and his generation is dead." When he heard "Blowin' in the Wind," Van Ronk told Scaduto, he approved.

In his own role as a folksinger, Turner started performing "Blowin' in the Wind" at Folk City as a member of an interracial folk band, the New World Singers—one of whose members was already conversant with the song. Dylan would later refer to Delores C. Dixon, the group's Black singer, as a former journalist and dancer from Alabama, not all of which was accurate. Dixon was born in Savannah, Georgia, around the same time Dylan was; after her parents broke up, her mother went north to find work, and young Delores, or "Dee," lived with a grandmother until she joined her mother in New York. At age twelve she was playing classical piano and organ at a Baptist church in Harlem, and she eventually enrolled in the Performing Arts School in the city. At the Upper West Side home of a friend, Bob Cohen, she met Turner, who proposed they form a group and also named it. "We sat one day thinking of all the names, and Gil came up with that," Dixon said. "We were going to be in a new world, and things were going to change." Traum, who joined later, also thought it may have derived from a folk song with the phrase "a new world coming" in its lyric.

At Folk City and a few other venues, the New World Singers had a repertoire that came to include "If I Had a Hammer" and Guthrie's "This Land Is Your Land," along with reworked versions of "He's Got the Whole World in His Hands" (remade into a civil rights anthem that the group called "We Got the Power in Our Hands") and "Down by the Riverside" (now "Down on the Freedom Line" with revised lyrics like "I ain't gonna segregate no more"). Dylan had heard them at Folk City—Traum would remember him joining them now and then for a few songs—and witnessed one of the high points of their set: "No More Auction Block," an antislavery song Dixon would sing a capella. Given that she was one of the very few Black performers on the scene, Dixon's performance of it was musically and visually dramatic.

At some point, Dixon and Dylan grew close. In his memoir, he would refer to her as "my sort of part-time girlfriend," and he described at length a party they attended in the Village, Dixon in a fur coat. "We didn't call it a date," Dixon said. "We hung out together. We went to parties. We'd go walking." She did not recall that particular party, "but it probably happened," she said. She would remember that they were both eating at her mother's house when Dylan pulled out a notebook of lyrics and out came some of "Blowin' in the Wind," set to a melody that brought to mind the traditional "No More Auction Block." As Dixon recalled, "I said, 'Really? Look at that.'" When Turner brought the song to the group, she remembered it, and in performance she took the contralto voice while the men sang gentle harmonies.

Dylan recorded "Blowin' in the Wind" in the summer of 1962, and the New World Singers were next in line. By early 1963, Traum had joined the group, lending his guitar and harmony skills to what was now a quartet. With Dylan standing right in front of them and holding the lyrics, they recorded a version of "Blowin' in the Wind" for *Broadside Ballads, Vol 1*, a companion to the newly launched political-songs periodical *Broadside*, founded by Agnes "Sis" Cunningham and her husband, Gordon Friesen. With its plucky banjo and showcase for Dixon in the chorus, the New World Singers' rendition of "Blowin' in the Wind" felt very much in the Weavers tradition.

Still, the group didn't experience anything close to the Weavers' trajectory. *Broadside Ballads*, on a subsidiary of Moses Asch's Folkways, was issued with little fanfare, and the group's gigs—including one at the Bitter End in the fall of 1962 that was recorded for a live album but never released—were few and far between. Since they had to split their paltry earnings, Dixon decided that the numbers didn't add up for her. "I had to pay rent and food," she said. "The guys could always go to a girl and eat their food and spend the night or whatever. But I had to have my own money." She settled for a job at the board of education, although she continued singing from time to time.

Once she left the group, Dixon saw less of Dylan, although he would bequeath her with a souvenir of their time together: a signed copy of his first album. "To New World Dee," he wrote, complimenting her "brown eyes" that shed "light sun every day a the year in Gerde's and every nite with me at Gerde's. . . . From Columbia Records I can only go down I guess so meet me on your way up and be nice. Look out for that Gil guy and the other fellows in the dressing room." Neither she nor any of her former bandmates in the New World Singers knew that "Blowin' in the Wind" was about to get a sizable second gust of its own.

▌▐▌▐▌

Aside from Grossman and the trio itself, another beneficiary of the success of *Peter, Paul and Mary* was, ironically, one of the people who had turned down the job. In the summer of 1961, months before that album was recorded, Folkways unveiled a second Van Ronk LP. As an audio document, *Van Ronk Sings* felt like an urban field recording, but it also displayed his growing confidence as a singer and guitarist. Here was someone who could not only pull off a credible cover of Willie Dixon's salacious blues stomp "Hoochie Coochie Man" but also a sublime rendition of "Dink's Song." Van Ronk acquitted himself well on a version of "Bed Bug Blues" that he'd learned off a Bessie Smith album. The citified (and dark-humored) aspect that set Van Ronk apart also burst out in "Georgie and the IRT," about a worker on his way home to Brooklyn whose head is lopped off by a subway-car door that closes too fast.

Van Ronk Sings also includes a ditty that he himself would admit to hating. Dick Weissman, the banjo player who had since joined the Journeymen, had learned a song from a calypso singer he was accompanying—and who never paid him in full for his work. When Weissman later came across the song in collections of traditional Jamaican folk music, he exacted a form of revenge by copyrighting the song under the name of himself and John Phillips, his partner in the Journeymen, and the group recorded its own version.

On a Village street, Weissman ran into Van Ronk, who told him he had "screwed around" with the song, writing new words and using a line in the chorus, "River, she come down," in its new title. Van Ronk wanted to record "River Come Down" for his album and copyright it in both their names. Thanks to an issue between publishing-rights organizations, Weissman's name was dropped from the song's credits on *Van Ronk Sings*. But Van Ronk, taking the honorable route, continued to give Weissman his share of the royalties—funds that turned into an unexpected windfall when Peter, Paul and Mary included their own harmonized take on the song, retitled "Bamboo," on their first album. From the sales of that album alone, Weissman estimated that he and Van Ronk each earned in the range of $8,000, a sizable amount at the time; Thal put the total as high as $16,000 each.

Being listed in the credits of the most popular album in the country helped raise Van Ronk's profile nationally, but in his own neighborhood, he and Thal didn't need such validation. Although both were only in their early to middle twenties, they were already regarded as parental figures. In the summer of 1961, the couple made their partnership more official. "We agreed that if we lasted two years, we'd get married," Thal said. "Two years later, we were busy organizing the coffeehouses, so we postponed marriage." Thal's parents had stopped speaking to Van Ronk when they learned the two were sleeping together. But the night before the wedding date of August 4, 1961, Thal's brother called, asking for directions, then put their mother on the line. "She was crying," Thal recalled. "The only time I had ever heard my mother cry was when she learned that all of her relatives in Russia had been murdered. When I hung up the phone, David said to me, 'Call your parents back and invite them.' I was amazed. Those people hadn't spoken to him for years." Thal asked Van Ronk to call instead, which he did, and her parents, in what she called "an incredibly strong, generous move," attended the city hall service, where Paxton served as best man. A week later, the new couple walked into the Lion's Head bar, a regular haunt, and some of the Clancy brothers began cheering and buying them drinks. "We really felt weird," Thal said. "We felt uncomfortable. But there we were."

By then, Thal had taken over managing Van Ronk after a disastrous experience with a previous manager, who pushed the musician to play a new coffeehouse outside Philadelphia even though, as Thal said, "It was clear to Dave and me that he was going to get stiffed." Van Ronk did indeed fail to get paid, leading him to ask Thal to steer that part of his career. Thinking it would be an adventure, Thal dropped out of City College, where she had been pursuing a graduate degree in political science, and entered the folk management world— a rare woman in a field dominated by the likes of Grossman and Manny Greenhill, Baez's manager.

Coincidentally, Van Ronk's career did move up another notch soon after, when he signed with Prestige, a jazz label that had recorded Miles Davis and the Modern Jazz Quartet but was moving into folk. According to Van Ronk, label owner Bob Weinstock, an Upper West Sider who had started recording and releasing jazz records in his early twenties, wanted to call the album *Dave Van Ronk: New York's Finest*. Appalled, Van Ronk made the case that it made him sound like a cop, and they settled on *Dave Van Ronk: Folksinger*, complete with a cover photo of the singer chortling on the front steps of the Folklore Center. (In terms of branding, the album would prove as important to Izzy Young's business as the Village Vanguard live albums were to Max Gordon.)

Although its title was designed to link Van Ronk to the emerging folk boom, *Folksinger*, from late 1962, wasn't for the faint of heart. Van Ronk's most confident and visceral recording yet, it was steeped in what liner-note writer J. R. Goddard called "strife and violence." Making its first appearance on one of his records, "Poor Lazarus" was like a relentless, haunted murmur, Van Ronk's voice breaking into an intermittent growl that broke the spell. The album had its fairly lighthearted moments, like "Chicken Is Nice," and Van Ronk exhibited a new depth in an interpretation of Reverend Gary Davis's "Cocaine Blues." But Van Ronk's emerging power as a singer truly burst through in a version of "Samson and Delilah" and a cover of "Come Back Baby" that was far more downcast than Hester's come-hither take. Around this time, Oscar Brand took a shot at his competition—"Dave Van Ronk would like nothing better than to be a blind Negro folk singer," he told a reporter—but *Folksinger* proved that Van Ronk could honor and add to his influences.

Soon, one of Van Ronk's former students was back on the circuit and also back in touch. Dropping out of the University of Wisconsin, Danny Kalb returned to New York, "whose bright lights and painted women have never ceased to astound or amuse," he would later write. He ended up back in his parents' Mount Vernon home. He'd already reconnected with Dylan when both were part of a folk show at Riverside Church on the Upper West Side. "Other people put Bob down for being unmusical," he told Mitch Blank, "but I'd listened to a lot of country blues, starting in about '58, '59, to know there was something there with Bob."

Not for the first time, Kalb, who could be psychically fragile when he wasn't cocky, fell into a depression. But he also reconnected with Van Ronk and picked up where their bond had left off. During the Cuban Missile Crisis, in October 1962, Kalb, along with Paxton, was in Van Ronk and Thal's apartment, smoking weed for the first time, all of them wondering precisely when the world would disintegrate as tensions rose between the United States and Russia. As Kalb would recall, Van Ronk began spinning an album of Bulgarian folk music. When a scream emerged from one of the Eastern European singers, Kalb said he and everyone "freaked," assuming it was the sound of a hydrogen bomb. Van Ronk had a gig scheduled for the Gaslight, so everyone wandered over to the club, where manager Clarence Hood told them he had called his friend and former president Harry Truman for clarification; Truman said that everything was in order and that they needn't worry. Given that Hood had connections to the Democratic Party in the South, the idea seemed plausible, and he was right: the world didn't end that evening.

That year, the unraveling of the world seemed at hand. The Soviet Union tested a fifty-megaton hydrogen bomb, and deadly riots had broken out in Oxford, Mississippi, after Kennedy ordered federal marshals to help a Black student, James Meredith, attend the University of Mississippi there. Now a nuclear standoff was added to the list. The community was very much in sync with the times. Canadian-born Bonnie Dobson had been performing her song "Morning Dew" at Folk City; inspired by the movie *On the Beach*, about people in Australia waiting for nuclear fallout to engulf them, it was both melodiously gorgeous and chilling—a folk lament for a modern age. Eerily enough, the song, which would soon become a touchstone of the antinuclear movement, was included on Dobson's album *At Folk City*, issued around the time of the Cuban Missile Crisis.

Chapter 4

Violets of dawn

1963–1964

Anyone who sang or worked at the Gaslight knew about the other, secret Gaslight that awaited them if they chose. One flight up sat a one-room apartment where performers could play cards, leave their instrument cases, or crash between sets on a small bed—alone or with company. "People would take someone from the audience up there for a little visit," one regular said. "We were terrible people." Thanks to a wire run from the club into a small speaker, the musicians could also hear whoever was onstage and prepare to follow them. On a night when Bob Dylan asked to crash at her apartment in the neighborhood, Carolyn Hester, unsure about whether she wanted to get involved with him, told Anthony Scaduto that she fabricated a date and instead found herself alone in the auxiliary Gaslight room.

If inspiration struck, a typewriter, supposedly contributed by Hugh Romney, could also be found there. Unwinding in the room one night between sets, Tom Paxton noticed Dylan tapping away. When asked what he was writing, Paxton recalled, Dylan handed him five typed sheets of paper. "I said, 'This is terrific—it's like "Lord Randall" in 1962,'" referencing the Scottish folk ballad in which a mother speaks with a son poisoned by his lover. Dylan told him he wasn't sure of his plans for the work, and Paxton suggested he send it to one of the small literary journals—"and get 25 bucks for it," he counseled—or set it to a melody. At the Gaslight a few nights later, Paxton watched as

111

Dylan premiered the song, "A Hard Rain's a-Gonna Fall," now a conversation between parent and child in what felt like a nuclear wasteland, and Paxton realized it was never meant to be a poem. "When he got to the sixth verse," Paxton recalled, "I thought, 'What was I thinking?'"

The wider public would hear "A Hard Rain's a-Gonna Fall" in May 1963, part of Dylan's long-in-progress second album, *The Freewheelin' Bob Dylan*. By then, it wasn't merely his music that was the talk of the Village. Nearly two years before, he'd been introduced to Suze Rotolo, a vivacious then seventeen-year-old who, thanks to her proudly Communist parents, was already immersed in the worlds of art and literature. After they'd met at the all-day folk radiocast from the Riverside Church in the summer of 1961, where Dave Van Ronk, Danny Kalb, and Roger Sprung, among others, played, Dylan and Rotolo drifted into each other's arms.

Rotolo watched as her boyfriend's career began to intensify; eventually, she began to harbor doubts about his connection to the truth and sensed that his growing cult might overwhelm her. There were family issues as well: her sister Carla and Dylan famously did not get along. Barry Kornfeld would recall receiving a call in the middle of the night from Carla, telling him to get over to the apartment she and Suze were sharing at 106 Avenue B in the East Village. There, Kornfeld found Suze "sitting in a bed, almost oblivious to what was going on—she was stunned—and Bob and Carla were frothing at the mouth at each other."

Kornfeld never learned more about the origins of the fight, but he sensed the pressure that Rotolo was receiving from her family to break up with Dylan. In June 1962, Rotolo decamped for Europe with her mother and stepfather. When Rotolo returned to the city at year's end, people on the scene treated her coldly, as if she had done Dylan grievous harm by leaving him. But she and Dylan reconciled and started living together at 161 West Fourth Street. For the cover of Dylan's second album, photographer Don Hunstein captured the two walking down Jones Street, not far from their apartment, Rotolo huddled next to him, Dylan exuding his James-Dean-of-folk aura despite insisting on wearing only a light jacket in freezing weather. Even more than the photos that graced Peter, Paul and Mary's debut and Van Ronk's *Folksinger*, the cover of

Freewheelin' crystallized the Village's romantic ambience like none before—what Rotolo (who was startled to learn she was included on the cover) would call "the time-honored language of youth and rebellion against the status quo." Dylan had debuted some of his new songs at the Gaslight in the fall of 1962, when Albert Grossman funded a mysterious audition tape for Dylan over two nights at the club. (Dylan biographer Clinton Heylin suspected that Grossman may have needed such a tape to sever his client's relationship with Columbia and move to another label.) According to John Sebastian, "It was like he just changed the whole fucking atmosphere." Sebastian, a beatific, Village-born musician who was working his way into the scene by accompanying artists on harmonica, had met Dylan in the basement of Folk City, where they both caught a set by the blues singer Victoria Spivey. Having heard Dylan play harmonica on a Harry Belafonte album (another of his earliest recordings), Sebastian wasn't initially impressed: "I said, 'Holy Christ, I gotta bear down on this—this guy isn't a good harmonica player, it isn't his strength!'" (According to Columbia publicist Billy James, who was at the Belafonte session, Dylan was stomping his foot so hard on the floor that the recording engineer had to jam a pillow under it.)

But that night in the Gaslight told another story. Dylan played at least three ambitious songs, "A Hard Rain's a-Gonna Fall," "Don't Think Twice, It's All Right," and "Ballad of Hollis Brown," and the results were astounding. The naturally graceful "Don't Think Twice, It's All Right" was widely interpreted as his take on his separation from Rotolo, and the folksy use of words and phrases like "knowed" lent it a patina of authenticity. But the song also felt universal, something many others would soon start singing in coffeehouses. (When Ramblin' Jack Elliott included it in one open-mic night at the Gaslight, Dylan, who was in the house, stood up, waved his arms, and said, "I relinquish it to you, Jack," and it became part of Elliott's repertoire.) "All of a sudden, little English ballads didn't count," Sebastian said. "Suddenly it was, 'Now we're *here*. We're not *there* anymore.'"

The music inside *The Freewheelin' Bob Dylan* fortified Dylan's artistry as well as the evolution of the community that had nurtured and fueled him. As much as any record released up to that moment, it was the look and sound of the new Greenwich Village. Like his debut, it largely consisted of Dylan accompanying himself. But unlike *Bob Dylan*, it was dominated by his own material, and the leap he'd made in just over a year was nothing less than remarkable. A few moments, like "Down the Highway" and "Talking World War III Blues," retained the frolicking, jumping-bean energy of *Bob Dylan*. But opening austerely with "Blowin' in the Wind," *Freewheelin'* was a more mature and sobering record. Listeners were also confronted, seemingly out of nowhere, with a stern antiwar ballad, "Masters of War," and the lilting "Don't Think Twice, It's All Right." At a time when most pop songs didn't venture past the three-minute point, "A Hard Rain's a-Gonna Fall" stretched out to nearly seven minutes. A gentle, rewritten version of "Corinna, Corinna," a country blues that dated back to the 1920s, gave one of the earliest indications of how Dylan could adapt to a sympathetic backing band. His first album had gone nowhere fast on the charts, but *The Freewheelin' Bob Dylan* ascended to 22 after its release.

Among Rotolo's new comrades in the Village was Sylvia Tyson, née Fricker, a Canadian who'd moved to the city in early 1962 with her singing partner, Ian Tyson. The duo, who performed as Ian and Sylvia, had met on the Toronto folk scene in the late fifties and were musically and visually striking. Ian, who'd yearned to be a rodeo cowboy before an injury derailed those plans and led him into music, was movie-star handsome and had a wood-grained baritone; Sylvia sang in a lustrous contralto and was equally attractive. Their voices could blend in unearthly harmonies but also sound as if they were singing separately, like two people having parallel conversations on the same topic. Many assumed they were a couple, even though they were platonic partners at the time.

Thanks to a friend who worked at one of the leading Canadian folk festivals, Tyson and Fricker were able to land a meeting with Grossman in his New York office. At first, Grossman said he wasn't sure he could handle them, saying he had his hands full with "a new trio" he'd signed. But he eventually agreed to work with them and, during another visit, took them down to the Gaslight, where he introduced them to everyone in sight. At Folk City, Mike Porco, displaying his thick Italian accent once again, referred to them as "Enos and Sylvius." Grossman also sent them to one of the leading talent-booking agencies, the same one that handled the Kingston Trio. Waiting in the reception area, Sylvia saw a map on the wall sprinkled with red pins that indicated every college in the country that had booked the Kingston Trio. Clearly, the entertainment complex was keyed into something in the culture.

▌▐▐▌▌

Given Dylan's sponge-like ability to soak up all the influences around him, the social consciousness apparent in his avalanche of new songs could have been inspired either by the times or by his peers. Sylvia Tyson thought it was at least partly the latter. "It's my opinion that Dylan didn't have a political idea in his head until he met Suze," insisted Tyson, who by then had become close to Rotolo. "She introduced him to all the Beat poets. Suze was a red-diaper baby and was very familiar with the whole leftie scene in the Village, which was her background." According to Tyson, Ian also affected Dylan: after the two met, she observed, Dylan stopped rolling up his jeans because Ian told him that cowboys didn't do that.

What no one doubted was that Dylan's stock and abilities were both rising in ways that surprised those who remembered the funny, fumbling, somewhat chubby kid who'd shown up in town a mere two years before. Dylan clearly knew how to make an impression. When he and Kornfeld would play chess, Kornfeld picked up on his friend's wiliness. "I would characterize it as, 'I don't know what I'm doing—checkmate!'" Kornfeld said. "If we had been playing for money, I would have described him as a chess hustler." With the black chinos, cowboy boots, and frayed brown-suede jacket he often wore, Dylan was becoming so iconic in the Village that he was the subject of at least one affectionate parody. José Feliciano, a Puerto Rican teenager from the Bronx who'd been blind from birth, had learned to play guitar—or, rather, the guitar succumbed to his love of blues, flamenco, and jazz. Making his debut at Folk City in 1963, he would play versions of pop and folk hits like "A Taste of Honey" and "Walk Right In," often with his service dog with him. One of those evenings, the *Daily News* captured Feliciano and a beaming Suze Rotolo sitting next to him onstage; she likely escorted him on and off it. Rotolo was amused by his flawless impersonation of her boyfriend's speaking voice and wheeze. To

Feliciano's shock, Dylan witnessed it for himself during one of Feliciano's sets but shrugged it off, telling Feliciano it was fine and he could do whatever he wanted.

In light of his looming legend and aspirations for himself, Dylan needed a consigliere. Who exactly introduced him and Grossman would remain debated. It may have been Noel Stookey during one evening at the Gaslight, although the *Times*' Robert Shelton maintained he brought Dylan over to Grossman's usual table at the club the first time Shelton saw Dylan there, in 1961. (According to Shelton, Grossman said little and, after Dylan left, asked him how successful he thought Van Ronk, not Dylan, could be.)

Either way, Grossman had evidently been keeping both eyes on Dylan: as early as September 1961, he told Izzy Young (noted in Young's journals) that "Bob Dylan has a much better chance of making it" than others, especially in light of Shelton's review of Dylan's show at Folk City that month. Sylvia Tyson insisted it was she and Ian, along with Stookey, who convinced Grossman to add Dylan to his roster. "Albert was very hesitant about signing him," she said. "He wasn't that keen on his music. Ian and I and Paul basically pressured Albert to sign him." However it happened, Dylan informed a startled Thal that he was becoming Grossman's latest client in the summer of 1962.

Grossman immediately renegotiated Dylan's one-album deal with Columbia and, with his hand in the publishing income as well, pushed for his other clients to record Dylan's songs. Ian & Sylvia's first album for Vanguard relied heavily on traditional songs like "Rambler Rambler" and "Mary Anne" (the latter in a definitive version, their voices poignantly intertwined). But Dylan's "Tomorrow Is a Long Time" found a place on their second album, *Four Strong Winds*, and Peter, Paul and Mary included three of his songs, "Don't Think Twice, It's All Right," "Blowin' in the Wind," and the rowdier "Quit Your Low Down Ways," on their third album, *In the Wind*.

Although Dylan's version of "Blowin' in the Wind" was already in stores, it would be Peter, Paul and Mary's harmonies—which both caressed the melody and lent it a pained, long-suffering quality—that took the song to another cultural level. "How do you translate a Dylan tune that doesn't have much of a melody?" Travers said. "You make a very moving first harmony part. You construct the harmony part that becomes, then, the melody. Then the melody becomes sort of a solid base. And then you construct the second harmony off of the first harmony. So that all of a sudden, you've got movement. You have a part on top, and a part on the bottom, and the melody serving at the bottom."

Rolled out in June 1963, the trio's "Blowin' in the Wind" became the fastest-moving single in Warner Brothers' brief history, selling 320,000 copies in eight days, or so the label claimed. Radio stations in Philadelphia, Cleveland, and Washington, DC, began playing it hourly. At the Newport Folk Festival, a month after the record's release, Dylan—inserted into the bill at Grossman's urging—led a group sing-along of "Blowin' in the Wind." Behind him, Pete Seeger, Joan Baez, the Freedom Singers, and Peter, Paul and Mary formed an all-star, all-approving chorus. Not everyone on that stage knew every word to every verse, but the way the title phrase was turned into a wistful chorus made it easy enough to join in. By the end of the year, thanks to that song, Peter, Paul and Mary had three albums in the Top 10 of *Cashbox*, another of the music business's leading trade papers.

Meanwhile, the New World Singers could only watch from afar as a song they'd first covered became a milestone for another group with a more aggressive manager and a more prominent record company behind it. "We didn't stand a shot," said Happy Traum. "Our version was on Folkways. Peter, Paul and Mary were on Warner Brothers. We didn't have that kind of clout. Their version was better and more commercial." Added Delores Dixon, who had left the band by then, "I was a little jealous of Peter, Paul and Mary. But I had to move on."

Without Dixon, the New World Singers were signed to Atlantic Records that year, and their one and only album for the label included a rendition of "Don't Think Twice, It's All Right"—but not "Blowin' in the Wind." During their audition for the label, Atlantic head Ahmet Ertegun, sitting in front of them in a chair, listened intently as they sang "Blowin' in the Wind." According to Traum, he said, "I like that song. But could you change the words and make it a love song?" Knowing Dylan as they did, the group didn't bother to ask him for a rewrite.

From his vantage point at the Folklore Center, Izzy Young had witnessed the way folk musicians were competitively jockeying for traditional songs. But one day in 1964, he beheld a very different sight. A few of them, including Tom Paxton and Len Chandler, were trading songs they'd written themselves, and the excitement among them was palpable.

Judy Collins also started noticing the shift. In her first two albums for Elektra, she'd largely relied on traditional songs, as did many of her peers; it wasn't uncommon to see a few of the same ballads, such as "Poor Lazarus" or "Mary Anne," on records by different artists. But now Collins was seeing her new home base—she moved to an apartment on Hudson Street in the spring of 1963—becoming a breeding ground for material that adhered to folk traditions but spoke a more personal language. "Tom Paxton would say, 'I've just written this song called "Bottle of Wine"—want to record it?'" she said, referring to a partly whimsical, partly desperate ode to that libation that may have spoken to her own developing drinking issue. "I didn't write anything, but I had a record contract, and if they could get on my record, that was good for them. It meant their song was going to get out there." By the time of *Judy Collins #3*, Collins was including two songs by Dylan, the doleful "Farewell" and "Masters of War."

Certainly, Dylan's overwhelming and unexpected new stature, now as a writer as much as a performer, had lit a fire under many Villagers. "When Bob started writing, everyone took notice because *nobody* was writing songs at that point," Sylvia Tyson said. "And he was so prolific. The reason a lot of us started writing songs is we thought, 'If this kid can write songs, we could too.'" The financial rewards were also a lure: as businessmen like Grossman knew all too well, the real money in the business lay with publishing—and royalties that could extend for years, if not decades.

But the times were also calling out for material that hadn't been written a hundred years before. Beyond the Village, incidents like Governor George Wallace's attempt to block the integration of the University of Alabama in 1963 kept the civil rights movement on the nightly news and on everyone's mind. Appearances by Dylan and Peter, Paul and Mary at the March on

Washington that summer made the connection between topical music and the Village even clearer. To lure Villagers to the march, a pickup truck parked on West Third Street blared a recording of Peter, Paul and Mary's "Blowin' in the Wind." Meanwhile, the country's increased involvement in Vietnam—the United States now had more than fifteen thousand troops there—was leading to skepticism about the government at large.

The combined turmoil and outrage came spilling out in songs that could be heard in Folk City, the Gaslight, and the Bitter End. Dylan's "The Death of Emmett Till" honored the young Black man killed in Mississippi in 1955 after he was accused of disrespecting a white woman. Paxton's "When Morning Breaks" was a courtly ballad about a soldier preparing for war; his sprightlier "What Did You Learn in School Today" was a sarcastic commentary on the type of simplistic world history taught in schools. "We wanted to write about the life we were observing," Paxton said, "and we would sing those songs because they got a reaction." Paxton's "Daily News" mocked the New York tabloid and its squaresville approach to covering their world because, he said, "everyone hated that paper."

Ian and Sylvia also joined the growing list of singers who wrote their own material. In about twenty minutes, Ian dashed off "Four Strong Winds," which had a horse-trot gait and a message of rootlessness and moving into the unknown that spoke to a generation that suddenly wasn't sure what lay ahead for itself or the country. Another song of departure, "Someday Soon," was narrated by a woman in love with a rodeo cowboy who provided an exit ramp from her family life. Written during a stay at the Hotel Earle, Sylvia's "You Were on My Mind" was, at heart, an ebullient pop song, even more so when it was remade and restructured a few years later by the We Five.

Although Elektra's Jac Holzman had been unsure about Paxton, he eventually relented and brought him into the company. Two weeks before he was set to make his first album for the label, Paxton learned a different way to play the G to C chord progression and wrote "The Last Thing on My Mind" in under a half hour. By then, Paxton had married his girlfriend, Margaret Anne (Midge) Cummings, and when he played the lovesick song at the Gaslight, friends approached and asked him, "Everything okay? The song is so sad." His response, invariably, was "It's just a song!" ("I wrote in the first person a lot," he recalled, "and it's almost never me.") Songs like Paxton's "Ramblin' Boy" and "I Can't Help but Wonder Where I'm Bound," which both spoke to the restlessness of his generation, had melodies as sturdily crafted as a well-made cabinet. They felt like they'd always been there, in the air and in coffeehouses.

That creative drive would soon be fueled by newer songwriters flocking to the Village and blending the personal with the political. Raised in Buffalo, New York, Eric Andersen had been a premed student when he caught the folk-music bug and started gigging with a group called the Cradlers, who once opened for Peter, Paul and Mary. At a coffeehouse in San Francisco, run by his future wife Debbie Green, he met Paxton, who tipped him to the Village and its beguiling opportunities, and Andersen landed in New York in February 1964. With his intimate baritone and the way he looked like a male model on a day off, Andersen made his debut at Folk City almost immediately after. At the Gaslight in late February, he played originals that adhered to folk traditions, such as "My Land Is a Good Land," which evoked the Guthrie standard, but he also included "Come to My Bedside," a strikingly erotic song that made some, like the *Times'* Shelton, take notice.

The previous June, Shelton had written a roundup of "New Folk Singers in 'Village,'" which included another fresh midwestern refugee, Phil Ochs. Like so many others lining up for the hoot night at Folk City, Ochs had come from elsewhere—in his case, Ohio, where he'd been a journalism major at Ohio State and a would-be folksinger and writer. A shy man who could rabble-rouse when needed, Ochs had been immersed in politics for several years—outraged by the McCarthy hearings, inspired by Kennedy's presidential victory—when he arrived in New York in 1962. He reconnected with a college friend, Jim Glover, who had also come to the city and had formed a duo, Jim and Jean, with Jean Ray, that regularly played at the Cafe Rafio on Bleecker Street.

Very quickly, Ochs inserted himself into the community, beginning with wanting to join Jim and Jean and make the group a trio. "I didn't want to do that," Glover said. "Phil was kind of bossy. But his talent was amazing." After he moved into Jim and Jean's small apartment and overwhelmed them with his energy, intensity, and slobby ways, they concocted a plan to get him out by introducing him to their friend Alice Skinner. Soon enough, she and Ochs were a couple, and he moved into her apartment at 178 Bleecker Street, at the corner of Thompson. There, Ochs's slovenly habits continued: his sister, Sonny, who was three years older and a schoolteacher in Queens, observed what she called one of her brother's "favorite games"—sitting in the kitchen at night, the lights out, seeing how many cockroaches he could kill in a minute.

Anyone visiting that apartment—a list that would include most of the notables on the scene—could see that Ochs, who had a passion for songs triggered by current events, was plugged into current events. "He watched the news religiously," said Andersen, who met Ochs soon after he moved to Manhattan and spent time in that apartment. "Nobody could talk when the news came on."

On the surface, Ochs didn't look like any sort of radical: he kept his hair short and sang in a clear, vibrato-free tenor that recalled country singers like Faron Young. But his intensity spilled over into the songs he began writing and introducing at Folk City and at the Third Side, a coffeehouse on West Third Street whose owner guaranteed him twenty dollars for any set. By mid-1963, Ochs had already written over fifty tunes, including ripped-from-the-headlines zingers about the Cuban Missile Crisis, Black activist and journalist (and FBI target) William Worthy, and the Birmingham, Alabama, protest that resulted in police employing dogs and fire hoses to beat back the crowd of Black protesters. Bobbing and weaving while singing, strands of hair falling in his face, Ochs had a nervous, infectious energy; he was a musical crusade and parade that swept people along with it.

On the day of his audition for the Gaslight, Ochs developed a crushing headache and, to the surprise of Sam Hood, said he had to undergo a spinal tap. Although he was barely able to sing, he still showed up for his audition and became a regular at the club. "He developed an audience so quickly," Hood told Van Ronk. "Probably quicker than anyone else I had." *Broadside* would soon declare that he was "virtually alone in his field" in the matter of topical material—while also wondering, in light of the increased attention on him, "Can he maintain a sincerity of principle despite material prosperity? . . . For

Phil Ochs, on whom the future of topical music now rides, 'these are the days of decision,'" quoting one of his song titles. At that moment, those days had arrived for Ochs and his friends in the area.

Happy Traum was back in the Gaslight, attending an open-mic night, when what he called "this large guy with a Guild guitar and no teeth" walked through the crowd. "I thought, 'Who is this guy?'" he said. "It was unusual to see a Black guy among all those folkies."

Over six feet tall, Richie Havens made an impression on multiple fronts. Missing his top row of teeth before later implants, he used his left thumb to barre chords on his guitar and sang in a gravel-road voice that lay somewhere between folk, soul, and the gospel group he joined when he was in high school. At seventeen, he'd left home—dismantling his family's dream of him becoming a surgeon—to move to the Village, where he made a decent living painting portraits of the tourists who came to gawk at beatniks. He began working the basket-house circuit, strumming his guitar with a fervor that threatened to bust all its strings and made anyone who followed him sound flimsy by comparison. "There was no touching this, that rhythm thing," said Sebastian. "The pail would be passed around and the audience would empty its pockets. By the time you got on, there was nothing left."

People of color and of alternative lifestyles continued to make their way to the Village. The Moroccan Village, a club on Eighth Street, was home to singers and female impersonators. At the corner of MacDougal and Eighth, the Bon Soir was as much its own world as the Page Three, which had been a shelter for Sheila Jordan and Tiny Tim. The club had once been home base for Mae Barnes, a Black singer and dancer whose 1953 recording "(I Ain't Gonna Be No) Topsy" became an early Black-pride moment. The Bon Soir's emcee, Jimmie Daniels, was a gay Black man. (The spot was also known as the launching pad for a young Brooklyn singer named Barbra Streisand, who played engagements there until the fall of 1962.) Each night it was open, the Bon Soir would undergo a makeover after the largely white dinner crowd left and a primarily Black clientele took over for the second show.

At the same time, Black music fans and musicians alike were sometimes made to feel like outsiders. In 1961 Art D'Lugoff claimed he heard police make a "racially insensitive comment" about the Blacks in the audience at the Village Gate one night, which led to the Police Department launching an inquiry into the accusations. Black musicians, particularly on the folk circuit, were still considered so uncommon that one night during her New World Singers days, Delores Dixon and a friend were ordered to step into a patrol car as they walked along MacDougal Street. The women weren't told what they'd done wrong, but Dixon heard one of the cops say, "We'll take you someplace and then let you go." Dixon began crying so much that the cops told her friend, "Would you shut her up?" Ultimately, they grew so tired of Dixon's weeping that both women were asked to step out of the car. Only later did Dixon realize that the cops assumed she and her friend were prostitutes. "I used to think the police were my friends," she said. "But then I realized that they're *men*."

Havens was far from the only Black vernacular singer trying to carve out a living and a career on the scene. Odetta, who had joined Van Ronk for the opening of the Cafe Bizarre, continued to loom over the community, conveying enormous dignity and steadfastness. After seeing her perform before he moved to New York, Dylan ditched the electric guitar he'd had in Minnesota and traded it in for an acoustic model, altering the course of his music in the process. Odetta would regularly appear as a headliner on the scene, as when she played the Village Gate for several weeks in the summer of 1963.

The scene was also supported, in a sense literally, by at least two Black musicians. Bruce Langhorne, a guitarist who hailed from Florida but had come north after his parents divorced, played on Carolyn Hester's Columbia debut; Peter, Paul and Mary's first album; *The Freewheelin' Bob Dylan*; and Odetta records. On some of those occasions, he was joined by Bill Lee, the southern-born jazz upright bassist who was becoming the go-to bottom end for folk-music sessions. Tom Wilson, the sharp-dressed, laid-back Columbia staff producer who oversaw albums by Dylan, Hester, Pete Seeger, and others—and recruited Langhorne for some of that work—was himself Black, a rarity in the music business of that era. "There were no racial components at the time," Langhorne said. "At least, none that affected us." When he wasn't appearing on Broadway or film, in works like Lorraine Hansberry's *A Raisin in the Sun*, Louis Gossett Jr. sang in a folk duo.

Watching the community expand from his space inside the Folklore Center, Izzy Young felt those advances weren't enough. "There is a real wall of segregation in the folk music scene I'm part of," he said to Richard Reuss. "We'll listen to the old Negro singers, and a bit of the young Negro singers trying to sound right for the white audience, but nothing is being done about the young Negro kids that are speaking to real audiences, mostly Negro."

Few experienced the struggles as up close as Len Chandler, the Village's most prominent Black folksinger. Originally from Akron, Ohio, Chandler was no mere strummer. In high school, he played oboe and English horn (the oboe's alto sibling) and was introduced to folk by one of his teachers. After graduating from the University of Akron in 1957, Chandler won a scholarship to Columbia to study advanced orchestral instrumentation and moved to Manhattan. A professor took him on a Village walking tour, which included a stop at the relatively new Folklore Center, where he met Van Ronk. On the side, Chandler began working with troubled teens at a facility near Washington Square Park and began singing there himself. He even talked Van Ronk into playing for the kids, experiencing Van Ronk's taskmaster side along the way. "He was very critical of the way you would approach a song or the guitar," Chandler told author Elijah Wald. "He would come and look at me carefully. If you played a certain way with your thumb, he hated that."

In the park, Chandler also met Romney and was invited to join him for a show in Hartford, Connecticut, where a musician was needed to sing between poetry readings. That job, in turn, led to Chandler making his debut at the Gaslight on bills with Romney and John Brent (which included Chandler's impromptu song during the Fire Department bust in 1961). Taking Chandler under his wing, Romney suggested he ditch his slacks and sports jacket for black jeans and a work shirt with a turtleneck dickey underneath; the look became Chandler's uniform. "I don't try to make anybody believe I'm a sharecropper," he told the *Daily News*. "I came up through different musical schools. I try to clothe my thoughts in poetry." After he was offered a job on a television show in Detroit, Chandler left New York for four months. Upon his return, he noticed half the folksingers he encountered in the Village wearing the outfit he'd adopted.

Chandler quickly grew in stature on the scene. He was the first musician Paxton saw play in the Village, likely at the Gaslight, and it was Chandler who invited Paxton to join him for a guest set there. The week after the "beatnik riot" in the park, a pictorial in the *New York Post* included a shot of Chandler looking on approvingly as the Sunday sessions resumed. Gaslight manager Sam Hood would later say that Chandler was the first Black man he'd ever met, but that gave him no pause in booking him and paying him $175 a week—$25 more than most, and $50 more than Paxton.

Chandler sported a goatee and a hearty, husky voice born to lead sing-alongs on protest songs like "Which Side Are You On" and Pete Seeger's "Where Have All the Flowers Gone"; his was the first version of the latter song that some in town, including Paxton, ever heard. "The heart of the Gaslight was Len," said Noel Stookey. "If you were upset and left the stage visibly shaken, he'd come over and ask if you were okay. He was the most outwardly caring person in the Village." On Cynthia Gooding's *Folksingers Choice* radio show on WBAI, Dylan would say he "stole the melody" for "The Death of Emmett Till" from a song Chandler had written about a tragic collision between a train and a school bus in Colorado that left nearly two dozen children dead.

But as open-minded and tolerant as the Village could be, especially when it came to alternative lifestyles and musicians of different races interacting, Chandler's journey was never easy. Bitter End manager Paul Colby would recall the moment Chandler ran into his club after being chased by a group of white kids with baseball bats. Chandler had seen them hitting another Black man and tried to intervene, only to be hunted himself. Another evening on MacDougal Street, Chandler—who, Dylan would later write, had the physique of a football player—attempted to hail a cab, which started to speed up rather than slow down for him. As Hood watched (and told Van Ronk), Chandler reached into the front seat through an open window and began smacking the driver, running alongside as the car continued down the block. "He was crazy brave," Paxton recalled. "He wouldn't back down, ever."

Visiting a friend in a West Village apartment building in the summer of 1963, Chandler accidentally knocked on the wrong door, and the startled resident— whom Chandler would later describe as Jamaican, although Hood heard he was Hispanic—mistook him for a burglar and hit him on the head with a pipe. As Chandler tumbled down a set of marble stairs during the brawl, nerves in two of his fingers were severed. Since he was scheduled to perform at the March on Washington several weeks later, he prematurely removed the cast from his fingers. Dylan, who also became friendly with Chandler, visited him at Bellevue Hospital. Fortunately, he healed well enough that he was able to play on the steps of the Lincoln Memorial that day. With Dylan and Joan Baez behind him, he barreled through "Keep Your Eyes on the Prize," a decades-old traditional song that had taken on new relevance in the civil rights era.

Chandler even added to the growing Village songbook. With poet Bob Kaufman, he rearranged and rewrote "Green, Green Rocky Road," a traditional children's song, into something imbued with adult yearning. Before long, everyone seemed to be taking a crack at it during paid gigs or open-mic nights. Yet the industry didn't seem to know what to make of Chandler. He was the first musician booked into the Bitter End, months before Peter, Paul and Mary made their career-making appearances there. But at that point, he could be heard on only one album—*The Beat Generation*, a 1960 compilation recorded at the Gaslight, where he shared LP space with Romney and Brent. Still, two songs on an album were better than none.

As the mid-sixties came into view, friction remained between the businesses and residents who predated the music scene and the increasingly boisterous new cafés. The Mob still loomed over the area, although its presence could be almost comical at times. At the bottom of the steps leading into the Gaslight sat a cigarette machine. David Bromberg, a nimble guitarist from Tarrytown, New York, who had started venturing into the neighborhood, noticed that it never seemed to be operational and asked Clarence Hood about it. Without specifying why, Hood told him he had to have it there—but he rebelled by not plugging it in. The basket houses weren't exempt, either. With guitarist

Steve Weber, who shared his taste for the offbeat and arcane, Peter Stampfel formed the Holy Modal Rounders, who began remaking old-timey songs
with rewritten, skewed lyrics. While playing at one of the basket houses in
the neighborhood, the two were approached by what Stampfel recalled as
"the lowest-level Mafia people"—who tried shaking down the musicians for
the dollar they'd just earned.

Starting in March 1962, the License Department had been put in charge
of approving paperwork for those businesses. But thanks to miscommunica-
tion between that office and the Buildings Department over exactly which one
would sign off on licenses, only a handful of clubs, including the Cafe Bizarre,
the Bitter End, and the Cafe Wha?, were granted licenses to operate. Nearly
three dozen others, including the Gaslight, were still awaiting approval. The
basket houses, such as the Four Winds, the Zig Zag, and the Why Not, were
keenly aware that they were allowed to feature only three instruments and no
singers. The staff at the Four Winds worked out a system whereby the "drags"—
workers who stood outside trying to lure people in—would signal those inside
the club if they saw a cop walking in the café's direction; whoever was onstage
would immediately stop singing. Susan Martin Robbins, a performer who also
comanaged the space for a time, recalled how her guitar skills improved expo-
nentially because she couldn't sing during those moments.

But little about those regulations mollified the residents and shopkeepers
who saw sightseeing buses barreling down their narrow streets, their drivers
calling out the names of cafés as they passed. At least once, the tension turned
horrifically violent. On the last day of March 1963, Ronald Von Ehmsen, the
thirty-one-year-old owner of Cafe Rafio, where Jean and Jim had landed a residency, was walking his Doberman a few doors down from the café when he was
approached by seventy-three-year-old Simone Pepe. Pepe was not happy: Ehmsen was planning to expand the Rafio, which meant that Pepe would soon face
eviction. The two began arguing, and Pepe pumped three bullets from his .32
caliber revolver into the man locals called "Von." The café owner managed to
drag himself into a nearby liquor store, where he died; Pepe himself died a few
months later. The situation was also playing out politically. For the job of Democratic Party leader of the district that included the Village, Carmine DeSapio,

the longtime Tammany Hall figure, was running for reelection against Ed Koch, who was taking a much firmer stance against the commotion, including coffeehouse employees who stood outside and loudly attempted to entice customers. Koch handily won, ending DeSapio's power in the community.

The federal government now joined the list of Village overseers. On February 6, 1963, Martin Crowe, a special agent with the FBI, appeared at 190 Waverly Place, a five-story apartment building with fire escapes lining its front windows. As the Bureau knew, the address had been home to Van Ronk and Thal since the previous December. Their friend Barry Kornfeld had moved in first, in an apartment on the third floor, for all of $91 per month in rent, and the Van Ronks took a place catty-corner to his on the same floor. Van Ronk, Thal, and Kornfeld would soon by joined in the building by Patrick Sky, who'd grown up in Louisiana and become part of the Florida coffeehouse scene before moving to New York. There, his combination of tender ballads (like "Many a Mile") and sarcastic wit set him apart both onstage and off. *Times* critic Robert Shelton lived across the street, at 191 Waverly.

With the help of the building superintendent, Crowe verified that Van Ronk lived in apartment 3F. Then Crowe made his way to Folk City. There, he was told Van Ronk was, in the words of a later report, "not currently appearing nor scheduled to appear in the near future," although the club confirmed that Van Ronk had performed at Folk City in the past. Inspecting the Queens telephone books, Crowe determined that Van Ronk's mother, Grace, still lived in Richmond Hill; then he reached out to the New York branch of the Selective Service for Van Ronk's files. With the help of an employee of the New York Telephone Company, Crowe was also able to obtain Van Ronk's number, which was registered under Thal's name. A memo dated February 14, 1963— ironically, Valentine's Day—listed all the details of his wedding to Thal, down to the name of the city official who conducted the ceremony and the presence of a "Thomas R. Paxton" as Van Ronk's best man.

Two weeks later, Crowe rounded up all that background information on Van Ronk—whom he described as "a folksinger and guitar player" largely associated with the Gaslight—into a comprehensive report that detailed, with startling clarity, how much the Bureau was continuing to keep tabs on the musician. The write-up touched upon his connection to the New York branch of the Socialist Party, beginning in November 1962; how he had attended five meetings between then and a month before Crowe's visit; and his connection to the Socialist Youth League back to the late fifties. Crowe noted that Van Ronk had entertained at "various" Socialist Worker Party functions throughout 1962 and had given "a lecture on African music and jazz" at the Militant Labor Forum on University Place in November 1962. It was also pointed out that Van Ronk participated in an antigovernment protest outside the Waldorf-Astoria, where, during a banquet dinner, Attorney General Robert F. Kennedy was given an award by the American Jewish Congress.

One of several follow-up reports included a copy of an ad for Folk City, where Van Ronk—called "The Lion of the Blues" in the flyer—would be playing in late April. On May 22, Crowe stopped by the Gaslight, where he spoke with an "unknown individual" who confirmed that Van Ronk regularly played the venue. At that point, Crowe suggested the case be closed "inasmuch as there is no outstanding investigation in this case." FBI head J. Edgar Hoover was of another mind and pressed the Bureau to continue looking into Van Ronk. That July 1963, in a memo called "David Ritz Van Ronk—Security Matter—Socialist Worker Party," Hoover made it clear that the coast guard should be contacted in order to glean more backup on Van Ronk's time in the merchant marine.

The FBI also began monitoring Phil Ochs. In what would amount to a file more than four hundred pages long, the Bureau made note of his 1963 essays on Woody Guthrie, reported on his appearances at a 1964 rally, described his songs as "un-American," and, according to Ochs biographer Marc Eliot, "looked into his business associations, his membership in the American Federation of Musicians Local 802, his neighbors on Thompson Street, his credit rating, his driver's license and Motor Vehicle records, and his voter registration history." (Various attempts had been made to draft Ochs into the army.)

Even Dylan wasn't exempt. Suze Rotolo already had an FBI file that took note of her application for a passport in 1961 (for a European trip) and its renewal in 1964. During a trip to Prague, it was noted that she was associating with "Communists and Communist front groups," and she was tracked when she visited Cuba in the summer of 1964. When agents approached her at her new Avenue B apartment, she told them, "I have nothing to say to you. Bye bye." By then, she had broken up with Dylan, but her former lover wasn't ignored. Another report noted she had dated "Bob Dylan, the folksinger," and his performance at the December 1963 Bill of Rights dinner in New York, where he was handed the Tom Paine Award for his work for "civil liberties," was cited. That same report noted that in his acceptance speech, which was delivered a month after John F. Kennedy's assassination, Dylan said he "agreed in part with Lee Harvey Oswald and thought that he understood Oswald, but would not have gone as far as Oswald did."

Not everyone took the government surveillance seriously. "It was a given that under Hoover's FBI, you were going to be under the camera, or at least there was a likelihood," said Kornfeld. "It was sort of romantic." Dylan appeared to be aware of the situation, although it was hard to gauge how much it affected him. Years later, Shelton told Dylan about an unusual sight at Folk City soon after Shelton's first review of Dylan had appeared in the *Times*: a man in his forties or fifties, far from the usual age bracket for the club, was smiling at everyone. Shelton joked to Dylan that people thought he might be an FBI man, and Dylan replied that he remembered him and that the person in question was a cop. When Shelton asked if the stranger had been looking out for Dylan in particular, Dylan replied that cops had been on his tail for some time, but not so much during the previous year.

During this time, the Treasury Department wrote to the Bureau of Special Services at New York's Police Department, alerting them to an investigation underway to determine "the suitability of the above-named individual": Dylan. The Police Department was asked if it had any files that "contain any record of traffic or criminal violations or of subversive activities." The address the Treasury official was given for Dylan was Grossman's office on West Fifty-Fifth Street. The agency was thoughtful enough to include a "self-addressed envelope which requires no postage." No letter of response would surface in the city's archives.

In the summer of 1963, Van Ronk and Kalb found themselves sharing a stage, but in an unconventional setting and with an unusual lineup. In a twist that was even more unexpected than folk or folk-style songs wending their way onto the pop charts, jug bands were suddenly trending. Made with kazoos, washboards, and stringed instruments, jug was a type of roots novelty music that didn't take itself too seriously even if genuine musicianship was involved. In the Boston and Cambridge area, the Jim Kweskin Jug Band ruled the scene. Washington Square Park gave birth to the Even Dozen Jug Band, cofounded by two guitarists, Stefan Grossman and Peter Siegel, and eventually including other local talents such as John Sebastian and Van Ronk student Steve Katz, along with Maria D'Amato (later Muldaur), a sassy-voiced Italian American who'd also grown up in the neighborhood. After Izzy Young stepped in to manage them, the group made an album for Elektra while they were all still in their late teens. The mania for the music was akin to a shooting star; the Even Dozen Jug Band went straight from playing in the park to multi-act shows at Town Hall and Carnegie Hall.

Village Vanguard owner Max Gordon had witnessed the drawing power of the Kweskin band during a visit to Cambridge. As Van Ronk would recall, Gordon asked Shelton if there were any jug bands in New York, especially since the Even Dozen had quickly disbanded, and Shelton directed him to Van Ronk as a starting point. Game for anything, Van Ronk pulled together a group that included Kalb, Kornfeld, mandolinist Artie Rose, and his friend, multi-instrumentalist and historian Sam Charters. Gordon booked them for a week at the Vanguard in August 1963.

By then, Dylan and Joan Baez were in the heat of their romance. Baez, who was still based out of Cambridge, had been hearing about the Village and dropped by the Cafe Wha? on a night when Romney was reciting poetry. At someone's instigation, she began singing along with him during his reading. She and Dylan likely first met at Folk City in the spring of 1961, shortly after the "beatnik riot" when Dylan was appearing there. "It was what everyone was talking about, so I went in that spirit of, 'Okay, what's going on here?'" Baez recalled. "He was such a scruffy, funny-sounding kid, but then I heard the words. Eventually I got to like that voice, but these *words* were coming out.

I was with my boyfriend at that point, who was gritting his teeth because he could see I was fascinated with Bob and the music. I guess he could see the writing on the wall." Meeting in front of the club afterward, Dylan played a song for Baez and her younger sister Mimi. "I was so pigheaded that I didn't realize he had a crush on Mimi," she said. "I didn't realize until someone told me years later. I was so self-obsessed that it didn't dawn on me that someone would be interested in anyone other than me."

By 1963, though, the two were inseparable, a fact that Van Ronk and his new group couldn't help but notice at their Village Vanguard debut. "Goddamn, Bob and Joan showed up and were sort of going through their moment of a real passion," Charters said. "They were sort of fumbling with each other underneath the table, so all the people who came were really paying all the attention to Joan and Bobby, and not much attention to us up on the stage."

That year, the industry also turned its head, for the first time, to Van Ronk. After making three albums for Prestige—including *In the Tradition*, which found him returning to one of his favorite genres with the Red Onion Jazz Band—Van Ronk had signed with his largest company to date, Mercury. His jug-band excursion would be his first LP for the company. Released in time for its Vanguard gigs, *Dave Van Ronk and the Ragtime Jug Stompers* found the group romping through versions of songs by Fats Waller, Sonny Terry, and Jesse Fuller; Van Ronk's voice sometimes sounded like a kazoo itself.

As another relatively recent arrival to the city was learning, the Vanguard was hosting even more forward-looking music. In 1961 a bus from Chicago brought twenty-one-year-old pianist Herbie Hancock to Manhattan. In his home city, Hancock had been a child prodigy, joining the Chicago Symphony for a Mozart performance when he was a mere eleven. After attending college in Iowa, he played with Coleman Hawkins and, back in Chicago, Donald Byrd. Invited to New York to join Byrd's band, Hancock soon found himself playing with Byrd at the Five Spot, and he was enrolled in the Manhattan School of Music.

Then Hancock met an even more audacious boss, and in a new downtown setting. In the few years following 1959's *Kind of Blue*, Miles Davis had been outpaced by younger players and appeared to be in a creative depression.

Starting in 1963, though, he assembled a fluid new band featuring bassist Ron Carter, saxophonist George Coleman (soon to be replaced by Wayne Shorter), teenage drummer Tony Williams, and Hancock. With them, Davis's so-called "second great quintet" began undoing and reassembling standards and blues. In February 1964, the group was booked into the prestigious Philharmonic Hall in Lincoln Center to support a benefit for voter registration in Mississippi and Louisiana, but Davis also needed a smaller room to work out his revised approach.

Jazz continued to thrive, sometimes just south or east of the Village. The Five Spot had moved farther east, to St. Mark's Place, after the original space was demolished to make way for an apartment building. In the spring, Nina Simone held court, as she frequently did, at the Village Gate. D'Lugoff had booked her into his venue during its first year, after the former Eunice Kathleen Waymon recorded her first album and her version of George and Ira Gershwin's "I Loves You, Porgy" became the least likely song anyone would have expected to crack the Top 20. Although she would soon be bankable enough to headline Carnegie Hall and Town Hall, Simone returned to the Gate regularly, calling it her "home club."

A 1961 show was recorded for a live album, *At the Village Gate*, and the songs on it—light on the standards that made Simone's name, heavy on vernacular numbers, like a rumbling "The House of the Rising Sun" and a brooding version of the gospel standard "Children Go Where I Send You"—seemed to absorb the genres then associated with the neighborhood. Her Gate shows were equally notable for their attendant drama. Between songs one night, she looked up from her piano and glared at the crowd after what she considered an insufficiently positive response. "You're not giving one thing tonight," she told them. Among those in the crowd was budding actor James Cromwell, who worked as a maintenance man at the club and was able to get into shows for free.

Meanwhile, at the Vanguard, Hancock and the audience were able to witness Davis's genius up close. Onstage, Davis had a reputation for turning his back to the people in the seats or pointing his trumpet toward the floor or wall. Seeing it for himself at the Vanguard, Hancock noticed that there was an element of shtick to it and that some in the audience, possibly tourists, came to see the notoriously mercurial Davis ignore them. "People would feel insulted by that, and they would come down here to see him do it," Hancock said. "Part of him was thinking, 'Well, this is actually working for me, so I might as well actually do that!'"

But Hancock also observed that Davis wasn't belittling the audience as much as he was facing the band; he seemed less like a moody bandleader and more like a conductor. If Davis heard something Carter was doing, he might pivot to the bass player and launch into a musical counterpoint; the same would be true with Williams, Hancock, or Coleman. When Davis would point his instrument toward the ceiling or down at the floor, Hancock also realized he was essentially playing the Vanguard. "He was exploring how it sounded coming off of the wood of the floor or how it sounded coming off of the angles of the walls," he said. "I never saw him do that as a disrespect for the audience. And people just never understood."

Although Van Ronk's own stint at the Vanguard was brief, he was proud of *Dave Van Ronk and the Ragtime Jug Stompers*; Kalb called his jazz-derived solo on "You's a Viper" the best he'd ever recorded. But the jug-band craze came and went quickly, as pop-culture fads tended to do, and Kalb also felt that current events interfered as well. At the end of "You's a Viper"—"viper" being uptown slang for a toker—he and Van Ronk had fun with jive-talk riffing: "We could switch to junk," one of them said, while the other wise-cracked about how "junk" was spelled "JFK." When Kennedy was assassinated in November 1963, just as the record was being released, the timing couldn't have been worse, and Van Ronk's first attempt to cash in on a pop moment was ignored.

█ █ █ █

A week before Kennedy's assassination, an Associated Press reporter, in search of the folk-music escalation in New York, ventured into Washington Square Park. There, during the Sunday-afternoon hootenannies, he watched a "pale girl uniformed in jeans, bulky sweater and long blonde hair." Her song of choice was a plaintive version of "Blowin' in the Wind," which, after only a few months on the radio, had joined the repertoire for songs any upcoming folk-singer needed to learn.

The appearance of Dylan material in a gathering that tended to favor tra-ditional songs was just one of many indications that the scene was evolving in ways no one could have predicted. The Greenwich Village Inn, one of the earliest bars in the area, was now an apartment complex. The downtown Cafe Society had become home to off-Broadway plays, not music. After selling the Gaslight, John Mitchell was now running the Fat Black Pussycat, the new name for the Commons. There, Tiny Tim established himself as less of a freak and more of a music-geek novelty act that everyone needed to experience. But trouble seemed to follow Mitchell: asked to leave town by the Mob, which threatened to bomb or smoke out the club, he was soon gone. Mitchell was reportedly in Tangiers, Morocco, before resurfacing in Spain, where he opened a new Fat Black Pussycat.

As the *Daily News* announced that fall, though, "The folk music craze is sweeping New York," even citing an exact number of folksingers—100—who worked downtown. *Greenwich Village Story*, a potboiler movie that showed up in theaters in 1963, included contrived footage of beatniks dancing; it also re-created the inside of the Gaslight, with Noel Stookey making a brief appear-ance alongside a "Gaslight Cafe" sign constructed expressly for the film. Musi-cians from other parts of the country were curious as well. Johnny Cash, deep into his addiction to pills, popped into the actual Gaslight to catch a set by Peter LaFarge. Cash was so stoned and discombobulated that he walked right into the bare light bulb hanging from the ceiling of the combined kitchen and dressing room, smashing it, and the room went dark.

The days when it was possible to saunter into the Gaslight, the Bitter End, or Folk City to see Dylan, Peter, Paul and Mary, or Judy Collins were now over. They were all now being booked into larger uptown venues, such as Town Hall; Peter, Paul and Mary were commanding four thousand dollars per show. But enough musicians, singers, and writers remained downtown. In a *Village Voice* ad, Bitter End owner Fred Weintraub sarcastically apologized for the club's prices—"75 cents for espresso, 75 cents for a stein of dopey cider"—by saying he compensated by booking talents like the Weavers' Ronnie Gilbert and a new comic, Dick Cavett. "If you want coffee go to Riker's," he wrote, adding, "if you want coffee and swinging entertainment," the Bitter End was the destination, as was the Village itself. In the course of a few weeks in September and October 1963, it would have been possible to see Odetta or Cuban bandleader and percussionist Mongo Santamaria at the Village Gate, Bill Evans at the Vanguard, or Fred Neil and his singing and strumming partner, Vince Martin, at the Gaslight.

Opening for Clarence "Tom" Ashley and the Irish Ramblers at Folk City on October 22, 1963, was a new duo that called itself Kane and Garr. They weren't actually all that fresh, nor were those their real names. In their hometown of Forest Hills, Queens, they'd been known as Paul Simon and Art Garfunkel, then as Tom and Jerry, whose "Hey, Schoolgirl" made them one-generic-hit wonders in the late fifties. After the duo split and each had gone off to college and travel adventures, folk pulled them back toward each other. Simon had tapped into the folk scene at Queens College and then in England—writing songs that weren't remotely political but had the guitar style and melodic range down—and before long the two were playing open-mic nights at the Gaslight. One of those songs, "Bleecker Street," had a melancholy, gently floating melody that evoked the early-morning hours in the Village, after the clubs had closed and customers began making their way home on streets not nearly as crowded as the night before. When Simon (who would sometimes use the stage name Paul Kane) sang a new song, "The Sound of Silence" for Columbia Records producer Tom Wilson, the duo had a record deal. The label urged them to change their name—the Rye Catchers was one suggestion, since the J. D. Salinger novel it played off was now a generational touchstone—but they stuck with their given last names.

Barry Kornfeld, who had seen Simon around the Queens College campus they'd both attended, got to know him better when Simon remade himself, in the Village tradition, as a thoughtful balladeer with pop smarts. The two started spending time together playing songs, and at the Gaslight, Simon asked Kornfeld to accompany him and Garfunkel on their first album, *Wednesday Morning, 3 A.M.* In the Village, though, Simon and Garfunkel never quite fit in. Starting with Simon's short hair, they looked a little too well-groomed for the scene, and Simon was said to have been irritated when Dylan talked throughout one of their sets, likely at Folk City; Kornfeld said Dylan would dismiss Simon as "a friend of Kornfeld's."

The alternately convivial, carousing, and driven community that did fit in often gathered at the Kettle of Fish. Sitting above the Gaslight on street level, the Kettle—dubbed a "bohemian mecca" by the *Daily News* in 1958, eight years after it opened—now made for a convenient hangout and watering hole for musicians, before or after gigs. It still pulled in working-class regulars and locals who wanted cheap beer in a sawdust-floor setting. But neither the bar nor its owner, Guido Giampieri, were "mobbed up," as Van Ronk and others said, and the curtained windows offered a degree of privacy for the musicians gathered at the round front tables.

Van Ronk could still be found there, holding court and intimidating more than a few—like John Hammond, the son of the Columbia Records legend. The younger Hammond had grown up in the Village and was now playing his own form of blues. "Dave was kind of a gruff, opinionated guy, and to hang out with him was to get an earful of opinions about everything," Hammond recalled. "He was a little intimidating to me. I kept my distance. I was not one of his guys." Dylan, back in Van Ronk's good graces after their falling-out over "House of the Rising Sun," could be found there together, although they remained sparring partners. "Bob and Dave had big, long arguments over a giant bottle of burgundy wine, about everything and nothin'," said Ramblin' Jack Elliott. "They just liked to argue. Bob used to put a mark on how much they'd drink out of that gallon jug of wine." (To Anthony Scaduto, Van Ronk would refer to those evenings as "our wine-drinking nights of arguing.") When she was still living in her Village apartment, Judy Collins would watch as some of her fellow musicians straggled into the Kettle in the morning to sober up and start their day. Collins herself was not averse to letting it rip: after friends gave her a first-ever hit of acid, she drank an entire bottle of Jim Beam to come down from it.

Watching some nights from the bar on the left side was Woody Guthrie's teenage son, Arlo. Eager to see what a day in the Village was like, Guthrie had once parked himself in front of the Gaslight for twenty-four hours.

In the morning, he saw women opening their windows and shaking out the rugs, followed by the garbagemen. "Everybody had their five or ten minutes," he recalled. During the afternoon, the street remained quiet, very few people walking by him, but by six or seven at night, things grew crowded. At the Gaslight, Giampieri and his crew allowed Guthrie to sit at the bar and nurse a Scotch and soda, thanks to his lineage. He would see the gang—Dylan, Van Ronk, Ochs—"goofin' off and having fun." But the five- to seven-year age difference between him and them made them seem like the "serious guardians" of the form, and at that point he was never encouraged to join their table.

To some, like Buffy Sainte-Marie, the scene remained oppressively male. While studying Asian philosophy at the University of Massachusetts Amherst, Sainte-Marie found in the folk revival a style of music ideal for her impressive tremolo, the way her voice could fluctuate in volume. Sainte-Marie, who said she had Cree Nation ancestry, wrote songs like "Now That the Buffalo's Gone" and sang them in a coffeehouse near the campus. Visiting New York, she learned more about the blossoming downtown music world and went to one of the Monday open-mic nights at Folk City. There she met Dylan, who suggested she drop by the Gaslight, where Sam Hood booked her in August 1963. That performance led to a rapturous *Times* review by Shelton that called her "one of the most promising new talents on the folk scene" and cited two songs in particular, the historically minded "The Universal Soldier" and the harrowing "Cod'ine."

As a woman on the scene, Sainte-Marie was happy to land work in coffeehouses rather than bars, with their potentially boisterous male drunks. "A pretty woman standing on a stage with a guitar—are you kidding me?" she said. "I wasn't going to sing in a damn bar." The coffeehouses were more welcoming, yet the combination of her ethnicity and gender still made her feel, in her words, like "a guest," and she rarely wandered into the Kettle of Fish, where Van Ronk would often be found with Patrick Sky, the troubadour who'd moved to New York after meeting Sainte-Marie in Florida (the two became lovers, and he followed her north).

But to Sainte-Marie, the community was "controlled, misogynistic and really white," which became apparent when she premiered an uncompromising

song, "My Country Tis of Thy People You're Dying," at the Gaslight. It chronicled the way indigenous people in North America had suffered or been humil-
iated or marginalized. "The reaction was, 'Oh, the little Indian girl must be
mistaken—we wouldn't do nasty things like that,'" she recalled. "There was
a sense of being patronized. People were so unfamiliar with the American
genocide that they just couldn't believe it. Most people did not know anything
about indigenous anything." She found it hard to reconcile images of some of
the performers on the scene "having their pictures taken at a well-publicized
rally" and the reaction to some of her material. "I had something totally different on my mind than 'hang down your head, Tom Dooley,'" she said, "and I
didn't believe the answer was blowing in the wind, either."

Given the amount of alcohol and the late-night hours in bars, it was hardly
surprising when that same crowd turned libidinous. Paxton and Sylvia Fricker
went on a few dates, which, according to Paxton, precipitated her marrying Ian
Tyson in the summer of 1964. Collins had an intense fling with David Blue,
a would-be actor from Rhode Island who'd shown up in the Village in 1960,
when he was still David Cohen. Tall and roguishly handsome, Blue had started
washing dishes at the Gaslight, worked his way into the songwriting gang there,
and eventually began composing. At some point, Blue—who changed his last
name at the suggestion of Andersen, who thought the word "blue" defined
him—met and befriended Dylan, whose sense of humor matched Blue's. As
legend had it, it was at the Fat Black Pussycat that Dylan asked Blue to strum
chords as he wrote out lyrics for what became "Blowin' in the Wind." Collins
would describe Blue as "deliciously cute" while also remembering the cowboy
boots he didn't always remove when they found themselves in his single bed.
Hood would later tell Van Ronk that he caught the two of them going at it in
the kitchen of the Gaslight.

The atmosphere could also turn rivalrous. Paxton felt jealous when Eric
Andersen, who had come to New York on Paxton's advice, quickly scored a record deal with Vanguard. Andersen also benefited from a gleaming *New York
Times* review by Shelton—who, Andersen claimed, arranged for that Folk City
show and offered to manage him. "I'm saying, 'Wait a minute—no one's written about *me* in the *Times*!'" Paxton said. "What's wrong with this picture? It

was so competitive in that respect. You were happy for your friends' success but wanted some yourself." Dick Weissman of the Journeymen, who also made a living as a studio musician, felt a degree of contempt from the New Lost City Ramblers' purity-minded John Cohen when the two would encounter each other in the Folklore Center. "I didn't care for him, and I had no desire to defend myself against charges of commerciality," Weissman said. "That was an argument I had with myself that I had settled, and I wasn't into re-creating it. And I didn't think it was anybody's business."

That said, the community could be supportive, too, musicians going out of their way to support their friends. "If you were playing a gig at the Gaslight you'd have your break and you'd go running over to the Bitter End or Gerde's and see who was on," said Happy Traum. "And they always let you in because they knew you, so you never had to pay. It was competitive, but people were helping each other out." One night over beer at the Kettle, Dylan leaned over to Paxton and sang another new song into his ear—"Gates of Eden," a surrealistic dystopian ballad in the folk tradition. "People would be sitting at the bar at night and the next morning they'd come in with a new song," said Arthur Gorson, a college-age activist who, like Terri Thal, found himself managing a few of the locals (in his case, Ochs and Blue). "This whole crew of people were writing five or six songs a week and then they'd go downstairs to the Gaslight and show off the new songs. They were challenging each other and showing off."

In June 1964, Elliott was standing in front of the Folklore Center when a car pulled up, and Dylan, wearing what Elliott called "boots of Spanish leather, with high heels," ordered him into the vehicle: "We're gettin' ready to go uptown to do some recording." With Elliott carrying a few bottles of Beaujolais that were in the car, the two made it to Columbia's midtown studio, where Dylan's producer, Tom Wilson, and his road manager, Victor Maymudes, were prepping for Dylan to record his first new music since his headlines-oriented third album, *The Times They Are a-Changin'*. That disc, from February 1964, had handed the world the title song—another, more proactive anthem—as well as songs describing the murder of a Black woman named Hattie Carroll, the death of Black activist Medgar Evers, and a tragic, despairing midwestern farmer who killed his family and himself.

This time, over the course of just a few hours, Elliott observed as Dylan laid down on tape songs that reflected his breakup with Rotolo, including "It Ain't Me Babe," "Ballad in Plain D," and "I Don't Believe You (She Acts Like We Never Have Met)." On the cover of the album that would eventually be called *Another Side of Bob Dylan*—the title was Wilson's idea—Dylan was seen wearing jeans that Rotolo had cut to fit over his boots.

For the new legion of Dylan heads who looked to him for social and wardrobe cues, *Another Side of Bob Dylan*, released in the middle of the summer of 1964, was considered a letdown. Only one song, the elliptical "Chimes of Freedom," could have conceivably been sung at another march on Washington. Unlike the two releases that preceded it, it failed to crack the Top 40 on the album chart.

But the Village still spewed out enough topical songs to compensate, especially from the man many considered to be Dylan's closest rival. Phil Ochs's debut, *All the News That's Fit to Sing*, more than lived up to its title. With Danny Kalb's guitar making for a chiming, spunky sidekick, Ochs sounded like he looked on the album cover—someone who could absorb a TV newscast or an edition of a newspaper and turn its contents into songs. Some of them, like his talking blues about the Cuban Missile Crisis, felt dated almost as soon as they arrived. But with a steadfast, affectless voice that seemed to demand social justice with each syllable, Ochs could also turn a news event into a gripping narrative. In "Too Many Martyrs," he delivered his take on Medgar Evers's death, and the tale of a Black social worker who'd tried to break up a gang rumble and died provided the basis for "Lou Marsh." Ochs also revealed he had the heart of a poet when he transformed Edgar Allan Poe's "The Bells" into a twinkling beauty and wrote the rousing "Power and the Glory," which critiqued and celebrated America at the same time. Ochs played a few of those songs at a fall 1964 evening of protest songs at the Village Gate, where he shared the stage with Paxton, Sainte-Marie, Chandler, Andersen, and LaFarge (and, noticeably, not Dylan).

As the musical activity in the Village escalated, so did the city's issues with the cacophony of strumming, coffee machines, and smatterings of applause emanating from nearly every club, coffeehouse, or basket house. In March 1964, eleven coffeehouses, including the Gaslight and the Four Winds, were issued summonses for contributing a "honky-tonk atmosphere" to the area and were allowed to present only "musical entertainment of a limited nature." The fines were so small—twenty-five dollars in many cases—that most of the owners could afford to pay them; one coffeehouse, which was not named by the city, placed its summons in its front window as a point of rebellious pride. Such open defiance only made the authorities jack up their tactics. In November, officials pushed for injunctions against the Gaslight and the Cafe Rafio for violating zoning regulations, and the Four Winds and the Cafe Bizarre were cited for not having a "coffeehouse license" and for violating zoning rules over their use of "drags."

But the community also had bigger issues stemming from its own success. By the end of the year, oversaturation had taken its toll, and musical tastes were shifting. As 1964 wound down, neither the Kingston Trio nor Peter, Paul and Mary had seen any of their singles reach the Top 10 in about two years. "Folk music has gone from boom to bust," groused a concert promoter who'd laid out $50,000 for a festival that would eventually lose money. Village club owners had hoped that the New York World's Fair, held in Queens, would encourage visitors to stream into their venues, but that didn't happen. "New Yorkers' habits are changing," the Vanguard's Max Gordon told the *Times*. "Older people have stopped going to clubs and younger people are going to different places than they used to." The *Times* noted that "one well-known Greenwich Village club" didn't have a single customer one evening.

Simultaneously, anyone who'd tuned into *The Ed Sullivan Show* earlier in the year saw the writing, and the electric-guitar playing, on the wall. "The Beatles scuttled all of us," Sylvia Tyson said. "We still worked, but we didn't have the volume of work we had before." True to form, Dylan was among those who sensed the changes on the horizon: at the Cafe Figaro one night, he enthused to Kalb about John Hammond (Jr.'s) new album, *Big City Blues*, which he'd recorded with an electric rhythm section. In his West Village apartment, Noel

Stookey, on a break from his ongoing work as part of Peter, Paul and Mary, heard music coming from the courtyard of a nearby building. The ruckus came by way of John Sebastian, who appeared to be fronting a rock-and-roll band. As Stookey would soon realize, Sebastian, along with Kalb and a growing number of other musicians, was about to change everything up, with enormous ramifications for their music and shared neighborhood.

Chapter 5

trains running

1965–1967

Thanks to a case of mononucleosis, Danny Kalb's time
with Dave Van Ronk's Ragtime Jug Stompers had ended prematurely, but
then so had the ensemble itself, which only lasted six months. But the first
day of 1965 was bringing both a calendar change and a glimpse of the future.
On New Year's Eve, Kalb invited a group of friends to his family home in
Mount Vernon for a party. Among those who showed up was Roy Blumenfeld,
a handsome, athletically built kid who lived a block away and was dating one
of Kalb's cousins. A year younger than Kalb, he had attended the same high
school and played percussion in the marching band. To Blumenfeld, the teenage Kalb had been a loud-voiced, caustic, and opinionated kid—"it was his way
or the highway"—but he'd also kept tabs on Kalb's developing guitar skills,
especially a fingerpicking technique inspired by blues great Lightnin' Hopkins.

Since the party involved music making, Kalb wanted to try something he
hadn't done since his stint with his high school rockabilly band. The Ragtime
Jug Stompers had been a kick, and he'd made inroads as an accompanist, play-
ing behind Phil Ochs and Judy Collins. With Sam Charters, his bandmate in
Van Ronk's jug band, Kalb had also formed a folk, blues, and ragtime duo, the
New Strangers. *Meet the New Strangers*, issued by Prestige in 1964, revealed
Kalb to be more than a guitarist whose fingers could dance around a fretboard.
On their version of "Alberta," the Lead Belly–associated sultry blues, Kalb

sang in a husky, heavy-lidded voice that communicated burden, weariness, and hardscrabble feistiness. But now it was New Year's Eve, and as he said to his cousin and fellow musician, drummer Peter Kogan, he wanted to plug in. "He was very articulate about it," said Kogan. "I just remember him saying, 'This is the direction, to go electric.'"

Kalb was also partly inspired by something he'd absorbed in the Village likely a few months before, and right around the corner from the Gaslight. A street-level storefront, the Night Owl—at 118 West Third Street between Mac-Dougal Street and Sixth Avenue—was another one of those irregular music spaces in the area. At the dawn of the sixties, it had been home to Art Ford's Bowl-a-Gallery, a combination bowling alley and art gallery, before Joe Marra, a stocky Italian American, took it over. In keeping with the musical changes in the Village, Marra renamed it the Night Owl as a folk club. Like the Gaslight, it didn't have a liquor license, so its waitresses took orders for sodas and ice cream.

For all its quirks, the Night Owl was also distinguishing itself as the place for singer-songwriters who were pushing the form beyond the ballads and newspaper-headline broadsides that had so far typified Village folk music. Using musicians like guitarist and vibes player Buzzy Linhart, Fred Neil truly began breaking free of any previous stylistic restraints. Singing in a rumbling baritone that sounded as if it originated in the pit of his stomach, he would lead the musicians in long, incantatory jams where folk, jazz, and blues collided and frolicked. Another recently arrived transplant, Tim Hardin, was doing the same at the Night Owl. Born and raised in Oregon, Hardin had been in the marines and had become hooked on heroin during service abroad. Moving to New York in 1961 and hoping to be an actor—carrying on the tradition of the Clancy Brothers, Jimmy Gavin, and others before him—Hardin began spending time in the Village. There his love of music—both his parents had been musicians to varying degrees—overtook his thespian interests.

Hardin was an intense character: small, with an imposing forehead and a penetrating stare, he could be "a feisty guy . . . a mean guy" and "not terribly pleasant," as Marra recalled. But he also had a boisterous, phlegmy laugh, and his music defied categorization. Hardly a typical folk-crooning strummer, Hardin made music that was doused in blues, country, and jazz but owed allegiance to none of them, and he sang in a voice that could be tender one moment, boastful the next. In his mind he was more a jazz singer than a folk one, and he was also beginning to write songs, such as "It'll Never Happen Again" and "How Can We Hang On to a Dream," that hinted at his fragile and self-absorbed soul. "Oh, God, Jesus, what beautiful songs," as Marra also said.

As Kalb saw for himself one night at the Night Owl, Hardin played an electric guitar rather than acoustic and sang blues and R&B covers, and Kalb thirsted for a taste of those possibilities at his house party. "As soon as I heard those sounds, I knew that was what was happening," he told a Hartford newspaper in 1966, "and I had to be with it in order to express myself and my music." He and Blumenfeld already had several musical bonds: they'd both played together in a Dixieland combo, they'd both taken guitar lessons from Van Ronk, and both were hooked on *The Best of Muddy Waters*, a compilation of the bluesman's work that included "I Can't Be Satisfied" and "I'm Ready." Listening to Little Walter's harmonica solo on the latter gave them both chills. As Blumenfeld recalled, "Danny liked that power."

Although Kalb was playing a Gibson acoustic guitar that New Year's Eve, he invited Blumenfeld to join him on a version of "I Can't Be Satisfied." Blumenfeld took over the drum kit Kogan had brought with him, and the deep blues the two of them played sparked something creative in both young men. Van Ronk would say that the area around Bleecker and MacDougal transformed itself every few years—and Kalb and Blumenfeld would be among its next agents of change.

When Hardin played at the Night Owl, he would sometimes be accompanied by a cadre of like-minded musicians, including Neil, Linhart, and the newly ubiquitous John Sebastian. A Village native, Sebastian hailed from a family steeped in music and the arts. His father, John Sebastian Pugliese, had grown up in Philadelphia, studied at a university in Italy, and, upon returning to the States, announced he had no interest in his own father's financial world.

Instead, Sebastian decided to concentrate on the chromatic harmonica he'd been playing since he was a teen, and before long he was appearing at cabarets and clubs, including Cafe Society, where his son saw him perform with the folk-blues sensation Josh White. Along the way, he dropped his Italian last name professionally. In an attempt to warn his son about the dangers of weed, the elder Sebastian told him he'd shared a cab with Billie Holiday as she toked up during the Cafe Society days.

Sebastian and his wife, Jane Bashir, who worked in TV and radio, welcomed their son John in March 1944; another son, Mark, was born soon after. By the time John was ten, the family was ensconced at 29 Washington Square West, an elegant building at the park's northwest corner. One of their neighbors, albeit briefly, was former first lady Eleanor Roosevelt. Given the Sebastian parents' connection to the arts, their home became a gathering place for creative types: Woody Guthrie once stayed in a guest room next to the boys, although John's only memory would be the tones of Guthrie's harmonica. "As I was falling sleep," he recalled, "I remember thinking, 'Not as good as my dad.'"

Even though the family's spacious apartment on the fifteenth floor faced west, not directly over the park, the younger John Sebastian could still hear music, including the occasional bongo, from the windows. During his teen years in the late fifties, he would wander into the park to see and hear banjo players in one corner, a doo-wop vocal group in another, and a guitarist trying hard to sound like Lightnin' Hopkins. (His brother Mark, meanwhile, would take note of the junkies outside the Hotel Earle, just around the bend from their building.) When he started out in his own music career, as a member of the Even Dozen Jug Band, Sebastian went by "John Benson," his middle name, to avoid confusion with his illustrious father, who'd already recorded albums for Columbia and Decca.

By early 1965, Sebastian had become one of the scene's omnipresent accompanists. Starting with the first time he sat in with Neil at the Cafe Wha?, he left behind his father's classical technique and began developing a fulsome style of harmonica playing that sounded like a chugging train. He'd also seen how musicians were not always welcomed in the area. "That was an Italian neighborhood," he said, "so if you were going to try to have a little club in the basement, some woman on the second floor was going to be yelling 'get out of here,' in Italian, out the window." Sebastian had been floored when he heard Hardin's early demos wafting out of the next-door apartment at his own place on MacDougal Street, which belonged to Erik Jacobsen, a former member of the Knob Lick Upper 10,000 who was moving into production. Sebastian was equally taken aback when Hardin knocked on his door, said he'd heard Sebastian was going to be his harmonica player for an upcoming recording date, and informed his soon-to-be accompanist that he would never play better because he'd be supporting Hardin. "Modesty must have gone out of style somewhere," Sebastian thought to himself.

Like Kalb, Jacobsen had decided that electric music was the future and saw a hint of those possibilities in the Sellouts, a Long Island band that began working in the Village and was acknowledged to be the first local group to plug in and cover Beatles songs. Their name derived from the fact that their original bass player, Marc Silber, came from the folk world. Jacobsen and Sebastian had caught at least one of their sets at a space near the Night Owl, possibly Trude Heller's, and Jacobsen wound up producing a record with them.

But Jacobsen and Sebastian were more serious about the concept, "always scamming and scheming about something or another," Jacobsen recalled. Sebastian had been intrigued by the electric Les Paul that the Sellouts' guitarist, Skip Boone, was playing, and he now had a potential partner in electric-rock crime. Sebastian had already befriended Cass Elliot, a brassy-voiced Maryland native who'd sung in two folk groups—the Big 3 and the Mugwumps—and was working the cash register at the Night Owl, among other jobs in the Village. (In an in-joke about her size that bordered on insensitive, Marra had named its most over-the-top sundae after her.) In February 1964, she invited Sebastian over to her apartment at the time, in Gramercy Park, to watch the Beatles on *The Ed Sullivan Show*. Another guest was Zalman (Zal) Yanovsky, a wild-eyed and energetic Canadian guitarist who looked like a six-foot-tall version of Ringo Starr. "We sit down and the show begins, and by the end, we're like 16-year-old girls," Sebastian said. Their bond was instantaneous—they even began swapping licks on the guitars they'd each brought to Elliot's place—and soon enough, they were joined by a bass player, Steve Boone, who'd been in the Sellouts, and a drummer, Jan Buchner.

From sitting in with Hardin and others, Sebastian already knew Marra and was blunt about what his new band wanted. "There is a big changing coming in music," he told the Night Owl owner. "The wind is changing—folk is going to get a beat. It's going to get happy, and we want to be the first to do that kind of music here. When I sing, I want all the little girls to flip out." Marra agreed to host the band, which was dubbed the Lovin' Spoonful after a line in Mississippi John Hurt's "Coffee Blues" ("I wanna see my baby 'bout a lovin' spoonful, my lovin' spoonful"). Marra would later write that the inaugural show took place in January 1965; Boone would say February. What no one disputed was that the musicians smoked a joint together in the basement dressing room, made their way upstairs, and squeezed onto the stage. They played rough-hewn versions of the blues "Route 66," the folk-blues traditional song "Wild About My Lovin'," and Chuck Berry's "Almost Grown," but also the Sebastian original "Didn't Want to Have to Do It," a summer-breezy, softly sung tune that pointed to a folk-rock future.

By then, Marra had changed the setup of his club. The stage, which had been in the back, was moved to the front and against the right wall. A few rows of seats were in front, the rest on either side of the stage; the musicians now faced a brick wall. But the fact that the Night Owl hadn't been reconfigured for a rock-and-roll band with drums and amplifiers became immediately apparent. "They broke glasses, windowpanes and eardrums . . . ," Marra would write. "The audience left. Man, they weren't even polite. They flocked out." When water started dripping onto the stage from the ceiling, Marra assumed the neighbors upstairs were protesting in any way they could.

Afterward, Sebastian would recall Marra saying "You guys are no fucking good" before explaining to them, during a group meeting in the empty club, the precise problems. "Zal, that fucking amplifier—you're killing these people in the front row," Sebastian recalled Marra saying. "John, you're looking at your shoes. You gotta look at the *people*." (Eric Eisner, who drummed in another Night Owl band, the Strangers, recalled that Marra seemed to say "fucking" every fourth word.) Marra stuck with them for two more weeks, but by the end of that run, the place was empty; on the last night, the club took in only $7.85. Although Marra liked Sebastian and believed in the potential of the Lovin' Spoonful—and likely knew there would be money to be made in local rock and roll—he also had a business to run. Calling the band in one afternoon, he fired them and watched as they forlornly slunk back outside.

In Marra's words, the Night Owl then went "back to blues and rhythm & blues," but the movement in the Village, and elsewhere, was not to be halted. On January 13, Sebastian was invited to CBS Studios in midtown Manhattan to participate in the first sessions for Bob Dylan's next album. Starting in high school, Dylan had experimented with rock from time to time, particularly on the ill-fated 1962 single "Mixed Up Confusion," but with producer Tom Wilson onboard, he was plunging in deeper than before. In the studio, Dylan would first lay down new material by himself, then invite musicians to join him on subsequent takes. Although Sebastian wasn't a bass player by trade, he accompanied Dylan on "She Belongs to Me," which also benefited from Bruce Langhorne's refined guitar winding its way throughout the song, and Sebastian played harmonica on "Outlaw Blues." Kalb, who'd kept in touch with Dylan since their University of Wisconsin days four years before, later claimed he'd been invited to the sessions to play lead guitar. But in what wouldn't be the first time, he was recovering from another bout of depression, what he would call a "dark time" in his life, and he assumed Dylan had been unable to reach him.

Steve Boone, who'd driven Sebastian in from Long Island for the session and had stuck around in the studio, was handed the bass guitar when an actual skilled player was needed. Either he or Sebastian provided the bottom end on a take of "Subterranean Homesick Blues," and Boone had a feeling it was his bass line on the final take of the wonderfully scraggly "Maggie's Farm," although he couldn't say for sure. What no one could deny was the overwhelming possibilities of what they were hearing. That same January, another group of reformed folkies, renamed the Byrds, recorded an overhauled version of Dylan's "Mr. Tambourine Man" in Los Angeles. Very soon, the impact of all that activity would reach the part of town where Dylan, Kalb, Sebastian, and others had established themselves just a few short years before.

The fall day that Kalb walked into Fretted Instruments at 319 Sixth Avenue (and Third Street), no introduction was needed. Steve Katz, who was working in the store, already knew Kalb as the fastest player in the Village, and they'd both had a connection as Van Ronk students. About two years before, they'd even been on the same jug-band bill at Carnegie Hall that featured Van Ronk's group and the one Katz was part of, the Even Dozen Jug Band.

For musicians in the Village, Fretted Instruments, along with Matt Umanov Guitars, was a destination spot. With the help of Izzy Young, owner Marc Silber, who was raised in Michigan and was both a musician and connoisseur of stringed instruments, had found the second-floor space in the fall of 1963. He knew nothing about business but noticed the people playing acoustic instruments and realized that a market existed. Among his first customers were Dylan and Joan Baez, who came in to buy guitar picks. Silber would sometimes see Sebastian in the shop for hours on end. Katz and the Even Dozen Jug Band would practice there before Katz took a part-time job in the shop. Even though he was only twenty and enamored of folk music, Katz could sense things were changing in the tightly knit world of Village musicians.

In March, the Lovin' Spoonful returned to the Night Owl a more focused, less blaring unit. After their shambolic start, they'd secured a rehearsal space in the grungy basement of the Hotel Albert, at Tenth Street and University Place, where their new drummer, Joe Butler of the Sellouts, was living. To everyone's surprise, including his brother Mark, Sebastian had started writing songs and becoming a more authoritative front man, and the group in general tightened up its arrangements; it also helped that Butler could sing, which bolstered their harmonies. They played a set at the Cafe Bizarre—still in operation, years after opening with Odetta, Van Ronk, and others, but more than ever a tourist trap that sold "Bohemian Burgers." Marra saw the band there and was suitably impressed—and also stunned by the sight and sound of Sebastian's new instrument, an electrified autoharp. He rebooked them into the Night Owl, improved the sound system, and placed a huge blow-up photo of the Lovin' Spoonful outside the club, as if they were already stars. "We rehearsed at the Cafe Bizarre every afternoon until our show at night began," said Sebastian.

"That straightened us out real quick. When we came back to the Night Owl, we were pretty ferocious."

Suddenly, the club was jammed with teenagers along with mover-shakers such as Albert Grossman and producer Phil Spector, who spent the entire time with his head against the brick wall, for reasons no one quite understood. "When you put an ear against the wall," Sebastian considered, "you get that all-encompassing sound and can't hear anything else, so maybe that was an element of it."

For his part, Kalb was encouraged enough by his New Year's Eve blues jam to plow down a similar road. Not long after that party, Kalb and Blumenfeld ran into each other in the East Village, and Kalb invited his friend to join him at a club show on Long Island. It went well enough, but they needed a bass player for future work. By chance, Blumenfeld's roommate knew Andy Kulberg, a dry-witted kid from Amherst, New York, who'd attended music school in Boston, then NYU, and played upright bass and flute. With the addition of Artie Traum, Happy Traum's younger brother, the Danny Kalb Quartet (sometimes billed as the Danny Kalb Four) was born in the early months of 1965. The quartet played one of its first performances—what Kalb would call, rightly or wrongly, "the first electric blues show in New York"—at a free-speech benefit for striking Ohio students, held at the Empire Hotel on the Upper West Side in April.

Thanks to Kalb, whose fluidity as an acoustic musician was easily translating into the new format, the group had a raw, nascent approach—Kalb sang a more than credible "I'm Troubled"—and Marra booked them into the Night Owl. Arthur Levy, a young folk fan who'd begun making trips into the Village, already knew Kalb's name from his work with Van Ronk. But seeing Kalb's own combo at the Night Owl, where the musician was both lead guitarist and front man, was an entirely different experience. "There was nobody in that folk scene who could go from playing Chuck Berry guitar to Muddy Waters guitar to Lightnin' Hopkins guitar, and back again," said Levy, who came to befriend Kalb. "He was totally in control."

Quickly, word of mouth about the band was growing louder, and the high-end Morris Agency expressed interest in booking it. But that next step was put on pause, and by Kalb, who instead decided to spend the summer in Europe. Visiting England that season, Silber ran into Kalb, who was hanging with the new-folk crowd in Cambridge.

In August, Kalb returned to the States after receiving a telegram about a possible record contract for the band. Within those few short months, the music world as he knew it had changed even further. *Bringing It All Back Home*, the album for which Dylan had recruited Sebastian and Boone, was released in the spring and served as an initial warning signal that the musician was changing course. In June, Dylan's evolution accelerated when he recorded "Like a Rolling Stone," a volcanic six-minutes-plus message "telling someone something they didn't know, telling them they were lucky," he said at the time. When Kalb first heard the track—an acetate that Dylan played for him, likely before Kalb traveled overseas—he didn't know what to make of it. Dylan's performance at the Newport Folk Festival in July, where he startled some in the crowd with a short, scraggly, overamplified set of his new rock and roll, was another shot across the bow. That same month, the Lovin' Spoonful unveiled its first single, a romp called "Do You Believe in Magic," written after Sebastian watched a girl dance to their songs at the Night Owl; the tune would quickly ascend to the Top 10. The idea of either ditching folk or electrifying it was now legitimized.

After Kalb returned and tried to reconvene his quartet, he was suddenly down one member, as Artie Traum (who also went to Europe for the summer) opted not to return. In search of a replacement rhythm guitarist, Kalb tracked down Katz that fateful day at Fretted Instruments and asked if he wanted to audition. Even though Katz didn't have an electric guitar and didn't know how to play one, Kalb was going with his gut more than any business savviness. "Danny knew Steve had worked with Van Ronk and he could do certain picking," said Blumenfeld. Katz said yes and, after borrowing a DeArmond pickup from a friend, made his way to the Night Owl for this tryout. There he met Kulberg, "the practical one," as Katz called him, and Blumenfeld, "the goofball clown but very bright and fun." Plugging his guitar into an amp, Katz was unaware the pickup was turned up high, and out came a loud, riotous squalor. "I felt like I was being chased by a herd of rhinos," he said. "The sound was just so horrible." He turned his volume down to zero and could barely hear himself, but Kalb said he liked the way he played and hired him.

When Katz auditioned, he noticed another name on the marquee announcing the band: "Featuring Tom Jones." Likely keeping an eye on the British Invasion that had overtaken the radio, Kalb—at the suggestion of a manager friend—had recruited a lead singer who, thanks to the popularity of a certain Welsh pop star, would soon revert to his given name, Tommy Flanders. Under the name Jones, he'd briefly been the lead singer of the Trolls, a Cambridge band. With his Beatles bangs, raw voice that conjured an American Mick Jagger, and stage moves that included splits, Flanders injected the fledging band with the showy rock-and-roll personality it needed, not to mention a dose of braggadocio. At the Night Owl one evening, Flanders told Marra he could sing better than anyone else he was booking, and Marra called his bluff, telling him to come back with a band. Flanders returned with Kalb, Blumenfeld, and Kulberg, and before long the new band was sharing a bill with the Lovin' Spoonful.

Kalb's concept also had a changed name. The year before, producer Paul Rothchild had pitched Elektra's Jac Holzman on a series of albums, each with "project" in the title, that would explore forms like blues, old-time banjo, and the new groundswell of singer-songwriters. To Rothchild, the concept gave Elektra a connection not merely with commercial folk but also with its origins. The first of these records, *The Blues Project*, was the result of one day-long session that featured Van Ronk, Kalb, Mark Spoelstra, Geoff Muldaur, Eric Von Schmidt, and others, with Dylan playing piano under a pseudonym, Bob Landy. Among its friskiest tracks were Kalb's "I'm Troubled," featuring Sebastian on harmonica, and "Hello Baby Blues."

The album, which cost just under $1,000 to make, sold more than 35,000 copies after its release, according to Rothchild, and it gave Flanders an idea: given Kalb's association with the album, why not name his new band after it? Kalb agreed, and on October 7, 1965, days after Katz's audition, the renamed Blues Project Featuring Danny Kalb and Tom Flanders (with "rhythm in blue" added beneath the name) made its Night Owl debut. In the quickened way in which record deals could happen at the time, Columbia's Tom Wilson brought them into a studio that same month.

With the pop charts in mind far more than any blues credibility, the band chose to record Eric Andersen's "Violets of Dawn," a florid and borderline erotic love song that made others by his peers sound chaste. The band quickened the tempo and made it into an effervescent piece of folk pop, all with the help of a studio musician recruited by Wilson. Only twenty-one, Al Kooper, born Alan Peter Kuperschmidt, already had serious credits to his name, from playing guitar with the Royal Teens to cowriting "This Diamond Ring," the biggest hit that would ever be associated with Jerry Lewis's son Gary and his band, the Playboys. Equally talented as a musician and studio hustler, Kooper had attended the recording sessions for Dylan's *Highway 61 Revisited* and inserted himself into the proceedings over Wilson's initial objections; it was his organ that Kalb heard when Dylan played him the final version.

For Kooper, accompanying the Blues Project for a potential single was merely another gig in a schedule filled with them. But to his surprise, Kalb and Kulberg took him out for a meal later and offered him a full-time role in the band. "At sessions, I had to play what people wanted me to play," Kooper recalled. "I appreciated how that improved my training, but it robbed me of things I wanted to do. When they asked me to join the band, I had the notoriety, and I thought, 'This will be great.' They weren't nothing, but we built it at rehearsals until we could finally play a set in front of people. That was much more enjoyable to me than playing sessions."

In various apartments downtown, they began to work up a collection of songs to play—until, that is, they were booted out of each place for playing too loud. By his own admission, Kooper hardly knew anything about the blues, and Kalb had to drill the music into his head by inviting Kooper over to his downtown place and playing him blues records again and again. The two men were wildly different in musical backgrounds, but they were both Jewish, young, and hungry, and the Village—as well as the record business—were open to whatever they had to offer.

As the scene was growing more amped up, in every way, its unofficial clubhouse remained the Kettle of Fish. But with Dylan's success and the pressure and attention that came with it, the dynamics at those gatherings began to shift. In 1964 Robert Shelton of the *Times* watched—with a sense of wonderment rare for such a fixture on the scene—as Dylan entered the Kettle one night with the Supremes and members of the British band the Animals, whose sulking, electrified makeover of "The House of the Rising Sun" had given the ballad an audience far beyond the coffeehouse crowd. Those pop stars were a departure from the small, insular posse Dylan generally preferred, one that protected him and, many thought, egged him on as he dissected the peers and strivers at the Kettle on any given night. For extra privacy, Guido Giampieri would close and lock the front door at a late hour.

Dylan's gang was usually led by Bob Neuwirth, his road manager, sidekick, and would-be bodyguard. An artist by trade and education, the Ohio-born Neuwirth had attended art school in Boston, where he learned to play guitar and banjo and eventually made his way into the Village; Dylan would recall first seeing him in the audience at the Gaslight. Neuwirth's barbed-wire gibes and hipster persona were also of a piece with Dylan's. As a source told *Rolling Stone* a few years later, regarding Neuwirth's arrival in New York in 1964, "Dylan started to change at that time. Part of it was Neuwirth; he was a real strong influence on Dylan. Neuwirth [was] stressing pride and ego, sort of saying, 'Hold your head high, man, don't take shit, just take over the scene.' He was the kind of cat who could influence others, work on their egos and support those egos." Neuwirth's striped pants would soon be seen behind Dylan on the cover of *Highway 61 Revisited*, the album that announced, as much as any, that the folk revival had passed its expiration date.

Thanks to his work with Dylan on records and on stage, including playing with him at the chaotic Newport Folk Festival, Kooper was often at Dylan's table and saw how perilous it could be for anyone in the vicinity. "If Dylan focused on you, you were in trouble," he said. "He could out-think anybody." David Blue was a recurring member of the posse, although, as Ramblin' Jack Elliott would recall, he was rarely if ever the brunt of Dylan's withering gaze or comments. "Blue had a certain kind of stature," said Elliott. "He was a large guy, way bigger than Bob, and he had a certain composed personality."

By 1965, Van Ronk was holding his own. The Ragtime Jug Stompers hadn't worked out, but he retained his Mercury Records contract and, that year, released *Just Dave Van Ronk*, which again pared his music back to just his voice and guitar. There, he was finally able to unveil his arrangement of "The House of the Rising Sun," along with a moving rendition of "God Bless the Child." Though far from a household name in any home, he was nonetheless growing in stature. Shortly before a *New York Post* reporter showed up at 190 Waverly Place for an interview—where the writer found the apartment strewn with battered guitar cases and a sizable stone owl—a teenager had knocked on Van Ronk's door. It had happened before, some of the fans coming from Cambridge, but this one was from Montreal and wanted to meet Van Ronk for himself. At the Kettle one night, Dylan began offering advice on how Van Ronk could become a far bigger name. Increasingly irritated, Van Ronk finally shot back, "Dylan, if you're so rich, how come you ain't smart?"

To Dylan biographer Anthony Scaduto, Van Ronk theorized that Dylan zeroed in on particular targets for a reason: in Van Ronk's mind, they all wanted to "get rich," too. Whatever the motivation, the atmosphere could be fraught. "The level of 'rapping,' as we called it, was tough," said Arthur Gorson, the manager who sometimes found himself amid the Kettle gang. "People fell by the wayside. They would talk about songs and someone would say, 'Hey, man, you can't use that word—*I* used that word.' Eric Andersen was slightly damaged by Neuwirth's taunts." Andersen would later pen "The Hustler" about Neuwirth and those times in that bar. In the fall of 1965, Dylan himself would unveil "Positively 4th Street," a stern single that sliced and diced someone—or some group—who hadn't supported him. He never specified who, but some in the Kettle posse wondered if it were one of them.

One especially tense evening, Andersen witnessed Dylan lacing into Phil Ochs. As Dylan drifted from topical writing, Ochs fully embraced it—and was being lauded for it within their world. Reviewing Ochs's performance at Newport in 1964, Shelton opined that he was "rivaling Bob Dylan as a protest spokesman." *Broadside* also weighed in, commenting, "Ochs is much more deeply committed to the broadside tradition." With one album under his belt and a second, *I Ain't Marching Anymore*, due in the early months of 1965, Ochs was primed to be an even more socially conscious voice of his generation than Dylan was, and the two men had a "love-hate thing," as Paxton put it.

At the Kettle one evening, Dylan and Ochs got into a verbal match that ended with Dylan dismissing Ochs as merely a singing journalist (which, in Dylan's defense, wasn't too far from the truth at that point in Ochs's career). Andersen, who had grown close to Ochs (he had encouraged Andersen to add more verses to "Violets of Dawn") and would often crash at the apartment where Ochs lived with his wife, Alice, was suitably offended. As Andersen observed (and Scaduto also reported), Dylan turned on Ochs another night as well: "You oughta find a new line of work, Ochs. You're not doin' very much in this one." As an appalled Andersen recalled, "He said it right to Phil's face and really insulted him, and I said, 'Stop picking on him. Cut it out.'" Dylan, said Andersen, retorted, "Look, I'm buying all the wine here. I can say whatever I want to say. What do you want me to talk about, the sunset over the Hudson and the deep blue sea?"

For a brief period, Ochs and Dylan were both managed by Albert Grossman until Ochs felt he wasn't receiving the attention he deserved, and late in 1965 he asked Gorson to take over. (In a poke at the name of Grossman's company, ABG, Ochs asked Gorson to use his initials for his own management firm, which became AHG.) But Ochs had an emerging star power of his own: covering his January 1966 debut at Carnegie Hall for the *Times*, Shelton felt that Ochs still needed some seasoning and admonished his melodies and guitar playing but noted that the audience was "predominantly teenaged."

Later that year, in preparation for recording *Pleasures of the Harbor*—a lavishly produced record intended to be his moment of arrival as a full-on recording artist—Ochs introduced songs like "Outside of a Small Circle of Friends" and "Flower Lady" at Carnegie Hall. The latter—seemingly about a mysterious middle-aged woman who would walk into Folk City and sell bouquets of flowers, supposedly purloined from cemeteries—was set to one of his most sumptuous melodies. He and Dylan weren't far apart in some ways: they'd both grown up with rock and roll and eventually turned to acoustic music. With Kooper adding one of his recognizable keyboard parts, Ochs even recorded a plugged-in remake of his antiwar rouser "I Ain't Marching Anymore." But he and Dylan remained mirror images of the Village, the acoustic and the electric, the old world and the new world, circling each other and staring each other down.

Starting in the fall of 1965, Roy Blumenfeld would leave his apartment in the East Village, at First Avenue and East Fourth Street, and begin making his way west toward 152 Bleecker Street, between Thompson and LaGuardia. "As I'd get closer to the Village, everything was lit up," he said. "It was like going to the carnival."

On nights like those, Blumenfeld's destination was a striped, half-circular canopy, where he would walk down two flights of stairs and enter the Cafe Au Go Go, the Blues Project's home base and—along with the group itself—the embodiment of the Village's musical makeover. The club began as anything but the Village's rock-and-roll heart. As a teenager, Ella Lefkowitz, a vivacious redhead, had left home in Brooklyn for the Village, where she devoted herself to poetry, taking acting lessons, and ingratiating herself with the Beat writers she loved. Lefkowitz waited tables at the Cafe Bizarre and the Figaro, where she met and would soon marry Howard Solomon, a theatrical agent turned stockbroker who had small, deep-set eyes. In time, she convinced him to open what she first envisioned as a coffeehouse and then a nightclub in the basement of 152 Bleecker.

At that point, the space had been empty for so many decades that it took nearly a year to clean it out after the Solomons filed with the city, in May 1963, to open a business. And as the couple soon learned, it was one thing to prepare to open a club seating four hundred, quite another to grapple with New York paperwork and hassles. Ella Solomon didn't want to serve alcohol—the thought of coping with angry drunks didn't appeal to her—but the city nevertheless pressured the couple to obtain a liquor license, according to their son Jason. In turn, they sued the city and were able to open without a license, serving only ice cream, coffee, and soda. Professor Irwin Corey, an unconventional and zany stand-up comic, opened the Au Go Go with a six-week run in February 1964. Subsequent bookings—comics Mort Sahl and George Carlin, jazz artists Stan Getz and Bill Evans, the long-established

Josh White—put the venue more in line with the Village Vanguard than a pop club.

Two months into its run, the Au Go Go suddenly became notorious. Just as he was preparing to go onstage, the famously freewheeling and opinionated Lenny Bruce was arrested and charged with violating obscenity laws; Howard Solomon was also arrested for allowing a supposedly indecent performance to proceed in his club. Six days before, the police had obtained a club soundboard recording of one of Bruce's performances, which a grand jury heard as part of the evidence against him. Both Bruce and Solomon were found guilty of their respective charges, with Bruce sentenced to a year in a jail and Solomon fined $1,000. (In the end, Bruce served four months, and Solomon's conviction was reversed upon appeal.) The only positive development to emerge from the ordeal was that the Cafe Au Go Go was now pinned on the national map. Its size also made it more suitable for rock and roll, bookings for which largely began in July 1965, when the Paul Butterfield Blues Band, the Chicago band led by its street-tough harmonica player, appeared there.

Still calling itself "The Blues Project with Danny Kalb and Tommy Flanders," Kalb's expanded band opened at the Cafe Au Go Go in November. Because comedians were sometimes billed with folk or rock acts, their opening act was a young Black comic, Richard Pryor, who had also been spotted getting high on whippets (nitrous oxide) at the Gaslight. For the moment, their set relied heavily on blues, R&B, and early rock and roll, some sung by Flanders and others by Kalb: Willie Dixon's "Back Door Man" and "Spoonful," Muddy Waters's "Louisiana Blues" (retitled "Goin' Down Louisiana"), Jimmy Reed's "Bright Lights Big City," and Mose Allison's "Parchman Farm." The quintet's varied musical backgrounds played out in their stage persona, as Flanders strutted and spun around, while Katz looked the sensitive, withdrawn troubadour. They didn't put much thought into their clothes; as Kalb would later tell a reporter, "We don't wear any set costumes when we play. We all wear just what strikes our fancy." The crowds were sparse and the band still learning about stagecraft. "One stamped his foot, another did little knee bends, a third shook all over, a fourth gaped at the others, and the last rocked back and forth over the drums," groused a critic of one of their early performances. But their lack of collective stage experience didn't seem to trouble Solomon, who was hungry to put people in the seats: as Kooper wrote, "Business stunk and Solomon was desperate." To their surprise, Solomon booked them for additional shows.

For several years, there had been no shortage of actual blues legends in the venues south of Fourteenth Street. Happy Traum took lessons from Brownie McGee, and the New World Singers shared bills with Reverend Gary Davis, who later complimented the guitar that Katz used to audition for the Blues Project. It was possible to see Mississippi John Hurt or Lightnin' Hopkins at the Gaslight, or later Howlin' Wolf at the Cafe Au Go Go. "You could sit at the feet of people like John Hurt, who was a master," Andersen recalled. "It was like going to Adelphia, where the gods lived in Greek mythology. You were watching one god after another come down to play shows and you could sit there and soak it up." At the Allan Block Sandal Shop—the leading destination for handmade sandals in the Village and also an impromptu performance space for pickers who had to leave Washington Square Park by a certain time—Sebastian would watch as Delta bluesman Son House transformed from subdued to raving after a few drinks. When the blues artists would come to town, some would stay at the Broadway Central Hotel, on Broadway and West Fourth Street, and retreat to their rooms for parties after their shows. Sebastian and John Hammond (Jr.) both found themselves in Hopkins's room as one party was underway. "It was very wild times," Hammond said. "Guys would get really drunk and there were all kinds of scenes. It was crazy."

For those fledgling musicians, it was hard to determine how the blues players, some under-recognized before the folk and blues revival, felt about playing to largely white audiences in coffeehouses and clubs in downtown New York. Some were honored, others not so much. "There were guys who were like fish out of water, like 'What am I doing here?'" said Hammond. "Son House was a little recalcitrant. Lightnin' Hopkins was full of himself and wanted to be a big star. It was the whole gamut." Others were seemingly happy to be out of the South. Patrick Sky and his girlfriend, Lucy Brown Karwoski, got to know Hurt, whose career had languished before he was rediscovered by the folk-festival crowd. Walking down MacDougal Street with him one day, Karwoski noticed Hurt continually turning around and looking behind him.

When she asked why he was doing that, he told her that if he were walking with a white woman in the South, someone would likely grab and lynch him.

As the name accidentally implied, the Blues Project comprised students enamored of a style of music far removed from their own backgrounds. But to their credit, they didn't attempt to mimic the vocal styles. "Danny didn't do anything just by rote," said Terri Thal. "He put himself into the music. He could adapt arrangements well and intelligently. If he did blues, he never tried to sound like an old Black man from Mississippi or Georgia or Alabama. He never tried to sound like anybody but himself."

The same gradually became true for the band as a whole, which was aiming to expand on the music they all loved. Kalb would later tell an interviewer, "Our idea is to combine the emotion of the blues with the power of the rock band. Naturally we take advantage of all the new electronic musical resources." Kalb didn't use the effects increasingly common to guitarists, opting for a clean sound, but his fingers clambered all over the fretboard during solos, adding a loose, almost psychedelic edge to his notes. Although he was using a cheap Farfisa organ, Kooper pulled squeals and squeaks from its keyboard. Flanders's delivery was more garage-rock Jagger than ersatz Delta blues, and Blumenfeld's rhythms had the looseness of jazz. When one of Blumenfeld's drum pedals broke at an Au Go Go show, Katz filled the time between repairs by playing "Catch the Wind," the forlorn ballad by Scottish singer-songwriter Donovan that became a regular part of their repertoire—and another sign that they were stretching the definition of a so-called blues band.

Signaling how the music business was now eyeing the electric Village, the Blues Project soon found itself with a record contract. MGM Records wasn't a player like Atlantic or Columbia (which had passed on the band), but its roster included the Animals, Herman's Hermits, and Roy Orbison; the Lovin' Spoonful was part of its Kama Sutra subsidiary. The company soon after launched two separate labels, Verve Forecast and, with Folkways' Moses Asch, Verve Folkways; the Blues Project was signed to the latter.

Capitalizing on the roots-music rumble, Verve Folkways, working with *Cavalier* magazine, assembled what it called the "Blues Bag," four nights at the Cafe Au Go Go starting November 24, 1965. The lineups brought together authentic blues acts (John Lee Hooker, Bukka White, T-Bone Walker) with Village troubadours (Eric Andersen, Fred Neil, David Blue); the Blues Project would close out each night. With an eye toward using the Blues Project's sets for their first release for the company, MGM recorded each night. The streets were now teeming: as Blumenfeld would remember, the recording engineer for those nights kept his machines in a van parked outside the Au Go Go, with his German shepherd standing guard. Kooper would later admit to being embarrassed that Black musicians so much more seasoned and iconic would open for the Blues Project.

In an optimistically titled story "Blues-Rock Gains Foothold," *Billboard* reported that the Blues Project had been "signed by Verve Folkways in a move by the label to strengthen its singles image." In January 1966, in keeping with that plan, the label rolled out the first Blues Project 45: their cover of Andersen's "Violets of Dawn," which *Billboard* enthused had "possibilities for a smash folk-rocker." Unfortunately, there was a glitch: "Violets of Dawn" featured Flanders, who was no longer in the band.

Kalb felt that Flanders's delivery, especially on a rave-up version of Bo Diddley's pummeling "Who Do You Love," was "fucking fantastic, monumental—a monster." But as the band would tell it, Flanders had a persuasive girlfriend who demanded that his name precede the band's and also urged him to start his own career. "She said, 'You don't need these guys, this backup band,'" Kalb recalled. "Me, a backup band!" Matters came to a head in the first week of January 1966, when MGM flew the Blues Project to Los Angeles for the label's annual sales convention to introduce them to its staff. The band played at a company party, was invited to a screening of *Dr. Zhivago* (MGM had the rights to the soundtrack), and was wined and dined. According to the band, Flanders informed them he wasn't going to pitch in to help buy new gear for them because he was the singer and didn't *have* any equipment. Accounts vary about whether Flanders quit (as Kalb would remember) or was fired (as Katz and Kooper maintained). Either way, Kalb would describe Flanders's exit from the band as "great and sad at the same time."

Without its front man, the Blues Project carried on. Starting in January 1966, it became, in essence, the house band at the Cafe Au Go Go, playing roughly once a month, several days in a row each time. The arrangement was especially beneficial in the wake of Flanders's departure. MGM had concerns about releasing an album featuring a singer who was now out of the band. With Kooper and Katz stepping up as occasional lead singers along with Kalb, the Blues Project recorded more songs at the Au Go Go, saving themselves and their record contract.

When it was released a few months later, *Live at the Cafe Au Go Go* could or should have been a train wreck. On the cover, the venue name was larger than "The Blues Project." The words "Featuring Tommy Flanders," in an even smaller font, practically proclaimed that the Blues Project was not what it once was. At times the sound quality was so thin that the album sounded as if were emerging from a tinny car radio, not a stereo system. "You Go and I'll Go with You," a loose shuffle, seemed more like a practice tape than a fully developed performance.

Still, no record of the moment captured the thrill and potential of the new, gone-electric Village more than the Blues Project's debut. The array of genres on it—troubadour folk, Chicago and Delta blues, primal rock and roll—reflected what could be heard throughout the Bleecker and MacDougal vicinity. But the Blues Project took each style, put it through their collective mincer, and emerged with something all their own. With Kalb's voice taking on a more sensuous moan, "Alberta" was more seductive than his previous rendering with the New Strangers. Thanks to Flanders's borderline salacious delivery, the band's take on Willie Dixon's "Back Door Man" approached the Howlin' Wolf version as much as a bunch of white kids from the suburbs ever could. Andersen's "Violets of Dawn" and Donovan's "Catch the Wind" rocked the folk, rather than the other way around. Kalb's guitar scraped and wailed, Katz's harmonica chugged, and Kooper's organ lurched the song into the present. Coming across green but hungry, they sounded as if they were ready to conquer the block, the whole neighborhood, and maybe the rest of the world.

In the Village Vanguard's kitchen one evening, Herbie Hancock and drummer Tony Williams began goofing around with a martial-arts routine. Onstage was Charles Mingus, who finished his set and walked into the kitchen. Mingus remained an imposing presence—the Van Ronk of jazz, in some regards, although Van Ronk was nowhere near as volatile—and Hancock sensed that aura as Mingus stood behind him. To his relief, Mingus backed off. "He said, 'I ain't gonna fuck with those guys—they're doing some karate shit,'" Hancock recalled. "I looked at Tony and we were amazed: 'Wow—Charles Mingus is afraid of *us*.'"

They were all united in a sense of fearlessness. The middle of the sixties would be among the most electrifying in jazz history, and the Village was one of its central hubs. As a kid from Brooklyn, Gary Giddins had ventured into the Village and witnessed Dylan at Folk City and Phil Ochs and Son House on separate nights at the Gaslight; he'd also bought copies of *Sing Out!* at the Folklore Center. But his mind was suitably blown when he discovered jazz. At the beginning of his senior year in high school, Giddins borrowed a friend's ID to get into the Vanguard, which became a second home to him; he even asked his father to take him there for his eighteenth birthday. One night Miles Davis didn't show up with the rest of his second quintet, and the audience stood up to leave, as if they'd heard that a stand-in would be performing at a Broadway show. But Giddins stayed and heard Hancock, Williams, Wayne Shorter, and Ron Carter playing on their own, which was staggering in itself. On a subsequent evening when Davis did make it, he passed Giddins on the left side, near the piano, and extinguished his cigarette in the ashtray on Giddins's table. "Keep this, kid," Davis said. "Someday it'll be worth something."

The offerings were overwhelming during the summer of 1965 alone: Mingus at the Village Gate, John Coltrane and Thelonious Monk at the same venue, Sonny Rollins and Cecil Taylor at the Vanguard. One weekend in August, one could have chosen between Rollins at the Vanguard, Monk and flautist Herbie Mann at the Village Gate, and a jam session at the Vanguard that brought together Shorter, Roland Kirk, Max Roach, Freddie Hubbard, and Clark Terry. On a double bill with Coleman Hawkins at the Vanguard, Rollins, who was into the fourth year of his return to performing, began with a forty-five-minute version of "Take the A Train"; for the second set, he emerged, in typically dramatic fashion, from the kitchen at the back of the club.

Much like rock and roll, jazz was pushing the boundaries once again. Hancock's thematic *Maiden Voyage* was inspired by the sounds of the ocean and conjured that mood with his fluid interaction with members of the Davis band. Coltrane, who regularly played the Village during this time, recorded *Ascension*, its two forty-minute improvisations wandering even further out. But there were implications that came along with all this innovation. Jazz was growing so experimental that it threatened to alienate some of its audience, and rock players were dipping their toes into improvisation, potentially luring some away from jazz and toward the epic jams of bands like Cream and, starting nationally in 1967, the Grateful Dead. The consequences of that shift in jazz were exhilarating but still unknown.

By early 1966, the West Village coffeehouse world had become so overexposed that it was ripe for an entire book of spoofs. *From the Folk Bag*, by Brooklyn artist and musician Marcus Uzilevsky (but credited to Ry Cooper), took merciless aim at the voguishness of the Village. In one cartoon, a white guitar player was seated on a couch in a living room, surrounded by an attentive group of men and women: "Yeah! This is a song I wrote last night when I was down an' out in Greenwich Village!" he told them. In another, two young men were huddled in a railroad boxcar, one saying to another: "Man, this is not the fun like it sounded in that song you used to sing back on McDougal [*sic*] street."

But those jokes already seemed dated, as more and more folk acts in the area opted for amplified instruments and rock and roll. The same year the Lovin' Spoonful started at the Night Owl, the Magicians, a quartet that emerged from an interracial pop and doo-wop band called Tex and the Chex, also played there, and Columbia put out a single of theirs, "An Invitation to Cry." But the Spoonful loomed large, and now on a national level. After "Do You Believe in Magic," the Spoonful had returned to the Night Owl once more in the fall of 1965. But after they landed three more hits in the Top 10—the bubbly "You Didn't Have to Be So Nice," the sauntering "Daydream," and the winsome "Did You Ever Have to Make Up Your

Mind?"—they were swept up in national touring and promotion. They never played the Bleecker Street circuit again.

Another band that succeeded the Spoonful at the Night Owl, the Blues Magoos, was several more rattling steps removed from owner Joe Marra's original vision for the club. According to Peppy Castro, the band's uptown-raised singer and guitarist, Marra was less than supportive when the band made its own leap from primitive rock to indulgent psychedelia. That transition was egged on by a tape-delay machine that accidentally fell off the stage, emitting a godforsaken screech that became part of their act. "We were starting to do freakouts," Castro said, "and Joe comes up to us and says, 'It's too loud. If you play this fucking music like this, you're out of here.'" The band was ultimately fired for the racket—much like another band getting its sea legs in the Village that same year. Booked into the Cafe Bizarre just before Christmas 1965, the Velvet Underground was hardly folk or folk rock or anything easily definable. Their one show was notable for their future mentor Andy Warhol seeing them for the first time and drummer Maureen Tucker not being allowed to play her instrument due to owner Rick Allmen's objections; they were promptly fired.

In keeping with Sebastian and Kalb, many other folk musicians were eager to relegate their acoustic guitar to a closet and go electric. Perry Miller, a silky-voiced singer and guitarist who'd attended the same Queens, New York, elementary school as Art Garfunkel, had transformed into Jesse Colin Young after college in Ohio and then New York University. Until that point, his exposure to Greenwich Village amounted to the times his mother dragged him there for her dental appointments. Dropping out of NYU, he took a railroad apartment across the street from the Five Spot, where he once saw Thelonious Monk lingering outside. He eventually began working the basket houses and recorded an album, *Soul of a City Boy*. By then, he had changed his name, based on Old West outlaws Jesse James and Cole Younger and race-car driver Colin Chapman. Playing in Boston, he met another like-minded singer and guitarist, Jerry Corbitt, who introduced him to musician Lowell "Banana" Levinger and a drummer, Joe Bauer. Inspired by Paul McCartney, Young decided he would sing and play bass.

Moving en masse to New York, the musicians named themselves the Young-bloods and landed an early job at Folk City, where the club was so unprepared for amplified music, and the stage so small, that Levinger and his electric piano had to be set up in the audience. But whether they were taking a crack at Blind Willie McTell's stomping "Statesboro Blues" or Young's originals, they sounded like few other bands in the Village. Young's sweet, sometimes churlish voice was balanced by Corbitt's tough, snarling guitar, Bauer's locked-in drums, and Levinger's piano and velvety guitar parts.

In the spring of 1966, the Youngbloods were booked into the Cafe Au Go Go, where they were able to rehearse in the afternoons when the Blues Project wasn't doing the same. There, the Youngbloods heard the song that would eventually rewire their lives. A gentle tune espousing brotherhood, "Let's Get Together," written by Dino Valenti under the name Chet Powers, had been kicking around for a bit; the Kingston Trio had recorded a version in 1964. At the Au Go Go, either Young alone or the band together, depending on who relayed the story, heard Buzzy Linhart singing it. "I felt the heavens open," Young said. "I knew. I felt instantly that I had found something that would be a key to my path forward. I felt my life change." Even though at least one recording was on the market, Young asked Linhart to write down the lyrics and, in teaching it to himself later, tweaked the melody. With the Youngbloods, the song, now called "Get Together," went electric, complete with Levinger's spiraling guitar solo.

Even Kalb's sibling was swept up in the change. Like the brother three years older than him, Jonathan Kalb had gravitated toward music making at an early age, starting with classical piano before shifting to guitar and making his way to Washington Square Park, where he was stunned to see Lightnin' Hopkins behind him. He too had paid Van Ronk for guitar lessons, marveling at how his playing was poignant in its simplicity, and he also enrolled in the University of Wisconsin. In the summer of 1966, just before the start of his senior year, Jonathan, nineteen, returned to New York, now playing more electric guitar than acoustic. The entire scene struck him as so different from the one he'd left a few years ago, when he would watch Erik Darling play banjo in the park. "You still had some of the same places, like the Kettle of Fish," he said, "but all of a sudden it had changed dramatically."

During a jam session at the Cafe Au Go Go, Jonathan was approached by Ed Sanders, poet, writer, and owner of the iconoclastic Peace Eye bookstore on East Tenth Street. Sanders was also the cofounder (with Tuli Kupferberg) of the Fugs, the anarchist band that melded guttural rock, near-psychedelic folk, and lyrics that veered from tender to raunchy to politically subversive. Peter Stampfel and Steve Weber of the Holy Modal Rounders had been early members, and the Fugs had shared a bill at the Au Go Go with the Blues Project. The Fugs, too, were being monitored by the FBI for their "four-letter filth words," as one letter to the Bureau complained. Bringing their Lower East Side rock performance art to the Village, the Fugs rented out the Players Theatre, next to the Cafe Wha? on MacDougal. In need of a guitarist, Sanders asked Kalb, still a college student, to become the band's musical director, and the guitarist was soon adding musical muscle to the Fugs' verbal mayhem and parodies. Keith Richards and actress Kim Novak were among the stars spotted in the crowd.

When the band took breaks, a Black guitarist playing next door at the Wha? would talk with Kalb about effects boxes, like the fuzz box Kalb used on his guitar. Then going by the name Jimmy James, he was fronting a band called the Blue Flames and burrowing deep into the music and vibe of the Village after having been a sideman for the Isley Brothers, Curtis Knight, and others. That same guitarist, who was about to change his name to Jimi Hendrix, was playing songs from John Hammond (Jr.)'s album, and Hammond went over to the Cafe Wha? to see him. Soon after, he was playing behind Hammond at the Au Go Go.

Lenny Kaye, a student at Rutgers College who was writing music reviews for his college paper, attended a blues night at the Au Go Go and watched Hammond introduce someone he called Jimmy James. "The guy comes out and starts doing all these tricks, biting the guitar and playing behind his head," he recalled. Kaye had seen the Blues Project, Richie Havens, and others. But here was a musician taking his art to another level—and another instance of the Village as that incubator of change.

∎∎∎∎∎

In the summer of 1966, the Blues Project had just finished a four-night run at the Cafe Au Go Go, but to a guy in a pirate hat outside the club, something was off. "These teenagers have spoiled everything," he told UPI writer Aline Mosby. "City Hall sent cops from the riot squad down here. They have submachine guns in their trunks."

During the pre-electrified days in the Village, Dave Van Ronk would situate himself in front of the Gaslight and watch the same people walking back and forth on MacDougal Street. With each passing year, the escalation of street traffic was noticeable. In the summer of 1965, the *Chicago Tribune* was lamenting how "Greenwich Village every weekend turns out to be like Times Square on New Year's Eve." Twelve months later, the situation had grown even more suffocating. "Oh, we're from the Bronx," a young woman—dressed, along with her friends, in "fashionable printed cotton suits"—told one reporter as they stood in front of the Cafe Figaro. "Everybody comes to the Village now." Runaways were also beginning to flock to the area, and one of the regular and respected beat cops, Jimmy Byrnes, would guide some of them to the Cafe Au Go Go for ice cream and sodas. Some eventually landed work as waitresses there.

The corner of MacDougal and West Third Street became a particularly overrun intersection, thanks partly to the Night Owl and its street-level configuration. "You could look in the window and see people play," said the Blues Magoos' Peppy Castro. "That corner was packed. You couldn't move." Milling about outside of clubs like the Night Owl, the young men, with their long hair, flowered shirts, pinstriped bell bottoms, and chinos, wanted desperately to resemble a Beatle or a Rolling Stone; with their kohl-rimmed eyes, the women looked like clones of Cher, who had become a pop star along with her husband, Sonny, in L.A.

With the influx, new aromas began to linger in the air. "The smell of piss was all over," said the Blue Project's Steve Katz. "It went from a nice Italian neighborhood with folk music to this goofy, crazy thing, all these kids who wanted to go into the Village and see what the fuss was about. And the fuss was rock and roll." Van Ronk would later tell writer Mike Jahn that stern measures were sometimes required. "We used to have to defend our old ladies," he said. "The crowd I used to hang around with, everyone carried a knife. Those clods would come and assume that every 'beatnik' girl would go to bed with anybody."

The influx of tourists, along with wealthier sorts, was starting to drive less financially secure artists to the East Village, where a loft could be rented for as little as $40 a month. When a publicist set up an interview on WOR radio for his client Art D'Lugoff of the Village Gate, he sent along a list of "suggested topics" to the station that included "changes in taste and entertainment: the electronic revolution" and "expansion to the East Village due to high-rise apartments and NYU aggrandizement making inexpensive living in old Greenwich Village a myth. Creative writers, artists, et. al. can no longer afford the old Village."

The pirate in front of the Au Go Go may have exaggerated the hordes of law enforcement, but the teens and twenty-somethings swarming the Village streets did make for a sizable and viable market for drug dealers, and the police presence shot up accordingly. In March 1966 the city's mayor, John Lindsay, announced a sweeping plan to clean up both the Village and Times Square. On March 24, officers disguised as beatniks—complete with pins attached to their coats that trumpeted legalizing drugs—slipped into the Village. After scoping out the streets around Bleecker and MacDougal, the undercovers went into action and, by midafternoon, had arrested twenty people for sales of heroin, pot (including one dealer with ten thousand dollars' worth on him), barbiturates, and weapons; another dealer had weed, a gun, and a teenage runaway in his apartment. A month later, a new play, *Wait Until Dark*, opened on Broadway, and suddenly its plot—burglars breaking into a West Village apartment to steal fifty thousand dollars' worth of heroin that was hidden there—didn't seem so far-fetched. A doorman at the Cafe Wha? was busted for weed when police walked by the club, smelled the telltale aroma, and chased him down the street before collaring him.

In June 1966 the *Village Voice* published an account of "teenage hopheads" lured to MacDougal Street for heroin and amphetamines. Several months later, detectives swooped into the midtown apartment of Harvey Backer, a mysterious writer who slept in a coffin and was on the verge of selling fifteen pounds of heroin and pot to Village-bound teens. Crime was even impinging on the Folklore Center. When Izzy Young and Jack Prelutsky, another fledgling guitarist and Van Ronk student (and future poet and author) who began working at the store a year after it opened, would take a break to play chess in the back room, several times someone grabbed an instrument right out of the window and dashed away.

The availability of first-rate weed and speed was an aphrodisiac to musicians on many levels. To Mitch Blank, Danny Kalb would recall the night in 1966 when Dylan—"on speed or something," he said—came by Kalb's apartment with David Blue and talked for several hours, almost nonstop, about his parents and upbringing in Minnesota. Bob Neuwirth would make his way to the Village to obtain the quality weed he'd heard about. To make ends meet during his pre–Lovin' Spoonful days, John Sebastian would sell pot. "You're buying a shot glass of pot that had been through a fucking grinder so the seeds are in it," he said. "But it was the social exchange, too."

The harder drugs infiltrating the community were affecting the musicians in far worse ways. Tim Hardin soon became the scene's most chilling example of addiction. When Hardin would appear at the Night Owl, often late, he'd ask Marra for two dollars for a taxi. "No cab," Marra noted later. "Heroin." During one rehearsal for a recording, Sebastian, who was backing him on harmonica, watched Hardin casually shoot up as he was instructing Sebastian on the song they were about to learn. Erik Jacobsen's apartment on MacDougal, next door to Sebastian's, was the place where Hardin would shoot up. ("Oh, no, it's Tim," Jacobsen would say to his visiting friend, musician, and photographer Henry Diltz when he'd look through the peephole and see Hardin on the other side.) One night at the Cafe Au Go Go, Hardin went onstage, after a lengthy delay, with a fresh needle mark evident on his arm.

No one denied Hardin's talent, especially as it was heard on *Tim Hardin 1*. Here was someone equally at home with ballads as fragile and delicate as rose petals and blues that were cocky and swaggering—someone who could compose as pained a song as "Reason to Believe" and slip effortlessly into the role of a "Smugglin' Man." Not intent on re-creating his songs live, Hardin would play with the phrasing, lending him the feel of a jazz singer. "As weird as it was, the heroin and all, there was a core of something I was getting from this guy," Sebastian said. "It was a singular vibe, the combination of his skills and the heroin. That was what made it like Ray Charles." But it didn't make Hardin any easier to deal with. When Hardin and the Youngbloods shared a bill uptown, Levinger returned to the band's dressing room and found his guitar missing. Jesse Colin Young assumed Hardin had taken it to sell it for drug money. At a subsequent Village show, Hardin showed up with Levinger's guitar, and Levinger merely took it back without question, but the incident was just a reminder of how challenging it was to cope with Hardin.

Heroin also engulfed the lead singer of the band that took up a residency at the Night Owl after the Lovin' Spoonful had moved on. James Taylor had arrived in the city in the summer of 1966 with mental-health issues. As a teenager growing up in North Carolina, he'd dealt with depression as well as his father's alcoholism, and, after dropping out of high school, had spent part of the previous year and into 1966 at McLean, the psychiatric hospital in Massachusetts. Taylor had already begun making music in North Carolina and at the Martha's Vineyard home where his family summered; there he met a fellow guitarist and sparkplug, Danny Kortchmar. Ten months into his stint at McLean, Taylor reconnected with Kortchmar, who was now in New York and forming a band. Taylor bailed on the hospital by telling the staff he was simply moving "heavier stuff" out of his room, when in fact he was the one leaving.

Kortchmar was initially thinking of calling their band the James Taylor Group: his friend was clearly the lead singer, and the British band Spencer Davis Group was on a roll. Instead, they settled on the Flying Machine. Despite little in the way of performance experience, they were hired by Marra to play several sets an evening at the Night Owl, for $12 a night; at least once they were also booked into Folk City, opening for bluesman Lonnie Johnson. The band worked out the songs Taylor had written, including one, "Knockin' Round the Zoo," about his time at McLean, and "Steamroller," a parody of the young, white blues singers gravitating to the Village. "Their idea of soul was to crank up the volume on the amplifiers their parents bought 'em," Taylor told writer Susan Braudy a few years later. "They were all singing these heavy blues numbers that sounded really pretentious in their mouths." Revealing Taylor's appreciation for prerock standards, the Flying Machine also assayed Hoagy Carmichael's "Baltimore Oriole."

But even with his parents paying the rent for his Upper West Side apartment, Manhattan was jarring for Taylor, who was eighteen and couldn't say no to anyone, from dealers to runaways who wanted to crash in his home. Before long, he'd begun using heroin. His family predilection for addiction played a part, as did the nights he would crash in Washington Square Park, where savvy dealers would descend on him. One day Taylor came into the Night Owl carrying a crutch. Marra naturally asked if he'd injured his foot, but Taylor answered no, he hadn't, but he'd found the crutch and thought he might "need it someday." Realizing he had a problem, Taylor called his father in North Carolina, who drove up to the city and walked into the Night Owl looking for his son; when he found him, he brought James back home to recuperate. The Flying Machine, which soon crashed, left behind a tape of their songs, one of which, "Night Owl," was written in honor of their residency.

In an advice column in a Pennsylvania newspaper, a young woman wrote in to confess that her new boyfriend was urging her to move to the Village. The move felt like an important escape: her family was in turmoil, and her mother was coming home drunk most nights. But the columnist warned her against the plan. "Young love in the Village may sound romantic, but it can be deadly—and perhaps you'll be the unlucky one who ends up dead," she wrote. "The Village environs are where the drugs are and these don't just stop with weak 'tea.'"

It was yet another fraught night at the Kettle of Fish, but this time it didn't involve Ochs, Andersen, or Van Ronk, but rather the Blues Project. According to Kalb, Dylan had wanted Al Kooper to join his band for a European tour that summer of 1966. Given that Kooper's organ had become a recognizable part of Dylan's sound, it was hard to blame Dylan for asking. But the Blues Project convinced Kooper to stick with them, and as Kalb later recalled, Dylan had a tense exchange at the Kettle with Blues Project manager Jeff Chase. During one of the band's gigs at the Cafe Au Go Go, Katz then watched as Dylan and David Blue heckled them from the audience; he assumed they were irked that Kooper hadn't taken Dylan up on his offer. "At that time, we thought we were the bees' knees," Kalb told Mitch Blank. "He was Bob Dylan, okay, but we thought we could be the new Rolling Stones, or something. It goes to your head sometimes, especially if you're 23 years old."

Whether the Blues Project would ever rise to the level of the Stones was uncertain. In spite of MGM's hopes, neither of their singles—"Violets of Dawn," followed by "I Wanna Be Your Driver"—made it anywhere near AM radio playlists, and *Live at the Cafe Au Go Go* sold a respectable, but not chart-crashing, twenty thousand copies in its first few months. As Kooper would recall, the band members weren't always greeted like conquering heroes when they ventured outside of the Village; parts of the rest of the country treated them like freaks, booed, and hurled things at them. They were making a living but just barely. Each member had a weekly salary of between $115 and $123. For a week's run at the Au Go Go that summer, the band was paid a total of $1,500.

But their reputation, both in the city and beyond, was growing, and their peers were taking notice. In July 1966 the band shared a bill at the Cafe Au Go Go with the Paul Butterfield Blues Band. To Kalb's relief, the notoriously critical Butterfield gave them his seal of approval. "The second night, Butterfield comes around drunk and says to me, 'We heard your guys were pussies, but you're not—you can really play,'" Kalb said. "To hear that from Paul, one of the greatest musicians ever, was very important to us." During a two-band jam on the third night, Kalb and Mike Bloomfield, the Butterfield band's own guitar hero, found themselves in an impromptu duel. "Then God reached down, I kid you not," Kalb said. "And for reasons not known to me or anyone, the two bands break into 'When the Saints Go Marching In,' as an instrumental. It was su-*poib*!"

The band's increasing bravado and confidence would play out in the making of its second record. "We're never satisfied with our sound," Kalb told a reporter while promoting *Live at the Cafe Au Go Go*. "Our next one is going to be even better. Live albums in a club such as our first one can't match a good studio sound." When the group assembled in New York and Los Angeles to

Lionel Kilberg and his homemade Brownie bass (complete with miniature fire hydrant in honor of his dog) at a Washington Square Park jamboree, 1955. *Graphic House/Archive Photos/Getty Images*

ave Van Ronk, portrait of the blues singer as a young man, late '50s. *Ronald D. Cohen Collection, South- n Folklife Collection, the Wilson Library, University of North Carolina at Chapel Hill*

Miles Davis during one of several engagements at the Village Vanguard in 1958, the year he released and recorded *Milestones*. *Dennis Stock/Magnum Photos*

Poet Dick Woods exiting the Gaslight Poetry Cafe, February 1959, shortly after John Mitchell had converted the space to a hangout for poets and writers. *Bettmann Archive/Getty Images*

"Beat Poets, Jazz, Crazy Bongos, Congos" (or should that be "congas"?) and "Live Beatniks" at the newly opened Cafe Wha?, May 1960, six months before Bob Dylan made his first appearance there. *Bettmann Archive/Getty Images*

Izzy Young and protesters at the start of what would become the calamitous, so-called "beatnik riot" in Washington Square Park, April 1961. *Dick Kraus/Newsday RM/Getty Images*

The inimitable Nina Simone confronts the camera and her makeup table in her dressing room at the Vi lage Vanguard, late '50s. *Sam Falk/The New York Times Co./Getty Images*

Judy Collins at one of her earliest Gerde's Folk City shows, 1961. *Courtesy Irwin Gooen Collection*

John Lee Hooker at Gerde's Folk City, circa 1961, the same year one of his opening acts was Bob Dylan.
Courtesy Irwin Gooen Collection

Mark Spoelstra and Bob Dylan warming up in the downstairs dressing room at Gerde's Folk City, November 1961. *Ted Russell/Polaris*

Dave Van Ronk and the Ragtime Jug Stompers at the Village Vanguard, November 1963. *Left to right:* Kornfeld, Van Ronk (taking a solo on a glass bottle), and Danny Kalb. *Jack Kanthal/AP Images*

ter, Paul and Mary at the Bitter End, 1962, in an outtake from Bernard Cole's photo shoot for their
st album. *Michael Ochs Archives/Getty Images*

The New World Singers, 1962. *Left to right:* Gil Turner (with banjo), Happy Traum, Delores Dixon, and Bob Cohen. *Maurice Seymour for Prestige International Records*

Eric Andersen and Phil Ochs trading melodies on a Village stoop, 1964. *Kai Shuman/Michael Ochs Archives/Getty Images*

Bob Dylan and Suze Rotolo during their stroll up and down Jones Street on the *Freewheelin' Bob Dylan* cover shoot, early 1963. *Don Hunstein*

Tom Paxton ponders life and another possible song in a Village coffeehouse, August 1964. *David Gah Getty Images*

Len Chandler and Bob Dylan at the 1964 Newport Folk Festival. © *Jim Marshall Photography LLC*

rowds converge upon the Cafe Au Go Go, September 1965, for one of the "Blues Bag" shows featuring ie Blues Project, Eric Andersen, and others. John Hammond, Jr., in boots, center left. *Don Paulsen/ lichael Ochs Archives/Getty Images*

he original lineup of the Blues Project on a Village street to promote its early Cafe Au Go Go shows,)ecember 1965. *Left to right:* Danny Kalb, Andy Kulberg, Tommy Flanders, Al Kooper, Steve Katz, Roy lumenfeld. *Kai Shuman/Michael Ochs Archives/Getty Images*

Paul Jacobs, Christopher Guest, Chevy Chase, and John Belushi rehearse for *National Lampoon's Lemmings* at the Village Gate, 1973. *Michael Gold/Getty Images*

Rob Stoner, Joan Baez, Bob Dylan, and Eric Andersen at the loose and unexpectedly dramatic Mik Porco sixty-first birthday gathering, Folk City, October 1975. *Fred W. McDarrah/MUUS Collection Getty Images*

Willie Nelson and band joined by *Saturday Night Live*'s Gilda Radner and Bill Murray for a typically animated evening at the Lone Star Cafe, 1980. *Stephanie Chernikowski/Michael Ochs Archives/Getty Images*

Maggie, Suzzy, and Terre Roche gear up their harmonies as they prepare for the release of their first trio album, 1978. *Irene Young*

The next generation gathers in front of Folk City, circa 1981. *From left:* Lucy Kaplansky, Rod MacDonald, Gerry Devine, Martha P. Hogan, Tom Intondi, Jack Hardy, Bill Bachmann; *bottom,* David Massengill. *Brian Rose*

Suzanne Vega during her Folk City and Speak Easy era, New York City, 1982. *Irene Young*

make its first album of studio material, Kalb's prediction came true. *Projections*, as it would be called, didn't simply move the band beyond the genre in its name. Reflecting the varied influences of each member, the album aimed to show that the Blues Project was arguably the most versatile band to emerge from the Village.

Blues were represented, of course. For an Elektra compilation dubbed *What's Shakin'*, Kooper had remade "Lord I Just Can't Keep from Crying," a traditional gospel tune, into "I Can't Keep from Crying Sometimes." With the Blues Project, especially Kalb's guitar, the song shook off its roots and became a brooding psychedelic shuffle. There was folk rock: Kooper's jangling "Fly Away" resulted from the breakup of his first marriage, and Katz contributed a song originally called "Twelfth of December," which started like a medieval madrigal before blossoming into a pained song about his relationship with Mimi Fariña, Joan Baez's sister and a singer herself. When the label asked Chase for the title of the song as the record was about to get pressed, he replied, "What song? You mean Steve's song?" To Katz's chagrin, "Steves Song," complete with a missing apostrophe, became the title. Kooper had also been hooked on a lick at the end of a number by jazz guitarist Barney Kessel and turned it into "Flute Thing," which had elements of jazz but also a swirling solo from Kalb. Kulberg had drilled a hole in his flute, adding an echoplex and also connecting it to a fuzz pedal. "Andy invented the electric flute," said Kalb. "He put it through an amp so you could make it faster or slower. When he played 'Flute Thing,' he could play three lines at the same time. It was fucking weird and amazing."

About fifteen years earlier, Muddy Waters had recorded "Still a Fool," whose narrator grappled with an illicit affair and, in general, felt out of control and directionless. In 1966 Butterfield and his band recast it as a frisky romp now called "Two Trains Running." Now, on *Projections*, the song was more dramatically reinvented. Kalb clearly related to something in its lyrics (Kooper would remember that Kalb's apartment, which had a hot plate for a stove, was enough to give anyone the blues). The Blues Project transformed the song into a dramatic, personalized epic, with peaks and valleys that lent it the feel of a manic-depressive episode set to a slow-burning blues.

The song became a breathtaking peak of their sets and a spotlight for Kalb. "Danny was an amazing guitar player," Kooper said. "His technical facility was amazing. He could do anything. He was more original than [Mike] Bloom-field. He took more chances than Bloomfield." In the studio, though, the song nearly went off the rails. The band was deep into what felt like a nearly perfect take when, Blumenfeld recalled, "all of a sudden there was this really strange pause." A string on Kalb's guitar went out of tune by a half tone, but as the band continued to play, he retuned it, turning that glitch into a phrase all its own, and slid back into the song. The moment was preserved in the version heard on *Projections*.

But beneath the bravado, the band was starting to disintegrate. They fired Chase and hired Sid Bernstein, the promoter and impresario who had booked the Beatles into both Carnegie Hall and Shea Stadium. Onstage, the compet-itive drive between Kooper and Kalb became noticeable. "They were both so *loud*," Katz said. "Al would go up the high keys on the piano and Danny would be screaming [on the guitar] and they would be fighting each other. It was like the Punch and Judy show. Roy and I would look at each other like, 'Oh, my God.'" With his fondness for flowery shirts and a taxi-driver hat, Kooper was also the most fashionably flamboyant of the bunch.

Because Kalb was seeing a psychiatrist, the apparent solution was a group-therapy session with the shrink, Arthur Eaton, at his Park Avenue office. Eaton was, to say the least, progressive—he brought a joint to the session to loosen everyone up—and they all let out their issues with one another. As they left, they realized that it was effective but perhaps too much so: if they had another session, the band could fall apart.

Kooper and Kalb's clashes weren't centered only on volume. Around them, debate continued to rage about whether Village musicians should be authentic and pure or aim for pop crossover. A variation of that argument played out in a feud between Izzy Young and Robert Shelton, who appeared to have noth-ing but disdain for each other. One particularly testy dustup began in January 1966, when Shelton published a *Times* roundup of "folk-rock" albums—the latest from Dylan, Judy Collins, the Byrds, and others—and called it a "healthy movement." A few weeks later, in response, the newspaper ran what it called a

"Folk-Rock Symposium" including letters from *Sing Out!*'s Irwin Silber, writer Nat Hentoff, and Paul Nelson, the opinionated editor of the folk magazine *Little Sandy Review*. Notably, Silber called Shelton's piece a "self-conscious apologia" and the genre "a Tin Pan Alley gimmick."

In a letter to Howard Klein, the music editor at the *Times*, Young went even further, questioning Shelton's folk knowledge and accusing him of being compromised by writing liner notes for albums. "Now that they call it 'folk-rock,'" Young wrote, "the Negro is easily separated from rock and roll and Mr. Shelton can write paeans to all the white imitators and ignore every Negro group as he did" in his roundup. In a seven-page letter he sent to Young, Silber, and Hentoff, along with Albert Grossman and Pete Seeger, Shelton responded that he had considered suing Young for libel. But upon realizing it could financially ruin the Folklore Center, he decided against it and instead offered to put up a hundred dollars toward what he called Young's mental-health care.

When it came to the bands on the scene, the Blues Project most embodied the choice between purism and the pop charts. "There was always a battle for control between Danny and Al," said Katz. "Danny was very stubborn, a purist in those days. Al had to have everything his way. It was about Kooper's ego and Danny's intransigence." Nor was Kooper alone: the band took notice when the Youngbloods, their peers at the Cafe Au Go Go, scored a minor hit with their first single, a jaunty jug-band rocker called "Grizzly Bear." "We were jealous of that," Blumenfeld said. "We didn't have a tune like that. We tried." *Projections*, which Verve Folkways released in late 1966, also suffered from its occasionally guitar-pick-thin sound: the band had been allotted only a few hours of studio time at a time, depending on which of MGM's other acts wasn't working.

With his background in Top 40 and his fascination with horns and rococo arrangements, Kooper was eager to expand the group's palette, and he wrote two songs expressly constructed to be pop hits, "Where There's Smoke, There's Fire" and "No Time like the Right Time." The gambit almost worked—the latter peaked at 96 on the *Billboard* Top 100. The band even hired Emmaretta Marks, a Black waitress at the Au Go Go, to sing with them on "Where There's Smoke, There's Fire." Kalb played along, literally, but disliked both songs. Blumenfeld recalled a Cafe Au Go Go rehearsal where they worked on one of those numbers. "The whole band was ready to kill each other," he said. "It wasn't blues enough. Danny was rough on Al. I started to do a 6/8 time thing, big, bombastic drum stuff, and everything came together." At one point, he later wrote, Kooper also took to carrying around a cane for additional affectation—but soon stopped when he realized he could have pounded Kalb on the head with it out of frustration.

Kooper remained undeterred, pushing for the group to add a horn section to beef up its sound. Kalb rejected the idea, saying it didn't make sense to add overhead to a band that wasn't making much money to start with. He also argued that they'd only begun to explore what the five of them could do together. Kalb remained a classicist, shooting down producer Tom Wilson's idea of recording a cover of Dylan's "If You Gotta Go, Go Now." During the making of *Projections*, he also dismissed a suggestion that they cover the stomping "Wild Thing," which would soon become a ubiquitous radio hit for the Troggs.

To complicate matters, their love lives were in disarray. Katz was still recovering from his brief affair with Fariña. One day, Blumenfeld received a call from Katz asking him to come to his apartment in the West Village. "I didn't know what was going on," Blumenfeld said, "so I went over and opened the door and there's a woman with blond hair, sitting with her back to me, playing guitar. I thought this human being was gorgeous. We left there pretty quickly and skipped down the street and went to her place in Chelsea." It was Joni Mitchell, a Canadian singer and songwriter who had appeared at the Gaslight with her then husband Chuck Mitchell. Now in the city alone, she'd hooked up briefly with Katz. The only issue was that Blumenfeld already had a girlfriend, who was in Europe at the time. "I fell in love with Joni, but we had to break up because my girlfriend was coming back," he said. "Joni knocked me out, I fell in love with her. But she was beyond me, in a way."

Despondent when she heard the news about Blumenfeld's other relationship, Mitchell ended up at the Tin Angel, a bar next to the Bitter End. Kooper offered to take her to his place, to console or otherwise; instead, she sang him a bunch of her songs there, including one called "Michael from Mountains" that he thought would be ideal for his friend Judy Collins. He felt compelled to call

Collins and tell her about Mitchell—and ask her to maybe give Mitchell a ride to the upcoming Newport Folk Festival. Collins came through with the car and gained a potential source of new songs for her next album.

In 1967 Phillip Namanworth, a jazz-leaning keyboard player then living far uptown, answered a musician-wanted ad for a band. He turned up at a rehearsal space in the West Village, where he set up his Farfisa organ. Immediately, Namanworth—whose nickname, Pot, came from his job as a dishwasher, not from marijuana—knew the project would be far from a traditional folk record. Guitarist Dave Woods asked Namanworth if he could play a blues in B flat. He could and did, and was hired immediately.

The band for which Namanworth was enlisted was the latest in Van Ronk's search for ways to musically stretch his legs. In 1966 Van Ronk had become the next area musician to sign with Verve Forecast. His first album for the label, *No Dirty Names*, was an exuberant acoustic affair with a saucy version of Josh White's "One Meatball," where he pushed his voice into a growly scat, while one of his first originals, "Zen Koans Gonna Rise Again," was a dreamlike depiction of the Village underbelly with a double-tracked vocal that lent the song an added eeriness. His jazz jones emerged in a rendition of Dizzy Gillespie's "Blues Chante" and his love of Kurt Weill in "Alabama Song"; with added accompaniment from Woods, both songs were fully remade in the Van Ronk mode.

At the same time, Van Ronk had never been averse to augmenting his voice and guitar, and like many around him, he felt the pull of rock and roll, with all its creative and financial opportunities. "Dave wanted an electric band," Thal said. "He thought it would make good music. And there were groups forming all over the place and they were getting rich. So he thought he could have a good band and, perhaps, do better financially than he did as a solo performer."

Similar makeovers of acoustic musicians into amplified ones were happening all around Van Ronk. By 1967, in addition to Kalb and Sebastian, the list would include David Blue, who'd fully made the transition from actor to troubadour. *David Blue*, his 1966 Elektra debut, very much followed in the folk-meets-rock footsteps of Dylan's work and featured originals such as "So Easy She Goes By" and "Grand Hotel" that held promise for Blue's own future. But the album hadn't sold, and soon enough, Blue had formed a four-piece band, the American Patrol, that pushed his sound even further into rock and roll. And despite being firmly entrenched in the unplugged world, brothers Happy and Artie Traum—along with guitarist Marc Silber, owner of the still-thriving Fretted Instruments store—formed the Children of Paradise, which aimed to simulate the British Invasion groups on the radio. They landed work at the Cafe Au Go Go and a contract with Columbia Records that included free electric guitars and amplifiers.

Unlike the Children of Paradise, Van Ronk's crossover dream didn't need an outside cash infusion. The royalties he had made on Peter, Paul and Mary's version of "Bamboo," which Thal had tucked away in a bank account, would now underwrite his electrification. By the time Namanworth was invited to join, the band had a name—the Hudson Dusters, after the New York City street gang that had formed in the late 1800s—and two other members, bass player Ed Gregory and drummer Rick Henderson. For a producer, Van Ronk turned to his friend Barry Kornfeld, who had largely left the coffeehouse scene behind and was venturing into session work and even publishing. In 1965, Kornfeld and Paul Simon had become business partners by forming a publishing company, Eclectic Music, with the intention of snapping up Village songwriters and signing them to deals. Among the first songs they published was David Blue's "I Like to Sleep Late in the Morning," an ode to the lazy life that would become his best-known and most-covered song.

If Van Ronk was aiming to sell records, he would do it his own way. Among the songs he and the Hudson Dusters put on tape were a version of the Hollywood Argyles' novelty hit "Alley Oop"; a demented piece of folk rock called "Head Inspector"; a version of the Bing Crosby–linked "Swing on a Star," with intentionally lush, corny harmonies; and an electric, full-band remake of "Cocaine," which had become a staple of Van Ronk's repertoire. "He didn't mean it to be an album of eclectic stuff," said Namanworth. "He said, 'Let's gather things from around me from all different influences.' Dave could take something in a song and make it his own."

At one rehearsal, Van Ronk asked Namanworth if he wanted to hear a new song. With just his guitar, Van Ronk played "Both Sides Now," with what Namanworth recalled as a "young blonde lady" sitting in the corner, listening. Van Ronk had met Joni Mitchell in Detroit, where she was living at the time. He loved the tune—he had a fondness for ruminative songs about life, aging, and regrets—and decided to include it on the album. He called it "Clouds," although Mitchell preferred her own title, "Both Sides Now." They compromised by calling it "Clouds (From Both Sides Now)." Woods arranged it as twinkly folk pop and also lent a plusher, more pop-chorale feeling to an arrangement of another Mitchell song, "Chelsea Morning."

For her part, Thal had her doubts about the entire project. "I thought it was a lousy idea," she said. "I didn't think Dave belonged in any band. He wasn't a group-conforming person. But he wanted it, so we went ahead with it." Besides, Van Ronk and others associated with the record felt that no matter what it was called, "Clouds" would be the song that would finally give Van Ronk the hit that he—and many of his peers—secretly coveted.

By the summer of 1967, the musical electrification of the area between Fourteenth and Houston Streets had all but consumed it. As the Cafe Au Go Go demonstrated, it wouldn't merely be local acts that flocked there. The Grateful Dead and Jefferson Airplane would rattle its walls, as would Cream, making its Village debut at the Au Go Go. Sitting a few rows back, the Youngbloods took in the pulverizing, electroshocked blues of Eric Clapton, Jack Bruce, and Ginger Baker; Levinger said it was the first time he'd ever experienced a stomachache from a bass guitar. Upstairs from the venue, owner Howard Solomon opened the Garrick Theater, which hosted off-Broadway musicals but most notably Frank Zappa's Mothers of Invention, who brought their shows, a theater of the musically and politically absurd, from Los Angeles. Their one-week gig became such a must-see that they stayed in the city for several more months.

In ways it was beginning to be hard to count, the vestiges of the previous Village world were starting to fade. In August 1967, the city abolished its odious cabaret-card system, including the fingerprinting of musicians. As License Commissioner Joel J. Tyler announced, a department study determined that "a need to be suspicious of top-flight artists," along with wait staff and "go-go dancers," was no longer necessary. To keep the live-music world in some semblance of order, licenses for the venues themselves would suffice.

But even with those restrictions lifted, the neighborhood was still roiled. The Night Owl closed in early 1968. In a blow to coverage of the scene, Robert Shelton, at work on a major biography of Dylan based on his years of interviewing and chronicling him, left his job at the *Times* and relocated to London that same year. Had he remained, it's unlikely Shelton would have devoted much space to the latest club to open on MacDougal Street. Situated a few doors down from the Cafe Wha?, the Answer was run by a sandal-clad twenty-four-year-old and decorated with flowers and graffiti. In fact, it was a Salvation Army–operated "coffeehouse ministry," as it was called, which aimed to convert runaways to Christianity with the help of no-name folksingers.

Ed Koch, then a city councilman, continued his quest to ensure that unlicensed music-connected businesses were monitored and not disruptive to those living in the neighborhood. Cafe Feenjon, a coffeehouse where Dylan and José Feliciano had played during their formative New York days, had started on Seventh Avenue South and eventually moved to 105 MacDougal, formerly home to the Fat Black Pussycat. There, the space made room for largely acoustic world-music groups; its owner, Manny Dworman, even fronted the Feenjon Group, which included musicians from Greece, the Middle East, and Turkey. Although the music was hardly abrasive or rattling, police slapped the coffeehouse with a summons in late 1967.

Some of the old-guard musicians remained. After years in or around the Bleecker Street vicinity, Richie Havens, the Black singer and strummer who'd made such a lasting impression during his basket-house days, finally started commanding attention outside the area. Unlike his peers, Havens hadn't ridden the Village wave as quickly as some of his peers. He'd signed with Albert Grossman in 1963 and made early recordings for a small label. But it wasn't until 1967, when he joined the Blues Project and Tim Hardin on Verve Folkways, that Havens's career began to take shape. On *Mixed Bag*, he displayed the deft way he could dip into the Village repertoire, recasting Dylan's "Just Like a Woman" and the Fugs' "Morning Morning" by way of his masculine but tender delivery. "Handsome Johnny," cowritten with actor and fellow musician Louis Gossett Jr., showcased the rhythmic guitar approach that set him apart in his early days, and its haunting evocation of a soldier who fought in war after war, like a roaming ghost, proved how much he could contribute to the topical-song world.

But Havens was now starting to look like the last musician standing in his neighborhood. Up in Woodstock, where he had moved and was still recovering from a mysterious 1966 motorcycle accident, Dylan was spending the summer of 1967 with the Hawks, recording new songs (in their rented, salmon-colored house) to pitch to other artists. After his early shows at the Night Owl, followed by ones at the Cafe Au Go Go and the Bitter End, Fred Neil had become one of the Village's most admired and most enigmatic troubadours. *Tear Down the Walls*, a collaboration with Vince Martin, set the table, but Neil's own 1965 debut, *Bleecker & MacDougal*, announced a newly liberated songwriter who could whoop it up on the title track and, on "Little Bit of Rain," dip into a deep well of regret. But never fully comfortable on stage or with the music business, Neil was soon living and recording in California before transferring for good to Florida. Tom Paxton and his wife, Midge, left their apartment on West Tenth Street and found a house in East Hampton, Long Island, where they could raise their family.

From early shows at Folk City to a headlining set at the Bitter End, Arlo Guthrie was beginning to construct his own path in the Village, apart from his father's legacy. At one of those Folk City shows in 1966, he'd premiered an early draft of "Alice's Restaurant," a long, comical talking blues about a Thanksgiving Day littering bust; by the time he was playing it at the Gaslight, it had expanded to include the way he'd avoided the military draft as a result of being arrested for that littering. Now the differences between the scene he'd experienced in the late fifties and the one a decade later were impossible to deny, especially from his vantage point of an apartment at the corner of MacDougal and Eighth Streets. "It used to be that you could just walk in and sit down [at clubs or coffeehouses] and people would know you," Guthrie said.

"Then they started havin' people outside at the doors to watch who's comin' and who's goin'. It changed from bein' easygoin' to more organized, more militaristic. The tightening up made it not feel quite as welcoming. I remember thinkin' it became more like Disneyland, with people lookin' to see hippies. We're in a zoo, and that didn't feel as comfortable as hangin' out with your own kind." Before long, Guthrie and his family sold their apartment and moved to Massachusetts.

The wounds in the community could also be self-inflicted. If Dylan could break into AM radio and into the album charts, why couldn't they? With visions of hit records and warmer weather in mind, many other songwriters left the Village and headed west, draining the scene of some of its visionaries. John Phillips, part of the Journeymen with Dick Weissman, soon relocated to Los Angeles with his new pop band, the Mamas and the Papas, which also included former Night Owl employee Cass Elliot. Los Angeles was also now populated with young folkies like Stephen Stills and David Crosby, who had each given the Village coffeehouses and basket houses a shot before heading out west. Phil Ochs subsequently moved there, as did Tim Hardin and, soon after, Carolyn Hester. David Blue's plugged-in band, the American Patrol, recorded an album so unappetizing that Blue asked Elektra to shelve it, and soon after he followed a girlfriend to California.

Andy Wickham, a Los Angeles record executive who'd befriended Ochs and encouraged him to make the transition out west, made the same pitch to Eric Andersen. In 1966 Andersen's second album, *'Bout Changes & Things*, heralded the Village's next apparent star. Steeped in the sensuous romanticism of his voice and tender guitar, the album included his original version of "Violets of Dawn" and "Close the Door Lightly When You Go," an elegant fare-thee-well love song. Andersen sounded less like someone at a rally and more like a man mulling over life choices. Like more than a few of the songs by his peers, "Thirsty Boots," also on that second album, felt like something written decades before in a mining camp. In fact, it was inspired by the sight of the New World Singers' Gil Turner walking into the Gaslight with mud-caked footwear after returning from a civil rights rally down south. (Hearing the tune in an early stage, Ochs told Andersen, "Man, that's a great song—finish it," which only made Dylan's putdowns more infuriating to Andersen.) Meanwhile, Andy

Warhol had cast Andersen in a small role in his film *Space*, although Andersen was so embarrassed when he saw the close-up of his crotch that he sank low in his seat as he watched it in a theater.

Andersen made all the crossover moves anyone needed to make at the time. At one of his Cafe Au Go Go shows in 1967, writer Glenn A. McCurdy noted the mix of "high school and campus-set hippies, twisted intellectuals [and] dropped-out establishment couples" who filled every seat. To satisfy the British market (and to Ochs's unhappiness), Andersen rerecorded that sophomore, largely acoustic album but with a folk-rock–leaning rhythm section and keyboards, calling it *'Bout Changes 'n' Things Take 2*. He then left his manager, Arthur Gorson, and was about to sign with the Beatles' overseer, Brian Epstein, just before Epstein's death. Given all that had transpired, New York had little left to offer him. "The scene kind of stopped," Andersen said. "I found Vanguard Records a little stultifying, and they didn't really promote anything."

Although Columbia had signed Len Chandler and put out his first album, *To Be a Man*, in 1967, sales were minimal, and Chandler also packed up for the West Coast, for a job with KRLA in Los Angeles. There he wrote and sang three topical songs a day as part of the station's news programming. After the Youngbloods had recorded their first of several albums for RCA, with a repertoire of blues songs and Jesse Colin Young originals they'd sharpened at the Cafe Au Go Go, the group toured out west and beheld the difference between California and Manhattan. "In New York in those days, you felt that anyone who smiled at you on the street was going to ask you for money," said Young. "In San Francisco everyone was smiling at me on the street and everyone was high. It was a beautiful thing." After their third trip west, they asked one another why they kept returning to the grime of the Village and Manhattan in general and decided to make Marin County their new home base. Two years after its release, "Get Together" would belatedly become the Youngbloods' breakout hit—but by that point, no one thought of them as a Village-associated band.

For a band that projected such a good-timey image, the beloved Lovin' Spoonful experienced what amounted to a slow-motion car wreck. In San Francisco in mid-1966, Zal Yanovsky and Steve Boone were busted for pot after leaving a party; told they had little choice but to cooperate with police, they brought along an undercover agent to another bash. For a while, the incident gained little to no traction. "Summer in the City," a collaboration between the Sebastian brothers that injected a jolt of urban tension and grit into their sound, ruled that summer.

But after the San Francisco police arrested someone at the party that Boone and Yanovsky had mentioned, word of their collaboration spread through the underground press. The fact that the two musicians were essentially forced to work with the police *didn't* leak, however, and the Lovin' Spoonful became outcasts, especially in their East Coast stomping grounds. Walking down Village streets, Boone would later write that he felt as if people were shooting him death-ray looks. The Spoonful never recovered. Tension between Sebastian and Yanovsky led to the band firing its lead guitarist, and despite replacing Yanovsky, the Spoonful didn't last that much longer. Eventually, Sebastian also left the city and moved to Los Angeles.

Those who remained found streets littered with beer bottles and broken dreams. The Children of Paradise, the Traum brothers' rock band, released a single, "Hey, You Got Somethin'," that was largely derivative and went nowhere, as did a full album. "It was very Beatle oriented, but not *good* Beatle oriented," Happy said. When they played a free concert in Tompkins Square Park in the East Village, the musicians were told to load their gear into their car within five minutes of finishing their set. Parking it near the stage, they began packing their guitars and amps into the back of the vehicle, unaware that "some locals," as Marc Silber put it, were extracting equipment from the *front* of the car. Disillusioned by that experience, Silber quit. With his wife, Jane, Happy Traum moved to Woodstock, and Artie followed. Nancy Sinatra and her creative partner, songwriter, musician, and producer Lee Hazelwood teased the perceived crass commercialism of protest songs and the area identified with them in "Greenwich Village Folk Song Salesman," a jaunty mockery of a song peddler hawking folk-rock tunes about Vietnam and LBJ. For added ridicule, they pronounced the title word "*Green*-witch."

For anyone who'd followed the scene, though, the collapse of the Blues Project was the most disheartening development. In her *Rock Encyclopedia*, the first such undertaking in publishing, writer Lillian Roxon had called them "New York's first band—first band of its own, that is." As before, they appeared to be making strides. *Projections* had outsold *Live at the Cafe Au Go Go*, with tracks like "Flute Thing," "Two Trains Running," and "Steves Song" making headway on the fledgling free-form FM radio. The band was slotted into a multi-act bill in midtown in April 1967, alongside the Who, Smokey Robinson and the Miracles, and Simon and Garfunkel. A month later, the Blues Project headlined at the prestigious Town Hall, a performance that MGM and Verve Folkways recorded as the band's follow-up to *Projections*.

But the volcanos within the band began erupting with more frequency, and their bond, a shared Jewish heritage, wasn't enough to keep them together. Kooper was calling the others "fat and lazy" for not being, in his mind, more musically adventurous and for sticking with the identical set list night after night. When the band played in Montreal, Kooper and Katz found themselves in a fistfight. As Katz wrote in his memoir, Kooper accused him of nabbing a sandwich, which led to fisticuffs. Kooper, who had already had a nervous breakdown, had another soon after, going into something resembling a comatose state in his apartment. Frustrated, Kooper, who was also coping with a recurrent ulcer, quit the band in May.

In June the band had been scheduled to play the Monterey International Pop Festival in California, another prestigious gig that would have them sharing the bill with the Byrds, Otis Redding, Simon and Garfunkel, Big Brother and the Holding Company, and Jimi Hendrix, who had moved to London in the fall of 1966 and fully transformed into the psychedelic guitarchitect he'd long promised to become. (Hendrix was one of the few musicians who found his voice once he *left* the Village rather than after he'd arrived there.) To replace Kooper, the Blues Project hired a Black lead singer and keyboardist, John McDuffy, who'd previously played in the King Bees. In an interview just before the festival, Kalb sounded optimistic: "There's been a discrepancy between the power of the electric band and the puerility of the lyrics. Well, we're trying to fuse the power with meaningful lyrics. We think we're coming very close." But those prospects proved short-lived. "The band was disintegrating on a certain level at Monterey," said Blumenfeld. "Losing Al was a really big deal. He brought a certain upbeat craziness and flair and a charismatic attitude. People were drawn to that. He was an entertainer. Danny was more of an inside guy, serious about the tunes, demanding people listen to him."

For Kalb, the splintering of his band was proving to be especially disorienting. "We played Monterey, but it wasn't a happy scene," he said. "I was almost suicidally depressed." Following a new girlfriend on a side trip to San Francisco, he met up with Owsley Stanley III, the Grateful Dead's sound wizard and LSD chemist. When Stanley offered to sell him LSD, Kalb was not averse, calling it "the sacrament—not just a drug, but a religious test." But as he realized too late, digesting acid was the last thing he should have done, especially once he found himself in the midst of an horrific trip. "All of a sudden, the world explodes into the most gorgeous experience of my life," he recalled of the initial moments when the LSD hit. "The beauty of the colors was exquisite and a half. It's like I'm in heaven, for about eight hours." Unfortunately, that high didn't last. "It started to turn into something else," he said. "The dark side happens. The sky turns black, and I know I'm heading straight to hell."

Kalb returned to Stanley's house and attempted to come down over the course of a few hours, after which Stanley took him to what Kalb called a "gathering of freaks" where no one smiled and all Kalb heard was incessant and increasingly loud drum beating. He wound up running through the streets of San Francisco all night, yelling, "Can you be my executioner?" (as he later told a bandmate, John Berenzy) before being picked up by police. Brought to a hospital, he was put in a room alongside another acid casualty. "I'm scared shitless," Kalb recalled. "I'm in hell." With the help of Kulberg and Blumenfeld, he returned to New York, but he was still suffering from the experience. "The acid had come down, but I was insane," he said. Back on the East Coast, a wealthy friend, he said, took him to a facility for recovery.

Meanwhile, the Blues Project staggered on into the fall of 1967, with Kooper returning for a series of Cafe Au Go Go performances. Kalb was largely missing in action, a few times temporarily replaced by his brother, Jonathan, who played a different style of blues. That same season, Verve cobbled together a third and shockingly slipshod Blues Project album, *Live at Town Hall*. No one who bought it knew, but only some of the record had been taped at that venue. To fool listeners into thinking the rest of it had been, applause was tacked onto studio recordings (Kooper's two attempts at hits and a Katz-sung version of Patrick Sky's "Love Will Endure"). A more anticlimactic finale for such a promising band was hard to imagine.

"Strangely enough, the death of the Blues Project hit New Yorkers badly," wrote Roxon in her *Rock Encyclopedia*. "They still feel wounded and betrayed by it all. Those nights at the Au Go Go were a big part of the musical coming of age of a lot of people in the audience, as well as of the performers." Because the band owed MGM one more album, Kulberg and Blumenfeld recruited new members and produced a faux Blues Project record, *Planned Obsolescence*, before folding the group. They couldn't have picked a more sadly fitting title for both the band and, as 1968 approached, the scene that had birthed them.

Chapter 6
down in the flood
1968–1975

lthough he didn't know it yet, Dave Van Ronk was about to meet his next and perhaps most promising protégés. Arriving at 321 Avenue of the Americas that day in 1968, John Roche parked the family station wagon and, with his teenage daughters, Maggie and Terre, stepped into the narrow row house just north of Bleecker Street.

For Roche, known to many as Jack, returning to the area must have felt like old, comforting times. Three decades before, he was living in Buffalo, New York, with his first wife and children and working as an English teacher. But while acting in a local play, he met and fell in love with one of his costars, Jude Jewell. The couple—John eleven years older than Jude—eloped as soon as they could and moved to the West Village, ending up in an apartment on Commerce Street; John took a job at Ross Roy, an advertising agency. Their first child, Margaret (Maggie), was born in October 1951 in Detroit, where John had been temporarily transferred. Returning to New York, the family settled in Queens, and another daughter, Theresa, nicknamed Terre, arrived in April 1953. As the family grew—daughter Suzzy was born in September 1956 and son, David, soon after—the Roches migrated to the suburbs, eventually settling into a split-level home in Park Ridge, a New Jersey suburb thirty miles outside Manhattan.

The family may have been removed from what Suzzy would later call her parents' "bohemian life" in Manhattan (a world John was unhappy to leave), but their artsy and liberal-leaning outlook was ingrained in them. John would read poetry to his children and write songs to be sung at rallies for local Democratic candidates. Jude, who also composed poetry and worked on an unpublished novel, had what she called a "reading hour" at home; their kids would have to sit quietly for that amount of time and listen to classical music as their mother prepped dinner. The ritual felt torturous, but Maggie, demonstrating a driven side even at that age, would use the time to practice piano.

As self-described nerds, the sisters always felt a little removed from their Jersey environs. Their friends were immersing themselves in the latest rock-and-roll bands, such as Led Zeppelin, but Maggie and Terre had grown up on their parents' Bob Dylan, Joan Baez, Judy Collins, and Simon and Garfunkel records, and preferred the folk bins of their local department store. One day Suzzy, then about five, planted a garden of watermelon seeds in their backyard. A neighborhood boy who seemed to have a crush on her came by to see if the seeds had sprouted into fruit. As Suzzy watched, horrified, he stomped out all the nascent watermelons. It felt like yet another reason for the Roche sisters to distance themselves from their surroundings.

In high school, Maggie and Terre learned to play guitar by way of *Folk Guitar with Laura Weber*, a public-television series, and began playing the songs Maggie had started writing or ones their father wrote for fund-raising events. Maggie was reserved and spoke softly but quickly, her dark hair dropping to her shoulders. Terre, a sandy blonde, was chattier and more outgoing than Maggie, who would make charts out of her mood swings. Maggie had a lovely, plain-spoken singing voice, while Terre's was higher and sweeter, drifting more toward a soprano. But the blend worked, and Maggie pressed her younger sister into learning harmonies for the early tunes she'd written. "Simon and Garfunkel were my favorite group," Maggie said. "I felt passionately about them, listening over and over again in my room and feeling like they were talking directly to me."

During John Roche's bus rides into New York City, one of his fellow commuters, who knew his daughters were fledgling singers, told him about a man named Izzy Young, who had a connection to a radio show on WBAI. Apparently, folksingers could audition for the program; perhaps the sisters could do the same. John, who by then had left the ad-agency world and had developed a language-skills class on tape for high school graduates who couldn't read well, could be enveloped in dark moods at home, according to Terre. But he always seemed in a better frame of mind when he would bring his family into the Village, so a return visit felt like the right idea.

Climbing the two flights of stairs at 321 Avenue of the Americas, Roche and his daughters found themselves inside the new Folklore Center. In 1965 Izzy Young had relocated the store there from MacDougal Street, also moving into an apartment above it. The cheaper rent and the increased square footage, which made live performances inside more feasible, were two factors. So were the Mob guys in the building near his old location, who'd pressured Young to turn his business into a numbers front. One of them, a tall and gray-haired sort, came to be nicknamed "The Admiral" since he always wore a navy uniform.

As the Roche family had hoped, Young was there—and so too was Van Ronk. The sisters had never heard of him before, and his now expanded girth and beard reminded Terre of Santa Claus. As their father watched, the sisters sang and played a few of Maggie's songs. Young seemed to enjoy them, but Van Ronk was even more enthusiastic and told them he wanted to have them meet his wife, Terri, who was a manager. Following him outside, they all found themselves several blocks away, at 190 Waverly Place.

The Roche sisters weren't the first neophytes encouraged by Van Ronk and Thal. Somewhere along the line, they'd met Janis Fink, a small-framed teenager from New Jersey who wrote and sang delicate and prematurely wise songs about the generation gap, suicide, and other outré subjects. Eventually rechristening herself Janis Ian in the tradition of the Village, she made several beelines for Washington Square Park's Sunday-afternoon sessions. "What a great metaphor the fountain was," she said, "spouting new water all the time from old water—that's folk music." Thanks to the Gaslight's lack of a liquor license, which made it easier for a teenager to land work there, she was able to perform, although she was frequently taken aback by the sound of the toilet flushing while she was onstage.

Thal and Van Ronk eventually took Ian under their wings, inviting her to dinner at 190 Waverly. Wary of her daughter spending time with what she called a "boozing Irishman," Ian's mother made her bring a friend. But Ian discovered that Van Ronk was actually more traditional than his image let on—a gentleman, not quite the brawler he appeared on stage. Winding up with a record deal with Verve, Ian recorded "Society's Child," sung in the voice of a young white high schooler who has to break up with her Black boyfriend thanks to the disapproval of her friends and family. With its haunted blend of girl-group pop and chamber folk, the record became a belated hit in 1967. Van Ronk strongly advised her to scrutinize her royalty statements to avoid being ripped off by the heinous music industry.

Van Ronk and Thal seemed to take even more to seventeen-year-old Maggie and fifteen-year-old Terre Roche, lending the sisters albums by artists they'd never heard of—Joni Mitchell, Tim Hardin, and Tim Buckley, a curly-haired, West Coast–based troubadour with a multi-octave vocal range. With their father in tow, the sisters dropped into the Kettle of Fish, where they took a seat at Van Ronk's table and watched as talk turned to the events of the day. For Terre, who'd never smoked a joint or even a cigarette, the experience was overwhelming. "I was a goody-two-shoes and all of a sudden I'm hanging with Communists in bars," she recalled. "We're sitting around in the Kettle and people are talking about Marxism and Trotskyism. I'd grown up thinking that I'm not supposed to *be* a Communist."

Van Ronk invited them to see him play at the Gaslight, where they were riveted by a throaty delivery that made Dylan's sound comparatively velvety. Van Ronk remained a daunting stage presence, appearing to say whatever was on his mind. He even made blunders work for him: when a guitar string broke mid-song, the Roche sisters watched as he paused and told the crowd, "My mistakes are *golden*," and the crowd ate it up. The sisters would sometimes crash at the Waverly Place apartment. By then, Maggie was a student at Bard College, just north of New York City, where she earned a *C* in English, but Terre would have to take an early-morning bus home in order to take her PSAT to prepare for college herself.

The Roche sisters practiced in their bedrooms in New Jersey and had played before a few audiences, including in a heart-fund benefit at a local restaurant.

But with their newfound Village connection, they, Maggie in particular, grew more serious about their craft. They were still novices, staring at their feet as they performed, but Maggie had acquired a penchant for aqua-blue tank tops and miniskirts—a change from the matching jumpers and white shirts they had worn at one show in New Jersey. As Van Ronk and Thal knew all too well, the Village music community felt like a tarnished gem. Maybe the Roche sisters could carry on a tradition after so much had changed around them.

When *Dave Van Ronk and the Hudson Dusters* was released in March 1968, the initial reaction was encouraging; *Billboard* approved of the single "Romping Through the Swamp," which, its reviewer noted, "borders on progressive rock." But although Van Ronk would call it one of his favorite albums, most critics didn't know what to make of it: "so saturated in whimsy that at times it almost threatens to float away," wrote one, adding, "What happened to the old, unamplified Van Ronk, hunched over his acoustical guitar, his teddy-bear face contorted with anger, bristling through each number whether happy or sad?" As Barry Kornfeld recalled, "This was a commercial album for Dave, but it wasn't very commercial."

Given its graceful melody and relatable sentiments, "Clouds (From Both Sides Now)" had the strongest chance of radio airplay, and plans were made to release it as a 45. But a last-minute snag arose. Phillip Namanworth was hanging out with Van Ronk at 190 Waverly when Judy Collins came to visit. Collins, who'd included her version of the song on her album *Wildflowers* the previous November, wanted to make it her own next single. Somewhat begrudgingly, Van Ronk agreed, and Collins's version—which, starting with Collins's more mellifluous voice, had a sparkling arrangement that lent itself to AM radio—peaked at number 2 in late 1968. "What could we say?" Thal said. "We liked Judy, and we wished her the best of everything. We were philosophical about it. It happened. But we weren't happy. What do you do? You say, 'Oh, shit.' And maybe you say it for a couple of days. And life goes on." Added Namanworth, "We were starting to get airplay. If she hadn't done that, we could have had a big record."

When the Hudson Dusters went on the road to promote their record, Van Ronk didn't encounter anything close to the adverse reaction Dylan received at Newport. Namanworth felt that he personally lost a degree of hearing thanks to the amplification, but audiences appeared to accept the idea of Van Ronk with backup musicians. But, in the end, the numbers didn't add up. "It was a very good group," Thal said. "But it wasn't enough of a rock group to become lucrative." By the end of 1968, the band was no more. The original Hudson Dusters street gang had fallen apart when the bohemians infiltrated the Village; now, the band of the same name collapsed just as the bohemians were leaving.

The year brought another, even more symbolic change when Van Ronk and Thal's marriage dissolved. As Thal would later detail in her memoir *My Greenwich Village*, the strain of working together, as manager and client, began taking its toll. When he was on the road and Thal remained in New York, both slept with other people. In typically idiosyncratic fashion, they didn't officially pursue a divorce at the time. "When we broke up, Dave said, 'Let's stay married, let's not get a divorce,'" Thal said. "And it didn't make any difference to me; I didn't intend to ever marry again. So I said okay." Van Ronk soon moved out of 190 Waverly Place and into his own place on Sheridan Square, and the breakup robbed the music community of an especially strong foundation.

∎∎∎∎∎

With the help of Van Ronk and Thal, the Roche sisters made it onto the stage for at least one Monday open-mic night at Folk City in July 1969. By then, the club was no longer the focal point it had once been. Indicating a desperate need for customers, the club's ads now announced a "new, no-minimum policy" for its "Best in Folk Entertainment." (Popping into the venue one day, Happy Traum witnessed the debut of Emmylou Harris, a southern-raised folksinger who'd dropped out of Boston University and made the Village her home for a short period.) The times had also changed, but Folk City hadn't fully changed with them; Mike Porco was reluctant to have electric instruments in his club.

When New York University took over and then condemned the West Fourth Street building that housed his club and restaurant, Porco was forced to close in September 1969. Luckily, he found a new space even closer to the Bleecker Street action. Formerly home to Tony Pastor's, the Italian restaurant and gay women's gathering spot, 130 West Third Street held 110 in the main room and 50 at the bar. Porco moved the stage from the far back corner to the right, just past the bar, but retained its most memorable decor—a mural, created to commemorate New Year's Eve 1939, that depicted New Yorkers gazing upon flamenco dancers, their eyes on fire. The new Folk City opened in November, a mere two months after the first location shut down.

At least it was still open, which couldn't be said for other local landmarks. Despite the coffeehouse busts of the late fifties and early sixties, the Cafe Figaro had survived and prospered, largely because it didn't officially present live music and didn't need any of the required paperwork. But in January 1969, another obstacle—a dramatic rent increase—caught up with the Fig, forcing it to close. The shutdown was accompanied by the city equivalent of a yard sale. The Ziegler family, which still ran it, took the lamps and checkerboard tables, but the public was invited in to buy its tables and chairs for as little as fifty cents each. Once it was empty, the new and telling tenant moved in—Blimpie, part of a Jersey-based chain of sub and sandwich shops that already had several stores in the city but was now bringing its vinegar-and-oil taste of suburbia to the Village.

Several streets down on Bleecker, the Cafe Au Go Go began to stumble. Beginning in 1968, the club had unexpected competition when promoter Bill Graham opened the Fillmore East, the New York version of his San Francisco venue the Fillmore West, off Second Avenue and East Sixth Street. The Fillmore could hold roughly five times the customers as the Au Go Go and paid better than Howard Solomon could. But the shady characters increasingly inhabiting the Village also left their mark. When an anonymous hood threatened to kidnap Solomon's two young children, Jason and Candace, for reasons Jason never discovered, their father decided it was time to leave. An ad in the June 12, 1969, *Village Voice* sought a "responsible tenant" for the space. In the end, the building owner, Moses Baruch, took it over and reopened the Au Go Go. Yet despite a few high-profile bookings, such as the Grateful Dead, the club couldn't find a revitalized groove and closed again in December 1969. As

Baruch told *Rolling Stone*, "The big groups go to the Fillmore East, and personally, if I wanted to see them, I'd rather go there since you see a show and it's not
too expensive."

A glimmer of hope—and rock glamour—announced itself in the summer of
1970, when Jimi Hendrix's long-planned studio, Electric Lady, opened on Eighth
Street, near the corner of MacDougal. That space had once been occupied by
a country bar and then a short-lived club, Generation, that presented soul and
blues acts like B. B. King and Muddy Waters. It was now an underground studio with tie-dyed pillows and lighting that could be adjusted to accommodate a
musician's mood. Hendrix died the month after it opened, though, and overall,
Bleecker and its surrounding streets were now being increasingly given over to
poster-art stores and a carnival atmosphere that made it seem even seedier than
it was. More of the old businesses began leaving. In 1968 Manny Roth sold the
Cafe Wha?, and Marc Silber closed Fretted Instruments, selling most of his
instrument inventory to Izzy Young and the Folklore Center. A *Buffalo Evening
Post* reporter wandering the MacDougal Street area one summer evening found
stretches that were "fairly empty," with clubs that "looked fun from the outside
but turned out to be luminously painted and vacuously dull" once he made his
way inside.

Given how hobbled the neighborhood appeared to be, it was ironic that
Dylan chose that moment to return. His departure from Woodstock had
at least something to do with Albert Grossman; after Dylan suspected that
Grossman had been taking a bigger chunk of his publishing income than he
thought, he'd finally broken with his manager. Woodstock was getting insuf-
ferable anyway; fans were showing up in Dylan's driveway, and Grossman, who
owned property, a recording studio, and at least one restaurant there, seemed
ubiquitous. Dylan bought a brownstone at 94 MacDougal Street, about a block
and a half south of the Gaslight. He and his wife, Sara, and their children were
now a few short streets from his first apartment in the neighborhood. The
building, whose front door was accessible to anyone who wanted to knock on
it, also shared a vast courtyard with several other structures, and locals began
spotting him walking up and down the block or, in one case, driving a van with
kids in the back seats.

Once more, Dylan could be seen huddled at a table at the Kettle of Fish. Catherine Todd, a Gaslight employee, would marvel at the up-and-coming acts booked into the space, including a young Bonnie Raitt. Todd would sometimes be sent upstairs to the Kettle to take drink orders for the musicians between or after sets and witnessed the unusual pecking order there. The front table, she noticed, would be populated by "everyone with a record contract," such as Dylan or another returning visitor, David Blue. "If you were a buzz act who was possibly getting a deal, they would be at the next table," she said, "and the next table were the nobodies."

Although Dylan was rarely one to look back, he appeared to be hunting for inspiration in more of his old environs than just the Kettle of Fish. He stopped by 190 Waverly Place, where he and Terri Thal, who still lived there after her breakup with Van Ronk, spent several hours talking. "I think he was looking for a piece of his past . . . ," Thal told Dylan biographer Anthony Scaduto. "He seemed stressed. He said he was uptight, told me he had all this money and didn't know what to do with it." Thal had held on to one of Dylan's corduroy caps from the early days, which he'd given to her, but when she offered to return it to him, he declined to take it back. In one of the few times he stepped into a studio in 1971, he recruited Happy Traum to remake a few older songs; "Crash on the Levee (Down in the Flood)" now felt like a commentary on the new Village.

Returning to the Gaslight to see Happy and his brother Artie, Dylan was seen wearing what comanager Susan Martin Robbins, formerly of the Four Winds, called a "big white Cossack hat," adding sarcastically, "like he doesn't want any attention." Robbins and Betty Smyth, who were comanaging the club under Ed Simon, were terrified that Dylan would be recognized and that a scene would result. As they stood at the doors watching customers leave, one said, "Do you know who's in there? Tony Glover!," referring to the Minnesota blues harmonica player who knew Dylan. Both breathed a huge sigh of relief.

But if he needed a reminder that one era had ended and another, stranger one had begun, all Dylan had to do was see one of his most obsessive fans, A. J. Weberman, picking through the trash cans located to the right of his front door. The canisters lay behind a small metal fence, easily accessible to anyone who cared to excavate them. On the day of Dylan's thirtieth birthday, in May 1971, Weberman, who felt his hero had abandoned songs that addressed social conditions and politics, organized a "Free Dylan" rally for his "Dylan Liberation Front" outside the building. Dylan himself was out of town, reportedly in Israel, but that didn't prevent hundreds from clogging MacDougal Street, which the police had barricaded for the occasion. "Bobby, come on out—we know you're in there," Weberman said into one of the three microphones before presenting Dylan with a birthday present—a new garbage can, this one with a lock. "Free Bob Dylan" buttons were handed out.

A new Gaslight regular was Erik Frandsen, a talented and dry-witted finger-picking guitarist who hailed from Sleepy Hollow, New York, and had started playing guitar with David Bromberg, a high school friend a year older than he. Around the time he graduated from high school in 1964, Frandsen and Bromberg visited the Village and grabbed a seat at the Gaslight for an evening with Doc Watson and Skip James, the Mississippi blues guitar great who was then in his early sixties. To his dismay, Frandsen watched as the crowd talked nonstop during James's opening set. Suddenly, Frandsen saw a hulking figure position himself in the door by the stage, taking up the whole frame. At the end of one of James's songs, the man—Van Ronk—glared at the crowd and said, "Shut the fuck up!" The audience complied, and afterward Frandsen approached Van Ronk, introduced himself, and shook his hand, becoming the latest to inquire about guitar lessons.

After a detour living and performing in California, Frandsen returned to New York. Sam Hood offered him work at the Gaslight, and Frandsen soon found himself at the Kettle of Fish as well. One night, one of those Dylanologists was there, extrapolating about the origins of Dylan's "Went to See the Gypsy," included on Dylan's just-released *New Morning* album. Frandsen himself had witnessed Dylan write a portion of the song, which, he recalled, made a reference to Chicago. "Lot of gypsies in Chicago, Bob?" Frandsen had wisecracked. Dylan wondered aloud if Las Vegas was a better idea and changed it. Elvis Presley's run of shows in Vegas may have also inspired the song, although Dylan would later claim the two never met. But here at the Kettle was someone holding forth on the way Dylan intentionally chose Vegas as a symbol for capitalism. Frandsen could only chuckle at the absurdity of it all.

Surveying the state of jazz in the city in 1968, critic Leonard Feather was less than optimistic. Playing off New York's nickname as the "Big Apple," he wrote in his syndicated column that the club scene in New York was "rotten to the core," particularly from Harlem to midtown. The year before, the Five Spot had discontinued presenting music, giving up its cabaret license and focusing on food. ("We used it for storage," Iggie Termini told the *Village Voice*'s Gary Giddins of the music area.) Although Feather didn't refer to it at all, Miles Davis's second quintet was coming apart; Herbie Hancock and Ron Carter had both left by summer of 1968. Feather detected a ray of hope in the Village Gate, but even those dreams were dimming. As Art D'Lugoff told him, "If we had to survive on just jazz, we'd be padlocked within a week." That year, D'Lugoff announced that he could no longer pay the bills and would begin recruiting rock acts, and soon Chuck Berry and a barely eighteen-year-old Stevie Wonder worked its stage.

The Village still played host to adventure, however. In November 1968, Hancock, now on his own, played the Vanguard with a new sextet that included Carter on bass and Pete La Roca, one of the drummers on Rollins's landmark Vanguard live album. The following year saw the opening of Boomers, at the intersection of Bleecker and Christopher Streets. As Mel Watkins would later recall, Boomers initially focused on piano and bass duos, but before long the Black-owned club was also hiring Charles Mingus, Pharoah Sanders, and Joe Beck. At the Vanguard, Chick Corea, who replaced Hancock in Davis's band, would debut a new lineup with bassist Dave Holland, drummer Barry Altschul, and saxophonist Anthony Braxton. But the increasing dominance of rock, the drop-off in jazz gigs, and the sense that the music was no longer being treated with the same respect was prompting musicians, including Dexter Gordon, to uproot themselves and move to Europe.

Even before rock began shifting to the East Village, the jazz world had started the exodus. Disillusioned with the jazz-club business, saxophonist Sam Rivers transformed his home at 24 Bond Street, just east of Broadway, into Studio Rivbea, a loose-knit performance space where players would wander in and out. It was eventually joined by other spots that were one neighborhood or street removed from Greenwich Village's traditional boundaries: Ali's Alley on

Greene Street (started in the apartment of former Coltrane drummer Rashied Ali), the Tin Palace on the Bowery, and Environ, south of Houston in SoHo.

The movement would eventually have a name—loft jazz, after the kind of spaces where the music would be made. In those rooms, which were cheaper than West Village property, free and avant-garde elements of the music flourished. Other loft-jazz venues materialized in Chelsea and the Lower East Side. What united them was that none were in Greenwich Village proper: the Vanguard and Boomers aside, the area seemed to have almost priced itself out of jazz.

With help from Terri Thal, who had taken the Roche sisters under her managerial wing, Maggie (or "Maggi," as it was mistakenly spelled in the ad) and Terre Roche made their formal Village debut on January 22, 1970, opening for Len Chandler. The show was at the space now sometimes called the Village Gaslight. Sam Hood and his wife, singer and songwriter Alix Dobkin, had both left New York for Florida but returned and were working with Ed and Penny Simon, the club's current managers. Other than the name, everything remained in place: the overpriced glasses of apple juice filled with ice, the envelope of cash that one of the staff was told to give to a city inspector when he came by. With the Hudson Dusters consigned to the dustbin of his history, Van Ronk also returned, securing a regular Monday-night slot even as many of the artists who started shortly after he had—Judy Collins, Peter, Paul and Mary, Buffy Sainte-Marie, Phil Ochs—had moved on to large halls and venues.

By then, Maggie had a stack of roughly fifteen finished songs. Fueled by the decade that had just ended and the Vietnam War that raged on, two of them, "War Song" and "Flag," had topical overtones—in the former, a soldier whose "battlefield is strewn with corpses"—that connected them to the Village's previous heyday. John and Jude Roche hadn't been shy with their political opinions: in June 1969 Jude had published a letter in the *Record*, one of their local newspapers, in which she declared she would vote for the independent candidate for governor of New Jersey. "As near as I can figure," she wrote, "the party system does little more than assure a great strength to a powerful few."

But in perhaps the first interview she ever gave, to the *Poughkeepsie Journal* in August 1970, Maggie made it clear she wouldn't be so easily categorized. "We're not trying to put across a political philosophy," she said, adding, "You can get pretty mad at the flag wavers and that kind of behavior." Most of her songs, in fact, were more personal and intimate, like "Malachy's," which chronicled the often indifferent response she received when performing at the Upper East Side bar during her Bard period.

In that regard, the sisters unintentionally embodied the altered singer-songwriter sensibility that had made its way into the Village. With the advent of a new decade, the socially aware songs inspired by headlines were tapering off, and a new approach—more inward, more personal, more resigned to the fact that the largely unlikable Richard Nixon was now president—was encroaching. In March 1970, James Taylor returned to the Village. Following his days with the Flying Machine at the Night Owl and subsequent meltdown, Taylor had moved to England. After he connected with Apple Records executive Peter Asher, Taylor was signed to the Beatles' company, which released his well-received if not commercially successful album.

Taylor's second album, *Sweet Baby James*, was just starting to appear in record stores in the early months of 1970, but he was already a symbol for the new retreat in pop, leading to long lines along MacDougal Street for each of his two nights at the Gaslight. The audience included music-industry types, critics, and even Taylor's father, up from North Carolina to see his still drug-hobbled but now more successful son. Staff worker Denny Brown was handed the responsibility of jamming in as many people as possible in a space that held only about sixty. It was so crowded that the opening act, the Traum brothers, couldn't leave the stage when Taylor began his set. Although the staff couldn't stop the notorious leaky pipe above the stage—leading Taylor to make a crack playing off of the Beatles' "While My Guitar Gently Weeps"—Brown made sure that a smaller rise was placed on stage so that Taylor could sit and still be elevated above the crowd.

To further support the Roche sisters, Thal agreed to help with contacts, starting with a suggestion to take a songwriting class at New York University with Paul Simon. In her typically goal-focused way, Maggie waited in the lobby of the NYU building in the East Village and introduced herself to Simon as he arrived for a class. At the peak of his Simon and Garfunkel phase thanks to the release of *Bridge over Troubled Water*, Simon invited the sisters to audition by way of singing a few songs for him and agreed to let them sit in on the classes, for free. After the first session, Simon drove them in his sports car up to the George Washington Bridge, where they took a bus home to New Jersey. As Terre watched, in awe of her sister, Simon asked Maggie if she considered herself as good a songwriter as Paul McCartney; she replied yes.

Beyond the thought of working with one of pop's most respected songwriters, the class appealed to the sisters in terms of Simon's success in a duo with Garfunkel and the gentle, introspective sound they'd created. "We were thinking that what we were doing is what they were doing," Maggie said. "We were patterning ourselves after them." The sisters watched as Simon carefully dissected the work of some of their classmates, including a local songwriter named Melissa Manchester, and observed how he didn't seem to flinch when a camera crew filmed one of the sessions. With the help of one of their father's friends, the sisters sublet an apartment on Charles Street in the West Village and landed a ten-week residency at the same bar, Malachy's, where Maggie had played on her own while at Bard.

Maggie's emphasis on the personal over the political in her new songs was evident in other incoming songwriters. The same season that the Roche sisters had driven into New York and met Young and Van Ronk, Loudon Wainwright III made his debut at the Gaslight. Beginning with his upmarket name and short-haired, straight-arrow look, which incorporated buttoned shirts and slacks, Wainwright was far from anyone's cliché of a Village bohemian. Growing up in Westchester County, the son of journalist and *Life* magazine columnist Loudon Wainwright, he had been a rakish, boarding-school preppie. The first records in his collection were Fats Domino singles, but he caught the folk bug around 1960, forming a jug band at St. Andrew's school in Delaware and, during weekends back home, taking the train into Manhattan to see the likes of Van Ronk and Clarence Ashley at Folk City. He studied theater at Carnegie Tech, where he and his fellow student and pal George Gerdes played some early attempts at rock. Winding up in San Francisco during its vaunted Summer of

Love in 1967, Wainwright indulged in psychedelics and other aspects of that culture, but he came to realize he wasn't meant for the hippie life and made his way back to the East Coast.

Busted for weed on the drive back, Wainwright retreated to his grandmother's house in Rhode Island and began writing songs and playing them to Japanese tourists in a Village basket house. In the summer of 1969, Wainwright began working the open-mic nights in Cambridge, Massachusetts, and at the Gaslight before landing opening slots for some of its name performers, such as Carolyn Hester and John Hammond.

Compared to acts like those and their peers, who took themselves very seriously, Wainwright wrote and sang songs that were comic and caustic, often taking the knife to his own wrist in the process. "Glad to See You've Got Religion" took aim at the escalating self-help movement. A breakup song like "I Don't Care" wasn't remotely maudlin or nostalgic, and his ode to his prep school period, "School Days," wasn't afraid to brag about the girls he took to his bed. In "Uptown" he even complained about the squalid conditions in the Village and dreamed of leaving it all behind for a day and taking in Central Park, a basketball game at the Garden, and a museum visit or two. In performance at the Gaslight, Wainwright wasn't always a genteel folkie either. To fend off stage fright, he would whip his tongue in and out; at times, his face could twist into grimaces that made one reviewer compare him to a "Quasimodo-like derelict."

Still, the music business continued to sniff around for post-Dylan troubadours. Milton Kramer, who ran the publishing company Frank Music, caught a Wainwright set at the club and was duly impressed, and after the *Village Voice* called him "unquestionably great," record executives, including Atlantic's Ahmet Ertegun, could be seen wedged behind the Gaslight's tables. Very quickly, Wainwright ended up with a contract with Atlantic, which outbid Columbia.

Like many who came aboard the scene, Wainwright found himself befriending Van Ronk, who, for all his surface sternness, could still be supportive and welcoming. After hearing Wainwright's "Plane Too," a deadpan list of everything he experienced on a flight, from a copy of *Time* magazine to "earphone music" and "airplane booze," Van Ronk told him it was either the best or the worst song he'd ever heard. Wainwright wasn't sure what to make of that comment, but he came to view Van Ronk and Patrick Sky as older brothers, joining them on various escapades in and out of the city. Although Wainwright could throw back his share of drinks, he couldn't always keep up with Van Ronk and Sky. Some nights at the Kettle of Fish, he would take a shot of whiskey and, when Van Ronk wasn't looking, pour it out on the sawdust floor.

On June 28, 1969, Van Ronk was two days from turning thirty-three and having an early birthday meal with friends at the Lion's Head on Christopher Street. The Lion's Head remained a magnet for writers, musicians, and artists; it wasn't uncommon to find one of the Clancy brothers, Art D'Lugoff, or other local luminaries inside. But once he began hearing police sirens, followed by some type of commotion, Van Ronk knew tonight would not be his usual evening at the bar.

Stepping outside to gauge what was taking place, Van Ronk saw a crowd outside the Stonewall Inn two doors down. At 53 Christopher Street, a few streets south of the Village Vanguard and a quick walk to the Sheridan Square area once home to Cafe Society, the Stonewall had become a hub for gay men and women and runaways. A Mob-owned joint, the Stonewall didn't have a liquor license; gay dancing and kissing were considered "disorderly" and therefore illegal. Instead, it was dubbed a private-membership "bottle bar" (as in "bring your own"), and as with most of the gay and lesbian bars in the Village, the Mafia also routinely bribed police to keep those businesses open.

Tonight, though, a full-on raid was taking place, the street outside the Stonewall filled with gay men who'd been told to leave while the police went through the bar and dragged others out. As each person was pulled out and emerged on the street, the crowd outside cheered him or her on. Once the paddy wagons arrived, though, the mood turned defiant, and the crowd, expressing its pent-up anger at the harassment, began hurling bottles and coins at the cops.

As Van Ronk told author and Stonewall historian David Carter, he was happy to add his voice and whatever else to the protest. "What I saw was another example of police arrogance and corruption," he told Carter. "As far as I was concerned, anybody who'd stand against the cops was all right with me, and that's why I stayed." Van Ronk admitted to Carter that he too had "tossed a quarter or just some pennies" in the direction of the cops. As he was preparing to head back into the Lion's Head (or, according to one policeman, retreat into the crowd), a cop grabbed him. The two fell over, and Van Ronk was arrested and pulled inside the Stonewall, where he was handcuffed. Since it took three cops to overcome Van Ronk, none remained on the street, which, according to an initial report in the *Village Voice*, intensified the protest. Along with others who were arrested, Van Ronk was booked at the Sixth Precinct for second-degree assault for allegedly hurling an "object" at one police officer. His court dates were scheduled and rescheduled several times, up through February 17, 1970, when he appeared in court and charges were dismissed; Van Ronk ultimately pled guilty to harassment and paid a fine.

The antagonism between authorities and gays in the Village had been fomenting for years. In 1964 Police Commissioner Michael J. Murphy, with the approval of then Village Democratic leader Ed Koch, assigned more police to the Village to curb, as the *New York Times* put it, "loitering and solicitation by homosexuals." In one form or another, music venues that catered to a gay audience were also affected. By the time of the Stonewall riot, the Page Three, the basement space with the cross-dressing crowd that had nurtured talents like Sheila Jordan, had shut down. Dating back to 1937, Tony Pastor's, the restaurant on West Third Street into which Folk City had moved in 1969, had originally been a nightclub, complete with a gay clientele, a large dance floor, and live, small-combo music. But in March 1967 the city revoked its liquor license after determining it had allowed, in the words of the State Liquor Authority of New York, "homosexuals, degenerates and undesirables to be on the license premises and conduct themselves in an offensive and indecent manner." The Bon Soir, the cabaret on Eighth Street that had been the launchpad for Barbra Streisand a decade before, was also history.

In the wake of the Stonewall Riot, the gay-rights movement grew and became emboldened, and a new wave of venues began springing up to cater to both gay and straight crowds—and for those in search of modern rock and roll and pop. Named after a character in Cole Porter's musical *Anything Goes*, Reno Sweeney took up the basement of two brownstones on West Thirteenth Street. The decor was art-deco–chic, with palm trees flanking the stage. From its opening in October 1972, the club was envisioned as a successor to the Bon Soir, even down to hiring that club's former emcee, Jimmie Daniels, and it aimed for both gay and straight acts and audiences.

It would be gay acts—which included Australian singer, songwriter, and pianist Peter Allen, who would came out as gay, and early transgender and Warhol Gang darling Holly Woodlawn—that especially came to be associated with the club. As *Rolling Stone* would report, "This year the gays dominated the club scene with places like Reno Sweeney, where Barbra Streisand lookalikes (male and female) sing smoky ballads and people primp and parade in ice-cream outfits under lighting that makes everybody a star." Three months after it opened, Reno Sweeney hosted a party for Bette Midler, who'd sung backup for another act during the club's earliest weeks and was now a brassy, red-haired hurricane of a star, with a gay following she'd developed playing at the Continental Baths uptown.

The same year Reno Sweeney launched, David Johansen heard about a new opportunity for the band he'd just joined. Although he'd grown up on Staten Island—and had the brusque accent to prove it—the hardened-faced Johansen felt more than plugged into downtown life. When he was a child in the fifties, an aunt would take him to a restaurant in the West Village where waiters would do the limbo; as a teenager, he took day trips to MacDougal Street and the Night Owl, where he saw the Lovin' Spoonful and the Blues Magoos. The atmosphere and security in those venues were so casual that when he saw Van Morrison at the Cafe Au Go Go in 1968, Johansen was able to walk into the dressing room and chat him up. A natural performer with the strut, swagger, and comic leer of a front man, Johansen soon had his own bands. His first, the Vagabond Missionaries, played R&B covers and a few originals during afternoon shows at the Cafe Wha?. "We were not very good," he said, "but we made up for it in enthusiasm."

In late 1971, Johansen joined what would become the New York Dolls, which owed more of a debt to garage rock and glam than any of the other bands that thrived at the intersection of Bleecker and MacDougal. Johansen was also friendly with Eric Emerson, the front man of what Johansen called a "gypsy rock and roll" band called the Magic Tramps and also a bisexual member of the Warhol gang. "Eric said, 'I'm playing at this new place—do you want to come and play before we play?'" Johansen recalled. "And I said yeah. We were just starting up and trying to get any gig we could get. We weren't *choosy*. Our first gig was in a welfare hotel, so this was a step up."

Located just west of Broadway and a block north of Bleecker, the Mercer Arts Center wasn't strictly a music venue. Carved out of the back half of the Broadway Central Hotel, where young folkies like John Sebastian and John Hammond had once watched visiting bluesmen party, the Mercer had been converted into a series of small theaters, a sort of avant-garde downtown version of Lincoln Center. Over the previous century, the space had been home to venues like the Winter Garden, where John Wilkes Booth and his brother had acted in *Julius Caesar* the year before Booth shot Abraham Lincoln. In 1966 the Village Gate's Art D'Lugoff had leased the space, but in 1971 air-conditioner magnate Seymour Kaback took control, taking over the first two floors of the back of the hotel and converting them into the Mercer Arts Center. "I mix my air conditioning people in with it, so we've got five on the staff altogether," Kaback explained at the time. Even the city lent an unexpected hand: the Economic Development Office contributed money for improved street lighting, more regular trash pickup, and a new sidewalk.

The Broadway Central, renamed the University Hotel in 1969 but often referred to by its previous name, was a $5.70-per-night dump known for housing addicts and criminals. But the Mercer Arts Center, which opened in January 1970, was its own universe. The entrance, at 240 Mercer, led to a staircase and a narrow corridor with a labyrinth of rooms, with a capacity ranging from fifty to several hundred people. Rooms that once were rented for bar mitzvahs and wedding banquets were home to off-Broadway plays such as *One Flew Over the Cuckoo's Nest* and video installations. But two of its theaters, the 299-seat O'Casey and the 200-seat Oscar Wilde Room, weren't merely performance spaces. With the Village rock world never shakier, the theaters provided work for musicians, possible salvation for the scene—and a haven for a sexually liberated music community seeking to define itself in a new decade.

In the summer of 1972, the Blues Project resurfaced on Bleecker Street, and in their old haunt. But a mere half-dozen years after they'd recorded their first album at the Cafe Au Go Go, neither the band nor the venue that had established them was the same. Ever since it shuttered at the end of 1969, the Cafe Au Go Go had remained vacant, a depressing symbol of how hollowed out the scene had become. Then, in the spring of 1971, it suddenly reopened, but with a new and mystifying name—the Gaslight at the Au Go Go—that only added another layer of confusion.

In spite of higher-profile bookings like James Taylor's, the original Gaslight had struggled. Local lore had it that Sam Hood and his father, Clarence, had placed a $100 bet on the Mets to win the pennant and World Series in 1969. To everyone's surprise, the Mets pulled out a miracle. But the bookie didn't pay up—he was supposedly fished out of the East or Hudson River—and Hood allegedly never collected on his $100,000 windfall. In the spring of 1971, the Gaslight briefly closed, and Hood moved his business into 152 Bleecker Street, once home of the Cafe Au Go Go, and rechristened it the Gaslight at the Au Go Go. To complicate matters, the first Gaslight then reopened in its original MacDougal Street location, now managed by Ed Simon, who had run the Four Winds basket house.

The reconstituted Gaslight at the Au Go Go, which held about three times as many people as the original Gaslight, launched auspiciously with Miles Davis and an electric band. After each show, Denny Brown, who had moved from his job washing dishes and other tasks at the Gaslight to help manage the new place, had to pay Davis nightly, in cash, and with a Davis valet watching carefully. "Miles didn't trust anyone," Brown said. "I'm counting out cash and there are guns in the room. And they weren't mine. He wanted to get paid."

Among the familiar faces seen on the stage was Danny Kalb, making his return to the club that had launched the Blues Project. Since the dissolution of the group in 1968, Al Kooper had instigated his plan to merge rock with jazz and big-band horns, emerging with Blood, Sweat & Tears, which also included his former Blues Project adversary Steve Katz. Moving to Marin County, Roy Blumenfeld and Andy Kulberg formed Seatrain from the remnants of the Blues Project's final lineup. As for Kalb, he was still recovering from his debilitating drug experience but was attempting to pick up where he'd left off. Early in 1969, he'd formed Danny Kalb and His Friends, sharing vocal duties with Karen Dalton, the early Village fixture who had moved out west and grappled with heroin and alcohol issues before making her way back east. The group played at the first Cafe Au Go Go but dissolved by summer.

A few months later, Kalb revived the name that had established him: "The Blues Project II featuring Danny Kalb" debuted at the new Au Go Go, with only Kalb remaining from the original band. That same year, Kalb finally reemerged on record. With Stefan Grossman, the guitarist who had played in the Even Dozen Jug Band with Steve Katz and John Sebastian, he made an album, *Crosscurrents*. Most of the songs were sung by Grossman, whose adept fingerpicking, with its roots in Celtic music, dominated the album. Vocally, Kalb stepped out for only two songs. His version of Son House's "Death Letter Blues," about a man who receives a letter from a woman after she died, was stark and chilling. But his guitar, and the way it intermingled with Grossman's, hadn't lost its sting or sparkle.

In August 1970, Kalb and his friend Ron Radosh attended a Muddy Waters show at the Museum of Modern Art, which held concerts in one of its gardens. Kalb had long worshipped Waters and felt redeemed when the bluesman commended Kalb on his version of "Two Trains Running." "Muddy heard Danny do it and he said, 'You got me with that one—you reached me,'" said John Berenzy, a local college student and guitarist who befriended Kalb during this time. "Danny said it was the high point of his life." But after approaching Waters at the museum and having a quick chat with his idol before the set, Kalb announced he had to leave, for reasons never made clear to Radosh. Maybe it was all still too much for him.

Berenzy, a Blues Project aficionado, had randomly called Kalb one day. To his surprise, Kalb invited him to a restaurant where he was playing a gig. "He was part of that tradition, like the Weavers—he would play anywhere,"

Berenzy said. "He loved playing for people and he loved the folk tradition of telling stories." Later Kalb invited him to his Village apartment for a guitar lesson. Berenzy took note of the studio apartment with its large windows, record and book collection, and eat-in kitchen. Kalb would down many cups of coffee, smoke, and tell tales, such as the one about the time he showed up at Van Ronk's for a lesson and instead gave *him* one. Berenzy found Kalb's stories about his hallucinatory meltdown heartbreaking.

In 1971 Kalb and Blumenfeld, who had left Seatrain and the music business and was working as a lumberjack, reconvened and revived the Blues Project as a trio with bassist Don Kretmar, landing a contract with Capitol. Released in 1971, *Lazarus* had its moments; the title song, the same traditional tune Van Ronk had taught to Kalb, was transformed into eerie, simmering electric blues. (On the cover, in contrast to his smiling bandmates, Kalb appeared sullen and more disheveled than during his Blues Project days, another sign that he was still coping with the aftereffects of his bad trip.) But while opening for the likes of Black Sabbath and Yes, the new Blues Project found itself confronting the new rock world order that had arisen since they'd dissolved. Before each set, Blumenfeld would stand up from his drums, flash a peace sign, and scream, "You wanna rock and roll?" The audience would scream back in unison—and then the band would open with an unhurried blues. "You could hear the yawning and see people talking among themselves," Blumenfeld recalled. "It was a different game."

In 1972 original front man Tommy Flanders returned for one more album, but the resulting record, simply titled *Blues Project*, again failed to relight the old fire. The band made it through a few shows, including one at the Gaslight at the Au Go Go, but at their Los Angeles performance at the Troubadour, Kalb was missing in action. Joni Mitchell, who was in attendance, asked Blumenfeld where he was. After one last show, in New York's Central Park, Kalb, depressed over the latest incarnation's lack of liftoff, left the band. Knowing how much the label had invested in the group, a Capitol executive asked Blumenfeld if he wanted to keep it going without its founder. Blumenfeld declined, and the Blues Project as an active band was laid to rest.

At times, the Gaslight at the Au Go Go remained a destination. In May 1972 a blossoming Jersey talent named Bruce Springsteen auditioned there for John Hammond, who would soon sign him to Columbia. But that same year, the original Gaslight finally closed for good, as did the Gaslight at the Au Go Go the following year, seemingly taking Village rock and roll with it.

▌▐▐▐▌

In Park Ridge, New Jersey, in early 1972, the Roche family had just settled down for dinner when the phone rang. The caller was none other than Paul Simon, and he was asking for Maggie. Given what the sisters had been through in the years since they'd taken his class, the call came not a moment too soon for their salvation.

On the recommendation of Terri Thal, the sisters had dragged their guitars and cases over to the Bitter End early in 1970. By then, owner Fred Weintraub had handed the keys to his club over to its manager, Paul Colby. Starting with early bookings like Joni Mitchell, who made her New York debut at the space in June 1968, the Bitter End was supplanting Folk City and the Gaslight as a leading showcase for the new wave of troubadours from around the country, including Randy Newman in 1970 and John Prine in 1971. During one of his sets, Kris Kristofferson invited a friend in the audience, Steve Goodman, to come up and play his newly written "City of New Orleans."

The Bitter End had also become the place for those eager to break into music and show business to audition for what was called the Coffee House Circuit (which, at various times, had the word "College" or "Campus" preceding it). Established pop and rock acts with hit records or large followings could make a good living playing colleges and universities, but the market had become so lucrative, and the artists had begun demanding such exorbitant fees, that some schools could no longer afford them. Established by Weintraub in 1966 and run by his company's vice president of special projects, Marilyn Lipsius, the Coffee House Circuit would offer unsigned or nascent musicians to colleges, which would pay two hundred dollars per year to Weintraub's organization; in turn, the Coffee House Circuit would book and promote the shows. The musicians would be paid a few hundred dollars a week and had to play two sets per night for a week in a school's cafeteria, student union, or similar space.

With the Bitter End's famed brick wall behind them, the one immortalized on the first Peter, Paul and Mary album, the Roche sisters sang a few of Maggie's songs. Their voices weren't as tightly blended as those of their heroes Simon and Garfunkel; sometimes the harmonies would circle around each other as if they were each singing their own separate melodies. But the blend of Maggie's and Terre's different tones was unique, and with John and Jude Roche's approval, they were offered one of those college touring jobs, even though Terre was still a senior in high school. Starting in Fargo, North Dakota, the duo traveled to schools out west and down to Louisiana, and to spaces that would sometimes be reconfigured to look like something familiar. Revealing what a brand the "Village" had become, said Terre, "They would turn the cafeteria into a coffeehouse patterned after the Gaslight or the Cafe Wha?." During their show at Louisiana State University, a student reporter compared Maggie to "a very tranquil Janis Joplin" who "might weigh 80 pounds with guitar," and described their music as "up-to-date folk."

At a school in West Virginia, the sisters, along with Derek, a friend they'd met in Louisiana, got high on mescalin and were fired from the circuit. That escapade would be nothing compared to the wild and sometimes traumatic times to follow. After one last show in Idaho—and a gig opening for, of all people, the Vegasy pop belter Gary Puckett, in Missouri—the sisters kept going west, ending up in San Francisco. With contacts supplied by Thal, they ended up at a newly opened, three-hundred-seat club, the Boarding House, where they began gigging regularly starting in May 1971. At open-mic nights at other clubs, they would play to small crowds who didn't know who they were and didn't seem interested in songs that were lovely but decidedly quirky.

The music soon stopped, though, once Maggie fell in love with the club's bartender and Terre with their soundman. As Terre would recount in her memoir *Blabbermouth*, the sisters began living a lifestyle that felt, at least to an outsider, like a rebuttal to their strict Catholic upbringing; Terre would remember taking acid daily for a month. They also crisscrossed the country, Maggie falling pregnant along the way, and eventually returned to their quasi-base in San

Francisco. After putting her sister on a bus back to New Jersey, Terre remained in San Francisco but found herself with a drug-dealer boyfriend, his nefarious friends and associates, and a black eye after getting into a fight with a Boarding House employee and another woman. When she took a detour down to Los Angeles to see Van Ronk, who was playing there, he took one look at her and said, "I'd like to see what happened to the other guy." Terre's time out west would soon come to an end; after a devastating sexual assault in the middle of the day in Golden Gate Park, she too returned to the family home in New Jersey.

Undeterred, Maggie began phoning Paul Simon's office daily, leaving a message each time. When he finally returned her call during the family meal, Simon, who remembered them from his class, asked what was so urgent. Maggie filled him in on the songs she'd written and that the sisters had been performing, and Simon suggested she reach out to his lawyer and business partner, Michael Tannen. At his Upper East Side apartment, Tannen didn't know what to make of the women who showed up at his door. Maggie was eight months' pregnant—she would soon give birth to a son, in March 1972, whom she would give up for adoption—and Terre looked to him as if she were twelve. Tannen listened as they went through their repertoire, then told them about the publishing company he and Simon had started. Soon, the sisters were signed to DeShufflin Music and provided with an apartment on Sullivan Street in the Village, the rent paid by Simon and Tannen's company. Simon also took them record shopping and hooked them up with music teachers to hone Maggie and Terre's chops on piano and guitar, respectively.

The sisters also went back on the road for further college-campus work. In Pittsburgh they learned from Tannen that Simon had expressed interest in having them sing on his second post–Simon and Garfunkel album, which he was recording in Muscle Shoals, Alabama. Without alerting Simon of their plans, Terre and Maggie took a bus to that city and showed up at the famed Muscle Shoals Sound Studio. Simon and the ace session musicians he'd hired were out to lunch, and when they returned, the sisters were waiting for them outside the studio. For a Caribbean-flavored amble, "Was a Sunny Day," Simon told them he'd been absorbing Jimmy Cliff's soundtrack to *The Harder They*

Come and wanted the sisters to add harmonies similar to those on that album. They did their best and were soon back on a bus to Pennsylvania.

Months later, in May 1973, Maggie and Terre received a finished copy of Simon's album, *There Goes Rhymin' Simon*. Cracking open its gatefold sleeve, they were shocked to see a photo of themselves inside; Simon's camp had somehow gotten hold of a shot and had kept it a complete surprise. After a tumultuous three years, it was hard to imagine a better reintroduction for the sisters to a world they thought had tossed them aside.

Starting in the first month of 1973, Dylan, Baez, and James Taylor made return engagements to the Village, but not in the way anyone would have expected or predicted.

As he began making his way daily from his apartment on Bank Street to the Village Gate, Christopher Guest still recognized much about his neighborhood. The thirty-one-year-old son of a British United Nations diplomat had grown up at 160 Waverly Place, down the block from Van Ronk and Thal's home, and had played stoopball in Washington Square Park as a kid. For a time, his babysitter was Mary Travers, a family friend; later, she would later drop off copies of the latest Peter, Paul and Mary records at the Guest family home. (A folk purist who gravitated toward Alan Lomax field recordings, Guest admitted he wasn't initially taken with Peter, Paul and Mary records: "I never opened one of them. They were always put in the closet because I thought, 'This is just not my thing. These are ostensibly folk songs, but this isn't real folk music.'") After learning to play guitar, the teenage Guest picked out a regular spot around the fountain and discovered the Folklore Center, where he once saw Dylan asking to try out a guitar hanging on the wall. He was too scared to say anything to him or to Van Ronk, whose beard and lumbering gait reminded Guest of a pirate.

When the Bleecker and MacDougal intersection became overrun with out of towners, Guest, like many locals, learned to walk in the middle of the street to circumvent the gawkers. He eventually landed a job at the Village Vanguard, where he worked the cash register until Max Gordon relieved him of those responsibilities after a few incorrect-change flubs. He also helped escort the blind multi-instrumentalist Rahsaan Roland Kirk from the dressing room to the stage; Kirk would hold onto Guest's arm, bob his head back and forth, and say, mysteriously, "Chris, where I am right now, you can't write to me."

Before his family moved uptown in 1963, Guest and his friends would often run over to Washington Square Park, with his mother's approval, and return home on their own when dusk fell. Now, the park was a place to avoid—filled with, as he put it, "people sleeping on the sidewalk and broken bottles." Mark Sebastian, John's brother, was playing the clubs himself at the time and would notice the junkies in Washington Square Park as he walked from the family's apartment on Washington Square West down to Bleecker Street. At the Gaslight, Catherine Todd took note of customers nodding out at tables. "I thought they were just falling asleep," she recalled. "I'd say to the girlfriend, 'Is your friend all right? He can go lay down if he's tired.' She would say, 'No, he's all right.' I didn't understand heroin. *Nobody* understood heroin or cocaine at the time." The Hotel Albert, once an affordable retreat for musicians, was now populated with addicts and derelicts.

Izzy Young told *Village Voice* writer Ira Mayer that his store was doing only a third of the business it had done during the mid-sixties. Rightly sensing that the Village music community was in decline—concerts in the store would sometimes only attract a dozen people, recalled Mayer—Young set his sights on Sweden. His wife, who was French, was intrigued by the Swedish women's movement, and Young had met Swedish musicians in his store who filled him in on their scene and their nation's progressive politics. In 1973 he closed the Folklore Center and moved there.

The grime and gloom overtaking the city as a whole, making it feel psychologically overcast, also left its mark downtown. In 1973 the number of burglaries in the Village was 31 percent higher than in other parts of the city, and grisly stories seemed everywhere. A Macy's copywriter was robbed and stabbed in the foyer of her Hudson Street apartment by a heroin addict who took seven dollars from her; a week later, an aspiring actor was also fatally stabbed outside his Ninth Avenue home. Store owners along Bleecker began closing early for the night after the city placed hundreds of Rikers Island inmates at a hotel on the block. In response to the crime wave, four hundred Village residents marched on the Sixth Precinct to demand more police protection. St. John's Lutheran Church, on Christopher Street, launched what it called Operation Eye-Opener to take in runaways being lured into addiction and prostitution. When it came to drug dealers, "the staff from the church has often had to fight to get a runaway from them and back to the safety of the church," it reported. In a wildly overstated number that still spoke volumes about how the Village was being perceived, St. John's also claimed that "85 percent of the residents take drugs."

In 1970 Guest had received a call from Jerry Taylor, the publisher of *National Lampoon*—and also Mary Travers's husband at the time. At that point, Guest was in acting school and hadn't written much of anything, but when Taylor asked if he wanted to contribute an article to the magazine, Guest soon became part of a stable of gonzo-satirical writers and editors. A gifted musician and mimic who could submerge his low-key personality into his characters, Guest took acting jobs—including one soap opera where he was asked to portray a dope-smoking, bongo-playing hippie—but truly came into his own with the *Lampoon*. Overseen by writers and editors Tony Hendra and Michael O'Donoghue, the 1971 *Lampoon* album *Radio Dinner* didn't remotely spare the music heroes of the previous decade. Guest's parody of Dylan—"Those Fabulous Sixties," an ad for an album, *Golden Protest*, of vintage topical songs—was so spot on that the magazine received a threatening call from Dylan's lawyer.

Having ventured into magazines and albums, the *Lampoon* bosses decided to franchise their success and create a stage production that could tour around the country. As *Radio Dinner* suggested, the new big-money business of rock and the increasing insularity and wealth of its superstars were easy targets. As casting proceeded, it turned out that some were skilled at mocking rock: Guest for one, but also John Belushi, recruited from Second City in Chicago, who nailed the hot mess that was Joe Cocker. "A bunch of us got together and started kicking this thing around," said another newly hired cast member, Chevy Chase, a twenty-five-year-old comic-ensemble actor and writer who was skilled at acting, drumming, and piano playing. "We discovered what each of us could do and built the show around these individual abilities."

Lampoon editor Hendra, a thirty-two-year-old Brit with long blond hair and a subtle wit, would direct the show, and Guest and Canadian-born *Lampoon* writer Sean Kelly, along with the show's musical director, Paul Jacobs, would write the parodies. The actors would serve as the band, with Guest on guitar, Chase on drums, Jacobs on assorted instruments, and Belushi attempting bass. The *Lampoon* secured the Village Gate, which had been hosting off-Broadway and often-irreverent theater productions for years, including the hot-ticket revue *Jacques Brel Is Alive and Well and Living in Paris* and *MacBird!*, a satire of Lyndon Johnson and Vietnam that was shut down at least once by the Fire Department during its nearly year-long run. Art D'Lugoff suspected that the latter show's leftist bent offended certain department officials, but he was never able to confirm his suspicions.

The first half of the show called *National Lampoon's Lemmings* comprised a series of random sketches, such as Chase playing a Hells Angel who wanted to take down a "peace creep" for daring to touch his motorcycle. Chase delighted in those moments when he would push his way into the seated crowd and get a bit too up close and personal with some in the audience. "I remember some guy was like, 'Don't touch me!'" Chase said. "It was wonderful." Other sketches mocked *Jesus Christ Superstar*, the ubiquitous gospel-rock musical.

But by the early seventies, no more enticing pop target existed than Woodstock. As chaotic as it was, the 1969 festival had spawned a cottage industry all its own, including a lucrative feature film and two best-selling albums. Guest himself hadn't attended the gathering. "I thought, 'This is just going to be a bunch of these fucking bozos from New Jersey—it's going to be a nightmare,'" he recalled. "I wouldn't go near there." He wasn't the only one who thought it ripe for savagery; Chase also found the Woodstock legend lacking, saying at the time that it "didn't really work—it was the peak of the acid era, and everyone there was wiped out on drugs."

The second half of *Lemmings* delivered on that scathing assessment. Called the "Woodchuck Festival of Peace, Love and Death," it skewered the idea of mass rock gatherings, starting with the premise that the fans who flocked to them were a brain-dead herd being sent to their death. In his role as the festival's emcee, Belushi encouraged fans to climb the sound towers so they could leap to their demise; an "All Star Dead Band" comprised Jim Morrison, Janis Joplin, Duane Allman, and Paul McCartney, who, according to a conspiracy theory, had supposedly died four years before. "The *Lampoon* always had this other side, which was pretty out there," Guest said. "And this was the music version of that."

The Village Gate had had troubles of its own; six months before, D'Lugoff held a benefit, with music by David Amram, to bolster its finances. "The Village nightlife scene isn't what it used to be," D'Lugoff told *Newsday*, "but I believe it's on the upswing now." Still, when the cast and crew of *Lemmings* gathered at the club for opening night on January 25, 1973, they found the doors padlocked. The club had fallen behind in its taxes, and only a last-minute cash infusion from one of the *Lemmings* producers kept it open. *Lemmings* could be equally chaotic backstage. During its run, Hendra introduced Belushi to cocaine; Guest would glimpse Belushi's dealer at the backstage door, and he watched as his costar overdosed twice. Hendra fired Belushi for being out of control, only to rehire him. "We needed him," Chase said. "I'm sorry he was an asshole, but we needed that asshole!" Chase freaked out one night when an actual Hells Angel was in the audience, brandishing a weapon in case he saw anything offensive in the show.

Lemmings not only had an edge that had long been missing from the artists who played Bleecker Street; it also had more buzz than just about anything apart from the occasional event, like Stevie Wonder's run at the Bitter End in 1972. The *Daily News* called the revue "generally hilarious," and the show, which ran every day of the week except Mondays, began doing brisk business. Dylan, who still had a home around the corner on MacDougal Street, was never spotted in the audience, but Dustin Hoffman was, along with James Taylor and Carly Simon, pop's reigning soft-rock power couple. (Simon and Chase had also briefly dated during their high school years in New York City.) Guest was about to play "Highway Toes," a devastating parody of Taylor ("Farewell to Carolina, where I left my frontal lobes," went one line), when he saw the couple take front-row seats. "James is sitting there looking up at me," Guest said, "and I'm thinking, 'Wait a minute, have I fucked up? I love this guy. I love his songs. What am I doing?'" Simon laughed hysterically at the satire of her husband, but Taylor, who was in the grip of addiction, seemed catatonic to Guest. Afterward, Taylor and Simon visited backstage, but Taylor merely stood there, never saying a word.

Guest also noticed an occasional person in the Village Gate audience, possibly on heroin or another drug, nodding out in his or her seat. "It was a dark time because the surrounding area was very much changed, and even the people who came to the show were those 'other people,' as I called them," said Guest. "It was not like doing a show in the Sixties. It had all changed. It was all on the verge of some other thing."

Although *Lemmings* served as a commentary on major-league rock, it also, in its way, skewered the Village and the style of music most associated with it. Guest reprised his Dylan parody, this time with a guitar and harmonica rack and having him play the Woodchuck Festival only after Belushi, as the emcee, flashed a wad of cash. As first heard on the *Radio Dinner* album, Mary-Jennifer Mitchell sang a devastating satire of Baez and liberal piety, "Pull the Tregros," written by Hendra and arranged by Guest. A sitcom parody starring Mimi Fariña was tabled as being too arcane, but even without it, a show that mocked some of the stars of the Village became the show to see in the area throughout 1973.

Lemmings closed in November 1973, moving on to Philadelphia for the first stop on a planned national tour that didn't come to fruition. That cast included only Belushi and Chase from the Village Gate production, but did add former Lovin' Spoonful guitarist Zal Yanovsky, who was still grappling with life after the band and who got into fisticuffs with Chase. Before it ended its New York run, the cast gathered in a Village bar to do one more interview to promote the opening of the Philly version. Chase cradled a glass of beer that, in Village tradition, had a cockroach in it. "Would you bring me another glass?" he asked the waitress. "Either another glass or another roach."

Lenny Kaye, a twenty-five-year-old guitarist and rock critic working at the Village Oldies record store on Bleecker Street, began noticing flyers on the wall of the store for the New York Dolls. Having seen the Blues Project, Hendrix, and the Fugs the previous decade, Kaye had witnessed the Village's first rock era rise and sputter out. But the handbill for the Dolls, advertising a show at the Mercer Arts Center, promised an outlandish new dawn.

First in the Oscar Wilde Room and then in the larger O'Casey, Kaye and a few hundred others saw a band that, musically and visually, made everything about rock and roll in the Village at that time look and sound as dated as a Vietnam protest ballad. The Dolls were a battered-bridge-and-tunnel version of the Rolling Stones, with none of the white-blues jamming, progressive-rock excursions, or troubadour balladry that had overtaken FM radio. "They were resurrecting values in rock and roll that myself, along with many other rock journalists at the time, felt were in need of revisiting," Kaye said. "The Dolls brought it right back to the hard beat and sense of humor and a lot of bouncing around on a stage that was informed by this pansexual atmosphere of New York City at the time." Kaye ended up going to see them every week.

The Dolls themselves—David Johansen, guitarists Johnny Thunders and Sylvain Sylvain, bassist Arthur Kane, and drummer Jerry Nolan (replacing original member Billy Murcia, who overdosed in late 1972)—were straight men who all looked as if they'd been on a bender, woken up in the home of a woman they didn't know, and left in her clothes. Johansen could come onstage with his hair in a bun or wearing a gold bodysuit, and some of the other band members sported eyeliner and makeup. Nothing about it, musically or visually, would ever be associated with the Bitter End or Folk City, which made it all the more enticing to kids like Lance Loud and his high school friend Kristian Hoffman. In California, Hoffman had seen a photo of the Dolls in *Melody Maker*, the British music newspaper, and he and Loud—who was becoming semi-famous as part of television's first reality show, *An American Family*— moved to New York. The Dolls were one of the first groups they saw play live, and Hoffman was especially entranced. "They were theater of outrage," he said. "They were playful with sexuality. Lance didn't come out on the show, but he started putting on eye makeup during that time." Even the songs stood out: "Vietnamese Baby" was antiwar, but not in the old-school Village sense. "It wasn't a folk song," Hoffman said. "We hated those songs, and the albums with a stupid jam on one side and three tone-deaf blues covers on the other side. We were completely reactionary against that, and so were the Dolls."

One of their opening acts was the Planets, an equally stage-storming and also interracial band featuring guitarist Binky Philips and front man Tally Taliaferrow. Like Kaye, Philips had checked out the Dolls and was instantly hooked; he was especially moved by "Frankenstein," which felt like Johansen's commentary on how he would be teased about his looks as a kid. "Nobody was booking rock bands with original material," said Philips. "You could be a folkie and get a gig at the Bitter End and play an entire set of songs you wrote. The Dolls were the first band in my memory who could get away with playing nothing but originals. They opened the door for all of us."

By the time the Planets were able to share the stage with the Dolls at the Mercer Arts Center, the Dolls were very much a sensation, with a growing and increasingly flamboyantly dressed crowd. By Philips's estimate, "About 30 percent of the audience was decked out in high-heeled boots and satin pants, up from 10 percent." David Bowie, in his full-on Ziggy Stardust phase, was spotted there at least once. The audience wasn't heavily gay; many remember it being largely hetero, including plenty of women lusting for a Doll of their own. But the freedom to be whatever one craved was in the air. Paul Nelson, the music critic then working as a publicist for Mercury Records, became a relentless champion of the Dolls and called those nights "a benign *Clockwork Orange* filmed in a packed-to-the-rafters Hollywood Mutant High wired for massive sound." As Johansen recalled, "The subway went through it. You could feel it. But not when we were playing—the subway could probably hear *us*."

The music rooms of the Mercer Arts Center held out hope that rock and roll could maintain a grip on the Village the way it had once before. But late in the afternoon of August 3, 1973, ominous sounds started rumbling through the hotel that housed them, and just after 5 p.m., a chunk of the building caved in and collapsed, the wreckage overtaking Broadway. Since the theaters were empty at that time, musicians or actors weren't injured or even on the premises, but four people trapped inside the hotel were killed and more than a dozen injured. Most of the theaters inside the Mercer Arts Center were not seriously damaged, but the four plays in production had to find new homes, and several offices and a studio were buried.

When a friend called to tell him what had happened, Philips couldn't quite grasp what he was hearing and went to the site a few days later. "It was pure, unadulterated rubble," he said. "I looked at it and thought, 'Well, that's that. *That* was fun while it lasted.'" Lawsuits alleging building violations were filed, and it turned out that the hotel had been cited for sixty-three violations during its sixty prior years. The cause of the crash was ultimately determined to be a destabilized support wall in the hotel that had been weakened by an unapproved drainpipe installation. The Mercer was ultimately condemned, and within a year, the Kitchen—one of the performance-space rooms at the Mercer—had relocated several blocks south, to SoHo.

Major rock acts had started playing the Academy of Music, a theater on Fourteenth Street, at the northern border of the Village. But the end of the Mercer Arts Center as a music hub proved to be the next step in rock beginning its gradual move east. Just months before the collapse, the Dolls were booked to play the Gaslight at the Au Go Go. On the afternoon of the show, Johansen arrived with Thunders. As the two were about to walk down the two flights of stairs to the entrance, a large man with a knife jumped out from nowhere, screaming he was going to kill Johansen because he had "impregnated" him from the stage. "Apparently I had been looking at him in such a way that he became pregnant," Johansen said. Thunders pushed the intruder down the stairs from street level, and the man ran away.

Later that year, bar owner Hilly Kristal opened CBGB on the Bowery—an unintentionally symbolic move, since that street could be found at the eastern end of Bleecker, home to the previous decades' folk, rock, and jazz heyday. The lifestyles, music, and culture that a venue like the Mercer Arts Center had supported and encouraged would survive, but they would now do so blocks removed from the heart of Greenwich Village.

As if their owners were convinced of a pending rebirth, new venues still periodically arose. At 188 West Fourth Street, between Sixth and Seventh Avenues, a short walk from the new Folk City, the Metro Cafe became a new base for acoustic music. Starting in late 1973, its bookings included Mimi Fariña and the man who continued to live nearby, Dave Van Ronk.

The last few years had been thorny for the local legend who'd been dubbed the Mayor of MacDougal Street by a Kettle of Fish bartender in the early sixties. In 1969 Van Ronk put his signature on an MGM Records contract that called for three albums in a year. None appeared, but in the fall of 1970, label president Mike Curb dropped eighteen acts from the roster for supposedly promoting drug use with their music. Van Ronk was not publicly mentioned, yet neither was he on the list of those who were retained. (Perhaps Curb or someone else at the company heard "Cocaine.") In 1971, Van Ronk did finally return to making records, three years after the Hudson Dusters and now with Polydor, which had bought MGM. *Van Ronk* was among his most opulently produced LPs. As usual, it tossed together songs by modern writers (Joni Mitchell, Leonard Cohen) with compositions by Jacques Brel and Van Ronk's Village friend Peter Stampfel. He also comically tipped his hat to his past in "Gaslight Rag," a self-penned homage to what he called "Mitchell's Café" with its rats, fellow tunesmiths, and "grunge on the floor." Given that the Gaslight was teetering and its founder John Mitchell was long gone, the era he sang about seemed even further back than ten years.

By then, Van Ronk and Terri Thal had divorced, although it had taken a few years. "We stayed married for about five more years," she said. "Finally, he was acting weirdly, although not to me, and I called him up and said, 'I'll bury you because you're my friend, but not because you're my husband. So let's get a divorce.'" In a new relationship, with Joanne Grace, he was still living at his apartment on Sheridan Square, right across the street from what was once Cafe Society. In interviews or with friends, Van Ronk remained loquacious and intellectually voracious, whether talking about Greek history and French literature or the batting average of the New York Mets. Like a bear prematurely woken from hibernation, he could still be his cranky self. During an interview in the Village with writer Mike Jahn in 1973, he pointed out the businesses now shuttered or replaced and grumbled about the state of the area and the sightseers who still flocked to it. "I don't like the tourists," he said. "It's

becoming almost pathological with me, I hate them so badly." He grimaced
when he heard people at the next table ordering a "drinky-poo." Being the curious person he was, however, he took a seat at their table and started grilling
them on their stories.

Van Ronk wasn't the only one who was landing work at the Metro into
1974. Starting January 24, Happy and Artie Traum and their band settled
in for three nights—and with a mystifying opening act. Having left her New
Jersey upbringing behind somewhere on the Garden State Parkway, Patti
Smith was now a poet, writer, and playwright. With accompaniment from
Lenny Kaye on guitar, she was increasingly pairing her poetry with rudi-
mentary rock and roll. At Max's Kansas City, just north of the Village, on
New Year's Eve 1974, Smith opened for Phil Ochs, who was in the midst of
a debilitating period of his life and career. Ochs's dreams of a new America
and pop success had both crashed after the 1968 Democratic Convention;
he was drinking heavily and seemed depressed and rudderless. His father,
a doctor, had suffered from manic depression and, according to Ochs's sister, Sonny, would have meltdowns every three years; Ochs was starting to
exhibit some of those same signs. Kaye's most enduring memory of the show
was seeing Ochs at the Max's bar, where Ochs apparently left his pay without
realizing it.

Still managed by Albert Grossman, the Traum brothers were specializing
in singer-songwriter folk. But the crowd at the Metro seemed to be there to see
Smith, who was joined by an early version of a band with Kaye, pianist Mat-
thew Reich, and actress and Warhol regular Diane Podlewski. Set against the
venue's brick-wall backdrop, the show lay halfway between cabaret rock and
performance art. Happy's wife, Jane, was mesmerized by Smith and admired
her gutsiness on stage. "Compared to the long-haired girls who played Joan
Baez songs," she said, "I thought, 'We need this.'"

Jane Traum's admiration for Smith did not translate to the small dressing
room, where both bands were crammed. Kaye recalled one of the Traums, likely
Artie, approaching him and barking, "What do you know about music? You
just know three chords!" ("I was quite taken aback," Kaye recalled. "I didn't
know where it came from. They were a little protective of their universe.")

When one of the Traum players asked Smith who she was, she replied, "I'm a little bit happy and a little bit arty."

Matters soon grew physical. In Happy Traum's recollection, Kaye borrowed an amplifier from one of the Traums' musicians and blew it out. (Kaye had no recall of that moment.) How physical it became depends on the source. Guitarist Arlen Roth, who'd been hired for the show, wound up arriving late and was told he'd just missed something. "You wouldn't believe what just happened!" another Traum band member told him. "We just had a fight with Patti Smith's band!" The scuffle was trivial but also revealing: a new wave of rockers was being shunned by a world that once had welcomed them.

Morgan Studio in London was a far cry from Folk City and the college coffee-houses where Maggie and Terre Roche had worked to fine-tune their songs and stage presence. Much like the legendary Abbey Road building, its control room looked down upon the recording room, which could make musicians feel dislocated from their producers. Glancing down at the sisters, Paul Samwell-Smith, the balladeer-sensitive British producer who often worked there, wondered if they found it overwhelming. "I thought, 'It must be tough for them,'" he said. "They seemed like a couple of nice, innocent, naive girls who came over not knowing anything, really, about the recording business. But they seemed really eager for this."

For the making of what would be the duo's first album, the stars appeared to finally be aligning after a difficult few years. Paul Simon had connected them with Samwell-Smith, the former bass player for the Yardbirds who'd shifted to record production and had worked on "American Tune" on *There Goes Rhymin' Simon*. The sisters' album would be put on tape in the same studio where Samwell-Smith had recorded Cat Stevens's *Tea for the Tillerman* and Carly Simon's *Anticipation*, two of the best-selling singer-songwriter records of the time. "They thought, 'Maybe Paul Samwell-Smith can do what he did with Cat Stevens for you guys,' and we were into it," Terre said. "We were like, 'Oh, that'd be exciting, wouldn't it?'" During their stay the sisters made the most of their temporary London home, exploring the pubs and inviting their mother,

Jude, over for a visit. According to Terre, Maggie, unhappy with her songs up
to that point, had torched all the tapes of her earliest material. But she had
written a whole new set of material that reflected her and her sister's adventures
and struggles of the last few years.

In what would prove to be a litmus test for how the next generation of
Village-rooted songwriters could fit, or not, into a particular music box, the
making of the album would be anything but a breeze. Maggie's songs had intricate chord and tempo changes that resisted conventional arrangements. (When
their sister Suzzy later tried learning to play "Jill of All Trades" on piano, she
realized that every chord on the right hand was a different chord on the left.)
Samwell-Smith felt the need to make the sisters' album more amenable to radio
airplay. "That might just have been me doing the normal pressures," he said.
"But I thought, 'Why are they coming in and paying for all the airfares and the
studio time?'"

After several weeks, the sisters and Samwell-Smith had several finished
songs, including "West Virginia," an elliptical, Terre-sung look back at their
time (and drug taking) on the campus tour, set to a delicate string arrangement. But one day they received a call from Michael Tannen, telling them that
no one was happy with the rough mixes that had been sent back to New York
and that the sisters should return to the States. Dejected but momentarily free
of any need to conform, Maggie sat down at the studio piano and, with Terre
playing along, worked out a new song, a downcast ballad about dashed hopes
called "Down the Dream." "Maggie was able to relax and sing and play just like
she wanted to," Samwell-Smith said. "It was lovely. We had the attitude of, 'Oh,
well, we should be doing more of this.'"

The sisters found themselves back in America and at the same Alabama studio and with the same studio musicians who'd worked on parts of *There Goes
Rhymin' Simon*. "That was Paul's doing," said Tannen. "He was trying to make
them more commercial." But almost immediately, another conflict flared up.
Keyboardist Barry Beckett, their new producer, preferred that the sisters not
play their guitars and have the musicians handle the instrumental tracks. Such
was their traditional method for recording, but the Roches protested—Terre
in particular was becoming a skilled guitarist—and Beckett quit. Hurriedly

stepping in to salvage the project, bassist David Hood and guitarist Jimmy Johnson, the new producers, realized it was best to let the sisters be more involved. "I worked with Aretha and she didn't do great until they sat her down in the studio at a grand piano and she played when she sang," Hood said. "And that's what made it work with Maggie and Terre. Their singing wasn't as good when they weren't playing."

Challenges remained. Simon, who wasn't present, sent word that from the tapes he heard, the sisters should "sing more in tune," as Hood recalled. At that time, Maggie didn't write down chords or have notated sheet music; she preferred to teach a song to the musicians by playing it for them on the piano. She also had a vision for her music that adhered to the complexity of her writing. "You couldn't get her to change anything," Hood said. "She never wanted to hear the word 'commercial.'"

Seductive Reasoning, its title suggested by Maggie, reflected the scattershot way in which it was made. Wrestling with melodies that would switch tempos without advance warning, the Muscle Shoals musicians made the songs either jaunty, melancholy, or country-fried. On the final version of "Down the Dream," the augmented instrumentation heightened the song's melancholy, but in "The Mountain People" and "Wigglin' Man," the Roche sisters came off as an Appalachian version of the Andrews Sisters, the cheery World War II–era entertainers. The songs helmed by Samwell-Smith were set to sparser arrangements, like "Jill of All Trades," which featured only Maggie's piano. "If You Empty Out All Your Pockets You Could Not Make the Change," the one song on the album produced by Simon, reflected his rhythmic sensibilities and, with its harmonies by the white gospel band the Oak Ridge Boys, his own eclectic sensibility.

Although Maggie demurred from talking about the stories behind her melodies and strongly discouraged Terre from doing the same, the songs alluded to the sisters' lives over the previous five years. "Malachy's," Maggie's song about playing that bar, made the cut. With its references to men wanting virgins and leaving them in ruin, "Underneath the Moon" could have easily been about Maggie's tumultuous personal life. References to pills and Louisiana, where they'd traveled during their San Francisco period, had the same effect in "Down the Dream," and lyrics about bus rides and "a needle and a kid" in "Jill of All Trades" could have been inspired by Maggie's return home when she was pregnant. She and Terre took turns on leads, Terre's voice swooping in and around her sister's when Maggie was in the forefront.

The finished album in hand, Simon and Tannen shopped it around. The sisters met with David Geffen, whose Elektra/Asylum label felt like a suitable home but who struck Terre as pompous. Ultimately, they signed with Columbia, Simon's home.

But even then, the promotion for the sisters' launch into the mainstream would be as taxing as making their record. Asked in her 1970 interview about why she apparently didn't wear makeup, Maggie had shot back, "I don't like to be kicked around by anybody. But I'm not in any organization of any kind." The years hadn't affected Maggie's uncompromising nature. Before the album was unveiled, the label had an executive take Maggie and Terre clothes shopping at Macy's and arranged for a high-end photo shoot in which the sisters, rarely prone to posh outfits, were dressed in black velvet. "They tried to tell them what to wear—all the stupid things people say to young women," said Suzzy. "That was not going to happen. Any rule given to Maggie and Terre, they would break." Rejecting the photos, the Roches opted for a far more casual shot of themselves in sleeveless white blouses, lounging on a couch, Terre in a buzz cut that lent her a boyish look. "We and the record company jointly tried to get them to dress a little better," Tannen admitted. "They would dress in ankle-length dresses, like from a thrift store. In hindsight, it was very cool, but what the fuck did we know?"

Columbia sent Maggie and Terre to Los Angeles to play a few early shows and hobnob with its California staff. The sisters thought the encounters had gone well, but upon their return to New York, they went to Tannen's office after hours one night; they'd been told they could use the piano there to practice. On his desk, they saw a folder labeled with their names and couldn't resist peeking inside. To their horror, they saw a report from a West Coast Columbia executive that harshly criticized their stage skills and looks and, as Terre would recall, disparaged "Maggie's ever-present Wallabees," the earthy, moccasin-style shoes in vogue. "Maggie and I said, 'We're in over our heads—we don't know how to hang with this high-powered thing,'" Terre said. "We started to feel like, 'We don't sing well enough, we don't play well enough, and we're not good enough. We're making fools of ourselves.' We were swimming upstream."

Released in March 1975, *Seductive Reasoning* began garnering airplay on WLIR, the Long Island progressive radio station. *Billboard* cited Maggie's "perceptive writing" and called the album "remarkably well done and versatile" and "quite different from anything happening in a big way today," with a "strong commercial possibility." In the *Village Voice*, critic Robert Christgau found them a bit arch but overall approved of their "assured, relaxed and reflective" women's sensibility.

But as Tannen saw for himself, repeatedly, Maggie and Terre tended to react the same way when a decision had to be made: they would go off, talk between themselves, reach a verdict, and stick with it, no further discussion allowed. In this case they opted to leave New York and the record business and head to Hammond, Louisiana, where a friend had opened a kung fu temple. "Maggie was very fragile, always," said Tannen. "She was kind of a mystery, which was part of her appeal. But the record is released and there's no Maggie and Terre." Tannen freaked as well, telling them they were making a huge mistake, but it was too late; the sisters gave up their downtown apartment and were soon out of town.

"Don't be afraid to flop," Van Ronk had told them when they were spending time with him a few years before. When Terre had heard that advice as a teenager, the thought was liberating and, as she put it, took the pin out of the grenade when it came to career pressure. It seemed the essence of the bohemian world they'd engaged with after that drive into the city to see Izzy Young. They were outsiders who flourished in an outside world, and for the time being they would choose to remain that way.

By the summer of 1975, it wasn't merely the Village that seemed under siege; the entire city felt as if it were capsizing. In the spring, New York had defaulted on its billions of dollars of debt, plunging it into the worst financial crisis in its history. The first week of July, Abe Beame, a Democrat who'd been elected mayor the previous year, was forced to lay off 40,000 city workers, including 5,000 police and 1,500 firemen. In protest, the Sanitation Department went on strike, allowing 28 tons of daily trash to start piling up on seemingly every block, with accompanying odors to match. "Stay off the streets after 6 p.m.," warned a four-page pamphlet, *Welcome to Fear City*, published and distributed in the city by a group that included unions of firefighters and police.

The same week Beame ordered the municipal job cuts, Allan Pepper witnessed something neither he nor anyone else had seen in several years. Bob Dylan was back in the Village, and one of those sightings had taken place at the Bottom Line, the club that Pepper and his partner Stanley Snadowsky had opened the previous year.

For all the pessimism engulfing the city, the Bottom Line had injected a degree of hope for the future of the Village. Both thirty, Pepper and Snadowsky had known each other since grade school in Brooklyn and were oddly complementary. Pepper, a sociology teacher, was short, garrulous, and music-focused; Snadowsky, more inclined toward business and already running his own entertainment-leaning law firm, was more oversized. When they were barely out of college, they'd started Jazz Interactions, a nonprofit that organized jazz shows at, among others, the Five Spot and the Top of the Gate. In 1968 they began booking shows at the Village Gate proper, bringing in rock acts like Seatrain, the Blues Project spinoff. Pepper and Snadowsky left the Gate and, in 1971, moved over to Folk City at its second locale, on West Third Street.

Given their interest in acoustic music, Pepper and Snadowsky were a good fit for that space, even if they had once clashed with two of its nascent talents. In their club-haunting days before their trip to London, Maggie and Terre Roche had been given an assigned open-mic slot at Folk City and expected to be let in for free, as Mike Porco had done before his new bookers had been hired. "Maggie and I acted like we owned the place," she said. "No one ever *charged* us to go in. We were late and suddenly these two guys at the door are giving us some trouble. I remember saying to Allan, 'Fuck you!'"

Porco didn't know what to make of some of the amplified acts Pepper and Snadowsky signed up for the place, and the men also made subtle changes, like ordering the wait staff not to take orders during the performances. But Folk

City was still struggling to reinvent itself and book name acts; Milton Kramer, Loudon Wainwright III's manager, chose to place his client at the Gaslight rather than Folk City, which he considered small time.

At his law firm, one of Snadowsky's clients leased the Red Garter, a Dixieland- and jazz-inclined club at 15 West Fourth Street, across the street from the original Folk City. In 1973 Snadowsky heard that his client was about to renege on the deal. Pepper's wife, Eileen, had an uncle who worked in the sportswear business, and with his financial aid the two men raised around $250,000 to buy and gut the Red Garter and start their own live-music business. The intersection of West Fourth and Mercer was far from the Bleecker and MacDougal crossroads, and the area around the club would be quiet and unsafe at nights. The first Folk City was now a parking lot, and the Mercer Arts Center, which had been catty-corner from the Red Garter, was closed. Anybody who parked their car in the vicinity risked a break-in or theft.

Still, Pepper and Snadowsky were intent on establishing an upscale, four-hundred-seat music venue, and timing was on their side. Soon after the Traums and Patti Smith show, the Metro shifted from music to comedy. At their embryonic venue, Pepper and Snadowsky installed an upgraded sound system and monitors that would allow the musicians to hear themselves on stage as best as possible. Ringless cash registers and phones would make sure that nothing encroached on the music during the shows. The new owners also built soundproofed dressing rooms behind the stage; that way, the acts wouldn't have to walk through the crowd to get to their space, as they did at the Village Vanguard, the new Folk City, and others. "It's much different when we say 'ladies and gentlemen,' and they walk out onto the stage rather than pass through the audience," Pepper said. "It's more dramatic and professional."

Professional would remain the operative term for the Bottom Line. From the moment it opened, the club noticeably injected the big-money, high-living rock world of the seventies into the Village. The venue had a soft opening with Labelle, a year before "Lady Marmalade" made the trio a glitter-funk sensation. The official opening night, February 12, 1974, presented New Orleans voodoo rocker Dr. John. Photographer Peter Cunningham sensed that he needed to be there—"there was a buzz that this was going to be the next big place," he said—and he and his camera weren't disappointed. In the crowd were Mick Jagger, Carly Simon, and Albert Grossman, among others; Stevie Wonder and Johnny Winter joined Dr. John onstage for a jam session. As Carol Klenfner, who was handling publicity for the club, recalled, "I was very focused on the opening. We tried to get everybody who was anybody who was in town."

Local talents like Van Ronk, Wainwright, and the Traum brothers each played the Bottom Line during its inaugural year. At the same time, bigger rock stars began dropping in. That first summer, Stephen Stills stopped by to sit in with Bonnie Raitt. His sometime bandmate Neil Young, in the house for a Ry Cooder show, sent a member of his posse to Pepper's office to ask if Young could play an impromptu set of his own after Cooder's. For those who remained, which was most of the house, Young ran through eleven songs, including several, such as "Long May You Run" and "Pushed It Over the End," that few outside his circle had heard before. Tom Scott and the LA Express, which had worked with George Harrison, Joni Mitchell, and others, head-lined one night, and Mitchell, a backstage guest, was asked by Scott to sing with them. When she proved resistant, a microphone was run to where she was standing, at the bottom of the steps at the back of the stage, and she sang out of sight of the crowd. With an elevated stage that was set higher off the floor than those in other Village clubs, the Bottom Line also unintentionally demon-strated the way that rock stars were now cultural gods placed on pedestals.

In April 1974 the New York Dolls took over the Bottom Line. Their first, self-titled album had rolled out at almost the same time as the hotel next to the Mercer Arts Center collapsed, and they were now releasing a second one, tellingly titled *Too Much Too Soon*. Their music was not to the tastes of the club owners: as Pepper told the *New York Times* shortly after, "We detest that kind of music." But he and Pepper wanted to serve up as much variety as possible at that early point in the club's existence. The night of the Dolls' show, a bomb threat cleared the club, but even more rattling for Pepper and Snadowsky was a visit to the dressing room, where they found a smashed mirror. "I was just furious," Pep-per said. "I felt personally aggrieved. We had spent so much time and here these guys were in their own world and couldn't give a crap." The owners deducted the cost of the mirror from the band's pay—along with, as club policy, half the cost of their beverages. "There was some sort of intramural brouhaha going on," the Dolls' David Johansen said. "Arthur threw a seltzer bottle or something at the back of my head and I ducked it and it smashed the mirror. I guess they call that 'trashing.'" The band was banned from playing the club.

The Bottom Line bosses soon learned the peccadilloes of their audiences. Bluegrass crowds brought their own wine and paid in pennies. Fans of Leonard Cohen, who played the club in the fall of 1974, left it spotless, whereas Deadheads left behind their share of vomit when Jerry Garcia (who was paid a higher-than-usual $7,000 for his show, according to the *Times*) brought along his own band.

Whether it intended to or not, the Bottom Line also affected the rock clubs in the Village and in nearby districts. In August 1974, Max's Kansas City filed for bankruptcy; that venue had been "the leading rock music club in New York City and hence the country," opined the *Times*. Sam Hood, of the Gaslight and the Gaslight at the Au Go Go, had been booking acts there. Max's had its share of issues—it endured several fires, and owner Mickey Ruskin spent a good deal of money remodeling it—but Ruskin explicitly blamed the Bottom Line's success for cutting his space off at the knees. A month later, in September, he sold it to a new owner, temporarily ending an era.

But nothing could stop the Bottom Line. Record companies began shelling out thousands of dollars for press parties in the venue, like the time Elton John hosted one for British singer Kiki Dee. In what Pepper called "a whole new world," the labels also bought batches of tickets to give to members of the press. Dylan had played Madison Square Garden the month before the Bottom Line opened, but his surprise appearance during a Muddy Waters show, where he sat in on harmonica, was likely the first time that anyone had seen him onstage in a Village club in years. (When Pepper and Snadowsky were booking Folk City, Dylan had stopped by with George Harrison to see David Bromberg, but he never set foot anywhere near the stage and even left early.)

The next month, a further coronation of the Bottom Line took place when Bruce Springsteen started a five-night showcase. Playing the same venue a year earlier, Springsteen had barely been able to fill it. "If you brought one hundred of your best friends, I could have gotten you seats," said Pepper. This time around, the shows were sold out, and Lou Reed and Robert DeNiro were in the house. To stress the connection between Springsteen and his fans, Columbia, his label, asked Pepper and Snadowsky to not let anyone from the press or the music business sit up front. "Bruce knew how to work the stage, but people thought it wasn't translating onto the records," Pepper said. "So their notion was that any disbelievers who thought it was all hype could see real people reacting to it, and that would make a statement and an impression. They wanted the fans up front. They knew what they were doing, like they were going into battle."

Pepper and Snadowsky also knew to fortify the front tables, since Springsteen would likely walk on them. It was a small repair price to pay for the euphoric talk generated from some of the most enthralling shows the Bottom Line had so far presented.

▌▌▌▌

Late in the evening of October 23, 1975, Van Ronk could be found where he often was, at the Kettle of Fish. Whether it was the alcohol or the passing of time, it took him a minute to recognize the twenty-seven-year-old who approached him. Along with Maggie and Terre Roche, Rod MacDonald was yet another musician who'd been raised on the troubadours and songs of the previous decade. Connecticut-born, MacDonald had played in a commercial folk group, the Lovin' Sound; enrolled in Columbia Law School; and worked as a reporter for *Newsweek*. Along the way, he'd also begun a solo performing career. Moving to Thompson Street in 1973, he'd met the Roche sisters in a local laundromat, and he'd also encountered Van Ronk during an out-of-town trip to Chicago, where the two wound up drinking into the night.

After MacDonald reintroduced himself, Van Ronk stood up, announced, "Come with me," and led MacDonald out of the Kettle and across MacDougal, where they ran into David Blue. Although still based in California, Blue had had a checkered career. Thanks in part to his friend Joni Mitchell, Blue became part of managers David Geffen and Elliot Roberts's roster of Laurel Canyon songwriters and had made several albums for Geffen's Asylum label. At the Bitter End in 1972, he'd introduced Springsteen to Jackson Browne, launching a long-running friendship between the two. But Blue himself hadn't achieved anything close to the success of Browne or the Eagles, who recorded one of his songs, "Outlaw Man." To promote his latest album, he was back in town for a few gigs in the Village.

Van Ronk and Blue, who struck MacDonald as wired, embraced, and the three proceeded to Folk City, a few doors down. The club was normally quiet—on Thursday nights and many others as well—but this evening, a small crowd hovered outside. Mike Porco was turning sixty-one, and Van Ronk was adhering to his tradition of stopping by, wishing Porco a happy birthday, and downing a shot of whiskey. Once that was done, Van Ronk, who later said he had an upset stomach, said to MacDonald, "I'm not sticking around, but you should." A couple of local songwriters MacDonald knew, including Van Ronk pal Erik Frandsen, were playing that night. But the real draw was the tables at the far left rear, partly subsumed in darkness, where MacDonald saw, to his shock, Bob Dylan, Phil Ochs, Joan Baez, Allen Ginsberg, and Ramblin' Jack Elliott, with more luminaries on the way.

As just about everyone in the downtown music community was aware, Dylan was once again a Village regular. On the heels of releasing *Blood on the Tracks*, with songs that hinted at marital turmoil, he'd left his wife, Sara, and their children behind in California and taken an apartment in the vicinity. A few days before sitting in with Muddy Waters at the Bottom Line, Dylan turned up at what was once the Bitter End. The same year the Bottom Line had launched, the Bitter End had run aground. Ultimately, manager Paul Colby found himself with the lease to both the Bitter End and the next-door Now Bar. Breaking through the wall that separated the two businesses, he merged them and renamed the expanded space the Other End, complete with a liquor license, tables and chairs replacing the bench pews, and a separate but connected bar area called the Other End Bar.

One night in June 1975, Dylan was inspecting the present and maybe future of rock. Patti Smith was most regularly seen tearing it up at Max's Kansas City and CBGB, but starting with her tense co-bill with the Traum brothers at the Metro Club, she also made her way into a few West Village clubs. When another act dropped out of a booking at the Other End for late June 1975,

Smith landed the slot and unveiled her full new band, featuring Lenny Kaye. The shows were nothing like the venue, or possibly all of Bleecker Street, had quite witnessed: an androgynous poet whose band could blend crude but still refined punk and garage rock with dollops of reggae and spoken word. Many of the acts who were playing the club seemed like prisoners of the past; Smith simply took no prisoners.

During one of those shows, Kaye saw a familiar figure walk in. It was unclear how Dylan knew of Smith, although she was already chummy with Dylan's pal Bob Neuwirth. "We'd been getting good press, so I'm not sure he was totally unaware of her," Kaye said of Dylan. "Bob is a little slicker than he would like to have one believe. He probably knew there was a brouhaha around a rock 'poet.'" For his part, Kaye tried to concentrate on his playing, including a guitar solo on a version of "Time Is on My Side," and thanks to a spotlight, he couldn't see much of Dylan, who took a seat, drank wine, and chain-smoked. Afterward, Dylan made his way backstage, and a photographer took playful photos of him and Smith together. "They kind of danced around each other," Kaye said. "Both of them were trying to be cool."

To Colby's delight and the astonishment of journalists and musicians alike, Dylan kept returning to the club, often wearing a black-leather jacket and a striped shirt, and accompanied by Neuwirth and lyricist and new collaborator Jacques Levy. When Ramblin' Jack Elliott started a multi-evening stand, Dylan sat in with him, returning two nights later with Smith and Neuwirth. During Elliott's performances and then bleeding into a series of July shows headlined by Neuwirth and others, Dylan made the Other End an unofficial second home. He could also be found at the tables near the adjoining bar, trying out new material, such as "Isis" or an ode to dead mobster Joey Gallo, for whoever was around.

"Bob was trying to reconnect with this scene that he'd been too far away from," said Rob Stoner, a guitarist and bassist who'd met Dylan before and been pulled into Dylan's circle when Neuwirth offered him a hundred dollars to back Neuwirth at the Other End. "He'd tried to [reconnect] when he moved back with his family earlier, but he couldn't do it with Weberman [the "Dylanologist" who'd gone through his garbage] and those cats. Now he was back, but this time he was unencumbered. He was there with his bodyguard—Neuwirth—and he went *crazy* with chicks. He was making up for lost time."

Back again in the city in October, Dylan was finishing up a new album, *Desire*, and formulating his next move. After another gig at the Other End, Elliott was in the back room collecting his pay when Dylan walked in, handed him a glass of red wine, and told him he was thinking of going on the road for "small gigs" with a gang including Neuwirth and Baez. Elliott said he was in, and on a call a few weeks later, Dylan said they would start in November. More name musicians began stopping by the Other End, jockeying for a role in whatever Dylan was planning. "There was a certain magic but at the same time a competitive ugliness to it," Stoner said. "They could see he was casting around to do something new, and whatever it was they wanted to be either witness or be part of it. People were trying to be cool and wanted to end up doing whatever crazy project he had in mind. But no one knew what it was yet."

By the time Van Ronk led MacDonald into Folk City on October 23, however, everyone knew: Dylan was making some sort of movie. A film crew had shown up at the club first, telling Porco they were shooting an "educational television" special. They began filming the entire evening, starting with Porco's birthday celebration, which was organized by another local talent, troubadour Jack Hardy. In a surreal start to what would be an equally strange evening, Hardy and Rosie Smith, a gregarious spitfire who emceed many of the club's hoot nights, dropped the birthday cake on the stage, splitting it in two. Soon after, a car pulled up in front of the club, and Dylan, Baez, Stoner, musician T Bone Burnett, and Dylan's longtime friend and road manager Lou Kemp emerged and filed in, making their way toward the back. Eric Andersen, who drove in from his home in Woodstock, entered with Smith. "The night held an expectation of fireworks excitement," Andersen said, "but also the feeling of broken glass."

Sporting a multicolored shirt for the occasion, Porco followed the gang to the back of his club, where he kissed Dylan and Neuwirth on the cheeks. Soon enough, Smith called "Joan Baez and her friend" to the stage. Looking taken aback as he walked onto it, the club's still gloriously tacky mural behind him, Dylan smiled shyly as Smith hugged and kissed him. With Stoner on bass, Dylan and Baez sang "One Too Many Mornings" before a moment of chaos ensued: the bridge on Stoner's stand-up bass broke halfway through, but Baez pulled him closer to her and Dylan so he could sing a harmony. "Let's get outta here," Dylan said to Baez after, but it wasn't to be: with Dylan now strumming along, Baez led the crowd in a birthday toast to Porco. "You can't go wrong with entertainment like this!" Smith said. Finally, Dylan spoke: "We're just really happy to be here and be able to wish Mike a happy birthday and many more."

For the expanding crowd inside, the evening grew only more Fellini-esque, with a mélange of folk, spoken word, and cabaret moments that recalled an earlier, headier time in the Village—a grown-up version of the old Gaslight. Patti Smith improvised a poem. Ginsberg recited from William Blake. Roger McGuinn of the Byrds, who'd become part of the Other End hang-out crew, materialized to play "Chestnut Mare" and "I'm So Restless," the latter with its sly dig at Dylan's semiretirement. Bette Midler, who'd also befriended Dylan, sashayed toward the stage and joined Buzzy Linhart on his song "Friends," which had become an anthem for her. (When she whispered her name into Rosie Smith's ear, the emcee mistakenly introduced her as "Betty Miller.") Accompanied by Burnett, Neuwirth made a crack about the guitar he was using—asking if Eric Andersen had tuned it, a dig that referenced the old Kettle nights—and played a rowdy version of his "Mercedes Benz," which Janis Joplin had popularized.

Watching it all from the stage was guitarist Arlen Roth, who'd been given a heads-up by Andersen to rush down to the club that night. "The survivors of the Seventies will be decided tonight," Andersen told him. His Martin and Telecaster guitars at his side, Roth opted to remain on stage for anyone who needed his accompaniment—and found himself grappling with a parade of counterculture heroes old and new. "It was obvious that everyone was vying for Dylan's attention," he said. "The fact that anyone could come up there and start singing—the whole thing felt weird and decadent and strange. It was very much New York in the Seventies."

With dawn rapidly approaching, Rosie Smith indicated that the night was wrapping up. But the woozy, boozy festivities would end on a sadly poignant note, a vision of the Village past. All night long, Phil Ochs had been a peripheral presence, sidling up next to Dylan and talking away; he too craved an audition to be part of the traveling tour Dylan had in mind. Ochs had just come off a summer of extreme bipolar behavior. Declaring that the Ochs everyone knew was gone, he had taken on the persona of an untidy, arrogant, and often physically threatening figure named John Train, often wearing a dirty leather jacket over untucked shirttails. Friends would steer clear of him on the street; Colby threw him out of the Other End. "There were times when you didn't know if you were talking to Phil or John Train," said writer Larry Sloman, who was chronicling the Dylan summer of 1975 for *Rolling Stone*. "It was kind of a hairy situation. He'd go into Folk City with an axe and knock the axe into the bar. Was he going to use it to kill someone in the Village? Of course not. It was a flamboyant display of who knows what." At times like those, Porco, ever the supportive father figure, would talk Ochs or Train down.

Ochs's former manager Arthur Gorson, who remained in touch with him, thought Ochs was trying to hark back to a time when he was relevant, when people talked about politics; John Train was his way of acting out those fears. At his apartment on Prince Street in SoHo, where Ochs stayed from time to time, Sloman would attempt to cheer Ochs up by inviting women over and, with their encouragement, asking him to try out the new songs he was writing about his alter ego. "He was so hesitant to sing," Sloman said. "So I'd say, 'Hey, Phil, what about that song where you check into the Chelsea Hotel?' And he would start doing them." Some were completed songs, others fragments, but a few that emerged, like "The Ballad of John Train," proved that Ochs could still summon his melodic gifts and entrancing voice.

By the time Ochs walked onstage at Folk City at the end of the Porco birthday bash, John Train had been vanquished—along with such sketchy plans as buying a building in Tribeca that he would turn into an entertainment complex. (Ochs, or Train, had given Sloman a check for $1 million toward that project, which Sloman knew shouldn't be cashed.) His face hidden under a white brimmed hat he'd snatched off Dylan's head, Ochs looked bedraggled and a little puffy. He made it clear to Roth he didn't need accompaniment, then had trouble tuning his guitar. Drama began even before he sang a note. Porco's birthday cake, its cutting knife still jammed in it, sat on the floor in front of Ochs. Suddenly, a mysterious man, who'd been spotted at the bar and was now in the front rows, pulled the blade out of the cake and seemed to threaten Ochs.

Glancing down at the man, Ochs appeared nonplussed: "You better use it quick or else I'll use it," he said, with a chilling matter-of-factness. But others were less sanguine as the night took on an element of seventies New York danger. "Like everything else, things can turn on a dime," Andersen said, "and things suddenly became a threatening situation." To defend his friend, Andersen tackled the man, the two of them tripping over into the tray with the cake. The would-be assailant was dragged out of the club as Andersen wiped icing off his face.

As if matters couldn't get any more fraught, Ochs finally started to perform. Over sixteen nonstop minutes, he wove his way through such folk songs as "Jimmy Brown the Newsboy," Johnny Cash's "There You Go" and "Guess Things Happen That Way," the Everly Brothers' "Maybe Tomorrow," and Marty Robbins's "Big Iron." At times, he sounded rusty; other times, hints of the rousing voice many had heard a decade earlier poked through. Whatever his voice was doing at any moment, the performance added up to a moving journey through Ochs's musical roots and life. It was as if he were trying to find himself again in song—to return to that younger, more eager kid who'd settled into that part of town a dozen years before. For some in the house, though, the set was difficult to watch. "Phil saw that night as his last chance at redemption," said Stoner. "But he didn't have it physically together. He was too far gone. Everyone was looking uncomfortably at each other." When Dylan got up at one point, Ochs implored him to stay. "Bobby, Bobby, Bobby," he called out. "Where you going, Bobby?" Dylan replied that he was just heading for the bar. By then, the Dylan crew had stopped filming, preserving some of Ochs's performance only in audio.

Once Folk City emptied out, the party moved to a loft apartment on Eighth Street and MacDougal, where Andersen saw Dylan and Patti Smith huddling in an upstairs bathroom, whispering conspiratorially. Downstairs, a visibly unhappy Ochs may have realized he had blown his chance to join what would become Dylan's roaming crew of musicians, the Rolling Thunder Revue—and maybe he wanted to make sure it wouldn't happen at all. "Phil was getting more antsy and quarrelsome," Andersen said. "David Blue and I tried to calm him down. He then began threatening to go down to the street to summon the cops for a drug raid." Given the amounts of pot and coke at the party, Andersen was nervous. When Ochs jumped up from a couch and made for the front door, Andersen followed him to calm him down. Ochs was adamant, insisting he would get everyone busted. After twenty minutes, though, he settled down, collapsed on the same couch, and closed his eyes. Andersen left soon after; it was the last time he would see Ochs.

Dylan himself wouldn't be in town much longer. His nights at the Other End stopped as mercurially as they'd begun, and the Rolling Thunder Revue buses were already preparing to leave for the tour's first stop, in Massachusetts, a few weeks later. But the memory of Porco's boldface-name party would linger. "It was such a microcosm of all these hopes and dreams and careers, crammed into one tiny space," Roth recalled. Dylan's Village summer, culminating in the Porco party, had drawn more attention than just about anything in the neighborhood in years. Perhaps the darkness that had enveloped the Village for nearly a decade was preparing to lift.

Chapter 7

down the dream

1976–1980

F or Maggie and Terre Roche, the first few months at
the Lotus Temple in Hammond, Louisiana, had proven to be restorative.
In a nondescript building that had once housed a telephone-company
headquarters, the sisters took classes in kung fu, tai chi, and yoga; in their
spare time, they earned extra income at a pizza chain restaurant. Reminders of
their flirtation with the music business lingered: in the fall of 1975, the same
period when Bob Dylan and his posse took over Folk City, the sisters watched
their mentor Paul Simon guest-host an episode of the newly launched *Saturday
Night Live*. Terre would compare the experience to watching the circus continue on after one had stopped working for it.

Still compelled to express herself with music, Maggie channeled her return
to Louisiana into at least one new piece, "Hammond Song." As if echoing a
family conversation or internal debate, "Hammond Song" made the case both
for going south and not, and Maggie set the lyrics to one of her most sinu-
ous chord progressions, in E flat. But those moments were proving to be infre-
quent: their experience with Columbia Records and *Seductive Reasoning* was
still so traumatic that Terre rarely played music or sang during their time in
Louisiana.

In the end, personal entanglements would send them back north. As Terre
would write, the head of the temple was in love with Maggie but married, and

Terre felt it was time, after a few months, for her and her sister to return to the Northeast. Opting to hitchhike, a potentially dangerous scenario for two young women in the South, they thumbed their way back to Manhattan early in 1976. Thankfully, Mike Porco remembered them, and both sisters were soon working at his club, waitressing and bartending. (As Terre learned, serving alcohol at Folk City wasn't terribly hard; Porco offered only one brand of beer, Budweiser.) The sisters heard about Dylan's conspicuous return to the Village the previous summer and fall, but the largely desolate nights at Folk City, with few name artists on the bills, confirmed that the Village music scene, especially folk and rock, was still struggling. "If anyone gave you any trouble, Mike was like, 'The customer is always wrong,'" Terre said. "But there weren't a lot of customers. I thought of it as the Dark Ages. The Sixties thing was over. Everyone had moved away. That whole group was not around anymore."

Reminders of the long-standing racial friction in the Village persisted—and, soon after the Roche sisters returned to the area, with fatal consequences. Although physically unchanged, Washington Square Park still felt home more to stragglers and dealers than families and singers. On the night of September 8, 1976, dozens of young men, reportedly of Italian and Irish backgrounds, declared that they were about to take back the park. Brandishing baseball bats and pipes, they entered the grounds. In the end, nearly three dozen people, most of them Black or Hispanic, were attacked and injured. Marcos Mota, a twenty-two-year-old Dominican Republic college student, was hit in the head, close to the volleyball court where he loved to play, and died. In the end, nine people were arrested and six ultimately found guilty of manslaughter. The following nights in the Village were desolate, especially in clubs that were already straining to pull in customers. "You could literally land a plane," said Rod MacDonald, who had been performing at Folk City with a small rock band that week. For some, the clubs hadn't been that empty since the weekend in 1969 when it felt as if everyone journeyed upstate for something called the Woodstock festival.

Starting with the crash of the Mercer Arts Center as a rock-and-roll mecca, the action continued to head east, where CBGB was regularly hosting the Ramones and Patti Smith. In the fall of 1975, Smith's *Horses* (recorded at

Electric Lady Studios, Jimi Hendrix's now-flourishing compound on Eighth Street) had declared her now fully formed rocker persona. Months later, the Ramones were making their first album under their major-label deal with Sire Records. Any typical weekend at CBGB in the early months of 1976 afforded the chance to see the Ramones, Television, Mink DeVille, or Johnny Thunders' post–Dolls band, the Heartbreakers—none of them yet stars, but the difference in energy levels from the Folk City world was palpable. In that climate, contemplative troubadours with harmonica racks around their necks were the last thing the music business had in mind.

One local songwriter, Tom Pacheco, had begun making records for RCA and would invite the locals over for songwriting sessions and wine at his Mac-Dougal Street apartment. But Pacheco was proving to be the exception; by and large, the type of balladeers who still gravitated downtown were men and women without a country. MacDonald had auditioned for Columbia's John Hammond shortly before Hammond retired, but nothing came of it. "The corporate labels weren't looking to sign anybody like us," said MacDonald. "We were persona non grata with the traditional folkies, and the country world in Nashville didn't care about us at all." A recurring joke among the musicians was Porco's formula for paying them: $500 a week if they were lucky, after Porco deducted expenses for newspaper ads and "the Lou" (his brother-in-law, who took tickets at the door).

Yet little about that bleak scenario stopped songwriters from continuing to make their way south of Fourteenth Street. The dream of writing an impeccable ballad—and having a record executive hear it and offer up a contract—refused to die. Every Monday, men and women dutifully lined up on West Third Street, guitar cases littering the sidewalk, for a shot at Folk City's ongoing hoot night. By 1976, one of them was David Massengill, a droll Tennessean who'd started writing eccentric modern Appalachian ballads and playing them on a dulcimer. As his surname signaled, he was a member of the pharmaceutical family known for its feminine-hygiene products. Diminutive but sturdy enough to have played football in high school, Massengill volunteered to work on George McGovern's 1972 presidential campaign during his college years, but when McGovern was slaughtered in the election, Massengill returned home. Thinking music could restore his soul, he remembered the dulcimer his mother had bought and stashed under a bed, and he began writing long, involved songs with three dozen story-like verses, singing them in a low-down southern drawl. When Lisi Tribble, a girl he'd dated back home, moved to New York to work for CBS News, he followed her up at the end of 1975, finding an apartment in the East Village.

Massengill's earliest experiences in the city weren't entirely encouraging: he was mugged in the stairwell of his apartment a week after moving in, and his first attempt to perform in the Village, at the grungy Mills Tavern on Bleecker Street, ended abruptly when he was told the owner wanted him to cease and leave the stage after one song. But Massengill still stood in line for the hoots, at Folk City and a few other venues. Everyone was still talking about Dylan and how, on the heels of *Blood on the Tracks*, he wrote better songs when he was unhappy. "Even though it was not happening in the big time, you couldn't tell people it wasn't going to happen again," said Massengill. "It had happened before, so it might happen again. It's like a dog that needs one little pat on the head to be happy."

Another regular spotted in that line was Steve Forbert, a twenty-two-year-old from Meridian, Mississippi, with a pug nose, swelling ambitions, and a reedy voice that, with its hint of molasses, conjured both swimming holes and subway rides. As a kid, Forbert had played in local rock bands and, with some friends in a band, had driven out to Hollywood, where producer Keith Olsen, then working with Fleetwood Mac, listened to some of their songs and passed. Forbert was undeterred. Taking an Amtrak train to New York in June 1976, he found a place to live, busked on Village streets as possibly deranged homeless people stumbled by, and stood in line for any and all open-mic nights. Forbert already had a few songs in his back pocket: "Goin' Down to Laurel," a melancholy reminiscence that nonetheless skipped along like a country song, and "What Kinda Guy," a sly bit of wordplay set to unplugged rockabilly. Ensconced in the East Village, he began writing new material that reflected his change of scenery ("Tonight I Feel So Far Away from Home"), his desire to make it ("Big City Cat"), and what he called his "manifesto" ("Steve Forbert's Midsummer Night's Toast," which saluted the everyfolks and took shots at the wealthy now all around him). The music settled into the house that folk rock built, but Forbert played his songs with a jittery energy and chugging harmonica that recalled early Dylan more than any of the so-called "New Dylans" had before him.

On his second day in town, Forbert came face-to-face with another part of the Village's past when he wandered into the Other End and came upon Tim Hardin. Still possessing his recognizable understated, clenched-jaw voice, Hardin was no one's idea of a manageable artist. After his Village heyday and move to California, he'd returned east, living in Woodstock, later England, still hobbled by a heroin habit. The spigot of songs that had once flowed out of him had shut off. Forbert had heard the stories of Hardin's drug use and unreliability, but with his Martin guitar in hand—Forbert always carried it with him for fear it could be stolen—he approached Hardin and asked if he could play him a few of his songs.

After Hardin listened politely, Forbert asked for advice on launching a career in the music business. To Forbert's surprise, Hardin had few words of wisdom. Given that he no longer owned his classic songs after signing away his publishing, perhaps Hardin felt he didn't have much to contribute. But he offered to put Forbert on the guest list for his show, where he saluted Phil Ochs with a version of "Pleasures of the Harbor," Ochs's song about a sailor's adventures and misadventures on shore, inspired by John Ford's film *The Long Voyage Home*.

The timing amounted to a eulogy. Two months before, after exhausting his John Train persona and returning to a subdued version of his old self, Ochs had hanged himself in the Far Rockaway home of his sister, Sonny, on April 9, 1976. Dave Van Ronk had last seen Ochs during his Train phase, when he'd shown up unannounced at Van Ronk's home, drunk and demanding to be let in. Van Ronk refused, and the two hadn't spoken since. At a memorial concert for Ochs, at New York's Felt Forum in May, the lineup—Len Chandler, Pete Seeger, Peter Yarrow—evoked another era. Van Ronk offered a growled but poignant rendition of "He Was a Friend of Mine." Danny Kalb played a touching original, "Mournin' at Midday," and Eric Andersen sang his own "Thirsty Boots," which brought everyone back to the time when he and Ochs were tenderfoots haunting Village clubs. Looking shaken, Hardin debuted his emotional version of "Pleasures of the Harbor."

As the old guard gathered to pay respects to one of its own, their potential successors were settling in and scoping out what was left for them. At the Other End one evening, Forbert wound up double-billed with Van Ronk. As with Maggie and Terre Roche, he found himself in unfamiliar political territory in Van Ronk's company. "A lot of those older cats were Commies," he said. "The next thing, you'd be talking about socialist politics." Forbert had no way of knowing that, in the near enough future, Van Ronk would be asking Forbert to record one of his songs.

Starting in the fall of 1975 and continuing into the following spring, Bob Dylan had taken his Rolling Thunder Revue on the road. Joan Baez, Bob Neuwirth, David Blue, and Ramblin' Jack Elliott were part of the carousing crew, but mirroring the way he had bailed on the Folk City party for Porco, Van Ronk would not be along for the bus rides. As someone disinclined toward grueling tours and who preferred sleeping in his own bed, Van Ronk hardly salivated at the idea of hopping aboard. It's also possible that he wasn't taken with the idea of being reduced to a cameo at a Dylan show, and he wasn't even sure the so-called revival would amount to much. "When Dylan and all those guys were having their semi-formal party in New York a few years ago, and everyone was talking about another folk revival," he told writer Terry Lawson, "I knew it was all media hype."

Creatively, however, Van Ronk was on the verge of a revival of his own. For his next record, he opted to return to the unaccompanied acoustic approach of his early work rather than the sometimes ornate records he'd made starting with the Hudson Dusters. Available not long after the Rolling Thunder Revue was underway, *Sunday Street* opened with its title song, a rare Van Ronk composition, and an utterly charming twelve-bar blues about the "king of tap city" who dreams of a larger-living life but knows it will never happen. His ever-evolving guitar skills were on display in Scott Joplin's instrumental "Maple Leaf Rag," and he accomplished the rare feat of making a Joni Mitchell song feel like one of his own. Built on his gentle but rumbling strums, Van Ronk's version of "That Song About the Midway" no longer sounded like Mitchell's paean to Leonard Cohen. It now felt, even obliquely, like Van Ronk's meditation on his life and career, especially when he bit into her lines about hustling for "one more dime" and slowing down at the midway point. It would be one of his most poignant and affecting recordings.

As true to Van Ronk's essence as the album was, he was also turning into an artifact of the Village past. Reviewing a show in Philadelphia in 1974, writer Jack Lloyd compared it to "hopping in one of those time capsule things and going back about 14 years." That same year, Van Ronk performed at a "folk revival" concert at Long Island's Nassau Coliseum alongside Odetta and the latest iterations of the Kingston Trio, the Hillside Singers, and the Highwaymen. In the words of a *New York Times* review of one of his shows at the Other End in 1976, he was "teetering on the brink of 40," at the time a music-industry death sentence. That he was still playing the same Bleecker Street–area clubs where he'd started embodied the way Van Ronk appeared to be spinning his own wheels. Like the *Songs for Ageing Children* album before it, *Sunday Street* was released on an independent label—the Vermont-based Philo, which signed him to a one-year, eleven-song contract. "It was the absolute low point of his adult life," said Elijah Wald, a musician and NYU student who befriended Van Ronk during this period. "The bottom had dropped out of everything. He was just trying to make ends meet."

When it came to earning a reliable income, Van Ronk had little choice but to keep teaching guitar. As he'd been doing for well over a decade, he continued to open his apartment door to students, still charging fifteen dollars per lesson. Starting in 1976, one of those apprentices was Christine Lavin, a twenty-something songwriter, singer, and guitarist from Peekskill, New York, who was beginning to write witty, clever, urbane, modern folk songs about relationships, upheavals, and the feelings brought up by attending friends' weddings.

Lavin had met Van Ronk earlier that year at the Caffé Lena in Saratoga Springs, an out-of-town favorite of the Village crowd. On his way back to New York City after a show in Montreal, he'd stopped by the next-door Executive

Bar, where he sat down in a booth with Lavin, club owner Lena Nargi Spencer (a steadfast folk supporter who'd given Dylan one of his earliest jobs outside of Manhattan), and others. To Lavin's surprise, Spencer practically ordered her to sing Van Ronk a song she'd written about Ramblin' Jack Elliott. Although she was competing with a jukebox, a TV, and a pinball machine, Lavin proceeded. Halfway through the song, she noticed that Van Ronk had closed his eyes. Lavin assumed he'd fallen asleep, but Van Ronk was in fact listening carefully to her lyric and guitar technique. Opening his eyes, he told her, "You should come to New York—I'm a teacher."

After relocating to the city, Lavin began making the weekly trip to Van Ronk's apartment. Like everyone else, she would walk down the narrow entry hallway into a small living room, where an imposing, eight-foot-tall wooden sculpture from New Guinea—a bird with its wings spread out—hovered between two bookcases. At the start of many of the lessons, Van Ronk would place a large glass of Amarone wine on the coffee table in front of him, along with the occasional shot of whiskey, a batch of cigarettes, and often his inhaler; his laugh was an asthmatic wheeze.

No matter the student, Van Ronk never took that part of his work less than seriously. As a left-handed musician who played right-handed guitar, he had his own system of tablature. "Your left hand will be slightly smarter than the average guitarist, but the right hand is slightly dumber," he told Lavin, who often typed out his peculiar notations in lieu of payment. Van Ronk would often introduce his students to fingerpicking by way of Mississippi John Hurt's "Spike Driver Blues," a variation on the story of Black railroad worker John Henry told from another point of view. When Wald came for his lessons, which were scheduled for late in the afternoon, Van Ronk would often cook them dinner and break out a bottle of whiskey. Before the local liquor store closed, he'd send Wald out for a second bottle, and Wald would stagger home around dawn.

The classes were not always limited to technique. Van Ronk told Lavin about the Hudson Dusters, describing it as one of the few periods he ever played in a group. To bolster that tale, he told her about the time his kinder- garten teacher had sent a note home to his mother that read, "Dave does not play well with others." Owing to his love of a reflective ballad, he made Lavin listen to Janis Ian's "Stars." After the days of "Society's Child," Ian had been confronted with the other side of fame. Successive albums faded quickly, and it wasn't until 1975's "At Seventeen," a detailed snapshot of a teenage girl's angst, that she rebounded. Released the year before "At Seventeen," "Stars" was about those who were "crowned" and those who were "lost and never found." Its lyrics clearly spoke to Van Ronk, who played it for Lavin about twenty times in a row during one lesson.

During this period, Van Ronk had another one of his occasional brushes with wider recognition. As tired as he'd grown of performing Reverend Gary Davis's "Cocaine," he would still play it upon request; he knew it was one of his signature songs. In 1977 that became particularly clear when Van Ronk encountered Jackson Browne at a Los Angeles show. Browne told Van Ronk that he'd just recorded a version of "Cocaine" for his next album, *Running on Empty*, and asked Van Ronk where to send the publishing money. "I told him Gary Davis wrote that song and he'd better get out of the room right now or I was gonna kill him," Van Ronk said later. "He's a nice kid, but jeez."

Through a connection in the business, Van Ronk also heard country songwriter Don Schlitz's "The Gambler" and likely related to its title character, a wizened drinker and smoker who passes along his words of advice to the narrator. Although he was convinced it would be the hit single he'd long hoped for, Van Ronk wasn't able to convince anyone to give him a shot at the song. Ultimately, it would be recorded by a handful of acts, including Johnny Cash and Schlitz himself, before Kenny Rogers made it a country standard in 1978.

By the spring of 1977, Phil Hurtt thought he knew what to expect from Jacques Morali. Part of the Philadelphia crew of Black songwriters, arrangers, and record producers dubbed the Young Professionals, Hurtt brandished an impressive résumé; he'd worked with Philly Soul producers Kenny Gamble and Leon Huff, been a staff producer at Atlantic, and had cowritten the lyrics, with Thom Bell, for the Spinners' glorious "I'll Be Around." In 1976 Hurtt heard about one of Morali's schemes: the French producer-songwriter and a creative partner, Henri Belolo, needed lyrics for a disco record by the Ritchie Family, a trio of Black female singers who weren't actually related. Hurtt pitched in, helping with the brassy tribute to nightlife and dance songs called "The Best Disco in Town." While working with Hurtt on another Ritchie Family project, at Philly's Sigma Sound studio, Morali said he had a new idea—what he called a "gay group," a notion that had lodged in his head just a few months before in Greenwich Village.

Whether the genre was jazz, blues, folk, or rock, the Village was still seen as a destination for people who craved listening to music seriously and intently, seated at tables, chins resting on fists. But in keeping with the idea of the neighborhood as a getaway for outsiders, dance clubs and early discotheques that catered to its gay community were, to varying degrees, a vivacious part of the mix, the sound of the Village loosening up. In 1967 the Sheridan Square basement where Cafe Society had once resided turned into its latest incarnation, Salvation, a high-end disco with a small dance floor and celebrity clientele. (In a rare instance of rock pushing its way in, Jimi Hendrix played a last-minute night show there in September 1969.)

The following year, Salvation owner Robert Wood was found dead in Queens from a bullet to the head, not long after he'd informed the Police Department that the Mob was muscling in on his and other spots. But the idea of a dance club survived, and that same year—Valentine's Day, 1970—another more casual but more influential gathering would launch on the southwestern tip of the Village. To help pay the rent on his second-floor, 1,850-square-foot loft at 647 Broadway, just above Houston Street, twenty-five-year-old David Mancuso began hosting private-invite parties at his home. Raised for a period in an upstate orphanage, Mancuso had the long hair and beard of a *Jesus Christ Superstar* cast member, as well as his own flock. At what became known informally as the Loft, dozens, then a few hundred, would show up at his building's unmarked door and lose themselves in the darkened space amid R&B and funk. Balloons bounced around the floor; guests downed fruit juice, nuts, and raisins set out on tables; and others took (but didn't sell) acid. Although he disdained the term "DJ," Mancuso would spin a range of records, from Santana and the Rolling Stones to Aretha Franklin, blasting them on the secondhand speakers he'd bought.

Some would remember the crowd as largely gay, others as more sexually diverse. "There was no one checking your sexuality or racial identity at the door," Mancuso told author and Loft historian Tim Lawrence. "I just knew different people." No matter the preferences of its invited guests, the Loft was a sanctuary, especially as city life grew grimmer and sootier. In 1973 Mancuso was able to break through the wall separating his space from the one next door, and suddenly his parties could hold five hundred people. Spinning vinyl, Mancuso favored lengthy deep cuts with extended instrumental breaks that would build into ecstatic climaxes, like "Listen Here" by Brian Auger and the Trinity or "Land of Make Believe" by Chuck Mangione. At a Brooklyn record store, Mancuso came upon a copy of "Soul Makossa," a throbbing piece of Afrobeat by Cameroon saxophonist and songwriter Manu Dibango. The song became a favorite at the Loft and soon crossed over to dance and then pop radio, busting into the Top 40 in 1973. In that regard, at least, the Village could still have a national impact.

In 1975 Mancuso moved the Loft to a space on Prince Street in SoHo, just south of the Village. But as Morali and Belolo discovered, gay clubs had begun proliferating in the Village. Manhattan South was the new name for what was once the Salvation club. Infinity, a few unmarked doors up from where the Loft had been, was a large, open space dominated by straight men and women. Flamingo, slightly farther south, near Houston Street, attracted an upscale gay crowd and had particularly high standards for admission. "You had to have a great body and be young," recalled D. C. LaRue, a disco singer and club-hopper who lived on Sheridan Square and frequented them all. Like Flamingo, 12 West, on West Street between Jane and Twelfth Streets, was a private-membership club and drew a largely gay clientele. What the nightspots had in common were drugs, disco records (some of the best and most underground anyone heard at the time), and that part of town. "All these clubs were in the neighborhood," said LaRue. "Sometimes we'd go to Studio 54, but we'd have to take a cab there. Midtown discos were just the beginning. Everything moved downtown."

The Casablanca-born Belolo, who was straight, had been a DJ and promotion man in his home country before moving to Paris and working as a producer for Polydor Records. Morali, who was gay, was a former employee of the record store at Orly Airport in Paris. What both men shared was a fascination with disco as well as show-biz glitz: after the two ended up on the East Coast in the early seventies, initially in Philadelphia, they conceived of the Ritchie Family as the Carmen Mirandas of the dance floor.

The two men—or just Morali, depending on who was telling the story— were in the West Village when they noticed a man dressed in Native American garb walking down the street and followed him into the Anvil, the gay bar on West Fourteenth Street. The man, Felipe Rose, turned out to be a bartender, and Belolo and Morali watched as he and others danced atop the bar to disco records. A week later, the two record makers were at 12 West, where they again saw Rose, as well as one man dressed as a cowboy and another in a construction hat; Belolo wrote down the different archetypes on a napkin. With those characters in mind, Morali and Belolo had the idea for a pop group. As Morali would recall to *Rolling Stone*, "I think in myself that the gay people have no group, nobody, to personalize the gay people, you know?"

Morali, who knew a gimmick when he saw one, also considered a "very good-looking, preppy [character] ... the plain straight guy with his attaché case, the businessman going from Wall Street." He soon dropped that idea but continued with the concept for a novelty dance group, placing an ad in the *Village Voice* for singers to join Rose, whom Morali had already asked to be part of the nonexistent band. "Jacques said that he saw in the Village the way people dressed in different ways," said Hurtt. "They were all part of the culture, but they would dress in different ways and come from different walks of life."

Morali also had an idea for a group name—the Village People—and for the format of their first album: four extended dance tracks, each named after a place with a prominent gay community. Hurtt said Morali told him that some of the lyrics written by their other collaborator, Peter Whitehead, were too sexually explicit and would need to be toned down to cross over to pop radio. Although he never visited the Village himself, Hurtt picked Whitehead's brain, resulting in songs named after Hollywood, San Francisco, and New

York's Fire Island, as well as Greenwich Village. The lead vocalist would be Victor Willis, a husky-voiced, gospel-rooted singer and actor who was part of the sessions.

Rolled out in the summer of 1977, *Village People*, the ad hoc group's first album, looked and sounded like a kitschy disco record, down to its artwork. Since there was still no actual full Village People band at that point, the cover photo featured a group of male models dressed in the garb of the archetypes Morali and Belolo had seen in Village bars. But as the huffing, puffing, and beat-heavy "Village People" proclaimed, the "time for liberation" had arrived. Compared to much of the music seeping out of West Village clubs at that time, *Village People*, like disco itself, felt alive, vibrant, pulsating. Even without a pop hit on it, the album sold a respectable 100,000 copies and was a favorite at the Village discos. Soon after, a full-on lineup of the Village People was finally assembled, with Willis dressed as a cop, Rose as a Native American, and other band members as a leather fetishist, a cowboy, a construction worker, and a GI.

As outlandish as the Village People were, the cultural significance of the group was momentous. If the folk music wafting out of coffeehouses the previous decade reflected its time, the first Village People album, and the following year's more cartoonish *Macho Man*, mirrored its seventies moment: gaudier, more hedonistic, less overtly political in their songs' subject matter. Not everyone in the group was actually gay (Willis, for one, wasn't), which came to incense the gay press of the time. But as if raising a middle finger to the Stonewall busts, the Village People proclaimed to the world that the neighborhood was proudly queer—and was ready to take that message beyond the area to the rest of the world.

When Maggie and Terre Roche had begun investigating the Village's coffeehouses and bars with Van Ronk and Terri Thal at the end of the sixties, their mother, Jude, thought their younger sister, Suzzy, wasn't ready for the experience. In Suzzy's words, Jude was afraid that her daughter would "get ruined or something" by the milieu.

Nearly a decade later, the time had come for that experience. Suzzy had her own distinctive look apart from her sisters—darker hair, physically ganglier, a bit of a gap in her front teeth—and her own path. After graduating from high school at sixteen, she'd enrolled in the State University of New York at Purchase to study theater. In class one day she stood up and, for reasons she never would understand, proclaimed, "I'm not coming back!" Moving to Manhattan, she took an apartment with a friend over the Pleasure Chest S&M goodies store on Seventh Avenue and Charles Street, the Village Vanguard directly in sight; her sisters had separate apartments nearby.

The decision would prove momentous for all of them. In June 1976 Maggie and Terre had gingerly returned to performing, playing at the National Woman's Festival at the University of Illinois in Urbana-Champaign, alongside new-generation troubadours Holly Near and Meg Christian. With Suzzy now living nearby and the holiday season approaching, the sisters needed an additional source of income. Coming upon a songbook devoted to three-part Christmas carols, they began singing holiday songs on the street and in Washington Square Park—even venturing into the Kettle of Fish and launching into a carol as startled drinkers watched. For added holiday cheer, they would sometimes adorn themselves with tinsel. By chance, Suzzy's roommate was dating *National Lampoon*'s Christopher Guest, who began making his way to the park to hear them. "They would stand there and sing carols, ending with Handel's 'Hallelujah Chorus,'" Guest said. "It became this cool thing that only maybe 20 people knew about. They were sort of the next generation of people who would sing under the arch."

When Christmas ended, the sisters decided to continue their new trio configuration. The rich blend of the three voices—Maggie's lower register, Terre's soprano, Suzzy's more conversational way with a phrase—couldn't be denied; Suzzy would refer to it as a "blending of souls." Given Maggie and Terre's interactions with Mike Porco as singers and employees, Folk City felt like an obvious destination, and Porco was open to the idea of hiring them as entertainers. But revealing the way the two eldest Roche siblings were still reeling after their collision with the major leagues, they informed Porco that they wanted to use a different group name each time so as not to be pinned down. "We didn't want

a following," Terre said, recalling the Italian-accented phrase Porco would use
with everyone. "Mike was like, 'You gotta get da-following.' He didn't want
someone in his club who didn't have one." Porco's other idea was to host a night
of all-female acts and call it either "Girls! Girls! Pretty Girls!" or "Girls, Girls,
Girls." The sisters hated it, as did some potential customers when an initial
ad appeared: bartender Peggy Duncan-Garner would take calls from irate
folk fans yelling, "They're not girls—they're women!" When Porco suggested
they call themselves the Roche Sisters, they listened but abbreviated it to the
Roches.

In that atmosphere, Maggie's songwriting ramped up once more. "People
thought of Maggie as an angel," Suzzy said. "She was an angel, but a dark angel.
It was not a hip scene, and I say that with affection. It had crested and was
going down, but in that valley a lot of seeds were sown. That's where the soil
was the richest for Maggie. Maggie liked to be down in the mud. She was fearless." For her part, Suzzy was underwhelmed by Folk City and its denizens. "It
was like going to the circus—a bunch of dark, shadowy people you never saw
in the light of the day," she said. "It seemed very decadent to me. I was much
more of a goody-goody person. I didn't want to get drunk and get involved
with weird guys." To Suzzy, those men all seemed to be in their twenties but
tried to act older and tougher than they were; one of them would refer to her
as "Toots."

As timing would have it, a new opportunity presented itself to the Roches
and others who'd recently migrated to the Village for their shot. In the late
nineteenth century and into the twentieth, the long, narrow room at 157
Bleecker had been home to the Slide, one of the city's most notorious gay bars.
Just as the Roches were coming together as a trio, the space had a new name,
owner, and mission. Pat Kenny, a larger-than-life jack-of-all-carpenter-trades
born in the Bronx in 1932 but raised in Ireland afterward, had first opened
Kenny's Castaways on the Upper East Side, where he booked the New York
Dolls and a young Bruce Springsteen, among many. Although he never fully
explained it to his daughter, Maria, she and others assumed the "castaways"
part hinted at the fact that Kenny's father had abandoned him and his mother
and siblings.

In February 1977, Kenny moved the club to the former Slide space and resumed booking music there. To lure customers, he opted against a cover charge; anyone could wander in for free. Kenny's Castaways lacked the storied history of its down-the-block competitors the Bitter End and the Village Gate—which, in a way, freed it up to be whatever it wanted to be. With its high, tin-slotted ceiling, lightbulb chandelier, and "Kenny's Castaways" life preserver mounted on one wall, the space felt closer to a festooned bat cave than a nightclub. But Kenny, a gregarious host who reminded regulars of Robert Shaw's hard-drinking shark hunter in *Jaws*, was open to booking just about anyone, whether they be local veterans, UK troubadours (like British folk balladeer Bridget St. John, who moved to the city that year and became a regular), or beginners working out their acts. In his wheelchair, Doc Pomus, the songwriter of hits like "Save the Last Dance for Me," "This Magic Moment," "A Teenager in Love" and others that defined the first half of the sixties, became a regular, always asking for his usual chicken vegetable soup. Thanks to Don Hill, who booked acts in the club's early days, Kenny was able to install a used, somewhat battered soundboard from the Who, which lent the club a touch of rock-and-roll lore and additional volume.

Unlike Porco, Kenny didn't seem to care if the acts he booked had followings or not. Paul Mills arrived in the Village from Massachusetts the same year the Bleecker Street Kenny's opened. Mills came to the Village expecting to find, as he put it, "a Greenwich Village honeycombed with coffeehouses." He didn't find any, or any performers in Washington Square Park; the Sunday-afternoon sessions had sputtered out by then. Undaunted, he continued the park's weekend tradition, reciting poems like Edgar Allan Poe's "The Raven" in a style more akin to a rock star than a poet, and Kenny hired him one night. Now known as Poez (a combination of poetry and jazz, plus veiled references to Dylan and Hendrix) and reciting urban-tableau spoken-word pieces with titles like "New Wave Pizzeria" and "The Disco Laundromat," Mills, a magnetic performer, didn't initially bring in a huge crowd. But Kenny didn't seem to care. "It doesn't matter how many people came—*I* came, I make the decisions," he told Mills. According to St. John, who would work at the club as well as perform there, the downturn in the Village helped the club because landlords were less willing to increase business rents and drive away whatever income they were making.

At the original, uptown Kenny's, Kenny had booked Danny Kalb, which he continued doing at the new Village location. Kalb was still in the midst of rebuilding his life and career. In 1973 the members of the Blues Project had each been in transitional periods: Steve Katz had left Blood, Sweat & Tears, Al Kooper's career as a front man had peaked, Roy Blumenfeld was living in Louisville, and Andy Kulberg was in Massachusetts, where he was writing film scores. That year, Kooper had unveiled his own record company, Sounds of the South. Aside from a rowdy new Florida band, Lynyrd Skynyrd, one of the company's first endeavors was a reunion of the Blues Project.

That summer, the core quintet, without original lead singer Tommy Flanders, decided to regroup for a few performances, including in New York's Central Park. By then, some of the old friction had dissipated, and Kalb spoke fondly of Kooper and his desire to bring the band together one more time. "No lie, Al and I get along great now," Kalb told Associated Press writer Mary Campbell. "My man." Still living downtown, Kalb had turned to guitar lessons for supplementing his income but, as he admitted, without as much success as his onetime teacher Van Ronk. "I wasn't giving kids what they should have in terms of theory," he told Campbell. "I'm a primitive musician. That's my strength and weakness."

After rehearsing for a week in New York City, the Blues Project rose anew, greeted with a reverence in line with its place in Village music lore. For the performance in Central Park, the opening act was none other than Maggie and Terre Roche, whose names were known to some of the few thousand in attendance thanks to their appearance on a Paul Simon album. During their set, the Blues Project stuck with the same set list that had dominated their days in the Village, opening with "Goin' Down Louisiana" as they always had. But thanks to their individual experiences since their breakup, they made the old material richer and more profound. The band that was heard on a souped-up version of Chuck Berry's "You Can't Catch Me," a more confident take on Kooper's

"Fly Away," and a locked-together "I Can't Keep from Crying Sometimes" was a tighter, sharper, and better-recorded one than the young group taped at the Cafe Au Go Go seven years before.

Kooper and Katz had attained degrees of rock-star fame, but Kalb remained the focus. His guitar sliced through the arrangements like an electric carving knife. "Two Trains Running" still stretched out over nearly fifteen minutes but benefited even more from earned wisdom and misfortunes. During its final section, when the band returned to the opening refrain after nearly a dozen minutes of pummeling highs and bottom-of-the-ocean lows, Kalb pushed his guitar into a burst of musical phlegm, and his voice into a pained yowl, as if acknowledging and purging the stormy times that had followed him the previous few years. More than ever, "Two Trains Running" wasn't just a cover; it was a musical exorcism.

After the Blues Project reunion shows in 1973, Kalb dedicated himself to his own bands and restarting his career. With guitarist John Berenzy, he started a new Danny Kalb Band, which premiered at a high school in Edgemont, New York, in 1974. The lineup showed promise. With Berenzy playing slide guitar and sharing the microphone with Kalb, the band played not only Blues Project repertoire like "Goin' Down Louisiana" but also a country song or two. They also recorded a few songs for a compilation, *The Guitar Package: The Great Rock and Blues Hits*, which placed Kalb alongside Eric Clapton, Johnny Winter, Bo Diddley, Chuck Berry, and Roy Buchanan.

But as with so many of Kalb's post–Blues Project forays, the venture would prove to be short-lived. Since the repertoire stuck largely with the classic blues Kalb loved, Berenzy came to feel that the group was limited, and he eventually left. During a 1976 show at CAMI Hall in uptown Manhattan, Kalb made a joke onstage about his "15th annual comeback." But as his tenure in the Blues Project had shown, Kalb exhibited little interest in playing the type of jacked-up blues that had catapulted contemporaries like Eric Clapton into arenas. With his heroes cutting back on their touring or passing away, Kalb settled even deeper into the genre. Did he consider himself the inheritor of the blues, or did he have conflicted feelings about becoming a rock star, with the resulting pressure and under-the-microscope attention? As they watched him playing to crowds of varying sizes at clubs like Kenny's Castaways, some of his friends couldn't quite answer that question.

Kalb's commitment to blues and his apparent lack of interest in show business arose anew not long after he started playing the Village edition of Kenny's. Reveling in their success on both *Saturday Night Live* and in films, John Belushi and Dan Aykroyd decided to live out their rock-star fantasies and front a blues and soul band. Longtime admirers of the Blues Project, they contacted Kalb for the lead-guitar slot. The money and exposure would have been undeniably beneficial. But when Kalb showed up for an audition, he was instantly turned off by the concept—Belushi and Aykroyd wearing hats and sunglasses that lent them the look of hungover FBI agents—and declined the offer. "I couldn't believe he wouldn't do it," said his cousin, drummer Peter Kogan, a member of Kalb's band at the time. "Danny was proud that he was asked. The band was really good. But it was kind of ridiculous. It was comedy."

Ron Radosh, who remained in touch with his college friend, felt that Kalb rejected the offer to demonstrate he was sticking with his principles. Realizing he may have made a mistake, Kalb went back to Belushi and Aykroyd to see if the slot was still available. By then, however, it was too late; Steve Cropper, the producer and former Booker T. and the M.G.'s guitarist, had been hired, and Kalb returned to his regular gigs at Kenny's Castaways.

Pat Kenny wasn't initially sold on the Roches, feeling they weren't upbeat enough for his crowd. But he relented, giving them a few bookings in the middle of 1977 and providing the sisters with an off-the-grid workshop. The combination of venue and act proved ideal. Just as Kenny's Castaways wasn't a conventional folk club, neither were the Roches standard anything. With her background in theater, Suzzy injected sarcastic patter into their sets: One love song, she would say, was about the time after "the initial romantic part has fizzled but it's before the real hatred sets in." Exuding wit and wary toughness, each could stare down anyone, especially hecklers. "You were dealing with a much rowdier crowd, and we learned how to go back and forth with the audience," said Suzzy. "The punk thing was starting to break right around the same time, over at CBGB, and we started to take on some of that energy, where we would do anything."

Whether at Kenny's or the occasional Folk City show, they also didn't conform to what women folkies should wear onstage. Maggie's peasant dresses contrasted with Terre's close-cropped punk cut and baseball jerseys and Suzzy's neckties and gym shorts with leotards. "We didn't coordinate what we were wearing—we didn't think about it," Suzzy said. "We'd say, 'That's cool, I'm gonna wear this!' Anything goes."

Their music also became almost uncategorizable. Dedicating themselves to regular afternoon rehearsals in one of another of their apartments, they worked out intricate vocal arrangements that built on what Maggie and Terre had started on their own. As their fellow songwriter and peer David Massengill noted when he saw them, their harmonies seemed to be written as if they were melodies themselves, each of them songs in their own right. The combination of music and presentation helped make the point that the previous, sometimes prim archetypes of women singers and songwriters in the Village were being tossed onto the curb like yesterday's bell-bottoms.

Offstage, Maggie could be chatty with her family or close friends. But standing to the left of her sisters onstage, she was now the most muted, rarely saying much and leaving the introductions and asides to her siblings. Of his eldest daughter, John Roche used to say, "She hides her bushel under a light," a play on "She hides her light under a bushel" that Terre interpreted as Maggie being in the spotlight yet keeping everything to herself. Terre wondered if Maggie's subdued presence signaled the effects of her tumultuous life experiences. "When we were on that coffeehouse circuit, Maggie was fearless," Terre said. "I was more about hanging back and being cautious. But after that, I feel like she changed. She got much quieter." For a fan base that seemed to increase with each Kenny's or Folk City performance, though, Maggie's silent side lent both her and the Roches a mystique that was impossible to ignore.

Song by song, they also pulled together a repertoire—mostly by Maggie, some by Terre and Suzzy—that reflected life as single women in the city, each song imbued with wry wit, self-defiance, and learned wisdom. Maggie had "Hammond Song" as well as "Quitting Time," which Terre had long assumed was about their father and the way he had left his ad-agency job, forcing their mother to return to work as a secretary. Suzzy's first attempt at writing a song, "The Train," detailed, with easily relatable sentiments, a surrealistic commute into the city; the melody itself chugged like a commuter rail. After Maggie and Terre had returned to New York, Terre became pregnant, and her abortion led to a gentle ache of song called "Runs in the Family." When the sisters needed a bio of themselves for a December 1977 club show outside the city, they wrote a whimsical press statement alluding to Maggie and Terre's false start and their New Jersey background. They liked it so much that they used it as the basis for a song, "We." They also slipped in a cover of "The Naughty Lady of Shady Lane," a fifties prerock pop hit about a sassy woman who "has the town in a whirl" but turns out to be a newborn baby.

At Kenny's Castaways, an Irish promoter and friend of Pat Kenny introduced himself and offered to fly the trio to his country for work—to sing in a department-store window, as the sisters interpreted it. The plan fizzled, to their puzzlement and relief, but what emerged was "The Troubles," which included everyday questions about such a trip (would strawberry apricot pie be available there?) and counterpoint harmonies that circled each other like airplanes awaiting a landing on the same runway. "Pretty and High," which Maggie and Terre had attempted but not completed during the *Seductive Reasoning* sessions, was resurrected for the trio, becoming a rapturous set piece. With its reference to a prince, a circus, and how "pretty and high and shy" a woman performer was, it could have been about any number of aspects of their biography, although Maggie refrained as always from an explanation. "In 'pretty and high and a lie,' she was dealing with the difference between an image you're projecting and who you really are," Terre said. "In a lot of her early songs, she was always walking that line."

Another of Maggie's songs, "The Married Men," walked a similar line. A list of illicit affairs, real or imagined—a man in Louisiana is mentioned but not named—it hinted at another side of Maggie's life. The song also made reference to a new member of their circle. Since his days at the Gaslight, Loudon Wainwright III had moved on to other record companies, a fluke hit ("Dead Skunk" in 1972), a recurring role in the TV series *M*A*S*H*, and an ongoing series of autobiographical, often self-wounding songs about his life, career, and affairs. He'd heard *Seductive Reasoning* and been impressed with the songs, considering Maggie Roche on par with Dylan, and he soon developed a crush on her but was rebuffed. "I was trying to go there, and was not invited," he said. One line in "Married Men," about one man who's "got a little boy," referred to Wainwright, who by then had had a son, Rufus, with his now ex-wife Kate McGarrigle.

After Wainwright met Suzzy—at either an apartment in the Village, as he recalled, or backstage at his 1975 show at Fisher Hall, as she did—he was smitten. His initial entreaty to her was admittedly awkward; he showed up at her home with a copy of the first album by Kate and her sister Anna McGarrigle, which puzzled Suzzy but didn't prevent her and Wainwright from soon becoming a couple. Continuing a tradition that extended back to tangled personal Village relationships of the past, Maggie was coupled with Mark (later Marc) Johnson, another denizen of the scene who could create one-man-band pop that harked back to the work of Brian Wilson.

Terre was in a relationship with George Gerdes, a singer, songwriter, and fledgling actor from Long Island who had met Wainwright when they both attended Carnegie Tech in the sixties. Gerdes (unrelated to the family who ran the original Gerdes restaurant) had made two albums of arch country and folk songs, *Obituary* and *Son of Obituary*, then moved to New York in 1975, meeting the Roche sisters when they were back in town. His performances, where he often seemed to be acting out roles with a permanently arched eyebrow, introduced a theatrical element into venues like Folk City. The worlds of troubadours and theater had overlapped since the days of thespians turned singers like the Clancy Brothers, Jimmy Gavin, and David Blue, not to mention the Revuers during the early years of the Village Vanguard. With Gerdes, Suzzy Roche, and Wainwright, who all dabbled in stage and screen roles apart from music, the tradition continued by way of the next generation.

His own complicated history with the sisters aside, Wainwright was stunned as he watched them coalesce as a unit. "It was just perfect," he said. "Maggie was the killer songwriter on stage left and beautiful Terre ripping off those guitar licks. And then the actress, Suzzy, at the center of it. It could have been argued that Maggie and Terre might have found a way to turn into something else, but when Suzzy came along, that was the missing piece."

No one knew what it would all amount to; Maggie and Terre had seen firsthand that idiosyncratic singers and songwriters, especially from downtown New York, weren't an automatic sell. But at that moment, little of that seemed to matter. "No rules," Suzzy said. "No trying to get a record deal. We didn't have any interest in trying to be like anyone else or picking material that would help us get on the radio, any of that. It was like flying on horses. We were just going on fire."

Mort Cooperman was tending to business inside the Lone Star Cafe when one of his employees approached him with the news that a truck with an iguana had pulled up. Cooperman, who'd opened his club at 61 Fifth Avenue at Thirteenth Street in early 1977, thought he knew what his worker meant. Bob Wade, the iconoclastic artist known for oversized works of art inspired by his home state of Texas, had called Cooperman and told him he wanted to find a home for his latest piece and thought the club would be a good fit.

What he hadn't mentioned was that the artwork—an iguana made of polyurethane on an aluminum frame—was forty-one feet long and sixteen feet at its highest, its lizard eyes made of red glass, spikes jutting out from its back. Walking outside, Cooperman was stunned by the sight. "I thought we were talking about something four or five feet long," he said. "I had no idea. I said the immortal French words: 'Holy shit.'" Since there was no other place for it, the iguana was soon mounted on the roof of the Lone Star.

By the late seventies, pop music was beginning to break into increasingly separate camps—disco, punk, heavy metal, progressive rock. Reflecting those changes, the Village music scene also began splintering, each new venue presenting or embodying a genre and its attendant lifestyle—some of it, like the iguana, oversized.

Jazz had played a prominent role in the scene for decades, but its electrified, boisterous offshoot, fusion, was now part of the soundtrack of the seventies. The same year Kenny's Castaways swung open its doors, that new jazz hybrid found a haven all its own. Named after the West Village street where it sat, Seventh Avenue South wasn't strictly devoted to fusion, a genre unafraid to incorporate disco shimmy, mile-a-minute guitar solos, and burping synthesizers. The club was the brainchild of two of the city's most prominent jazz session men and bandleaders, saxophonist Michael Brecker and his brother, trumpeter Randy. With Kate Greenfield, who worked for the counseling and job-placement program in the Brooklyn criminal court system but dreamed of owning a restaurant, the Breckers and Greenfield each pitched in $12,000 and bought an empty, two-floor eatery at 21 Seventh Avenue South. A mysterious local who went by the name Cha Cha was the liaison for the cigarette, sanitation, and jukebox businesses.

Everyone seemed to know or have worked with the Breckers. Randy had been a founding member of Blood, Sweat & Tears, and the Breckers had made albums together with their own band; individually, they were heard on records by James Taylor, Elton John, Steely Dan, James Brown, and Paul Simon, among many. Thanks to those connections, Seventh Avenue South, after some early soundproofing issues with neighborhood buildings, became a hang for their musician friends and industry peers. A playground for serious players, the upper-floor performance space became the place to catch a set by Gil Evans, the Average White Band, or a Michael Brecker–led band featuring drummer Steve Gadd and keyboardist Don Grolnick. Returning to the States in 1976 after living in Copenhagen, Dexter Gordon chose the club as one of his earliest stops. Donna Summer, the newly reigning queen of disco, stopped by one night, as did Stevie Wonder. At least once, the dazzling but mercurial Jaco Pastorius jumped onstage with his bass to sit in with a surprised band. Joni Mitchell, then in a relationship with New York–based percussionist Don Elias, was an occasional visitor. Wanting to bring Mitchell a special dish, Greenfield had the idea of a guitar-shaped entrée and settled on chopped liver, which, she said, had "the right consistency to sculpt." Observing it was *Saturday Night Live's* Gilda Radner, who found the sight of the liver guitar hilarious.

At the Bottom Line, Allan Pepper and Stanley Snadowsky continued to frown upon drug use, especially in the audience; it wasn't uncommon for

Pepper, worried about losing his lease, to kick out anyone who lit up a joint. Yet that didn't mean the excesses of the time or of the rock world were left behind entirely. In their office, Pepper and Snadowsky could sometimes smell pot wafting out of the dressing rooms beneath them, and Pepper once heard a manager comparing the quality of cocaine supplied by competing record companies. "There were promotion guys supplying their artists and disc jockeys with drugs," said Pepper. "You could only police it to a certain extent."

Not much policing took place at Seventh Avenue South. Jazz and substance abuse had long been partners, and the tradition carried on at the club with a distinctly Me Decade touch. It wasn't uncommon for musicians to snort coke in the refrigerated food room or off the Pac-Man video-game console, especially after the club closed at 4 a.m. and musicians lingered for a few more hours. "Come on, you white bitch," Miles Davis said as he approached Greenfield one night. "I know you got some of that powder in your pocket." The Breckers even had groupies, some dubbed the "Skank Sisters," who would travel to the club after meeting them somewhere around the world. "Back in those days, it wasn't unusual to get high, pick somebody up or get picked up and be wild," said Greenfield. The partying could go on until dawn, sometimes with people driving home in less than sober states. John Scofield would later tell writer Shaun Brady that Seventh Avenue South was "the center of the jazz world."

That same year, the talk of the Village was an unlikely but welcome return. At eighty-two, Alberta Hunter had had a career before World War II, writing "Downhearted Blues," which Bessie Smith had cut, and singing and acting. When her mother died in 1954, Hunter pursued and received a degree in nursing. But after retiring, Hunter returned to singing, now at the Cookery, a restaurant-turned-club on University Place run by Barney Josephson. Although the founder of Cafe Society had owned the spot for years, Hunter, a regal presence in gowns and earrings, made the Cookery a new destination spot. Supportive crowds watched as she sang blues and standards, some delightfully suggestive, with hard-earned conviction.

Starting with its own launch in 1977, the Lone Star Cafe didn't have the new-jazz gleam of Seventh Avenue South, the moneyed industry feel of the Bottom Line, or the old-world history of Folk City or the Village Vanguard.

In its previous life, it had been a Schrafft's ice cream parlor, as seen in its confounding layout: a revolving entry door, a tiny stage at the front that directly faced the bar, and a balcony that allowed a chosen few to look directly down onto the stage. The sight lines were, Cooperman admitted, "shitty." A former ad man at the Wells Rich Greene agency, Cooperman had no experience in music business, nor did his partner and fellow ad man Bill McGivney, but the two went ahead with their plan to remake it as a club. "I knew *nothing*," Cooperman said. "I didn't know what to pay a band. I had no contacts. I didn't know what a sound system was. If I had known all that, I wouldn't have done it." A month after the club opened, a cop or fireman—Cooperman couldn't recall which—came in and asked, "Are you gonna take care of me?" Cooperman was so clueless about payoffs that he asked if the service was bad.

The Lone Star's kickoff performer, in February 1977, was Billy Swan, whose breakthrough hit, "I Can Help," was an eerily perfect facsimile of an Elvis hit. But early on, with barely a few dozen people in a space that held about four hundred, Cooperman watched as a couple stood up to leave. When he asked them why, they said they wanted to hear traditional country, not the watered-down version of the time. Embodied by Willie Nelson and Waylon Jennings, outlaw country was offering an alternative to countrypolitan and mainstream Nashville. Cooperman went the same route, booking rebels or honky-tonk heroes like Billy Joe Shaver, Doug Sahm, Mickey Gilley, and Kinky Friedman. Friedman and his twisted songs, like "They Ain't Makin' Jews like Jesus Anymore" and "Asshole from El Paso," were especially at home at the Lone Star. The club soon became the unlikely place to see legends like James Brown. In the basement dressing room after his set, Brown insisted that Cooperman "feel my leg" to show off his muscle, and Cooperman watched as Brown dressed down his band for not playing well. On one of several nights that presented Willie Nelson, John Belushi and Nelson shared a joint, and Bill Murray made his way onto the cramped stage with Nelson and his band. When Roy Orbison was booked, Linda Ronstadt (who had remade his "Blue Bayou") showed up with her beau, California governor Jerry Brown. When Orbison and Ronstadt huddled in his dressing room, Brown, waiting patiently outside, finally began pounding on the door: "Let me in! I'm the governor of California!"

Painted above the club's entrance, where "Schrafft's" had once been embla-
zoned, was the Lone Star's motto: "Too Much Ain't Enough," taken from a
line in Shaver's "Old Five and Dimers like Me." That proved fitting in ways that
sometimes had little to do with music. Thanks to the proximity of the stage to
the crowd, especially up front, the atmosphere could be boisterous, the audience becoming as much a part of the show as the performers. The festivities
often extended to the roof, where it wasn't uncommon for musicians or fans to
get high. The iguana had, as Cooperman said, "a rather large aperture anus,"
and word got around that musicians would be blessed with a good set if they
had sex in it before a show.

Another Village tradition, harassment, was also on the Lone Star's set list.
The Fifth Avenue Association, which had existed since 1907 and monitored the
entire storied avenue from uptown to Washington Square Park, objected to the
sight of a fake lizard atop the building. "It's not just a matter of the iguana," Fifth
Avenue Association executive vice president Michael Grosso told the *Daily News*.
"If we did not respond to the warnings of some of our members, the iguana's
presence could establish a dangerous precedent. Who knows what might go up
on other roofs in the name of art?"

Although the piece was a registered work of art and had been in the Art
Park outside Niagara Falls, the Buildings Department ordered Cooperman to
take it down. After it had been removed, the Texas state legislature jokingly
passed a bill asking the club to cede from New York City and become part of
Texas. When a delegation from Texas visited the club in the summer of 1978,
Ed Koch, who'd been elected mayor the same year the Lone Star opened, was
also in attendance. Approaching Cooperman, he asked, "Where's the iguana?"
Told what had transpired, Koch said he was shocked. The next day, an official
at the Buildings Department called to say the office had made a mistake, and
the iguana was reinstated. The party, inside and on the roof, would continue.

To the record companies in far-off midtown offices, the West Village remained
a ghost town, a relic from another era. From time to desolate time, even the club
owners shared that feeling. At Folk City, the Monday-night hoots continued,

but with diminished expectations all around. Starting at 7 p.m., Mike Porco would, as always, place numbered cards on the bar, face down, and would-be performers would pick one and be added to the list depending on their digits. Some went home if their number was higher than twenty; by the last slots, at three or four in the morning, few remained. "Nightlife is diminishing," a seemingly depressed Porco told the *Daily News* in 1977. "They play up the crime in the Village and people are afraid to come."

Apparently, though, no one told the *New York Times* that venturing south of Fourteenth Street was a waste of time. John Rockwell, the paper's chief pop critic, the Robert Shelton of his era, became one of its champions. Catching an early Roches set at Kenny's Castaways in the fall of 1977, Rockwell found it "pretty wonderful, if ever-so-slightly coy." In subsequent write-ups, he applauded their sense of humor and the intricacies of their vocal interplay.

The same season, Rockwell was back at the venue, this time to see Bridget St. John, the British folksinger who'd released several beautifully wintry albums early in the decade and had made the Village her new home. Yet it was the opening act that most caught Rockwell's ears. Playing off a tag that had been attached to Wainwright, Springsteen, and John Prine, Rockwell wrote, tongue in cheek, that "Steve Forbert is the next 'New Bob Dylan.' He is also the 'next new Elvis Presley' and 'the next new Rod Stewart.'" Rockwell added that Forbert was "really none of those things" but was "a wonderfully talented and assured performer."

Another regular at Kenny's was Willie Nile, a Buffalo-born writer and singer who'd first arrived in the Village in the early seventies. "The ghosts of the Sixties were haunting the different venues," Nile said of that period. Moving into an apartment down the street from Dylan, he would sometimes see his hero walking along by himself, crossing to the other side to avoid interacting with passersby. After a bout of pneumonia and mononucleosis sent him back upstate, Nile returned later in the decade and gravitated toward the new Kenny's. "This is what I came here for—it's a scene, a community," he recalled Forbert telling him excitedly one night. Like Forbert, Nile accompanied himself on guitar but approached his craft with a dash of rock-and-roll verve. Matching his look—a dash of troubadour, a bit of fifties greaser—Nile was a rocker and showman at heart; leaping about the small Kenny's stage, he would take to introducing imaginary accompanists.

In the summer of 1978, Nile noticed a studious-looking, bespectacled man in the audience who turned out to be the *Times* music critic Robert Palmer. As with Rockwell and Forbert, Palmer ended up being taken with the first act on stage—Nile, who, in Palmer's words, "would seem to be the most gifted song-writer to emerge from the New York folk scene in some while."

With those write-ups, the music business again turned its collective gaze toward the Village. On the heels of his review, Forbert was courted by three major labels, including Arista. Label head Clive Davis appeared in what Forbert recalled as a "floor-length winter coat" and, with his team, took Forbert to a nearby café to talk business. "It was a little uncomfortable," he said. "We had this little scene and all of a sudden you're seeing it happen for me. There were cats who had been working it for years and were older than me." In the end, Forbert signed with Nemperor, a division of Atlantic. It helped that he was comanaged by Linda Stein and Danny Fields; in previous jobs, including as a publicist for Jac Holzman's Elektra, Fields had helped the Ramones, the MC5, and the Stooges land record deals. After Palmer's review of Nile was published, Kenny's was overflowing the following night, Davis again in the crowd. Within a week, Nile had a contract of his own; this time, Arista won out, and the Village now had two major-label signees emerging from Kenny's Castaways.

That number would soon jump to three. Covering the first show of the Roches' five-night stand at Folk City in March 1978, Rockwell declared the sisters "one of the most moving, charming, funny and original acts in the country." In the downstairs area that served as both a dressing room and Porco's office, the sisters were told one evening that Linda Ronstadt (a friend of Rock-well's) and Phoebe Snow were in the house. During the set, the two seemed enraptured, loudly praising the sisters' harmonies; afterward, Ronstadt walked down into the dressing room to compliment them.

The trio also attracted attention in other, unintentionally comic ways. When the Rolling Stones were touring to promote *Some Girls* in the summer of 1978, the group inserted a few secret club shows, often billing themselves as "The Cockroaches." When the Roche sisters were booked into the Bottom Line that summer, Stones fans swarmed the venue, thinking their favorites were in the house. To deter the crowd, one of the club's bouncers quickly had a T-shirt made that read, "This is not the Rolling Stones."

During the same period, another British musician was circling the scene and the sisters. In 1977, Robert Fripp, the proper and irascible founder and guitarist of King Crimson, had moved to New York from the small, rural town in England where he lived after King Crimson had dissolved. After working with Peter Gabriel in Toronto in 1976, he decided to give New York City a shot. At first, its intensity put him off, and he couldn't afford to live in Greenwich Village; he wound up subletting on the Bowery, across from CBGB. Yet he found the city more welcoming than his home country. "I'd be crossing the street in the Village, and someone would say, 'Hey, Fripp, how you doing?'" he recalled. "Whereas if I were crossing the street in London, it was, 'Who the fuck do you think *you* are?' I was prog rock scum."

In search of work as a producer, Fripp befriended several journalists in the city, including Rockwell—who, Fripp recalled, suggested he check out the Roches. Terre would remember the moment taking place at Kenny's Castaways, while Fripp thought it was the Bottom Line, where he stood backstage and praised them when they came off. (Suzzy would remember it there as well, thinking, "What an odd fellow.") The Roches' music was diametrically opposed to the knotty, roller-coaster ride that was King Crimson's style of prog rock, but it appealed to Fripp for that very reason. "I thought, 'Wow, that was stunning,'" he said. "I loved the authenticity and reality of the performance. I never looked on them as being part of a folk scene. They were always outside the category. They were a category of their own."

Unbeknownst to the sisters, Fripp had signed a production deal with Warner Brothers. That company's Karin Berg, one of the few female A&R executives in the business at the time, was both friendly with Fripp and an admirer of the Roches. Given Maggie and Terre's previous encounter with the business, the sisters again treaded carefully. "We were trying to *not* be in show business," Terre said. "Maggie and I felt a little burned by our experience in the big time, so we said we're not trying to jump back into the frying pan. We wanted to work on our arrangements, but people started to hear about us and come to the gigs. And now we were in a whole different situation."

When the sisters were told that Fripp wanted to meet them and possibly produce a record for them, none of them knew who he was. At the mention of King Crimson, Terre only flashed upon the painting of the wide-open mouth on the cover of *In the Court of the Crimson King*, the group's 1969 debut. But they agreed to talk, and Fripp visited them at one of their apartments, only to learn that he was the one being interrogated. "They said nothing," he said. "I realized that *I'm* being interviewed for this. I must have talked for a while and then I got the gig. Whatever I said or didn't say, the argument was made and accepted." With the Fripp production role in the mix, the sisters signed with Warner Brothers. Maggie had her doubts about the advance they were receiving—in the area of $10,000, as Terre would recall—feeling it would place too much pressure on them. But by the summer, they were, again, a major-label recording act.

In September, mere months after their local buzz had become noticeably louder, the Roches began congregating with Fripp at the midtown studio the Hit Factory to tape their first album as a trio. Wearing a three-piece suit and sporting an "I Am Not Robert Fripp" button that played off his notorious irritability, Fripp had the sisters sit in a circle and simply perform their songs, keeping the focus on their voices and acoustic guitars (and bass parts from Tony Levin). The technique was dubbed "audio verité" by either Fripp or, in Suzzy's memory, George Gerdes, who was still Terre's boyfriend. "In my view, a conventional American producer would put a rhythm section behind them," Fripp said. "And once you had that, you would need some sort of soloist, a guitarist or maybe a keyboard player. At that point, where are the Roches?" The only instrumental solo on the record would, in fact, be from Fripp, on "Hammond Song." As he was tuning up, he began playing one of his typically serpentine leads, then launched into the song for real. In the end, everyone was more satisfied with the impromptu section; Fripp himself came to call it "as fine a piece of playing as anything else in my musical life," and it stayed on the record.

Fripp also received an introduction to a scene that was unrulier than he'd expected. As sensitive as they sounded onstage, the new generation of Village folksingers could throw down as much as anyone. Mounted behind the bar at Kenny's Castaways was a German drinking horn, which Pat Kenny would pull down for special occasions, fill with beer, and pass around; since it was old and leaky, it would sometimes spill all over people's shirts. (To his horror, Roger Probert, an English music-business veteran hired to book the club after Don Hill, discovered that no one had ever cleaned the inside of the horn.) Over at the Other End, as he and his producer Steve Burgh were preparing to start his first album, Forbert pounded down so many drinks that he collapsed on the sidewalk and was hauled away by police; Burgh, who preferred weed, watched disapprovingly from the sidelines. The Roches would write a song, "Face Down at Folk City," fueled by the day Terre showed up at a band rehearsal horribly hung over from the night before, emptying her stomach in the club's toilet as a fistfight broke out around them.

The day their album was completed, the Roches took Fripp out to celebrate. Their night of barhopping would culminate with all of them arriving at a mysterious door—the entrance to an after-hours club that the sisters knew well. As daybreak approached, Fripp left, but the sisters remained. "Those girls could *drink*," Fripp said. "*Whoa*. I couldn't keep up with any of them. I'm from the countryside in England. The pubs close at 11." Those wild times had nearly derailed Maggie and Terre earlier in the decade, but at this point, the mood was decidedly more celebratory.

▌▐▌▐▌

Van Ronk's spirit hung over the first batch of records by the Village's new graduating class, which started rolling out in the fall of 1978. As the luck of the Village in later years would have it, Forbert's debut, *Alive on Arrival*, appeared amid a three-month pressmen's strike that halted the printing of the *New York Times*, the *Daily News*, and, later, the *New York Post*. As a result, no reviews of the record would appear in any of them, but the Long Island paper *Newsday*, which wasn't affected, was able to weigh in, calling Forbert "a cross between Dave Van Ronk and Rod Stewart."

The reference was to Forbert's voice, an instantly recognizable instrument with scrappy warmth and excitable-boy verve. Whatever one made of the Van

Ronk (or Stewart) connection, *Alive on Arrival* was undeniably rooted in an almost mythical past. Starting with a burst of low-down harmonica and a guitar strum, the record had the earmarks of a troubadour album from the previous ten to fifteen years. A few of its songs—the bittersweet farewell "It Isn't Gonna Be That Way" and "Grand Central Station, March 18, 1977," which captured the life of a New York street performer, complete with open guitar cases, coins, and warnings from cops to cease—had the coffeehouse intimacy of records Forbert had absorbed as a kid in Mississippi. The denim-jacketed twenty-three-year-old on the cover didn't look fashionably punk, either.

But if any album of that moment lived up to its title, it was *Alive on Arrival.* Unlike some of his peers, Forbert wasn't simply a words guy but also a music one. Producer Burgh beefed up Forbert's sound with rhythm sections, a dash of studio-musician saxophone, and electric guitars that had the freshly scrubbed sound of the *Saturday Night Live* house band. Burgh and Forbert also transformed "What Kinda Guy?" into sly modern rockabilly and layered "Goin' Down to Laurel" with a lyrical pedal-steel guitar for added country panache. A modest-scale rock finale, "You Can Not Win If You Do Not Play," broadcast Forbert's musical and philosophical ambitions. Yet it wasn't simply the arrangements that made *Alive on Arrival* rise to number 82—unheard of for a modern folk album in 1978—on the *Billboard* chart. Forbert wasn't enigmatic like Dylan, but his tales of yearning to make a place for himself in the world transcended the Village and Manhattan itself.

A few months later, Van Ronk's onetime protégés, along with their sister, were reintroduced to the world. As bare-boned as any major-label album was permitted to be in the early months of 1979, *The Roches* captured the sound and set list the sisters had been perfecting at Kenny's Castaways and Folk City over the previous two years. The arrangements on Maggie and Terre's *Seductive Reasoning* were often too varied for the songs' own good. *The Roches*, in contrast, adhered to Fripp's vision of an album that replicated what he and so many others had seen at their live performances. Thanks to Fripp's recording approach, their harmonies were massive, an instrument all their own. "The Troubles," their vocal rope-a-dope about their canceled Ireland trip, was included, as was their autobiographical calling card "We," where they came across like a daffy but guarded version of World War II female vocal groups. "Hammond Song" had blossomed into a vocally seamless piece of pop choral music, the three voices as one as Fripp's lead guitar slithered up into the chorus.

The Roches wasn't simply a sonically gorgeous record. The sisters' songs were alternately poignant, frisky, sad, droll, and whimsical, and the album was imbued with the feeling of family members who strove to support and protect one another. On "Runs in the Family," backed by a simple guitar part that could have been borrowed from a Simon and Garfunkel album, Maggie and Suzzy weren't just singing along with Terre but also holding her hand through a difficult moment in her life. In the stunning "Quitting Time," their overlapping voices shifted tones with each new chord, Suzzy and Terre then singing beats behind Maggie's lead, as if echoing her. Whether or not the song was about their father, it felt like a glowing send-off to a new phase of life. *The Roches* came across like the most eccentric folk mass at a church—sung by angels who'd been through it, whether it was a surreal train ride, unemployment, or crushed expectations.

In the New York–centric media world, the album was greeted in a way *Seductive Reasoning* hadn't been. Rockwell would eventually name it his album of the year in the *Times*. How they would be received outside that bubble was another story. During the making of *The Roches*, the sisters were taken aback when Fripp told them they likely wouldn't sell many records but would be seen as groundbreakers. In one regard, Fripp wasn't off base. As everyone from Van Ronk to early Dylan to the Blues Project had learned, translating a downtown attitude and integrity to the masses wasn't easy. When the sisters visited Warner Brothers' L.A. headquarters, a receptionist complimented their "demo," unaware that the music she'd just heard was their finished record. Even folk stalwarts could heckle them, as the Roches learned when they shared a stage with Tom Rush soon after *The Roches* was unveiled. "We were not easy to pair with other people," Suzzy said. "The folk music people really did not like us. We weren't 'girls with the guitar.' It wasn't recognizable to them. It was sassier."

The Roches went on to sell a respectable 150,000 copies and reach number 58 on the *Billboard* chart. With Warner Brothers eager to capitalize on the album's electro-charged reviews, an opening-act slot on a major tour was a natural next step. That summer, the trio was offered such an opportunity with James Taylor, who was about to embark on a series of arena-heavy shows. "Paul [Simon] and I thought, 'This is it,'" recalled Michael Tannen, now their manager (and, with Simon, still their publisher). "You couldn't have asked for anything better than opening for a major national tour for James Taylor. We thought, 'This is money in the bank!'"

But once more to Tannen's consternation, the siblings went off by themselves, discussed the idea, and returned with an unconditional answer, which was no. Terre felt that playing such oversized venues wouldn't be suitable for their relatively quiet sound. Suzzy sensed the tour would have been difficult for her boyfriend, Wainwright, who was experiencing rough career waters after being dropped by his third label. "I was young and didn't want to lose him," she said, citing one review that praised the Roches and mentioned Wainwright's struggles. "It was hard for him to take all that." Once again, Tannen was left holding the bag. "You couldn't have a conversation about it," he said. "The three of them spoke and then came back. If you're on the other end, like us, it would drive you *crazy*."

Realizing they may have harmed their relationship with their label after turning down the Taylor work, the Roches latched into the next offer that came along—a short West Coast tour opening for Boz Scaggs. None of the sisters were overly familiar with *Silk Degrees*, his white-soul breakthrough record, but on the surface, the combination seemed plausible. "We weren't soft girls with a male band singing love songs," Suzzy said. "We were defiant. But we thought we were more conventional than we were. We thought we were making music right down the middle."

Night after endless night on the Scaggs tour, they were proven wrong. As local newspaper critics observed, they received a "less than lukewarm" reaction in Sacramento and were "ignored" in Berkeley—and those were the encouraging moments. Elsewhere, Suzzy heard screams of "Sit on my face!" as she tried to concentrate on a harmony. After one male concertgoer yelled something rude at them, Terre walked to the front of the stage and, out of frustration, threw a glass of water in his face, to which he screamed back, "You fucking whore!" More than once, they were booed offstage. A write-up in a California newspaper referred to them as the group Los Angeles loved to hate. The experience was so scarring and triggering that Terre would never again attend another large-scale stadium show.

To their relief and surprise, Joni Mitchell showed up at one show to offer support, and Ronstadt, along with Jerry Brown, visited them backstage in L.A. Hearing about the negative response they'd received, Ronstadt reassured them that everyone went through such things, then shared her own experiences of being heckled while opening for Neil Young years earlier.

By their own admission, the Roches weren't adept at working the system. Maggie remained enigmatic: talkative with family and friends in one-on-one conversations but withdrawn with industry people. "Social interactions, or interactions in general, were difficult for Maggie," said Suzzy, who would recall a record-company lunch in L.A. where Maggie sat with her head down the entire time. If it were a man, Suzzy surmised, it would be considered eccentric, but with Maggie, "it translated as weird."

A few months after *The Roches* was released, Ronstadt and Snow were the musical guests on *Saturday Night Live*. As Paul Simon and Maggie Roche watched in the studio audience, Ronstadt and Snow sang Maggie's "The Married Men." Ronstadt had wanted to record it, and everyone knew her rendition would generate sizable income for the group. But Snow, still struggling for another hit to follow up "Poetry Man" a few years earlier, had asked first, and Maggie, who'd promised Snow she could have first dibs on the song, would not budge from her decision. "Maggie was the most ethical person I ever met," said Suzzy. "She would not do anything but the right thing. She would have had to say to Phoebe, 'We're going to go with Linda instead—it's better for us.' But because she had said yes to Phoebe, she had to stand by that."

In November 1979 the Roches were themselves rewarded with the hallowed musical-guest slot on *Saturday Night Live*. The show regularly served as a jet pack for music acts, and it was easy to imagine the Roches receiving a second wind for their months-old album. During sound check, as Suzzy recalled, producer and overlord Lorne Michaels stood and watched them with folded arms. From what they'd been told, another artist had cursed onstage in a previous broadcast, and Michaels wanted to make sure the sisters wouldn't do the same. But Suzzy found the sight of Michaels before them nerve-racking.

As one of their two songs, they'd been asked to play "Hammond Song," a natural choice that would promote the album. Instead, they chose their rendition of the "Hallelujah Chorus," appropriate given the coming Christmas season. In their second segment, they played an entirely new and unrecorded tune, "Bobby's Song," named after the clarinet player in retro musician Leon Redbone's band who they'd gone to see play in Eddie Condon's, one of the earliest Village jazz clubs. The song, which referenced that musician's crush on Suzzy, had a bustling, borderline-comic energy to it, and Maggie even danced in place.

But since neither song was included on *The Roches*, the appearance did little to sell records and may have only reinforced the idea to viewers that the Roches were kooky Manhattan types. "It was a self-sabotage thing," Suzzy said. "There was this innate rebelliousness against the way famous people behaved that we were on a crusade about. That was kind of stupid of us. But to be fair, famous people were pretty much jerks for the most part."

███

Early in his New York years, Steve Forbert had mostly completed a joyful ode to being smitten, "Romeo's Tune," inspired by a woman he'd known in Mississippi. Feeling it didn't fit with the story he wanted to tell on *Alive on Arrival*, Forbert put the song aside, then excavated it for his second album, *Jackrabbit Slim*, in 1979. Like the rest of that album, "Romeo's Tune" was given a sprightly, sunshine-bright arrangement by producer John Simon. To ensure that the album received airplay in Texas—some of the early reviews were critical of the production, which was seen as too lavish—one CBS Records employee delivered a copy to a radio station while wearing a bunny outfit. As it turned out, "Romeo's Tune" didn't need the boost; made a single in January 1980, it slid up to an astonishing number 11.

By the middle of 1980, Forbert's wasn't the only record being sold in stores, or even being heard on the radio, from a scene long considered obsolete. Carolyne Mas, a Bronxville, New York, native, had paid her dues at the Other

End, Kenny's Castaways, and Folk City starting in 1976. Sometimes backed by a band, Mas didn't always conform to the acoustic troubadour tradition, to the point where she heard that one record-company executive who saw her at Kenny's Castaways said he wouldn't sign her since "a woman playing rock and roll will never sell." After Ira Mayer of the *New York Post* and Palmer of the *Times* wrote enthusiastic reviews of shows at the Other End, Mas was signed by Mercury in 1979. (By coincidence, its East Coast head of A&R was none other than former Blues Project member Steve Katz, who had decided to take a desk job for a time.) On tracks such as "It's No Secret" and "Stillsane," Mas's self-titled first album had a Springsteenian spark (and saxophone) to its rock and roll, and the ballad "Snow" had the feel of a pop standard. Likewise, Willie Nile's eponymous debut, rolled out in early 1980 by way of Arista, demonstrated that crafted rock and roll, with a touch of boardwalk and a dab of city streets, could still emerge from the scene. The propulsive acoustic rock he'd crafted at Kenny's Castaways was heard in "Dear Lord," and "It's All Over" and "That's the Reason" sounded like jangly folk rock that had been roughed up on the streets of Manhattan.

Despite this newfound music-business awareness of the Village, the instability and turbulence that engulfed the neighborhood and its venues began to take their toll on Mike Porco. As he approached sixty-five, he remained his affable, heavily accented self, still employing family members to work the door and staying until the early-morning hours. But the time had come for him to detach, and in late 1979 Porco floated the idea of selling the place to two workers close to him.

Robbie Woliver, a thirty-one-year-old from Long Island and Queens, had all the qualifications for the job. He'd grown up in a family that was pro–civil rights and antiwar, had been mesmerized by an Odetta album as a kid, and had taken a crack at a songwriting career himself. In 1978 Woliver, initially working with music critic Leslie Berman, convinced Porco to let him launch a Sunday-afternoon songwriters workshop, in honor of Phil Ochs, at his club.

Woliver and his girlfriend, Marilyn Lash, whom he'd met when they worked at the same Long Island record store and was now a Folk City employee herself, had scoured the area for a club of their own. But they circled back to Porco and, in May 1980, twenty years to the month after Gerdes Restaurant had been renamed Gerde's Folk City, the couple took over the lease and bought the rights to its name (for an undisclosed sum) in partnership with Joe Hillesum, a friend with a social-work degree. Since it was hard to imagine a more out-of-date genre in 1980 than folk—at the time, new wave and the emerging synth-pop had made that music feel even more quaint—the trio briefly considered changing the name. In the end, they opted to stick with Folk City, along with the vintage black-and-white photographs encased in glass outside the club. The club's reputation might have faded, but the shots of the young Dylan, Simon and Garfunkel, and Judy Collins would hopefully serve to pull in foot traffic.

Inside, framed photos of Dylan, Ochs, Forbert, the Roches, Bette Midler, José Feliciano, and Peter, Paul and Mary still lined the walls. But reflecting their desire to revive the waning venue, Woliver, Lash, and Hillesum removed the tacky Christmas lights hanging over the bar and installed a new piano, sound system, and, eventually, video arcade. Folk City also had its first-ever jukebox, which would eventually include 45s by notable alumni like Dylan ("Rainy Day Women #12 and 35"), Simon and Garfunkel ("The Sound of Silence"), and the Blues Project ("Goin' Down Louisiana"), along with con-temporary singles from Dylan, Paul Simon, and even Lionel Ritchie and Diana Ross. Soon after the club changed hands, Dylan stopped by and gave the freshly purchased piano a spin.

The past would reappear in other ways. Within the first few months of the club's new management being handed the front-door keys, someone who introduced himself as a member of the city Health Department appeared and, in Woliver's phrase, "hinted strongly" that a payment was expected. Unsure of what to do, Woliver called Porco for advice. Afterward, he went downstairs to the basement, pulled a wad of cash from their safe, and pur-posefully handed the money to the employee in front of anyone who was around to ensure there would be witnesses to the transaction. Soon after, the club passed inspection.

The first show at the revamped Folk City included Lucinda Williams, a Louisiana-born singer and guitarist with an affinity for the blues who'd released *Ramblin' on My Mind*, an impressive set of covers for Folkways. When

Lash and Woliver were married in September 1980, a reception was held at the club, complete with entertainment by Odetta. In time, Sonny Ochs, Phil's sister, would come in from her home in Far Rockaway and emcee the club's open-mic nights, which kept another tradition very much alive.

The club's ads in the *Village Voice* now announced it was home to "Rock... Country... Blues... New Folk... New Wave... Folk." The fact that "folk" was listed last was telling, and in another break from what they sensed were past practices, Woliver, Lash, and Hillesum also put a premium on booking female artists. "Mike [Porco] was old school—there was an all-boys-club kind of feel," Woliver said. "There were a few female artists he liked, but the prevailing feeling at the time was that men sold tickets and records. When we came in, that's something that we were very conscious of changing." With Lash taking on the bulk of those bookings, the club that was once home to Tony Pastor's and its sometime gay clientele was now presenting women's-music pioneers like the North Carolina singer-songwriter Teresa Trull and, in time, the proudly gay troubadour Ferron. Woman played other roles as well: among those working the sound system was Deidre McCalla, a Black singer, songwriter, and guitarist who'd been raised in the city and was working her way into the scene. At that point, soon after the new owners signed the paperwork, three years remained on the Folk City lease. It felt like a lifetime away.

▌▌▌▌▌

A few months after Folk City employees found themselves with new bosses, an album with an unlikely cover made its way into select record stores. Its cover was a black-and-white photograph of the storefront of a café, a small woman, huddled and bent over on a bitterly cold day, walking past it. The trees out front were bare, and Bleecker Street was glimpsed down the block. *Cornelia Street: The Songwriters Exchange* looked more like the cover of an urban-photography book than an album, but it was in fact yet another sign of the area's rebirth.

In 1977 a cluster of unsigned songwriters aiming to keep the Village-songwriter legacy alive began congregating at the English Pub, a bar on Sixth Avenue that was a quick stroll from Folk City. At various times, the group included Mas, Terre Roche, Rod MacDonald, David Massengill, and Tom

Intondi, a bespectacled high school English teacher with a benevolent-cleric vibe who was known as one of the new scene's best harmony singers and most fervent champions. Securing a part of the bar for themselves, they'd play each other their new material, largely ballads about their love lives, life in the city, and whatever else, to the din of drinkers and bar noise.

Whether at the English Pub or at Folk City, the undisputed if not formally designated overseer of this community—"the pope," as Mas called him— was Jack Hardy, the troubadour with the raspy voice and intense squint who had been the host of Mike Porco's sixty-first-birthday gathering at Folk City in 1975. Born in Indiana in 1947, of German and Dutch lineage, Hardy had spent time as a child in Colorado; his father, Gordon, was an administrator at the Aspen Music Festival and School. Moving east to attend the University of Hartford in Connecticut, Hardy achieved a moment of counterculture noto-riety in the fall of 1968. As the editor of the *Liberated Press* student paper, he'd published a cartoon mocking the election of Richard Nixon: a fist with a middle finger made to resemble a penis, Nixon's name beneath it. Along with the publisher and the undergraduate cartoonist, Hardy was arrested on charges of violating state obscenity laws and libeling the president of the United States, with a maximum possible sentence of two years in prison. Hardy was unrepen-tant: as he wrote in an editorial in the student paper, "Everybody says that the cartoon was in poor taste—true. Everybody says that Hardy was irrational— not true. Hardy knew what he was doing." After Hardy was convicted and fined fifty dollars, his lawyer appealed, and the case was ultimately tossed out on a technicality.

Soon after his college life, Hardy, sporting a handlebar mustache that made him resemble an Old West ranch hand, released an album on his indie record company and began making the coffeehouse rounds. During another stint of their college-campus shows, Terre and Maggie Roche met Hardy in Pitts-burgh. When they told him about a new scene coalescing in New York and encouraged him to move there, Hardy did just that, in 1974.

What the sisters didn't know—and few at the time did—was Hardy's complete backstory. Although he rarely mentioned it to anyone beyond close friends, John Studebaker Hardy was a descendant of the family that made and sold wheelbarrows during the California Gold Rush of the 1800s and amassed a small fortune manufacturing covered wagons and early automobiles before going bankrupt in 1933; it was revived and continued manufacturing cars until the mid-sixties. Adhering to the Village tradition of reinvention, Hardy gave himself a makeover when he arrived in New York. Opting for the role of impoverished artist despite whatever money the family still had, he moved into a one-room apartment on West Houston Street, off the Avenue of the Americas. The bathtub sat in the kitchen, and the bathroom, in the outside hallway, could be entered only with a key. When his friend Brian Rose, a songwriter, musician, and photographer, later discovered Hardy's family roots during a joint trip to Colorado and California, he was taken aback. "I was stunned," Rose said. "He went around acting like he was Woody Guthrie or something, living hand to mouth. But Dylan was fake too. It's where you go with it."

Hardy soon became entrenched at Folk City, Porco regularly recruiting him as an emcee for the hoot nights. Rightly sensing that the music business was not open to lyric-driven balladry, Hardy recorded and self-released *The Mirror of My Madness* in 1976. Unlike the increasingly cushy singer-songwriter records rolled out by the big labels, Hardy's was akin to a tree stripped of its leaves but very much alive. "Houston Street" painted a grim take on New York in the seventies, a world of Nathan's hot dogs, would-be actresses looking for love in bars, and a dead body on the street. Hardy could also be scolding ("Murder," his indignant take on the Church, the Mob, and America in general) or tender, eager to build a vessel to take his love away with him in "The Boat Song."

From Hardy's harmonica playing to the furiously galloping drumming of Howie Wyeth, who'd been supplying Dylan's backbeat, the album sometimes sounded like a downtown version of *Desire*. But Hardy's sandpaper voice had a barely contained indignation that made it unique, and Suzzy and Terre Roche added divine harmonies to "Out of Control" and "The Tailor," the latter the tale of an outfitter ordered to disguise various Victorian England–style villains with new garb, even as he knows it won't change who they truly are. Hardy was also included in John Rockwell's "Folk Music Is Back with a Twang," a lengthy, reported overview of the new Village players published in the *New York Times* in April 1978. The piece—a survey of what Rockwell called a "folk

music revival" courtesy of Hardy, Forbert, the Roches, and George Gerdes—
accurately assessed the "folksingers of the post-Dylan variety" who wrote
"personal, pointed lyrics, infused with a sophistication and wit that seem
indigenous to New York." Terre Roche, then living with Gerdes, was particularly relieved that he was included in the story.

Hardy and his songwriter friends quickly realized that a boisterous bar like
the English Pub wasn't the most appropriate place to preview songs. (Some
of them were drinking too much, too.) Fortunately for them, a new work-
space soon appeared around the corner. On the July 4 weekend in 1977, three
partners—British actor and writer Robin Hirsch, Irish writer and director Charles McKenna, and Italian-Canadian painter and sculptor Raphaela
Pivetta—opened a new business at what was an empty storefront down the
block from Bleecker Street. Now called the Cornelia Street Café, the one-room
bistro at 29 Cornelia sported white-plastered walls, a wood-plank floor, and a
ceiling fan. At most, about thirty people could squeeze in, and the menu was
initially limited to coffee and tea, with food prepared in a toaster oven.

Nearly as soon as it opened its doors, the Cornelia Street Café became a
hub for playwrights, journalists, puppeteers, and a local flute player; one night
featured a reading of Inuit poetry. Mas, who lived on the same street, became a
customer, its second waitress, and, two years before her record deal, its first performer, playing songs on guitar in the space. Sensing that the café would make
for an ideal woodshedding spot, she asked Hirsch if she and her friends could
move their gatherings there. Starting in December 1977, a songwriting workshop, which came to be known as the Songwriters Exchange, took over the
Cornelia Street Café early each Monday evening. Here, at last, was a facsimile
of the sixties coffeehouse circuit whose legend still cast an imposing shadow
over them all.

Unlike the previous gatherings at the English Pub, the workshop would not
be casual. From the start, rules were put in place: each songwriter could perform only a tune written during the previous week. Absolute quiet would be
demanded, as would feedback. During the gatherings, which started at 6 p.m.
each Monday and ended in time for everyone to walk over to Folk City for its
weekly hoots, each musician would sit on a stool at the makeshift bar, place a

lyric on a chair, and play his or her new composition. "You worked with your peers and made the songs better," Mas recalled. "You'd bring in a song and they'd say, 'It would be better if you were clearer in the chorus,' and this and that. You had to be open to criticism."

At those weekly sessions and on the scene overall, Hardy was a particularly rigid taskmaster. He could be magnanimous, lending MacDonald a guitar after his was stolen or allowing Terre Roche to crash on his couch after she and Maggie first returned to New York from their detour to Louisiana. Hardy also had a flair for the melodramatic. Steering his music in more of a moody Celtic direction—he was an admirer of Irish poet James Clarence Mangan—he took to wearing a cape, eventually immortalized in the Roches' "Face Down at Folk City." In 1977 the *Times*' Rockwell positively reviewed one of Hardy's shows at Kenny's Castaways. When Rockwell followed the review with a more mixed write-up, friends threw Hardy a mock funeral in his apartment, placing flowers on him as he lay in his bathtub.

At the Cornelia Street Café, Hardy's severe outward demeanor and laser focus on lyrics and turns of phrase struck some as encouraging, others as intimidating. Without hesitation, he would call out a songwriter for playing a tune he suspected hadn't been written in the prior seven days. Once, he accused another of not even *writing* his own song. Terre Roche was so spooked at the thought of partaking that she bowed out early. "To me, that was a nightmare," she said. "Maggie and Suzzy and I were extremely gentle with one another in creating our songs. Nobody would pounce on anything. So the idea that you're going to go over there to the Cornelia Street Café . . . it would be, 'That's the end of *that* song idea.' Jack was extremely opinionated."

Joining the established clique—Mas, Hardy, Massengill, MacDonald, Intondi, songwriter Nancy Lee Baxter—were a few newcomers, including another of the new scene's first people of color. Lili Añel, a Cuban American raised in the South Bronx, already felt like an outlier in her own neighborhood: sitting on stoops and playing her acoustic guitar, she'd be asked why she wasn't singing disco or Latin music. "I wasn't part of the culture in that way," she said. "We had José Feliciano, but there weren't a lot of Hispanics that weren't just playing Latin music." Looking for a place to perform, she noticed ads for clubs like Folk City, which she'd never heard of before, and made her way down to the Village. There, she heard about the Cornelia Street Café and its weekly gatherings, showing up one evening with an original song, "Boxes," inspired by the disapproving looks she and her instrument would receive uptown. (In another throwback to earlier days, Añel had studied guitar with Van Ronk's friend Barry Kornfeld and singing with the Page Three's Sheila Jordan.) "All I remember is that when I looked up, everybody was bobbing along to the song," Añel said. "And I was like, 'Oh, this is good.' And everybody clapped. It gave me a feeling of community."

Also wandering in from time to time was the Village's leading folk-blues fingerpicker. Born Frank Caputo to an Italian family in Newark, New Jersey, Frank Christian had remade himself like so many before him, emerging with a new last name and a repertoire of ragtime and blues covers and originals. In a review of a Christian set at Folk City in 1979, the *Times'* Palmer expressed skepticism over the phenomenon of new, white musicians covering Black blues, although he at least noted that Christian "projects enough originality to make his sets of borrowed blues sound like personal statements."

With his frequent slim mustache and penchant for brimmed hats and caps, Christian was also charismatic, like a debonair drifter from the Depression era. His playing had such a supple and effortless poise—his left hand seemed to glide over the fretboard on air—that he, like Van Ronk, also made a living teaching guitar; one of his students, briefly, was Suzzy Roche. Van Ronk himself was such an admirer that when students would finish working with him, he would send them to Christian. "We thought he had the prettiest hands," said Andrea Vuocolo, Van Ronk's new girlfriend at the time. "We'd love to watch them play. His hands were so graceful."

Not long after the Songwriters Exchange began, the head of the Brooklyn-based jazz label Stash Records started attending with his teenage son, who was a songwriter. Telling Hirsch he was impressed with what he'd heard, the owner offered to make an album featuring the musicians—the first time anyone had made such an offer to most of them. Ever vigilant of being exploited, Hardy balked at the planned payment—fifty free copies, with the possibility of royalties coming down the line—and the project was delayed.

But it eventually resumed, without Hardy's participation, and a gaggle of the musicians gathered in a New Jersey studio and, in one long day, recorded an album of their songs.

Issued in midsummer 1980, two months after the new team took over Folk City, *Cornelia Street: The Songwriters Exchange* signaled a scene renewal. Compared to records by Forbert, Mas, and Nile, none of whom were on it, *Cornelia Street* was as low key as some of its spare ballads. MacDonald's "Songs of My Brothers," the first song he'd ever debuted at the Songwriters Exchange, started it off with a scruffy kick; Massengill's "Contrary Mary" blended the mountain-folksy and the profane; and Martha P. Hogan's "Connections" pegged her as an inheritor to the likes of Janis Ian. Two of the most alluring tracks came from Chicago transplants Elliot Simon and Lucy Kaplansky, whose group name—Simon and Kaplanski—sounded like a parody of their illustrious predecessors. (At the time, Kaplansky was spelling her surname with an "i.") Like seemingly every other aspiring troubadour in the country, the two had read Rockwell's 1978 scene roundup and immediately pulled up stakes and moved to the city in order to plug in to what was happening in the Village. Their chamber-pop contributions, "Say Goodbye Love" and "Moonsong," were made additionally alluring by Kaplansky's dulcet counterpoint vocal.

Cornelia Street sold only a few thousand copies, and some of the songwriters involved were miffed that its cover was taken up with a photograph of the café; a small group shot, all of four inches by four inches, was relegated to the inside packaging. Acknowledging that the album was missing its most prominent local stars, Rockwell gently called it "a memento of some of the other, lesser lights of a movement that produced a lot of strong music and pleasant nights in Greenwich Village bars."

But the record made the case that the scene potentially had more to offer, and at least one of its observers was cautiously optimistic. Sitting with Erik Frandsen at the Cornelia Street Café one evening, Van Ronk, in a T-shirt emblazed with "Garlic Is as Good as Ten Mothers," slouched over one of the small tables and pondered past and future with Joe Lauro, an NYU film student and bass player making a documentary about the revived scene. Thinking back to the sixties, Van Ronk recalled visiting the office of a major-label executive—"*el presidente*," he drolly called him—and hearing him chew out a producer with, "No, no, what I want is something that's different that sounds like everything else!"

Taking a drag on a cigarette, strands of hair falling in his face, Van Ronk continued, not so much with bitterness as with acceptance. "The mentality hasn't changed," he said. "They want something that sounds like everything else except different." But he added, with a degree of hope, "I think there's some kind of reaction settling into over-production. And hopefully that will amount to something—given a certain amount of time."

another time and place

1981–1986

In the seafaring world where Dave Van Ronk had toiled
nearly a quarter century before, it was customary to christen a new ship by
smashing a bottle of champagne across its bow. By the dawn of the eighties,
the Greenwich Village equivalent of that tradition meant having Van Ronk
partake in the opening of a new music venue. He was in the house for the
openings of the Cafe Bizarre and the Village Gate, and on the night of September
18, 1981, a rainy day that cleared up by evening, he was once again celebrating
a newfangled outlet for him, his peers, and anyone hoping to pick up where
he and his generation had left off.

In keeping with another long-standing neighborhood tradition, Speak Easy
was a quirky, eccentric space that felt like anything but a music club. The front
half of 107 MacDougal, around the corner from Folk City, was a mid-level
Middle Eastern restaurant. Anyone peering into its front window would
glimpse a slowly rotating pole with cooked strips of meat destined for souvlaki
sandwiches, followed by a modest, charm-challenged dining room. A few steps
down lay a small stage enclosed by wrought iron and, behind it, a wall-to-wall
fish tank, exotic species flapping by. Van Ronk's longtime friend and Village
stalwart Erik Frandsen wondered if the whiskey bottles behind the bar were
filled with cheap rotgut. "You could taste it—Van Ronk and I would joke that

they bought the stuff from Dutch Schultz," said Frandsen, referencing the notorious early twentieth-century gangster.

The Village had not been exempted from the recession—and accompanying rise in crime—that settled over New York City that year. When a group of West Springfield, Massachusetts, high school students requested a class trip into the area, their school board shot down the idea, citing the "raw lifestyles" and "depravation [sic]" in that part of town. After NYU intervened, the tour took place the following year, although the city ensured that Washington Square Park was a little less squalid than usual after supplementary police swarmed into it and chased away the drug dealers. Even offspring of the leader of the country didn't appear to be immune: the same year that Ronald Reagan was inaugurated, a burglar broke into a West Tenth Street apartment directly above one occupied by his son, Ron Jr.

The new proprietors of Folk City saw eighties grime up close themselves: whenever a car slowed down in front of Folk City, Robbie Woliver would watch as homeless people descended on it and jabbed their hands in any open windows, begging for change. The baseball bat that Mike Porco had retained behind the bar likely went with him, but Woliver did have a foot-long metal bar at the door in case the doorperson needed protection from vagrants or drunk customers.

Eager to lend Folk City a partial musical makeover, Woliver and his two partners immediately began revamping the type of acts and styles of music booked there: as part of a series called "Two Nights of This," one fall 1981 evening featured a set by early hip-hop artist Mr. Freeze. Reflecting the rise of synthesizer-dominated pop, one Saturday-afternoon showcase found the club doused in clattering electronic music. Meanwhile, a record store full of classic-rock mainstays had recently been dropped by their labels and been forced to return to the bars and clubs where they'd begun. With Folk City eager to hire national names, the timing couldn't have been better, and before long, the names of Eric Andersen, Levon Helm, and the Byrds' Roger McGuinn appeared on the club's marquee. "I couldn't book the same people over and over again, draining their mailing lists," Woliver said. "You're not getting new people in." In his mind, pairing Odetta with a local artist like Frank Christian would benefit both: Odetta's fan base would be introduced to new talent in the neighborhood, and Christian's followers would, in Woliver's mind, "make people see Odetta in a new, modern light."

Not everyone in the community was elated by the strategy; seemingly overnight, the Folk City regulars of the previous few years were no longer being rewarded with headlining slots. Some viewed the change as Woliver's means of taking back control of the booking of the club from Jack Hardy, who had become a dominant figure there. "The Jack-established clique ran all the nights and got to say who played and who didn't," said Vincent (Vinny) Vok, a singer-songwriter who had not only played Folk City but also worked as its soundman. "They were at odds with Robbie, who wanted to say, 'I'm in charge—*I* say who's playing, not you guys.'" Woliver himself admitted that his ambitions left some in the scene frustrated. "A number of them were people who were used to playing every night, when Mike had the club," he said. "And since that wasn't happening, there were some people we didn't hire when we took over."

As the locals became more and more frustrated, Paul Mills, the performance-art poet known as Poez and also Vok's roommate, suggested they go in search of another venue and start approaching nearby restaurants, just as Izzy Young had done in 1960. Because Hardy was in Europe, Vok teamed up with Angela Page, who had run a well-regarded coffeehouse at SUNY Oneonta; there she had met and booked Hardy, who invited her down to New York to live with him. Page and Vok focused on 107 MacDougal, a four-floor row house built in 1858 that had been a dance hall in the early twentieth century before becoming the Cafe Rienzi, a leading Village hangout in the fifties. Eventually, it was a French restaurant. In 1980 Joseph Zbeda, a Middle Eastern businessman with a thinning pate, a birthmark over his left eye, and white sideburns bought the business for a reported $300,000, and the renamed Speak Easy, in honor of the illicit businesses from decades past, began serving up falafels, gyros, and similar fare. Its back room was converted into a low-rent disco, complete with that fish tank, a glitter ball, a floor that could be lit from beneath, an encased platform for a DJ, and mirrors on each side of that area. When disco cratered soon after, Zbeda recast Speak Easy as a reggae club.

The money behind his Village business didn't stem from any previous restaurant experience. After moving to the States in 1975, Zbeda was approached by

Meir Zarchi, a film director and friend from Israeli in search of financing for his movies. Zbeda became an investor and executive producer of one of them, a low-budget revenge flick called *Day of the Woman*. The plot itself was grim: a woman from New York, seeking solitude to write a novel, rents a cabin in the woods, where she is stalked and eventually brutalized and raped by four men. She ultimately exacts pitiless retribution on them by way of castration and hanging. When the gruesome movie was completed, it couldn't find a distributor, but a producer who specialized in grindhouse, horror, and exploitation films soon bought the rights, gave it a grislier new title, *I Spit on Your Grave*, and released it.

When the film opened in his city in 1980, *Chicago Tribune* film critic Gene Siskel condemned it as "the most offensive film in my 11 years on the movie beat." His *Chicago Sun-Times* rival Roger Ebert agreed, and the film was pulled from its Chicago theater; other cities followed. But Siskel and Ebert's warnings, combined with the rapidly growing home video market, only served to turn *I Spit on Your Grave* into a need-to-see videotape. In 1981 the movie was a top-ten rental in America, a windfall that likely helped Zbeda purchase the MacDougal Street business. After Speak Easy had been up and running for a period, Rod MacDonald saw him walk into the restaurant with a rare smile on his face; he told the musician he'd just made a half-million dollars licensing the movie to drive-ins. "You would not believe how much these things make," he told MacDonald, who wondered if Zbeda had ever seen it. When Zbeda brought it up, he would only call it "beautiful movie—love story!"

Vok knew the place—he'd eaten gyros there—and he and Page investigated. The performance space held a respectable 120 people, which could be boosted to 130 if they grabbed chairs from the dining room. Walking into the restaurant one day, Page met Zbeda, who gave her the distinct impression he wasn't happy with reggae or its patrons; in a later interview with Joe Lauro, he also said he'd considered converting the space into a comedy club. But when Page pitched Zbeda on a folk venue, he gave the plan his go-ahead.

That summer, a deal, much like the one made by Izzy Young, Mike Porco, and Tom Prendergast at the original Gerde's Folk City, was struck. Zbeda—a restaurant owner in serious need of customers, much as Porco had been—would pocket the proceeds from food and drink; the musicians would take the money from the ticket sales. A Musicians Cooperative, modeled on food co-ops in the city, would book acts, work the sound system and lighting, handle ticket sales, and do whatever else was needed. "It was like Spanky and Our Gang," said David Massengill, recalling the thirties show. "It was, 'Let's do this!' It was actually possible to do those things." The first flyers for Speak Easy called it "New York's new club dedicated to quality acoustic music," and in a symbolic switch, Page had the disco ball taken down.

Van Ronk was rarely if ever nostalgic about the old days and wasn't afraid to voice it. "We had to twist his arm to go to MacDougal Street," said Frandsen, who still lived right across from Speak Easy, still played sly slide guitar, and had written songs like "Nobody Grieves for George Reeves," which was about the actor who played Superman on a TV series and shot himself in the head after the show ended. "Van Ronk just got sick to death of it: 'I hate that fucking street!'"

But Van Ronk sensed the scene might be experiencing a second, or third, wind, and he became a member of the Coop's executive board and offered to host its dollar-admission nights on Tuesdays. At the grand opening, he and Hardy shared cigars and toasted the music scene's anticipated revival.

███

After its "gala opening celebration"—the same weekend that onetime Village talents Paul Simon and Art Garfunkel reunited for a free concert in Central Park—the Speak Easy officially began presenting live music on the weekend of September 25, 1981, with the duo Willie and Annie Nininger and Lucy Kaplansky. Whether out of forgetfulness or a degree of fear, Zbeda failed to inform the reggae musicians he'd originally booked that their services were no longer needed. They were less than happy when they showed up to work, but they left without incident. The second full weekend featured Frandsen, with the opening-act slot given to a newcomer on the verge of graduating from Barnard.

In her phrase, some on the scene saw Suzanne Vega as a "stuffy princess" from uptown; her thin physique hinted at her time as a high school dance student, and she could be as guarded as any native New Yorker. Yet she had a more varied background than anyone would have imagined. Born in Santa Monica, California, in July 1959, Vega would eventually be raised in East Harlem and the Upper West Side after her parents moved to New York when she was two. At age nine, she learned that her father, Edgardo Vega Yunqué, a Puerto Rican writer who went by Ed Vega, was actually her stepfather. As she later learned, her birth father had broken up with her mother, Pat, who was white, soon after Vega was born. Growing up in way-uptown areas with a biracial couple, she was exposed to childhood games that incorporated the types of rhythms that would emerge in hip-hop.

Ed Vega was also a guitarist, and his stepdaughter began playing the instrument herself at age eleven. A fan of the Roches, Ed Vega suggested that his stepdaughter sound like them—or, alternately, funk-rock pioneer Nona Hendryx, whose music he also loved. But Vega was heading in another, less trendy direction. At a thrift shop when she was around fourteen, she came upon a Folkways compilation featuring Odetta, Ed McCurdy, and Cisco Houston, and became enamored of it. Revealing an early analytical streak, she began dissecting songs by Dylan and Janis Ian, among others. "I would study something until I could master what they were doing," she said, "and I would go on." As a teenager in the mid-seventies, her friends at High School for the Performing Arts, where she was studying modern dance, were in thrall of David Bowie and Lou Reed. Vega herself was more partial to Dylan, Cohen, Laura Nyro, and Simon and Garfunkel. When a friend asked her to accompany him to a Patti Smith concert, Vega passed, thinking it would be too loud or abrasive.

Given the music that was affecting her the most, it would only be a matter of time before the Village came into Vega's line of sight. The first time she ever sang in public was at the Tin Palace, the East Village jazz club. Her father was friendly with bass player Richard Davis, and one afternoon in 1976 they made their way to one of its afternoon showcases, where she sang two of the many songs she'd already written. She began playing a coffeehouse in a church basement on the Upper West Side and, with the confidence gleaned from it, made her way downtown to its mythical clubs. A male musician in her dance class filled her in on the Village club hierarchy—first the Other End, then Folk

City, then the big-time Bottom Line. The fact that the Village was out of style failed to deter her. "I was aware of that," she said. "I didn't care. I was like, 'No, no, you're all wrong.'" Adhering to her friend's instructions, she put on a pair of flared white pants and plastic Candies high heels and made her way to the Other End for their open-mic nights. The experience was vaguely humiliating: she played songs while a manager sat in front of her eating dinner. But in an early indication of how determined she would be, she kept going back to the club for two years even after being turned down every time.

After being awarded a scholarship to Barnard, Vega enrolled in 1977, focusing on English and theater. But like nearly everyone who had dreams of playing in the Village, she absorbed John Rockwell's 1978 *New York Times* story on the folk revival and eventually made her way back downtown, discovering Folk City and meeting the likes of Hardy and MacDonald. A tape of her early songs made it to Folk City's owners, and Marilyn Lash was so impressed that Vega was booked into one of the club's Sunday-afternoon songwriter showcases. After asking everyone who saw her play at uptown coffeehouses to supply their names and addresses, she already had a mailing list, and thirty people—an impressive showing for an unknown—arrived for that first Sunday spot. She tried playing Kenny's Castaways but was, she recalled, "too soft" for that crowd; even her hairstyle, which tended to drop to her shoulders and framed her face with bangs, suggested early Joni Mitchell.

Some of her uptown friends also filled her in on the Songwriters Exchange at the Cornelia Street Café. Initially terrified of debuting one of her compositions to a group that would dissect it, she put off signing up for months. When she did participate, she didn't always listen to what everyone said, but Hardy, whom she called "brilliant and charismatic," would take her to task for what he called lazy melodies, and she would scoff at his traditional approach. "I thought [rhythm] was as important as the Celtic melodies Jack was excited about," she said. "The other, older [music] was cool. Some of it was archaic and some of it was beautiful. But why does it always have to be that? It was the Eighties! Why not be modern? It didn't all have to be that William Butler Yeats thing." (She also learned of Hardy's backstory: "A lot of people thought it was a pose, but it never bothered me. That's what life is for—to reinvent yourself.") Ultimately she, like others, found the Songwriters Exchange experience exhilarating. "I don't know of any other place like it anywhere," she wrote in 1982. "It has the atmosphere of the local meeting place of an old tribe or village, a gathering place for those with a song in their veins that they must express."

After her family moved into a smaller apartment on the far Upper West Side, Vega decided it was time to move out, eventually renting a room in a sprawling apartment that was part of Barnard housing. To Vega's gradual realization, the woman living there was in the midst of a nervous breakdown after her husband had left her, and Vega would often find her drunk and lying in a fetal position on her bed. She wasn't sure what to do, but another recent experience would also feed into the situation. In the fall of 1979 a friend asked if Vega wanted his extra ticket to see Lou Reed at nearby Columbia University. Although Vega knew him only for "Walk on the Wild Side," Reed's sole pop hit, she decided to go. The show, pegged to Reed's album *The Bells*, shocked her: "Everyone was stoned and shouting, 'You animal!' and Lou was throwing lit cigarettes into the audience and kissing his lead guitarist on the mouth." But one song, his version of "Caroline Says Part II" from *Berlin*, stayed with her, and she began investigating his music.

Building on the breakdown she'd witnessed and the stark quality of Reed's music, Vega wrote a new song, "Cracking," that was unlike any of the strictly folkier songs she'd composed before. Playing a descending series of four repeating, different bass notes, Vega altered the standard one, four, five, and minor six chords of folk by skipping the fifth altogether. That approach, observed composer and musician Doug Silver, was "unusual, leaving us feeling like something's missing." That impression, in turn, fed into the lyrics: the words, describing a shattered person's numb walk through a park, were largely spoken until she reached "the sun is blinding." As with most of her songs, she sang it—or, here, half-talked it—in a voice that was translucent, direct, and affectless.

When Vega played "Cracking" for her family, an aunt asked if she was OK; a boyfriend at the time raised an eyebrow but also added it was "very good." Musicians in the Village didn't know what to make of it. "I try not to be another sappy singer-songwriter," she said in 1984. "Some people go so far as to say I'm very dry and that I sing with no feeling. I think I sing with a restrained style. Some people don't perceive the emotions. I try more to project feelings of, say, anxiety or shock. 'Cracking' is a song about shock." But clearly "Cracking" was neither rock nor folk but something in between, hinting at a future for its writer and for a community that was entering a new, starker decade and city.

Like virtually every other bar or venue in the Village, 131 West Third Street, directly across the street from Folk City, had had more than one life. In the six-ties it had been a burlesque club; by 1980, the two-story building was David's Harp, an Israeli-Mediterranean club and restaurant that, much like the first incarnation of Speak Easy, was floundering. Danny Bensusan, a former Israeli soldier who'd moved to New York in 1969 after completing his mandatory ser-vice in his country's military, had already owned a midtown restaurant and a disco, Gatsby's, in Brooklyn's Sheepshead Bay neighborhood. But Bensusan yearned to return to the Village, where he'd first worked as a bartender at a small jazz bar after relocating to America. Walking into David's Harp one day and finding few customers, he offered to buy it from its Turkish owners. On October 20, 1980, the restaurant, a stage tucked away in the back, was his for a reasonable $195,000.

While Bensusan was still deciding what type of business his new space would be, a local promoter approached him and offered to make it a gay bar. Eager for any steady income, Bensusan went along with the idea. "He says, 'I guarantee you it will be packed and you'll make money,'" Bensusan recalled. "I said, 'Go ahead. I'm not transferring it to you, but you can promote it.'" The makeover didn't last long. Certain menacing locals stopped by and made it clear they did not want any such establishment or clientele in that part of the Village. Gay clubs, they suggested to Bensusan, should be limited to Seventh or Eighth Avenue in the West Village, not in the heart of the district.

Wisely deciding to change course, Bensusan took another suggestion, this time from a friend who'd worked the door at a jazz club and suggested Bensu-san host that music as well. Bensusan knew next to nothing about jazz, but the idea seemed viable enough. In a bit of good fortune, the name "The Blue Note" was available; at that time, the legendary jazz label was out of business and the name was up for grabs. A week and a half after Speak Easy's opening-night event, the Blue Note added to the amplified activity in the Bleecker and Mac-Dougal area. Its earliest bookings, which veered more toward mainstream jazz, included trumpeter Nat Adderley, whose Village days dated back to early jam sessions at the Cafe Bohemia, and saxophonist Lee Konitz, a cool-jazz standard-bearer.

With the opening of the Blue Note, another glistening era of jazz in the Village—what the *Washington Post* called "the closest thing to a renaissance of jazz in the United States since King Rock eclipsed all other music in the '60s and '70s"—was underway. The Blue Note welcomed veterans like Dizzy Gillespie, Earl "Fatha" Hines, and Zoot Sims. But it now had plenty of company. First opened in 1974, Sweet Basil, just south of the Vanguard on Seventh Avenue South, was taken over by new management in the summer of 1981. For booking, the owners recruited Horst Liepolt, a German-born jazz producer and promoter who'd enlivened the Australian jazz scene. After moving to New York, Liepolt brought on Don Cherry, Arthur Blythe, and Doc Cheatham and inaugurated a recurring series, "Music Is an Open Sky," that presented avant-garde masters Henry Threadgill, Anthony Braxton, and Lester Bowie. The Village Vanguard remained home base for bop and post-bop musicians, and Seventh Avenue South continued to roar, even after some of its principals had cleaned up. Piano bars, including Bradley's, the Knickerbocker, and the Cookery, seemed to be on every other block.

But it wasn't merely the number of places; the revival also encompassed what was heard inside them. Blythe and forward-looking pianist Mal Waldron, returning to the States after a period in Munich, were pulling customers into the Vanguard. Sweet Basil revived the Village's jazz and poetry blend on Monday nights and also hosted a new-generation innovator. Arriving in New York from his home state of California in 1975, tenor saxophonist David Murray first embedded himself with the loft-jazz scene. Inspired by the likes of Sonny Rollins and Albert Ayler, he seemed headed for his own style of free jazz and became a member of the World Saxophone Quartet. But in the early eighties, he transformed into a new-jazz force. At Sweet Basil, he would sometimes lead a twelve-piece ensemble that was unafraid to swerve from a Sidney

Bechet–inspired New Orleans stomp to more dissonant pieces. Murray could also employ cellists and violinists, resulting in music that sounded less like jazz and more like soundtracks for unnamed film noir. With crowds lining up along Seventh Avenue for his shows at that venue and elsewhere, Murray wasn't just blending traditional approaches with avant-garde ones; he was reminding the scene, the press, and the world that jazz in the West Village could continue to innovate.

The reasons behind the renewed interest in jazz remained puzzling. The recession may have been a factor, since, as the *Post* also observed, "Jazz historically becomes popular when the economy turns sour. People like to cheer themselves up with jazz." Still, making music in the Village wasn't without its difficulties. Clubs could still avoid having a cabaret license if they avoided hiring percussions or woodwind and brass players. At Bradley's one evening, that meant drummer Frank Gant had to resort to keeping time with brushes, and on a thick atlas, as the *Post* reported. Another night, a fight broke out in front of Folk City, and Bensusan intervened, winding up in the hospital with bruises. But at least people were showing up in the area; from the music to the younger crowds, the Village felt alive.

At Speak Easy on the third weekend of October 1981, old and new circles collided. In the performance area, David Massengill, his dulcimer before him, sang "The Great American Dream," a panoramic ballad about an assortment of dreamers (a writer, a prostitute, a Native American, and an immigrant) trying to find their way in modern New York. Inspired by the time a Black foreigner approached Massengill outside the Other End and asked, "Excuse me, I am a foreigner—where is this place called *Green*wich Village?," the song was welcomed as one of the first standards to emerge from the new community.

Loudon Wainwright III was at the bar, and a noticeably pregnant Suzzy Roche, about a month away from the birth of her and Wainwright's daughter Lucy, sat at one of the tables with Tom Intondi. Wainwright and Roche would soon see their smiling photos in Liz Smith's gossip column in the *Daily News*, which announced they were now living together. Wainwright was in the midst of a creative rebirth as well; starting with *Fame and Wealth*, recorded in 1982, he would roll out a string of albums that finally found a middle ground between his solo performances and full-band studio production, with songs that dug even deeper into family history and his own foibles and complicated feelings toward family and relationships. Also in the Speak Easy midst that night was David Roche, the Roche sisters' young brother, who was developing his own, decidedly more rock-based style, and also at venues like Kenny's Castaways.

Intondi was now one-fourth of a group, the Song Project, whose repertoire consisted entirely of songs written by the next wave of Village troubadours. The first incarnation of the band included Hardy, Intondi, Carolyne Mas, and Nancy Lee Baxter, and the latest version (Intondi, Lucy Kaplansky, Martha P. Hogan, and Delaware-born singer and guitarist Gerry Devine) had many feeling that they could be their generation's Peter, Paul and Mary. Here was a harmony group whose polished versions of songs by their colleagues could potentially tap into a larger audience in the same way the earlier trio had popularized Dylan and Gordon Lightfoot. The *New York Times* praised them ("Seldom has the expression 'fresh blood' been more vividly personified," wrote Stephen Holden), and the Bottom Line's Allan Pepper began advising them on how to capitalize on the buzz around them.

Among the tunes in the Song Project's repertoire was Terre Roche's "Runs in the Family," a choice that testified to their stature on the scene. But starting with their interaction with Boz Scaggs fans, the sisters had run into headwinds even while they were still promoting their first album. When they'd played Los Angeles, Warner Brothers head Mo Ostin informed them backstage that they'd need to break into radio next time; the implicit message was that Robert Fripp would not be working with them again. Amenable to a more accessible sound for their second record, the sisters decided to use a rhythm section and recruited Roy Halee, the up-for-anything producer and engineer known for his work with Paul Simon and Simon and Garfunkel.

The Roches had never sounded more confident and more vocally liberated than they did on *Nurds*. Inspired by the Scaggs tour farce, its title track was a proud declaration of misfitdom, complete with a Suzzy vocal that sounded like a parody of Patti Smith and a grand finale with the sisters breaking into howls and barks. Maggie hinted at a degree of innate loneliness in "One Season," which was equal to any on her songs on their first record, and they included a tightly harmonized cover of Cole Porter's "It's Bad for Me," a song so self-aware of the dark side of love that it could have been written by them. Terre's "Louis" examined the impact of fame and success, from their mother commenting that Terre was wearing too much makeup onstage (she told Terre she resembled an owl) to the backlash Forbert was experiencing with his own sophomore record. "When you went back into a club, people would treat you differently," said Terre. "You realized not everyone was as thrilled as you were about your success. I remember the feeling of being betrayed by the support group: 'They turned on me!' You always had been part of that scene and now when you went back you weren't anymore." One way she sensed it was the moment she revisited one of their old haunts and encountered a guy at the bar singing a parody of "Hammond Song"—but substituting the name of John Hammond, the musician and son of the legendary music executive.

Their idea of marketable, for one thing, was not especially in sync with everyone else's. Their backup musicians were not the studio pros favored by Simon but former Patti Smith Group drummer Jay Dee Daugherty and former MC5 and Television bassist Fred "Sonic" Smith. "I think *Nurds* has a better shot at airplay," Terre told *Rolling Stone* when the album was released in September 1980, "but I still don't hear anything on the radio that sounds like it."

The comment proved prophetic. Less cohesive than *The Roches*, *Nurds* wasn't greeted nearly as euphorically as its predecessor. The *Village Voice*'s Robert Christgau, who'd graded their first album an *A*, slapped a *B* onto *Nurds*, writing that they were "trying too hard." The sisters also gave an awkward interview with late-night TV host Tom Snyder on his *Tomorrow* show. "Why would anyone write a song called 'My Sick Mind'?" he asked them, referring to Terre's song on *Nurds*. Unsure what to make of his questions, such as what it was like to open for rock bands, they gave terse, on-guard answers; Suzzy noticed Maggie looking down during most of it. Ultimately, *Nurds* sold about half the number of *The Roches*. "I don't think we operate as a group by trying to further our status in the music business," Suzzy told the *Boston Globe*'s Jim Sullivan. "That is not a priority of ours."

As Suzzy Roche sat with Intondi in Speak Easy's dining room that night in October, the topic of music venues from years past came up. "Ask Danny," Intondi said, gesturing toward the front of the club. "He's been around for a while." Sure enough, there was Kalb, a stout figure with aviator glasses, his hair longish on the side if mostly gone on top. Looking like a scruffy Buddha, Kalb, approaching forty, was still looking to regain his footing. Earlier that year, the Blues Project had done another one of its occasional reunions, at the midtown club Bond's, but Kalb was still adhering to his old haunting grounds, playing at Kenny's Castaways and returning to guitar lessons, which he advertised with ads in the *Village Voice*. He also remained one of the most politically outspoken on the scene. "America is on the path to nuclear war," he told a small group huddled with him one night at Folk City, Ronald Reagan now in the White House. "And I don't think it can be stopped."

Two decades since the Village's musical heyday had commenced, the past sometimes felt as if it were growing more distant by the month. After Joe Marra had shut it down, the Night Owl had become a poster emporium; a record store, Bonaparte's; and, in 1981, another record shop, Bleecker Bob's. The Four Winds coffeehouse was now an Indian restaurant; the Gaslight served up Mexican cuisine. Another night at Speak Easy in the fall of 1981, a couple sat at a table as one of Phil Ochs's finest ballads blanketed the room. "He lived here years ago," the man told his date. "He hung himself. You know that song 'Changes'?" The woman nodded and hummed a few bars. "No," the man said, annoyed, "not David *Bowie's* 'Changes.'"

Beginning with Ochs's death in 1976, the legends who had once prowled Village streets with their guitars were also starting to vanish. A few days after Christmas, 1980, an anonymous caller alerted the Los Angeles Police Department to a "dead body" in an apartment in Fairfax, saying that the deceased was Tim Hardin, only thirty-nine. Few were surprised. Even though he was attempting to clean himself up and preparing to record his first new material in years, Hardin had apparently relapsed; the coroner's report listed the cause as a heroin and morphine overdose.

Since making Los Angeles his own new home, David Blue, who'd partaken in more than his share of Kettle of Fish revelries, had had his own struggles with the music industry and drugs. The same year Hardin died, Blue was back in New York and in and around the Village. With his new wife, Nesya, a Montreal native making her way into the filmmaking world, Blue sought to reboot his career. He was booked now and then into Folk City (where he would make as little as fifty dollars per show). Returning to his roots as an actor, he took the role of a washed-up rock star in a play, *American Days*, directed by Dylan's *Desire*-era songwriting collaborator Jacques Levy.

Blue also became a semi-regular at Folk City and the Other End, where he frequently caught sets by a recent arrival, Shawn Colvin. Born in South Dakota and raised largely in Illinois, Colvin had played shows in Austin, Texas, and then Berkeley, California, before landing in New York in 1980. Not yet a songwriter, often more inclined toward country than folk, she made her way to the Bleecker and MacDougal area, where Van Ronk, in her words, "scared the shit" out of her. Colvin nonetheless carved out a niche for herself by singing covers of songs by male songwriters like Bruce Springsteen, Tom Waits, Sting, and Gram Parsons. Combined with a voice that was alternately earthy and ravishing and a look that recalled Linda Ronstadt, Colvin became part of the parade of women artists who were making the once male-dominated scene their own.

One night at Kenny's Castaways, Colvin played Rod MacDonald's "American Jerusalem," a depiction of a depleted city that captured the mood in New York at that moment. When Blue heard it, he asked Colvin who'd written it; club owner Pat Kenny told him the composer lived around the corner on MacDougal, and Blue found himself at MacDonald's door that night, where he complimented the surprised songwriter. Blue also hosted *Village Voices*, a low-budget documentary on which he introduced performances by Colvin, MacDonald, and Cliff Eberhardt, and conducted interviews at Speak Easy.

But Blue's own return would be sadly short-lived. On the first day of December 1982, he put on his new blue jogging suit, left his and Nesya's Prince Street apartment, and went for a jog in Washington Square Park. Tom Paxton had run into him there a few days before (jogging himself) and was pleasantly surprised to see his old friend attempting to get healthy after years of partying. But that day, Blue, forty-one, had a heart attack, collapsed, and died. Since he wasn't carrying any identification, Nesya didn't locate him at the city morgue until several days later. That week, Eric Andersen was booked into Folk City, waiting for Blue to show up; Blue had told his friend he could stay with him while he was in town. Onstage, Andersen glanced beyond the bar and saw, through the front window, Blue standing outside, stroking his chin. Once his set was finished, Andersen asked a bartender where Blue had gone and was told no one had seen him and Blue wasn't there that night. Andersen later learned that Blue had died earlier that day.

Of the other area legends, Richie Havens, who'd become a national figure after his riveting festival-opening spot at Woodstock was immortalized in the film of that event, steadily recorded new albums and still lived in the West Village. Dylan remained his usual spectral presence. When Lucinda Williams was on the bill at Folk City one night, Porco introduced her to Dylan—who told her, enigmatically, "Keep in touch. We're gonna be going on the road soon." Needless to say, she didn't hear from him again, at least for many years. When his friends Levon Helm and Rick Danko were playing the Lone Star Cafe, Dylan, in a cashmere coat and fur hat, wandered in during their sound check. In his first time playing with them since the Band's farewell *Last Waltz* show, he joined them for both their warm-up and full sets, playing what Helm would call "a rather liquid" version of Hank Williams's "Your Cheatin' Heart" and a medley of "Willie and the Hand Jive" and "Ain't No More Cane." As Helm would write later, Dylan was then "out the door, into the night."

In July 1982, Dylan again returned to the Village, this time in name and legend only. By then, Speak Easy was having trouble pulling in customers on traditionally slow days early in the week. Adhering to a tradition that extended back to the original Folk City, the club made way for open-mic nights on Mondays, and Angela Page, still involved in running them, began noticing that everyone who showed up was trying to emulate Dylan. "It pissed me off," Page

said. "I thought, 'Sound like yourself.' Mike Porco used to say, 'There already is
a Bob Dylan—we don't need another.'"

That combination of desperation and irritation led to the club's first Bob
Dylan Imitators Contest. To everyone's shock at the club, the idea worked. As
soon as the event was announced, the club was besieged with calls from around
the country and the globe, asking how to enter the contest and for directions to
Speak Easy. After rumors circulated that Dylan himself might show, the line
that night stretched down MacDougal Street. Inside, contestants—a blend
of amateurs and more seasoned musicians from the club itself—competed
in one of five categories: Folk-Protest Dylan, Amphetamine-Rock Dylan,
Post-Motorcycle-Accident-Voice-Change Dylan, Born-Again Dylan, and Freestyle Dylan. Whatever the grouping, they would have to sing in Dylan's voice
and within a five-minute limit. The judges included Porco, Cynthia Gooding, and *Village Voice* writer Geoffrey Stokes. The judges patiently, sometimes
impatiently, watched as dozens of fake Dylans traipsed onstage. The best—
including Frank Christian, who won in the Folk-Protest category, and George
Gerdes, who took the Freestyle award—were greeted with lusty cheers. The
worst were booed or heckled. When asked if one contestant should be booted
off the stage, Porco grumbled, "No, I think we should shoot him."

The evening was both an acknowledgment and a tweaking of the Village's
past, especially the sixties loyalists who would still appear and compare the current crop to Dylan, Paxton, or any of their contemporaries. "The fans of those
people would show up and look around and say, 'Oh, you should have been
here in 1962,'" MacDonald said. "We'd roll our eyes and say, 'Well, we're here
now and that's what matters to us and we're trying to make something happen
now.'" Jack Hardy had his own complicated feelings on the topic. The night of
Porco's all-folk-star birthday party in 1975, he had been the scheduled entertainment, and he came to resent the way Dylan's film crew essentially hijacked
the evening. Hardy was also convinced he and his peers were creating music
equal to anything that had come before. To the *Daily News*' David Hinckley, Hardy said, unapologetically, "When the smoke clears, I think artists like
Bob Dylan and Leonard Cohen will be seen as having opened some doors, but
not as definitive song-poets, because they didn't understand the performance

potentials—harmonies, textures, etc. That's why people like the Byrds interpreted them. I think you'll see things written in the next few years which will surpass anything from the Sixties."

The Dylan-contest festivities would come with an added element of stress. In the days leading up to the contest, the club received a surprise call from Dylan's office, announcing they wanted to film it. The thought was both amusing and a little terrifying, and on the evening of the talent show, a two-man crew showed up at Speak Easy. The Dylan staff then took the footage and edited it down to just under a half hour. From what the Speak Easy people heard, Dylan watched and loved what was now called *Battle of the Bobs* and subsequently agreed to donate a guitar to future winners.

Joe Lauro wondered if the club could benefit in some way from the arrangement; nearly two years into its existence, Speak Easy was in need of a few upgrades. Reaching out to the Dylan office, he asked if the venue could show a then rare copy of *Don't Look Back*, D. A. Pennebaker's penetrating documentary on Dylan's 1965 European tour, and charge admission. The Dylan team agreed, with the stipulation that it not be advertised. Arriving at the Dylan office, Lauro was handed a paper bag containing the movie—which, once he set it up in the club, turned out to be footage from Dylan's rarely seen 1966 tour film, *Eat the Document*.

With the $1,000 raised by the movie screening, Speak Easy was able to improve its sound system and buy new microphones. The annual contest would continue for several more years; at one, Van Ronk served as a judge, and one of the contestants offered him a dollar bill and a cigar to influence him. As far as anyone knew, Dylan never attended any of them.

When Andrea Vuocolo heard the doorbell ring at her and Van Ronk's apartment, the same Sheridan Square place where he had been living for over a decade, she assumed it was her boyfriend. The two had just returned from one of Van Ronk's concert road trips, and he'd ventured to a nearby grocery store in search of food. Opening the door, Vuocolo found someone holding a cactus plant in front of his face.

"Is Dave here?" said the voice.

It didn't take long for Vuocolo to realize it was Dylan, and she asked if he'd like to come in and wait, even offering to make him coffee. "Is Dave coming back?" Dylan answered, a little nervously. Luckily, Van Ronk returned soon enough to find Dylan sitting on his couch, the plant still covering his visage. "Hey, Bob," Van Ronk said casually. "Still the shy young boy." Van Ronk was pleasantly surprised; the two hadn't seen each other in years. Sensing Dylan was uncomfortable, Vuocolo left and went to an office to finish paste-up work for a medical book she was working on; when she returned, Dylan was gone.

Dylan wasn't alone in continuing to pay his respects to Van Ronk, who, unlike so many of his peers, had stayed put in the Village. He still gave guitar lessons three times a week, which allowed him to work clubs on weekends. Showing up late for a lesson of his own, Massengill was told he'd just missed Joni Mitchell. Van Ronk remained incorrigible, still smoking and refusing to see doctors, and he was drinking heavily at times. In a jokey April Fool's Day listing at Speak Easy, he was billed as "Dave Van Drunk," alongside "Suzanne Vague."

For a batch of Midwest shows, Van Ronk recruited Massengill. At the Bottom Line, the two had been introduced backstage by David Bromberg, who had told Massengill to bring his dulcimer. At Bromberg's urging, Massengill played "On the Road to Fairfax County," about a doomed liaison between a highwayman-robber and the woman he encounters. Van Ronk, who didn't have a driver's license, said he liked it, adding, "Kid, I think we're gonna get along. Do you drive?" On their rides to their concerts, Van Ronk would buy a bottle of Irish whiskey and finish it off in one sitting. Although he was unaccustomed to that level of drinking, Massengill would do his best to help finish one of those bottles; having Van Ronk gulp it all down himself didn't feel like a good idea.

But like the scene he had long been part of and now embodied, Van Ronk appeared to be on a better track than he'd been in years. Thanks to rent control, he'd been able to retain his apartment, which by then cost only about $350 per month. As the seventies wound down, he had met Vuocolo, a gentle New Jerseyan who'd grown up a Van Ronk fan after hearing him on the radio in high school; she was especially mesmerized by his version of "Both Sides Now (Clouds)." Throughout high school, Van Ronk was her favorite singer, and during her college years in Boston, she saw him play there several times. Just a few years earlier, she had ventured into the city to see him at the Other End and summoned up the courage to approach him at the bar between sets and chat. The two eventually became close, and she moved into his apartment in the fall of 1982.

As the decade progressed, Van Ronk gradually began cutting back on his drinking and smoking. He would tell Vuocolo that the sixties were "a ten-year party and everyone was always drunk or stoned." Now, he told her, people needed to clean up their acts because their shenanigans were no longer charming. Van Ronk preferred to be at home with his books, records, or an old movie, and sitting in a particular spot on his couch (on the left side) so much that Vuocolo would have to replace the cushions. Near the apartment where he and Suzzy Roche were living, Loudon Wainwright III ran into Van Ronk in the aisles of a health-food store; both were shopping for brown rice and green tea. "People shouldn't know we're in here," Van Ronk growled furtively. "It'll be bad for our careers."

Every so often, Van Ronk would rouse himself, hail a taxi (it was sometimes hard for him to walk, a result of the wear and tear on his body), and head down to Folk City or Speak Easy. There he was finally given the respect and reverence the music business still hadn't bestowed upon him. Hardy, never the easiest to please, admired Van Ronk, as did many of the younger songwriters who would stop by his and Vuocolo's apartment at seemingly all hours. Even during those nights when Van Ronk seemed more interested in staying at the Speak Easy bar than listening to one of the balladeers on its stage, he was impressed with the fortitude and talent of the community. He even told Massengill that his generation was being short-changed and not getting the attention their predecessors had received.

According to Van Ronk's FBI file, the agency stopped tracking him in 1973, although the impact of that surveillance was still felt in his circle. When Vuocolo would reach out to some of his friends, a few were afraid to talk on the phone for fear of a wiretap. When someone *did* seem to still be eyeing the scene, the circumstances were almost comical. At Speak Easy, one newbie songwriter started performing a song about assassinating Reagan, which was presented as satire in the song's spoken intro: "I'm a nice guy and I don't want to see any harm come to anybody. But if I were *not* a nice guy and *did* want to see harm come to anyone, I would sing"—then he launched into a verse—"Kill, kill, kill Ronald Reagan!"

Everyone thought it was funny until, one afternoon, several Secret Service agents showed up, saying they had heard a folksinger there had written a song calling for the death of the president. The agents were informed about the disclaimer, laughed off the report, and left. Still, the incident was an unsettling reminder of the ways that the government had had the scene in its sights, and maybe still did.

Sitting at the bar at Folk City, Lucy Kaplansky could hardly believe what she was reading. That night, she'd opened for singer-songwriter Jesse Winchester, who was back on the touring circuit after moving to Canada to avoid the draft during the Vietnam War. She'd heard that John Rockwell was covering the show and, grabbing an early edition of the next day's *Times*, read his write-up, which included a career-making mention of Kaplansky: "If we lived in a healthy time for the record business," he wrote, "it would be easy to predict stardom for her." In absolutely another time, such an endorsement would have led to calls from agents, producers, and executives, but Kaplansky heard nothing from anyone in the business. "I had this idea that something should happen, but no, nothing happened," she said. "Zero."

Starting at the end of the seventies, jazz musicians who emerged from the loft scene were being rewarded with major-label deals: Arthur Blythe, for one, started recording for Columbia. But the Folk City and Speak Easy regulars were still left out in the business cold, especially now that the wave that had swept up the Kenny's Castaways crowd had crested. Forbert's third album, *Little Stevie Orbit*, didn't include a hit on the level of "Romeo's Tune," and the same outlets that had praised his first two records now found his third one "uneven," in the word of the *Times*' Palmer. Nile's second album, *Golden*

Down, featured a title song that many interpreted as being about a prostitute, a theory Nile downplayed. No one doubted the song's visceral, punky power, but the album sold only modestly, and Nile wound up filing for bankruptcy and parting ways with his label. "I walked away," he said. "It became more about business than music. It should have been a happy time. But it was a really dark time for me." With his wife and two children, he moved to Buffalo.

In its den-like performance space, those fish tanks hidden behind a curtain, Speak Easy provided regular work for the Cornelia Street Café crowd as well as a spectrum of preceding-era Village talent. The pay wasn't always enough to survive. Unlike the days when Village musicians could live off club work, other means of income were required; Massengill continued toiling as a dishwasher at an uptown restaurant. The cooperative also managed to book Van Ronk, Tom Paxton, Eric Andersen, Washington Square Park bluegrass legend Roger Sprung, and even the Monkees' Peter Tork, who had played Village basket houses early in his career and was once photographed, complete with goatee, watching the Lovin' Spoonful at the Night Owl. At Speak Easy, it had to be explained to Tork that he wouldn't be making a substantial fee playing there.

But since no one seemed to want to record the new generation, the Musicians Cooperative at Speak Easy decided to take their careers into their own hands. "Jack always used to say we can't wait around for other people to let us make our music," MacDonald said. "We have to do it ourselves." Hardy's idea was to release a monthly, independent compilation of songs by his peers, to be sold at Speak Easy and by mail-order subscription. Having by then released several albums on his own Great Divide label, he was conversant in what it took to tape and manufacture records. For an additional seal of approval, he ran the idea by Van Ronk, who wholeheartedly supported it. "He'd come over and I'd say something like, 'What if we did that?'" said Page. "He would say, 'Just do it!'" Hardy wanted to call it *Fast Folk*; Van Ronk suggested the word "coop," much like the Harvard Coop.

All they needed was an inexpensive way to record the songs. Mark Dann, a bass player and all-around accompanist, had been initiated into the scene a few years earlier, backing musicians like MacDonald and Lucinda Williams. At Speak Easy one night in the final month of 1981, Hardy approached Dann, and, looking at his own fingernails, said, "Is it true that you have a four-track tape recorder?"

The story was correct. Dann still lived in his parents' four-story Victorian house on a maple tree–lined street in Flatbush, Brooklyn, just south of Prospect Park. In the attic, Dann had set up a recording studio with a TEAC machine. Beginning in the first month of 1982, the songwriters and musicians began taking the subway out to Brooklyn to put their music on tape there. The studio, such as it was, wasn't soundproofed, but the arrangement worked since everyone was playing relatively quiet music. But the operation still came with certain rules. After entering the house, the musicians would have to quietly climb the stairs to the top floor so as not to disturb Dann's parents. To conserve tape, no one was allowed a second take. Once a month, anybody and everyone would converge upon the Cooper Square apartment of musician-photographer Brian Rose, where the booklets would be edited, pasted up on boards, and taken to a copy shop for printing.

Propped up for sale at Speak Easy in January 1982, *The CooP: The Fast Folk Musical Magazine* was priced at $2 and resembled an illicit bootleg. Its plain white cover featured a grim photo of keeper of the political flame Ed McCurdy, who was heard on two tracks, and the inside booklet had the feel of a do-it-themselves fanzine. But the record amounted to a defiant proclamation that something was happening below Fourteenth Street. The first *CooP* included Frank Christian's "Where Were You Last Night?," an elegant blues that conjured an empty, smoky bar and showcased his effortless guitar, and Massengill's "On the Road to Fairfax County." Vega's "Cracking" made its official recorded debut, as did Van Ronk's "The Jersey State Stomp" (later retitled "Garden State Stomp"), a ragtime-inspired roll call of New Jersey town names. To further inspire him after he had the idea, Vuocolo had found a library book listing the state's towns and municipalities. The second volume, subtitled *The New Interpreters*, introduced Vega's more folk-minded "Calypso," rendered by Kaplansky, now one of the scene's most luminous singers; Rose's "Old Factory Town," a Celtic-flavored tale of working-class despair sung by Gerry Devine; and MacDonald's "Honorable Man," a tense Kennedy-assassination commentary that harked back to an earlier Village era.

Independent rock labels were sprouting up around the country, reenergizing the music and resulting in the first recordings by Black Flag, the Replacements, Sonic Youth, and many others. Even in that climate, what came to be known as the *Fast Folk* series (after the title was shortened) was frantically ambitious: a new compilation every month, each with a magazine tucked inside. The quality could suffer from that timetable, but scattered through the many albums that followed, which eventually came to include more than 150 songs, were more than enough keepers. MacDonald's "American Jerusalem" was there, along with Massengill's "My Name Joe," inspired by a real-life cook (and immigrant) Massengill knew at the restaurant where he worked. Christine Lavin's acerbic "Regretting What I Said" rattled off a detailed list of horrific things she *surely* wouldn't want to have happen to an ex, and Shawn Colvin's first issued recording, "No Friends to Me," felt like a sweetly sung but still stinging update of Dylan's "Positively 4th Street," this one aimed at a pal's backstabbing buddies.

The first volume of 1984 included another of Vega's songs, this time a striking a cappella song that derived from several different inspirations. As an Upper West Sider, she frequented Tom's Restaurant, an old-school Greek coffee shop at Broadway and 112th Street. Leaving Tom's one day, Vega was walking down the street and thinking about her friend Brian Rose and what she called "his romantic, alienated vision as a photographer and how he always felt that he had a pane of glass between himself and life." Vega decided to write a dramatic monologue from his vantage point, set to a sing-songy melody she'd thought up that refused to leave her brain. She'd also been watching French new-wave films, intrigued by their lengthy scenes of people staring out windows. That same season, the fall of 1981, veteran actor William Holden, apparently drunk, had slipped on a rug in his Los Angeles home, hit his head on a coffee table, and bled to death. That bit of Hollywood lore also made it into the song, as did a reference to someone with whom Vega was having a clandestine relationship, inviting her to midnight picnics at the Cathedral Church of Saint John the Divine on the Upper West Side.

Early in its gestation, Vega considered setting the song, "Tom's Diner," to a solitary piano. But by the time she began performing it in the Village, it became a spell-binding a cappella opener for her sets: in a noisy bar, it was the ideal way to silence the room. "It made people stop talking and drinking," she said. "When I started the show, everyone would stop and listen to me. And it worked every single time." Hearing her perform it at Speak Easy one night, *Newsday* music critic Wayne Robins dubbed it "the first folk-rap fusion song rather than just a talking blues." Once more, the Village was giving birth to sounds few had heard before.

▌▌▐▌▌

Even though she'd grown up on Dylan records, the last place Nancy Jeffries wanted to be that night in 1983 was Folk City. One of the earliest executives to make her mark in the male-dominated music business, Jeffries had started her career as the singer with the avant-garde band Insect Trust, along with future *Times* critic Robert Palmer. She then made the jump to talent scout, landing ultimately at A&M Records. As her tenure in Insect Trust demonstrated, her tastes weren't limited to acoustic music, but she had to comply when her boss, label head Gil Friesen, essentially ordered her to check out an unsigned folk act. "I was really annoyed," she said. "First of all . . . folk music, *eh*. I had very low expectations. I thought, 'This is a drag and a waste of my evening.'"

At that point, the actual definition of what constituted folk music had changed. One of the most undeniably riveting records of the year before was Grandmaster Flash and the Furious Five's "The Message," a modern-day protest song that came from the hip-hop scene gestating in the Bronx. As the *Fast Folk* records made clear, that community didn't hesitate to make social commentary, but it had a hard time competing for radio play or MTV time with "The Message," Nena's nuclear nightmare "99 Luftballons," or Prince's pestering funk "Ronnie, Talk to Russia." Modern folk protest songs were just as likely to be jokey and funny, like Tom Paxton's "Yuppies in the Sky," set to the same melody as the western classic "Ghost Riders in the Sky."

As much as anyone on the scene, Vega knew nothing was a given. Some in the same community—including Christian, Vega's boyfriend during this time—remained hopeful that a music executive would happen upon them and scoop them up, but Vega sensed that those days were over. "Frank and I used to joke, 'When are the fruit baskets going to start arriving?'" she said.

"But I did the work. I was always writing a new song or new bio or making a new demo tape." Carefully taking in what did and didn't make an impression onstage, Vega took note when a folk veteran playing Folk City was so drunk he sang the same song twice in a row, and she determined never to shout at or scold an audience that was talking during a set. When Vega opened for the legendary Rosalie Sorrels at the New York Folk Festival at Folk City in August 1981, she approached *Times* critic Stephen Holden. Aided by a glass of wine, she demanded to know if he was going to review the opening act—her. When she bombed and didn't receive any write-up, she resolved to never drink again before she went onstage.

By chance, Ron Fierstein, the brother of actor and playwright Harvey, had decided to leave the law firm where he was working on copyright and trademark cases and start a production company with his college friend and one-time band member, guitarist Steve Addabbo. Addabbo would handle the musical and production end; Fierstein would make the deals. One of Fierstein's law-firm friends told him about a songwriter he'd heard at Columbia, and after meeting Vega for lunch—where she came prepared with flyers for her next show—Fierstein felt there wouldn't be any harm in seeing her perform.

What he—and, soon after, Jeffries—saw was someone who was leaving behind the long-haired urban-waif image of her earliest shows. Vega's hair was now cut short, just below her ears, and she dressed in suits. The latter stemmed from her self-consciousness: she had felt uncomfortable exposing any part of herself onstage, cringing at the thought of someone admiring her legs if she wore a dress. Realizing that heroes like Reed, Cohen, and Dylan, along with Patti Smith and Chrissie Hynde, often wore jackets, she borrowed a tuxedo jacket with big lapels and wide shoulders from a male musician friend. She didn't quite resemble David Byrne in Talking Heads' concert doc *Stop Making Sense*, but the clothing lent her an air of new-wave cool, along with a hint of androgyny, that differentiated her from her peers on the scene.

As Addabbo noted, Vega's guitar technique was also unusual. Reflecting the minimalist aura of the songs, she was playing clusters and patterns—spikey plucked chords more like Morse Code—rather than strummed patterns intended to encourage sing-alongs. Accompanying Vega one night at Folk City, Addabbo brought along a drum machine for one song. "It was a little bit sacrilegious," he said. "We were on the edge of going too far with Suzanne."

"Tom's Diner" was just one of several songs in Vega's set that told their stories by way of characters instead of her own persona. "I was not happy with this idea that women wrote confessional songs about their feelings," she said. "I felt tired of that whole thing. Laura Nyro's *Eli and the 13th Confession* was an unbelievable album. But there was no way I was going to do that. So I invented this coded way of writing that I felt very comfortable with." Although not as bleak as "Cracking," the autobiographical "Straight Lines" painted a portrait of a woman chopping off her hair and "trying to make sense of my life," she said. Set to one of her zestiest melodies, "Marlene on the Wall" derived from a photograph of actress Marlene Dietrich that Vega hung on her apartment wall as well as a brief romance with George Gerdes, who had already broken up with Terre Roche. (The lyric referenced the time he and Vega had seen the Tennessee Williams play *The Rose Tattoo* as well as his hand motions, which approached mime gestures.) "Neighborhood Girls" was a half-spoken, dryly observed nighttime crawl that particularly reflected Reed's influence on her work.

Even when her songs wandered into traditional vernacular territory, they walked their own path. In Rose's apartment one day, she played "The Queen and the Soldier," which spun out of dating a man who'd cheated on her. In two hours, she'd written a story-song about a female monarch who, nearly lured into a relationship with a man, instead decides to kill him. "It's about a type of person who will cling to power and not do anything that threatens that power and makes her vulnerable," she said. "They'll just get rid of them. I still think it probably says something about me somewhere in there."

Coincidentally, Fierstein took a meeting with Cat Stevens's manager, who wanted to discuss a possible movie version of his brother Harvey's *Torch Song Trilogy*. Sensing an opportunity, Fierstein, a Stevens fans who envisioned Stevens's label A&M as a perfect home for Vega, gave the manager a copy of Vega's tape and asked if he could pass it along to Gil Friesen. After hearing it, Friesen, an old-school record type who'd signed everyone from the Carpenters to the

Police, Joe Jackson and Joan Armatrading, instructed Jeffries to see her first Vega show.

Jeffries had neither heard of Vega nor listened to her material, but she was immediately taken by what she saw and heard. In Jeffries's mind, here was someone who was part of a so-called folk scene but had the potential to make an impact beyond it, and Jeffries took note of the small but devoted crowd that listened intently to every lyric or bit of stage patter. Despite the venue and folk-club trappings, Vega was, she said, "flying in the face of everything," which also appealed to Jeffries—but not to many of her bosses. "People were hedging their bets," Jeffries said. "They loved her. But they were thinking, 'How much money can we put into a folk singer?'" A&M wanted her to keep playing other venues and work on her publicity and fan base. Other labels, including Geffen, passed.

But on a night in March 1984, Vega's prospects flipped on a dime. During the sound check, she played Fierstein a newly written song, "Luka." Sung from the point of a view of a child who hints at being hit and keeping it to himself, the song, Fierstein correctly guessed, was about child abuse. To Vega's shock, he also immediately thought it could be a hit single. As she rolled her eyes, he told her how his generation had ended the war in Vietnam with their music, so it was important to write an issue song.

What she didn't tell him—or anyone, for decades, starting with interviewer Kevin Burke—was that the narrator of the song, the young Luka, was in fact her. During her childhood, she and some of her siblings had had to deal with what she would come to call "these violent things" involving her stepfather. After telling her she couldn't tell anyone about it, Ed Vega changed his mind one day. "He said, 'You can write about it if you fictionalize it, and if people ask you about it, you can say part of it is real,'" she recalled (to this author). In a way, Vega was now following his instructions.

The *Times*' Holden saw the show and, two days later, wrote the review Vega had likely been dreaming about since she had buttonholed him three years before. "The most obvious influence on Miss Vega's writing is the work of the young Joni Mitchell," he wrote, "which combined a similar eye for detail along with an analytical self-absorption." That same day, Fierstein received a call from none other than David Geffen, asking why the supposedly new Mitchell wasn't signing with him—after all, he had managed Mitchell and guided her career early on—and insisting on a meeting with Fierstein and Addabbo. At an uptown gathering with Geffen label executives, the two men, who weren't accustomed to the big-money ways of the music business, were given the hard sell. The label, they were told, was going to sign her, even though, as far as Fierstein and Addabbo could tell, none of them had heard Vega's music. To demonstrate his connections and ongoing clout, Geffen also played them an advance copy of Don Henley's "The Boys of Summer."

Flattered and stunned, Fierstein and Addabbo left and pondered the offer. Not long after, a Geffen A&R executive took a limousine from New York City to Northampton, Massachusetts, to see a Vega show. At a meeting afterward, he told her, in her memory, "We'd like you to have one or two hits, for the kids, and then any artistic statements you want to make, you can do that on the rest of the album." Although they weren't inclined to go with Geffen, Vega's team was able to use that company's offer to leverage more money from A&M. The Village now had its first major-label recording artist in half a decade.

The news of Vega's signing ricocheted through the Village scene. As Van Ronk would tell younger musicians such as Lavin, "Never root against your competition if what they're doing is good music, because their success means more work for you." Yet Folk City co-owner Woliver—in the midst of writing *Bringing It All Back Home*, an extensive oral history of the scene and his club—couldn't help but notice the similarities to the reactions when Dylan had signed with Columbia twenty-three years before. Some musicians were openly jealous, asking Vega to her face why she was the one. Colvin admits she was "horribly jealous" even if she didn't yet know Vega. Partly as a result of her signing the contract, Vega and Jack Hardy had a falling-out, although they eventually reconciled.

The making of Vega's debut album, cut in the early months of 1985 at several New York studios, brought together disparate aspects and eras of the

Village scene. The debate between acoustic and electric, purism and commercialism, played itself out in myriad ways. No one wanted to detract attention from Vega's voice, guitar, and material, but neither did anyone want an overly musty troubadour record. To add a degree of what she considered a downtown New York edge to the tracks—something the West Village had been long rejecting—Jeffries hired her friend Lenny Kaye to coproduce the record with Addabbo. The timing was right; after the breakup of the Patti Smith Group a few years before, Kaye had started venturing into record production. Playing the benevolent guru, he could make his presence known in subtle ways: whenever he felt the arrangements were becoming too fussy, he'd reach into his back pocket, pull out a fine-tooth comb, and place it on the console. Frank Christian played on the album, but only on two songs.

Taking a break one evening, Vega dropped by Van Ronk's apartment for a party. Early on, she'd felt that Van Ronk was kind; carefully listening to her songs, he too compared her to Joni Mitchell. Vega, meanwhile, was impressed that he knew Dylan and referred to him as "Bobby." But that evening, she encountered a different Van Ronk, who seemingly had had a bit too much to drink. "He was saying I didn't give a fuck about folk music," she said. "I do, actually, but it didn't seem like the right moment to fight with him, in his own house. He just got belligerent." In his posthumously published memoir, *The Mayor of MacDougal Street*, Van Ronk would write that while he had heard that Vega had referred to herself as a folksinger, "I doubt Suzanne has ever sung [a folk song] in her life." Vega soon departed. "I didn't have to stay and take it, so I left," she said. "I never held it against him. He thought I had this big-time record deal and possibly he felt he was being left behind."

That night aside, Van Ronk, inspired by the renewed energy in the clubs around him, grew more creatively energized himself. Thanks to an offer to appear on a British TV show, he overcame his fear of flying (taking some tranquilizers on the plane first) and began performing in Europe and Japan. Van Ronk also decided to do something he'd never done before, an album devoted entirely to his own material. According to Van Ronk's manager, Mitch Greenhill, the idea was to showcase Van Ronk as a songwriter and encourage others to cover his songs so he could earn a decent living. Stretching back over his life and career, it included remakes of songs from past records, including "Gaslight Rag" and "Zen Koans Gonna Rise Again," as well as newly recorded versions of "Garden State Stomp" and the sad but affectionate adieu "Another Time and Place." *Going Back to Brooklyn* had originally been made for Philo, home of his previous two records. But when the label ran out of money, the album was suddenly homeless. Depending on the source, another prominent roots label either passed or expressed no interest in a collection of Van Ronk's own songs. In the end, the album would be issued on Reckless, an indie founded by singer-songwriter Bill Morrissey and Van Ronk's former student Elijah Wald, now a musician and writer. Van Ronk's voice was wheezier than ever, but his spirit and guitar were able and willing. Among the new songs recorded as additional tracks for the album was "The Whores of San Pedro," a novelty that dated back to his merchant marine days and, in a sense, took him full circle.

▌▌▊▌▊

"Ye gods!" joked Van Ronk to *Boston Globe* writer Jeff McLaughlin during an interview in his Sheridan Square apartment. "We're having another folk music scare! Serves us right."

For a heady moment, the dream of a Village music scene did seem to be a reality once more. The Bottom Line, still the preeminent neighborhood showcase for anything that wasn't connected to hip-hop or dance music, hosted an evening devoted to the *Fast Folk* (formerly *CooP*) crowd, including Lavin (who organized it), Hardy, Kaplansky, Christian, MacDonald, and Massengill. To the wonderment of co-owner Allan Pepper, both shows that evening sold out. "I was a little surprised, because they weren't being played on the radio," he said. "I'm thinking, 'Where does this audience come from?'" After several trying years, the Blue Note started turning a profit in 1984: bass player Ray Brown, who had played with Dizzy Gillespie, Oscar Peterson, and others, had stopped in and urged owner Danny Bensusan to hire the reunited Modern Jazz Quartet. That successful run led to the booking of other legends like Gillespie and Sarah Vaughan.

Intent on modernizing the image and feel of Folk City, Woliver had reached out to *NY Rocker*, the city's most underground-leaning music publication, to gauge whether its staff could recruit upstart bands to play the club. With the advent of "Music for Dozens," a weekly indie showcase organized by the magazine's Michael Hill and Ira Kaplan, it was suddenly possible to walk into Folk City and see early New York performances by the Minutemen, the Replacements, the Violent Femmes, and Sonic Youth. "The venue just seemed so completely *not* right for that," Hill said. "It was a ramshackle folk club that wasn't the kind of place where one would expect to hear Sonic Youth. But for one night a week, it was our room to do that." When Minneapolis's roaring Hüsker Dü was booked, soundman Vincent Vok found himself pushing all the tables to the side to make room for Folk City's first-ever mosh pit.

Even more surprisingly, music emanating from the Village began making inroads on the pop charts. Vega's self-titled first album, released in the spring of 1985, was the most arresting singer-songwriter debut since the heyday of the genre the previous decade. Although she decided to omit "Tom's Diner," feeling it didn't sit with the other songs, her strongest, earliest songs remained, and in fairly unvarnished form. Vega's roots in the folk clubs were evident; Christian's graceful playing adding a delicate underscore to "Knight Moves." But starting with "Cracking," an unconventional opener if there ever was one, *Suzanne Vega* was very much of its time. The lyrical edge in songs like "Undertow" and "The Queen and the Soldier" felt more like the New York of the eighties than the previous eras. Addabbo and Kaye added just enough in the way of additional instrumentation, drums, and even strings to blow away any folk-club mustiness; the concluding "Neighborhood Girls" had a hint of rock sleaze. The album respected traditions but cleared the way for a new type of future.

Jeffries's support for a woman artist—one of the reasons Vega felt comfortable putting her signature on a contract with the company—also salvaged another aspect of the project. At a photo shoot for the cover, Vega was remade with puffed eighties hair and enough makeup to make her resemble, as she would put it, "the girl who did the weather." The men working with her all approved, but Jeffries took one look at the photographs and rejected them; Vega didn't look like herself. In the end, they opted for a more washed-out black-and-white portrait, taken on a cobblestone street, that made Vega actually resemble someone with a Greenwich Village connection.

Released as a single that summer, which was dominated by A-ha's "Take on Me" and other synth pop hits, "Marlene on the Wall" didn't stand much of a chance. But *Suzanne Vega* tapped into something—a yearning for contemporary and more intimate music rooted in a vintage style. When the Roche sisters returned home for a visit, John Roche was reading the newspaper and asked his daughter Terre, "Have you heard of this girl Suzanne Vega? They're giving her a lot more space in the *New York Times* than you." Even without a hit single, *Suzanne Vega* ultimately sold more than a quarter-million copies in its first two years in the stores.

The community also soon had its first nationally high-profile rock band since the days of the Lovin' Spoonful. Although they hailed from New Jersey, the Smithereens established a following at Kenny's Castaways and the Other End Cafe. Playing several sets a night for minimal pay, they woodshedded and kept alive the Merseybeat tradition of pop songs hammered out with thunderous guitars. In Pat DiNizio, the band had a songwriter who effortlessly conjured sixties-AM-radio songcraft as the band blasted away behind him. When "Blood and Roses," which had a dank, unrelenting propulsion to it, was included on the soundtrack of a teen vigilante movie, *Dangerously Close*, both the song and the group's first full album, *Especially for You*, blew up. The Smithereens' music wasn't as across-the-musical-map eclectic as the Spoonful's or the Blues Project's, but like them, they electrified the scene. They even had an unusual connection to the past: on the Blues Project's *Reunion in Central Park*, a lone voice was heard exclaiming, "Yeah!" before "I Can't Keep from Crying Sometimes." That shout belonged to Dennis Diken, the Smithereens' drummer.

Continuing a tradition that extended back in a way to Tiny Tim, the Village of the eighties also had its own historically minded novelty act. Comprising refugees from the East Village punk and new-wave scene, the Washington Squares donned berets and striped shirts (and goatees for the men), as if they were dressing as beatniks for the annual Greenwich Village Halloween parade. The Squares—bassist Tom Goodkind and guitarists Lauren Agnelli and Bruce Jay Paskow—resurrected the folk and folk-rock classics of the past, like "If I Had a Hammer," "Samson and Delilah," and "I'll Never Find Another You."

They also wrote a handful of striking originals, like Agnelli's "Charcoal" and Paskow's "New Generation"; the latter aimed to be the motivational call to arms that the Village hadn't produced in decades.

Thanks to Goodkind, who knew how to hustle and attract media attention, the Squares were overnight press darlings; the trio were on MTV before they'd even made a record. Unsure if the Squares were a sincere tribute act or put-on artists, the Folk City and Speak Easy crowd welcomed them warily. But if that was what it took to lure more people back down to the Village, few could complain.

In one part of the West Village in 1980, the average monthly rent was $358, about $100 more than the typical cost of a Manhattan apartment. By the mid-eighties, that trend refused to let up. Increasingly, the Village felt less home to bohemians—or anyone aspiring to that—and more to those with eighties-fueled disposable income. Recovering from the recession, the financial sector added more than 100,000 new jobs by the middle of the decade, and the economic rebound also meant the neighborhood was becoming more exclusive and in demand. Construction projects began running wild as monthly rental rates for Village two-bedroom apartments started to creep toward $2,000, at least ten times what they had once been. Anyone interested in owning a condominium or coop there would have to lay out as much as $190,000 for a studio or $300,000 for a one-bedroom apartment. In June 1986 a townhouse on West Eleventh Street sold for $1.7 million, reportedly the highest price ever paid for a Village residence. Adding to the neighborhood's newfangled allure, a crackdown on drug dealers in Washington Square Park in 1985 helped drive some of the mangier elements out of the fountain area.

In tandem with the cash roiling the area, Folk City once again found itself in the crosshairs. During the "Music for Dozens" rock series, Michael Hill sensed that Woliver was fretting over the teeth-rattling volume, especially when the Replacements nearly decimated the sound system. It wasn't long before some of the residents of the apartments housed directly above the club began taking notice. Folk City's new owners installed makeshift soundproofing on its ceiling and added comedy and theater shows to reduce the amount of music (and noise) coming from inside; some bands, like the Smithereens, purposefully played at decreased volume. Actor James Cromwell, who lived directly above the club for a year, grew accustomed to the muffled beats that would make their way into his apartment. But Virginia Admiral—the painter, archetypal Village bohemian, and mother of Robert DeNiro who owned but didn't live in one of those loft-style apartments—wasn't as taken with the rock and roll emanating from Folk City. The Blue Note's Bensusan would recall that Admiral (or whomever was renting her place) "complained about it all the time."

Repeating another scenario from decades past, the Smithereens and Vega graduated to larger venues and national tours. But this time, record executives didn't seem all that interested in signing anyone else from the community. MacDonald was able to record his first album only when Speak Easy's Joseph Zbeda heard he didn't have a contract and handed him an envelope stuffed with several thousand dollars to pay for the recording costs. Despite a repertoire that showcased much of the most compelling material by the Folk City and Speak Easy pack, the Song Project still had trouble gaining traction, and personnel changes in the band doomed it to a breakup. Taking a temporary break from music, Lucy Kaplansky, the Song Project member once singled out as the rising star of the new-folk scene, returned to college in 1983 to become a psychotherapist; Devine devoted his time to the Floor Models, who kept alive the power-pop tradition in the Village.

In the eyes of the industry, it didn't help that Warner Brothers hadn't been able to make the Roches palatable to the masses. With Robert Fripp they'd made another, largely acoustic album, 1982's *Keep on Doing*, which included their rendition of Handel's "The Hallelujah Chorus," along with material by Massengill ("On the Road to Fairfax County") and Gerdes ("Steady with the Maestro"). With Fripp doubling up their voices even more this time around, Maggie's "Losing True" was transformed into a wall of vocal sound, complete with another sinewy solo by Fripp.

For the sisters' fourth album, the time had come to try to sell records, and after working with multiple producers, they wound up with 1985's *Another*

World, which blended their harmonies with glistening synthesizers and often jarring drums. The makeover had its moments: the wistful "Love to See You" had a gorgeous ache, "Weeded Out" hinted at their concerns about their place in the music world, and Mark Johnson's "Love Radiates Around" showed how rapturous a sonically upgraded Roches could be. But it was also the first Roches album without a single song written solely by Maggie, who seemed increasingly withdrawn. After the album again failed to make the Roches pop stars, Warner Brothers dropped them, the sisters hearing the news while on tour in Europe. "It was the beginning of that realization that what you were doing was passing out of popularity," Terre said. "We were starting to realize that things were not what they used to be."

With its high-end ticket prices and upscale menu, the Blue Note catered to those who could likely afford luxury apartments in the area; the club even had a gift shop that sold Blue Note merchandise. Other venues weren't quite so shrewd. Seventh Avenue South had never been a huge moneymaker, and the club began running into financial troubles—only exacerbated in 1984, when the owner of the building sold the property to people who tripled the rent. The Speak Easy and *Fast Folk* scene, meanwhile, was starting to feel stagnant— Brian Rose encouraged his friend Suzanne Vega to break out of it—and Zbeda would grow anxious or peeved when attendance dipped on slow nights. ("Why don't you have Tom Paxton *every* weekend?" he groused to Jay Rosen, who worked on the sound system at the club.) Maria Kenny, the daughter of Kenny's Castaways owner Pat, began working at the club and noticed the nearby cafés closing, one by one, thanks to rent increases.

In 1984 Folk City fell victim to a rent hike of its own that saw its monthly bill leap from $1,500 to $4,300. Admiral, who was well-regarded in the community, told the *Times* that the venue's owners had been offered a fifteen-year lease if the space were soundproofed. But the cost of more extensive soundproofing, along with the rent increase, was proving to be prohibitive, and Woliver, Hillesum, and Lash accepted a short-term, two-year lease and began the hunt for a new location. "They decided they wanted to spend their money looking for a new place," Admiral said to the *Times*. "We wanted to keep them, because they're a Village institution, but they wouldn't soundproof."

As it was becoming evident that the club could shut down or be forced to find a new locale, Mike Porco, who'd retired to Lauderhill, Florida, in 1982, visited New York and took Woliver to meet Dylan, who was playing *Late Night with David Letterman*. In his dressing room, Dylan appeared gracious and relatively normal, even in white makeup, and offered his condolences to Porco, whose wife, Ellen, had passed away after a long illness. Seemingly aware of the club's predicament, Dylan listened and was invited to participate in a concert being organized to commemorate Folk City's twenty-fifth anniversary.

When that concert finally took place—in September 1985 at Pier 84, an outdoor venue on the Hudson—Dylan wasn't on the bill. (He played only two shows that entire year, both benefits, Live Aid and the inaugural Farm Aid.) But the show brought together the older guard—Tom Paxton, Odetta, Arlo Guthrie, and Joan Baez—with later crew such as Vega, the Roches, Massengill, and Colvin. By then, the concert was more than a celebration; it had become a benefit to help pay for Folk City's increased rent for the remaining two years of its lease. Unexpectedly, production expenses ate up all the proceeds, leaving the club's owners with only a few thousand dollars.

By spring 1986, the time had come for Folk City to move on. Woliver, Lash, and Hillesum settled on 82 East Fourth Street in the sometimes-squalid East Village. A former speakeasy that had been raided during Prohibition, the place could hold four hundred, a step up from their current location, and a tentative opening was scheduled for May. Those plans in place, Folk City bid farewell to its West Third Street space on Wednesday, March 26, 1986. From early evening until close to dawn, musicians huddled, sang a song or two, and drank—so much that bartender Peggy Duncan-Garner had to run across the street to the Blue Note for additional beer. Reflecting Woliver's vision for a rebooted Folk City, musical worlds collided: members of Yo La Tengo and the Smithereens rubbed tight shoulders with Massengill, Christian, and other new- folk figures.

Finally, at 5 a.m., the doors had to close, and everyone was finally booted out after what turned into a group sing-along of Dylan's "Knockin' on Heaven's Door," with some of the musicians seated on the stage. The mood was downbeat but not entirely forlorn. By then, thirty years had passed since NYU had begun demolishing parts of the Village, making way for Gerde's Folk City.

Nearly thirty had gone by since Izzy Young had opened the Folklore Center, Van Ronk played at the new Cafe Bizarre, the Village Vanguard committed itself full-time to jazz, and the Sunday park hootenannies made the local papers. The scene had somehow survived it all—Sonny Rollins was back at the Vanguard that spring—and many inside Folk City that night felt as if they were bidding good-bye to an old office space and preparing to move to a new one. After all, the club had shut and reopened before, and everyone assumed it would rise again in just a few months. "We all thought they were reopening," said Duncan-Garner. "Nobody felt that was it, that that was the end."

Just a few months before, the Roches' "Face Down at Folk City," their cheeky take on the world that birthed them, had been included on *Another World*. Its veiled references to Jack Hardy and Duncan-Garner were there, but one line—someone on stage singing a song, but it "ain't the latest rage"—now felt less like a wisecrack and more like an elegy to the club and the community itself. After Folk City shut its doors that night, the owners helped themselves to souvenirs, including coffee mugs, barstools, and leftover liquor. Many years before, Mike Porco had bought a bottle of artichoke liqueur, a distasteful concoction that had long sat untouched behind the bar. The bottle had seen it all, and now it too was gone.

see that my grave is kept clean

2002–2004

Early in the evening of March 24, 2002, several hundred began filing into Judson Memorial Church on Washington Square
South. For the last few decades, the building, designed by Stanford White
and sporting the look of an ancient temple, had welcomed artists, civil rights
groups, antiwar activists, gospel singers, and musicians fleeing the 1961 "beatnik
riot" in the park. On this day, it would host a tribute service for another fixture of
the neighborhood, Dave Van Ronk, who had died just over a month earlier.

In the years after Folk City and Speak Easy presented their final nights of
music, Van Ronk had reconciled himself to a life of demanding work and few
financial rewards. If anything, he appeared to be artistically liberated from any
industry pressure. He recorded albums of songs by Bertolt Brecht and from the
Great American Songbook, he narrated *Peter and the Wolf* on another record,
and he contributed to tribute albums to Phil Ochs and Robert Johnson as well
as the occasional *Fast Folk* collection. In 1996 he received a Grammy nomi-
nation in the traditional folk category for *From . . . Another Time & Place*, on
which he revisited repertoire favorites from "He Was a Friend of Mine" to his
more recent "Losers." Returning to his passion for jazz and prerock pop, he

immersed himself in versions of "Thanks for the Memory," "As Time Goes By," "Puttin' on the Ritz," and others on the 2000 album *Sweet & Lowdown*, with friend and guitarist Frank Christian among the accompanists. With Elijah Wald, Van Ronk also began the process of writing a history of the Village folk era; Wald would handle the research and much of the writing, and Van Ronk, according to Wald, the "flavor and the first-person slant."

In 1988 Van Ronk and Andrea Vuocolo had married, and the couple continued to live in their apartment off Sheridan Square. Van Ronk's health remained a cause for concern. He still wasn't keen on seeing doctors, even for his asthma issues, and his eyesight had begun failing him. Rejecting contact lenses, he joked that he wanted to make an album titled *The Seriously Nearsighted Dave Van Ronk*. But Erik Frandsen also noticed Van Ronk cutting down on smoking and dropping some weight. "He was starting to slow down," Frandsen said. "But he had it under control, a lot more than it *looked*." To the relief of the devoted Vuocolo, he finally quit smoking on a dime, even if he didn't want to talk about it afterward.

In the summer of 2001, Vuocolo noticed that Van Ronk appeared to be grumpy and tired. What was first thought to be diverticulitis turned to be colon cancer. Soldiering on, he kept a commitment to two more shows, at a high school in Pennsylvania and the Maryland-based Institute for Musical Traditions, the latter on October 22. Despite his diagnosis, Van Ronk managed to complete an hour-and-a-half set.

To raise funds for his costly surgery and treatment, a benefit was held at the Bottom Line, where he had played that previous spring. The club itself was struggling after a citywide recession in late 2000 and the aftermath of September 11, which decimated nightlife in Lower Manhattan. But Van Ronk's fans and friends came out; Tom Paxton and Peter, Paul and Mary were among the performers, and David Massengill went from table to table collecting money. Another benefit, at Caffé Lena in Saratoga Springs, featured David Amram, who'd met Van Ronk those many years ago at the Five Spot.

To anyone prowling Village streets, he could still be found at nearby favorites like the Cornelia Street Café, sipping a coffee. Lili Añel, the early Songwriters Exchange participant now playing venues around the city, ran into Van Ronk as she and her young son were walking along Bleecker Street. Van Ronk was so thin that Añel at first didn't recognize him, and she wasn't sure how well he remembered her either. But after she introduced him to her eight-year-old, Van Ronk perked up. "Your mom take you to all the places where she sang?" he said, then, turning to Añel, added, "You need to take him—he needs to learn."

Those sightings would soon drop off. In November 2001, Van Ronk underwent surgery, but complications emerged. His longtime smoking habit had left his lungs compromised, so he was put on steroids to clear up any infections before chemotherapy. His doctors thought he had another six months to live, which would have given him time to finish his book with Wald. In the hospital, he whiled away the time writing new songs, one of which he was hoping to record with Bonnie Raitt.

But the steroids delayed the chemotherapy, and a third chemo treatment hit him especially hard. During a brief period when Van Ronk was back home, Mitch Greenhill, his manager, called to cheer him up, suggesting he treat himself to a shot of Irish whiskey. To Greenhill's surprise and dismay, Van Ronk said he would pass. Soon he was back in the hospital, and on the morning of February 10, 2002, he succumbed to cardio-pulmonary failure at the age of sixty-five.

Although the connection was entirely coincidental, Van Ronk's passing felt like the culmination of the downward spiral of a music community that had supported him for more than forty-five years. To the surprise and discontent of some of its employees, as well as musicians who'd appeared on its stage, Folk City failed to have a third act. After Woliver, Lash, and Hillesum had placed a deposit on the East Fourth Street locale—moving the club's piano and some of its decor in the process—an entertainment lawyer who'd spent time at Folk City strongly urged them to back out, saying shady characters controlled the building. On that advice, they broke the lease, and plans for a new venue collapsed. Eventually, Woliver was able to reclaim the piano, but Folk City itself simply vanished.

By the mid-eighties, the Songwriters Exchange at the Cornelia Street Café had migrated to Jack Hardy's apartment, where the rules stayed in place with one old-world exception: those who gathered to workshop new songs for their peers were told to snap their fingers, not applaud. "No, we are not cool beat-niks . . . ," read the instructions that Hardy passed around. "We are trying to be considerate of the neighbors."

Yet the closing of Folk City seemed to set off a chain reaction in the area. The following year, Seventh Avenue South, at the end of its ten-year lease, finally expired and became a gynecologist's office. The Lone Star Cafe continued to pull in name country and rock acts and, in 1982, hosted a wake for John Belushi, who'd become something of a regular. But in 1989, its lease was also up for renewal, at three times the price. Unable to come to terms with the landlord, then co-owners Mort Cooperman and Bill Dick closed the club after twelve years. During an auction of what remained inside, a Virginia real estate mogul paid $17,500 for Bob Wade's rooftop iguana. By then, Cooperman had opened the Lone Star Roadhouse, an uptown version of the club.

Partly a result of the shuttering of Folk City, its competitor but also sister in acoustic music, Speak Easy, suffered a far more ignominious fate. Once names like Suzanne Vega and Christine Lavin had moved on to larger venues, attendance began to fall off, and Zbeda, who had his eye on cash flow more than chord charts, kicked out the Musicians Cooperative and brought in a new booker. In the fall of 1989, only a few months after the Lone Star Cafe had become a Houlihan's chain restaurant, Speak Easy transformed into the Speak Easy Sports Bar. A few years later, it returned, briefly, to a music venue, the Spotlight, but that too didn't last long. That same year, Max Gordon, who continued to preside over the Village Vanguard and could still be seen at one of its tables on most nights, died at eighty-nine after complications from gall-bladder surgery. His wife, Lorraine, took over, meaning that at least one iconic venue in the area would survive.

The Bitter End (which had reverted back to its old name, from the Other End, by the early eighties) had its own close call in 1992. After city inspectors claimed they couldn't find a seating plan posted anywhere in the place, the building's landlord threatened to terminate its lease. After the club received a cash infusion (and a rent increase), it survived, but the neighborhood was still starting to feel more like a musical ghost town. After nearly forty years, the Village Gate had fallen on difficult times. With $500,000 in unpaid bills,

Art D'Lugoff had no choice but to declare Chapter 11. After the building that owned the club went into foreclosure, it was taken over by Chemical Bank, which offered to allow the Gate to stay—but with a jump in rent from $2,000 (what the *New York Times* called D'Lugoff's "sweetest deal") to $15,000. In 1993, the Gate closed; eight years later, the jazz club Sweet Basil followed.

In a biting irony, the genre that Greenwich Village had long championed, even after so many had given up on it, returned to vogue. The year after Folk City's final night, Vega issued her second album, *Solitude Standing*, which, after all this time, included "Luka." With her producers and new band, she'd finally settled on an arrangement that worked, one that opened with keyboard player Anton Sanko's series of ascending fourths on a synthesizer, followed by a firmer rock beat than she'd had before and a skittery guitar solo. Thanks to those sonics and a concerted push by A&M, "Luka" worked its way into the Top 10. As Fierstein had predicted, a song with a social issue made the charts and helped refocus attention on domestic abuse.

When Vega played the album for her father, he told her he wanted to talk with her about "Luka." Given the way her life with him had inspired it, she said, "My stomach dropped to the floor. I thought, 'Oh, boy, here it comes.'" He told her she was glamorizing an ugly subject and asked how she landed on the idea. "I thought, 'Holy cow, he didn't know?'" she said. She told him it was about a boy who lived in their building named Luka, all of which was true. "He put two and two together," she said, "and he let me off the hook."

Male troubadours, like Cliff Eberhardt and John Gorka, successfully launched careers out of the Village. But in a noticeable change from the sixties Village, the artists who made the biggest public impressions were women. Vega would be the first but not the last. Shawn Colvin—by her own admission "a self-medicating drunk" in the early eighties whose memories of that time could be a blur—pulled her life together, got sober, and finally began writing her own material. Working with Vega's same management team, she was signed by Columbia and made her major-label start in 1989. (She also sang backup on "Luka.") Nearly a decade later, Colvin would win Song and Record of the Year Grammys for "Sunny Came Home." Julie Gold, a native Philadelphian, moved to the Village in the early eighties and played many of its clubs, including the

Bottom Line and the Bitter End. When she turned thirty, she wrote a new ballad, "From a Distance," that was championed by Lavin and eventually covered by Nanci Griffith, Judy Collins, and Bette Midler, whose version was ubiquitous in 1990. That same year, Vega's "Tom's Diner" was remixed (without her initial knowledge) by DNA, two British electronic musicians—the beginning of a second wind for the song that would extend for decades.

Tracy Chapman, a Black Boston-based musician, injected the genre with even more righteousness and folk roots on her 1988 debut album and its modern-day topical song, "Fast Car." Talking about Chapman's unexpected breakout with Lavin—who, like many, was taken aback by the scale of Chapman's success—Van Ronk asked Lavin, "Is she good?" When Lavin replied yes, Van Ronk, who still believed what was good for one songwriter was good for them all, retorted, "Then shut up!" In a near miss for the Village, Chapman had actually recorded a song for one of the *Fast Folk* collections—this one documenting the Boston acoustic scene—before she had secured a deal of her own. But a persistent buzz throughout the recording led to her track being dropped from that collection.

In 1997 Vega, Colvin, and Chapman were all part of the first Lilith Fair, a tour entirely devoted to female musicians and conceived by Sarah McLachlan. The Roches would have been naturals for that lineup, but it wasn't to be. Since being dropped by Warner Brothers in the mid-eighties, the sisters had pressed on—recording several more albums for different labels, sometimes venturing into softer, more electronic-pop sounds. Yet as Robert Fripp had predicted long before, the Roches would have to be content with a role as pioneers rather than rich pop stars. The year of the Lilith Tour, they announced they were taking a break. Terre was tired of the road, as was Suzzy, who by then was raising her teenage daughter, Lucy (she and Loudon Wainwright III had broken up in the eighties), and also acting. The death of their father, John, in 1995, also weighed on them. In 2000 Maggie and Terre went on tour to reprise their songs from *Seductive Reasoning*, which had grown in stature since its release twenty-five years before.

Years before his death, Van Ronk had suggested the trio record his "Garden State Stomp"; he even gave Terre Roche a guitar lesson in his apartment so he could teach it to her. The parts proved too difficult for her to learn, but she would soon have another chance to sing it, under different circumstances.

Van Ronk's passing closed the chapter on his plans to write a Greenwich Village history book, but his memorial service told its own story, with a book of its own. On their way into Judson Church's main sanctuary, with its stained-glass windows and Romanesque columns and arches, several hundred friends, relatives, and musical colleagues stopped to add their signatures into an oversized guest book.

Starting with its front cover, which featured a welcoming note from his old Gaslight buddy Wavy Gravy (aka Hugh Romney)—"Let's honk for Van Ronk. He was our moose of the muse. Now loose in heaven"—the sign-in book was a tour through Van Ronk's life and the Village's musical heyday. Mary Travers's signature ("missing you," followed by a doodle of a woman with long hair and bangs) graced the top of the first page. Underneath and on subsequent pages were those from survivors of the coffeehouse days, such as Erik Frandsen, Tom Paxton (and his wife, Midge), Patrick Sky, Oscar Brand, Sonny Ochs, Peter Stampfel, and Sylvia Tyson, who thanked Van Ronk "for being the glue in those early days, and for keeping the faith."

More recent additions to the scene, the ones who'd admired and played with Van Ronk, also scrawled their signatures, among them David Massengill and Terre Roche ("For Dave, who 'discovered' me and Maggie and has always been a big inspiration to me," she wrote). The blank white sheets would also be peppered with signatures from Terri Thal, longtime folk-music manager Harold Leventhal, and some of the club owners who'd given Van Ronk work—Sam Hood of the Gaslight, Paul Colby of the Bitter End. Bob Thompson of the Red Onion Jazz Band, Van Ronk's collaborators of nearly forty years before, playfully wrote, "Recall 'Get Out of Here and Go On Home'? Well you did it!"). The ushers consisted of Van Ronk's current and former students.

At Van Ronk's request, the ceremony opened with a New Orleans–style rendition of Leonard Cohen's "Bird on a Wire," performed by a band led by Ed Polcer, the veteran cornetist and bandleader just a few months younger than

Van Ronk. Suze Rotolo, Wald, Massengill, and author David Hajdu read from Van Ronk's uncompleted memoir. Lavin, Paxton, Odetta, Brand, and Mitch Greenhill talked about his life and legacy. Polcer played "St. James Infirmary," the song that many had heard Van Ronk perform in Washington Square Park and that had remained part of his repertoire. When a recording of Van Ronk singing "Green, Green Rocky Road" came over the speakers toward the end, people began choking up. The tribute then ended with the Polcer band playing the gospel standard "Just a Closer Walk with Thee," followed by "Didn't He Ramble?," a ribald British song that had become a standard post-funeral march in New Orleans. As part of it went, mischievously, "Didn't he ramble . . . I said he rambled / Rambled all around . . . in and out of town / Didn't he ramble . . . He rambled till the butcher cut him down."

Van Ronk's ashes then made their way to a columbarium at the nearby First Presbyterian Church. To honor his fallen friend, Massengill took one of Van Ronk's cigars to a nearby park, dug a small hole in the ground, and buried it. Knowing the power Van Ronk could summon, he half expected a nearby bush to burst into flames, like something out of the Bible.

On May 18, 2003, more than a year after Van Ronk's death, a tribute concert took place in his honor at the Bottom Line. His widow, Andrea, had needed time to mourn, and now the time had come to pay musical respects. The lineup included former students Lavin and Danny Kalb, peers Paxton and Richie Havens, and the later crowd like Christian, Massengill, Vega (who had long since made up with Van Ronk), Jack Hardy, and Terre Roche, who finally had a chance to sing "Garden State Stomp." Tragically, Hardy's younger brother Jeff, who had played bass with him and so many others on the scene, had died in the World Trade Center on September 11; Jeff Hardy was working as an executive chef at Cantor Fitzgerald at the time.

Much like the scene itself, the club, which had drawn countless music lovers to the Village for nearly thirty years, was reeling. It had taken a hit starting in the eighties, when co-owners Allan Pepper and Stanley Snadowsky had stuck with their all-seated policy. Their 1979 Christmas card featured a photo of

Pepper and Snadowsky dressed in drag and selling ten-cents-a-dance tickets to sailors: "We always wanted to be a dance club," read the card, followed by "Seasons greetings from the club with the chairs." But thanks to that strategy, the club missed out on booking rap, dance music, and new-wave bands. Those acts opted for the nearby Ritz, on the other side of Broadway.

The Bottom Line also hosted the last-ever performance by the original Blues Project, which had played several reunion shows there starting in the early nineties. In 1994 the quintet came together again as part of a series of concerts for Al Kooper's fiftieth birthday. Before the show even began, Kooper and Steve Katz, who had been frosty toward each other since the days of Blood, Sweat & Tears, had yet another falling-out. Planning to film and record the shows, Kooper presented all the musicians with a consent form right before the sets, which infuriated Katz, who declined to sign. The shows went on, with Kalb summoning up his old command for a reprise of "Two Trains Running." But afterward, Kooper was forced to remove Katz's guitar and harmonica from the recordings and hire another musician to replace those parts on the eventual album. Katz and Kalb, and also Kooper and Kalb, would join forces onstage in the years after, but the band's most beloved lineup would never again find itself on the same stage.

Soon after the Van Ronk tribute show, the Bottom Line's financial crisis started coming to a disheartening conclusion. By then, Pepper and Snadowsky were behind in the club's rent by $185,000. For a while, they were able to pay a portion of that monthly nut of $12,500. But even with Bruce Springsteen and SiriusXM contributing cash to rescue the venue, the unpaid part of the club's debt was beginning to snowball. New York University, which owned the building, offered to preserve the Bottom Line but at market rate, roughly double its rent. According to Pepper, NYU also wanted the club to pay for an upgrade, including the removal of its outside marquee to make the front of the building architecturally consistent with the rest of the street. Pepper and Snadowsky claimed that the combined renovations would cost them $1.5 million for a building they didn't own; NYU maintained the club wasn't up to code and that the owners were ignoring the university's proposals. In December 2003 a civil court judge ordered the club's eviction over unpaid rent.

Weeks short of its thirtieth anniversary, as Pepper and Snadowsky were working on a tribute show that would feature many acts that had played there, talks collapsed. Pepper and Snadowsky decided they had no alternative but to walk away, and on January 22, 2004, the Bottom Line joined the list of venue casualties in the neighborhood. Pepper handed over the keys to a representative for the university and watched as a locksmith made sure that neither he nor any of his employees could walk back in again. At least one musician, David Johansen, came by to pay his respects. The club's final show, weeks before the closing, turned out to be a tribute to Woody Guthrie. More than sixty years had passed since Guthrie had arrived in the city, writing "This Land Is Your Land" as soon as he was there and eventually joining the Almanac Singers. Unintentionally, the tribute now had the feeling of a world that had come full circle—an old-world folk bookend for a scene that was now endangered.

Two years later, CBGB followed suit, then Kenny's Castaways. In 2002 founder and owner Pat Kenny died from prostate cancer, which he'd been privately battling for a decade; his children ran the club until rent increases forced them out a decade later. In the end, only a few of the storied clubs—the Village Vanguard, the Bitter End, and the Cafe Wha?, which had reopened in 1988 with new owners—would persevere; the Village Gate had become a new music outlet, Le Poisson Rouge, later LPR.

The vanquished venues, and others before and after, were brought down by money and valuable real estate, which had bedeviled the Village music world for decades. But those weren't the only factors. Perhaps the evisceration of the scene was inevitable. Thriving music scenes in cities and towns burned bright and blared loudly for certain periods, then quieted down: such was the case with San Francisco in the sixties; Athens, Georgia, and Hollywood's Sunset Strip in the eighties; Seattle in the eighties and nineties. If anything, the Village had held on longer than any of them—a decades-long run that defied the odds and fought for its life every step of the way.

Then there was the matter of music itself. With the new century came a shift from the vernacular-based genres linked to the Village, like folk and blues, toward genres rooted in rhythm, beats, samples, and tech. It was equally valid music for a different time, but the Village couldn't keep up or seemed uninterested in doing so. Maybe, too, there was something symbolic about the iPod launching in the fall of 2001, the same season Van Ronk started his cancer treatment. Generational debates would ensue as to whether streaming and the abundance of online music made the art form *less* vital in the culture, or if those raised on music in the new century were consuming and absorbing it in different but equally meaningful ways. But no one doubted that songs and albums were now fighting for attention with so much else, and the way the Village had specialized in genres of music that demanded complete and utter immersion also felt like a ritual from another time and place.

Given how long it had persevered and how much it still loomed over the scene, the end of the Bottom Line felt hugely symbolic. But a heartening coda played out five months later. Shortly after Van Ronk's death, Eve Silber, a singer and musician who lived in the Village and had been one of his guitar students, felt that his contributions to the neighborhood needed to be honored and had an idea for a special dedication. Owing to administrative delays that had lingered after the city had shut down after the September 11 attacks, the ceremony would be delayed two years.

Finally, on what would have been Van Ronk's sixty-eighth birthday—June 30, 2004—several dozen of his friends and colleagues gathered at the corner of Washington Place, Sheridan Square and Barrow Street, right outside his apartment building. As with his memorials, the group ran the gamut from his earliest Village colleagues (Danny Kalb, Tom Paxton, Oscar Brand, Odetta, Suze Rotolo, Happy and Jane Traum) to later ones and students (David Massengill, Frank Christian, Elijah Wald). There were reunions, laughs, and a group shot modeled on the classic "Great Day in Harlem" photo that had brought together a group of iconic jazz musicians decades before.

At the appointed time, Vuocolo and Paxton tugged on a string that pulled off a covering and revealed a sign—for Dave Van Ronk Street. Dave Van Ronk Way and Dave Van Ronk Road had been considered, but Silber decided it should also be a nod to "Sunday Street," one of his best-known original songs. No matter what came next in the neighborhood, Van Ronk would be there in spirit, welcoming whoever would follow.

acknowledgments

Although I'd first considered writing this book many years ago, it took one article to revive the idea. In the spring of 2020, my bosses at *Rolling Stone*, ever tolerant and supportive of my love of an off-the-grid story, allowed me to chronicle the life and times of the late singer-songwriter David Blue. Working on that story reminded me of all the mythical—in some cases, deceased—musicians who'd found their way to Greenwich Village over the decades. Combined with expeditions back into the neighborhood, where I was reminded how few live-music venues remained there by 2019, the idea of a Village music-history book made a comeback tour in my brain. Thanks to Ben Schafer at Hachette Books for immediately supporting the idea and my agent, Erin Hosier at Dunow, Carlson and Lerner, for working her usual magic on making sure the project proceeded.

Of those who generously gave of their time and allowed me to pepper them with questions about their experiences, lives, and work in the Village, I offer a sustained round of applause, in alphabetical order, to Peter Aaron, Steve Addabbo, Bruce Alterman, David Amram, Eric Andersen, Lili Añel, Joan Baez, Danny and Steven Bensusan, John Berenzy, Roy Blumenfeld, David Bromberg, Denny Brown, Peppy Castro, Chevy Chase, Shawn Colvin, John Conley, Mort Cooperman, James Cromwell, Peter Cunningham, Mark Dann, Christina Mitchell Diamente, Dennis Diken, Donna Diken, Delores Dixon, Sharon D'Lugoff, Bonnie Dobson, Dan Drasin, Peggy Duncan-Garner, Noam Dworman, Eric Eisner, Ramblin' Jack Elliott, Ron Fierstein, Steve Forbert, Erik Frandsen, Robert Fripp, Jim Glover, Debbie Goodman, Deborah Gordon, Arthur Gorson, Kate Greenfield, Mitch Greenhill, Christopher Guest, Arlo Guthrie, John Hammond, Herbie Hancock, Carolyn Hester, Michael Hill, Robin Hirsch, Kristian Hoffman, David Hood, Phil Hurtt, Janis Ian, Pat

Irwin, Erik Jacobsen, Billy James, Nancy Jeffries, David Johansen, Sheila Jordan, the late Danny Kalb, Jonathan Kalb, Lucy Kaplansky, Lucy Brown Karwoski, Steve Katz, Lenny Kaye, Maria Kenny, Aaron Kilberg, Carol Klenfner, Peter Kogan, Al Kooper, Barry Kornfeld, D. C. LaRue, Joe Lauro, Christine Lavin, Lowell Levinger, Arthur Levy, Rod MacDonald, Carolyne Mas, David Massengill, Paul Mills, Julia Ann Mitchell-Conley, Phillip Namanworth, Willie Nile, Sonny Ochs, Angela Page, Hap Pardo, Tom Paxton, Allan Pepper, Binky Philips, Jack Prelutsky, Roger Probert, Ron Radosh, Paul Rizzo, Susan Martin Robbins, Sonny Rollins, Suzzy Roche, Terre Roche, Brian Rose, Jay Rosen, Arlen Roth, Bridget St. John, Cristy St. John, Buffy Sainte-Marie, Paul Samwell-Smith, John Sebastian, Mark Sebastian, Eve Silber, Marc Silber, Larry Sloman, Jason Solomon, Peter Stampfel, Rob Stoner, Noel Paul Stookey, Steve Swallow, Michael Tannen, Jon Taplin, Terri Thal, Catherine Todd, Happy and Jane Traum, Lisi Tribble, Sylvia Tyson, Suzanne Vega, Vincent T. Vok, Andrea Vuocolo, Loudon Wainwright III, Elijah Wald, Dick Weissman, Jonathan Williams, Robbie Woliver, Douglas Yeager, Eve Young, Jesse Colin Young, and Tim Ziegler.

Several people deserve additional shout-outs. Thank you to Terre and Suzzy Roche for their time and insights. Andrea Vuocolo not only generously shared memories of her life with her late husband Dave Van Ronk but allowed me to sift through some of his papers and sit on the same part of the couch in their Village apartment where Dave always plopped down. Jonathan Kalb not only spoke of his memories of playing with the Fugs and so many others in the Village but also arranged for me to interview his brother Danny, with whom I spoke about a year before he passed away in 2022. (Jonathan is still a keeper of the blues flame, and his own performances are highly recommended.)

As I was constantly being reminded, history was being erased even while I was at work on this project. During those four years, we lost not only Danny Kalb but also Ian Tyson, Len Chandler, Bob Neuwirth, Alix Dobkin, Roger Sprung, Patrick Sky, Bill Lee, the Night Owl's Joe Marra, the Cafe Au Go Go's Ella Solomon, temporary Blues Project member Emmaretta Marks, and preeminent folk scholar Ronald Cohen—a list that will surely, sadly, grow in the years ahead. I was able to speak with some of those players before they passed, others not. I was fortunate to interview Maggie Roche in 2009, eight years before she passed away from breast cancer, and a few of her recollections of her early days in the Village are included here.

A huge archival tip of the hat to the legendary Mitch Blank, who tolerated my numerous visits to his home archive with its awe-inspiring documentation on all things Dylan and Village. Mitch also allowed me to quote from his vintage interview with Danny Kalb. With help from Mitch, Paul Lovelace shared with me interview footage of Izzy Young, Art D'Lugoff, and WBAI's Bob Fass. Philomène Grandin graciously allowed me to quote from some of the writings of her father, Izzy Young.

Bob Porco talked with me about his memories of his late grandfather Mike and the early days of Gerde's Folk City, even that mysterious apostrophe. Thanks to Andre Marcell for allowing me to quote from his late, legendary uncle Joe Marra's notes on his club, the Night Owl. Teddy Lee granted me access to his wealth of photos from Folk City in the eighties, which rekindled many of my own memories of that period and club. Aviva Frankel generously gave us permission to use a few photos from her late uncle Irwin Gooen's historic photography of Gerde's Folk City and the early Village.

For helping me connect with sources and pointing me in any number of right directions, all due respect to Eric Alpert, Judd Apatow, Paula Batson, Andrew Berman of Village Preservation, Amy Blume, Angie Carlson, Jayni Chase, David Cooperman, Jim Della Croce, Jesse Cutler, Katherine DePaul, Erick Feucht, Parker Fishel, Raymond Foye, Michelle Garramone, Noah Gest, Erica Glenn, Benny Goodman, Matt Hanks, Jennifer Harrington, Mara Hennessey, Terri Hinte, Gary Jacobson, Larry Jenkins, Lisa Jenkins, Michael Jensen, Carol Kaye, Alisse Kingsley, Venta Leon, Nick Loss-Eaton, Meredith Louie, Mark McKenna, Aiyana Partland, Susan Patricola, Roger Paul, Mark Pucci, Gaynell Rogers, Jeff Rosen, Lee Rothchild, Carol Rothman, Elaine Schock, Steve Schweidel, Victoire Selce, Johanna Shapiro, David Singleton, Mark Spector, Michael Steiner, Elizabeth Stookey Sunde, Virginia Tate,

Britnee Walker, Ken Weinstein, Judy Werle, Kathleen Whaley, and Howard Wuelfing.

A hootenanny-style shout-along to the fellow journalists and authors who allowed me to pick their brains no matter the Village era or genre of music. David Hajdu shared transcripts of his interviews with many Village luminaries, including the Mary Travers and Sam Charters quotations included here. Jesse Jarnow passed along his astoundingly detailed chronology of the Almanac Singers and the Weavers as well as the FBI's extensive file on Fred Hellerman, which he'd received while researching his definitive Weavers biography, *Wasn't That a Time.* Aaron J. Leonard did the same with Dave Van Ronk's FBI paperwork as I awaited my own FOIA request. (Aaron's books on government oversight of music, particularly *The Folk Singers and the Bureau* and *Whole World in an Uproar,* are worth seeking out.)

Doug Silver offered his astute analyses of chord and harmonic progressions, musical notation, and other detailed matters that enhanced my own understanding of this music. Hank Shteamer, Gary Giddins, and Dan Ouellette made sure I was on solid jazz ground. Jim Farber, David Hinckley, Ira Mayer, and John Rockwell allowed me to dig into their Village-beat brains. Belated gratitude to Helen Epstein, who, as one of my journalism professors at NYU, signed off on my idea to cover the Village music scene for our magazine-writing class. Thanks also to Richard Barone, Nick Canfield, Deirdre Cossman, Patrick Doyle, Fred Goodman, Andy Greene, Kory Grow, Joseph Hudak, Karen Kramer, Barbara Landreth, Jeff Place, Steve Schwartz, Sean Wilentz, and Dave Zimmer for advice, tips, and suggestions.

Scott Barretta shared memories of Izzy Young. Liz Thomson did the same about working with the late Robert Shelton. She and Cliff Pearson are doing their own formidable part to honor the neighborhood's history with their annual Village Trip festival. Olympia Kazi was a valuable resource for cabaret-law history in the city.

Few are as dedicated to chronicling day-by-day, week-by-week histories of classic venues and bands as Corry Arnold, and his detailed Cafe Au Go Go time line (https://rockprosopography101.blogspot.com/2010/01/cafe-au

-go-go-new-york-city-152.html) was essential reading. Bruno Ceriotti's nearly week-by-week reconstruction of the Blues Project (one of many such music archaeology digs on his site, http://brunoceriotti.weebly.com) is second to none. George Vellonakis made sure I had my facts straight about the life and times (and roadways) of Washington Square Park, and John Sorenson's walking tour of the park brought the past back to life in so many ways.

Michele Romero, who knows her way around photo archives like no one else, applied her formidable research skills to the images you see here. Mark Davidson of the Bob Dylan Center handled numerous queries with diligence and grace. Joe Lauro at Historic Films allowed me access to his incredible treasure trove of archival clips, especially his own footage of interviews and performances from the early-eighties Village folk scene. (Note to Joe: Finish that doc.) Thank you as well to Kevin Rice at Historic Films for making it technically possible for me to view it all.

Kathy Heintzelman, not only a friend but also one of the best editors with whom I've ever worked, untangled sentences, corrected glitches in grammar, and simply made this a better book than it would have been before she dove in.

Elijah Wald, Dan Katz, and Stephen Petrus gave of their time to read through an early draft of the book, offering pointed insights and corrections along the way. Needless to say, *The Mayor of MacDougal Street*, the Van Ronk memoir that Elijah completed after Van Ronk's passing, is as vivid a firsthand recollection as you'll ever read about the late-fifties and early-sixties Village. Dan's deep-seated understanding of New York and American history, labor issues, and race relations—as revealed in his book *All Together Different: Yiddish Socialists, Garment Workers, and the Labor Roots of Multiculturalism*— added to my understanding of the outside-music forces at work in the Village. Stephen and the late Ronald D. Cohen's *Folk City: New York and the American Folk Music Revival* should be on the reading list of anyone interested in the Village's contribution to music history.

Brenna Ehrlich helped me navigate the byzantine world of New York City court records and pointed me in valuable research directions I wouldn't have considered. Andy Abrahams and his diligent fact-checking saved me more than a few times. Lily Marks assisted with transcribing and, more importantly, on-the-ground research in the New York City archives. I thank them all for their help in what was, for me, an often-overwhelming project.

At the NYC Department of Records and Information, Kenneth Cobb, Marcia Kirk, and Katie Ehrlich sent me to the right microfilm drawers and files and navigated permissions paperwork with patience and professionalism. Janet M. Bunde at New York University guided me through the school's massive archives. Katie Morrison at the Indiana University Archives allowed me access to the school's invaluable Richard A. Reuss collection. Many thanks as well to Jessica Gavilan at the New York Public Library for the Performing Arts; Aaron Smithers at the Wilson Special Collections Library, University of North Carolina at Chapel Hill; Jonny Verbeten and Weston Marshall at the Southwest Music Archive, Southwest Collection/Special Collections Library, at Texas Tech University; Maya Lerman, Judith Gray, and Allina Migoni at the American Folklife Center at the Library of Congress; Kate Long at Smith College; Jonathan Kuhn of the New York Parks Department; Joe Marvilli at the NYC Department of City Planning; Joseph Jourdan at the NYC Department of Small Business Services; and the Business Department of the New York County Clerk.

An old-school five-star shoutout to my bosses at *Rolling Stone* throughout this process—Jason Fine, Sean Woods, Christian Hoard, and Noah Shachtman—for their support and allowing me some time off to work on this book. Also at Hachette Books, thank you to David Shelley and Michael Pietsch for signing off on this book and the encouraging words as I was completing it. As always, it's a pleasure working with the Hachette crew, including Michelle Aielli, Ashley Kiedrowski, Mary Ann Naples, Michael Giarratano, Carrie Napolitano, Fred Francis, Amanda Kain, and Terri Sirma. Thanks too to Donald Pharr for the sharp-eyed copyedit.

As always, none of this would have been conceivable or possible without my wife, Maggie, and our daughter, Maeve. In so many ways, Maggie was there from the start, including with this book: we met while we were both at NYU;

she accompanied me to shows at the Bottom Line, Speak Easy, the Village Gate, and Folk City; we lived together in the Village for years; and she probably knew I was going to write this book someday. During this project, Maeve joined me at a jazz club in the Village and a Suzanne Vega concert, where she recognized "Tom's Diner" and, in doing so, confirmed what a classic it had become. With any luck and changes in New York City, she'll venture back down to that neighborhood someday to take in the next generation of singers, songwriters, and musicians.

source notes and bibliography

This book is based on more than 150 primary-source interviews largely conducted between 2021 and 2024, along with several file-cabinet drawers' worth of archival documents and articles in the bibliography that follows.

Quotations that are unattributed come from my own interviews. I also delved into my files for related reporting I did between 1981 and the present for *Rolling Stone*, the New York *Daily News*, *Music & Sound Output*, and my long-ago New York University magazine journalism class (the article later printed in the late, lamented NYU *Courier*). Those include older interviews with Joseph Zbeda (1981), the Song Project (1981), Suzanne Vega (1984, plus 2021–23), Ian Tyson (1987), Allan Pepper and Stanley Snadowsky (1989), Lucinda Williams (2015), Peter Yarrow (2009), Bruce Langhorne (2015), and Ramblin' Jack Elliott (2019, plus 2022).

The archives of the *New York Times*, the New York *Daily News*, the *Village Voice*, the *Villager*, the *New York Post*, and other, now-defunct publications were accessed online or by way of the New York Public Library. The Village preservation.org site is an exemplary resource for anyone interested in all things historical on the neighborhood.

BOOKS

Ballon, Hilary, and Kenneth T. Jackson, eds. *Robert Moses and the Modern City: The Transformation of New York*. W.W. Norton, 2007.

Barone, Richard. *Music + Revolution: Greenwich Village in the 1960s*. Backbeat, 2022.

Barretta, Scott, ed. *The Conscience of the Folk Revival: The Writings of Israel "Izzy" Young*. Scarecrow, 2012.

Boone, Steve, and Tony Moss. *Hotter Than a Matchhead: Life on the Run with the Lovin' Spoonful*. ECW, 2014.

Carlin, Richard. *Worlds of Sound: The Story of Smithsonian Folkways*. Smithsonian Books, 2008.

Caro, Robert A. *The Power Broker: Robert Moses and the Fall of New York*. Random House, 1974.

Carter, David. *Stonewall: The Riots That Sparked the Gay Revolution*. St. Martin's, 2004.

Chevigny, Paul. *Gigs: Jazz and the Cabaret Laws in New York City*, 2nd ed. Routledge, 2005.

Cockrell, Dale. *Everybody's Doin' It: Sex, Music and Dance in New York, 1840–1917*. W.W. Norton, 2019.

Cohen, Ronald D. *Rainbow Quest: The Folk Music Revival & American Society 1940–1970*. University of Massachusetts Press, 2002.

Colby, Paul, with Martin Fitzpatrick. *The Bitter End: Hanging Out at America's Nightclub*. Cooper Square, 2002.

Collins, Judy. *Sweet Judy Blue Eyes: My Life in Music*. Crown, 2011.

Cooper, Ry. *From the Folk Bag*. Oak, 1966.

Cross, Charles R. *Room Full of Mirrors: A Biography of Jimi Hendrix*. Hyperion, 2005.

Dobkin, Alex. *My Red Blood*. Alyson, 2009.

Dunaway, David. *How Can I Keep from Singing: Pete Seeger*. Da Capo, 1990.

Dylan, Bob. *Chronicles Volume One*. Simon & Schuster, 2004.

Einarson, John. *Four Strong Winds: Ian and Sylvia*. McClelland & Stewart, 2011.

Eliot, Marc. *Death of a Rebel: A Biography of Phil Ochs*. Franklin Watts, 1989.

Forbert, Steve, with Therese Boyd. *Big City Cat: My Life in Folk-Rock*. PFP, 2018.

Giddins, Gary, and Scott DeVeaux. *Jazz*. Norton, 2009.

Gordon, Max. *Live at the Village Vanguard*. St. Martin's, 1980.

Grandin, Philomène. *Don't Forget Me*. Scribner, 2022.

Greenhill, Mitch. *Raised by Musical Mavericks*. Hillgreen, 2019.

Hajdu, David. *Positively 4th Street*. Farrar, Straus and Giroux, 2001.

Hancock, Herbie, with Lisa Dickey. *Herbie Hancock: Possibilities*. Viking, 2014.

Havens, Richie, with Steve Davidowitz. *They Can't Hide Us Anymore*. Spike, 1999.

Heylin, Clinton. *The Double Life of Bob Dylan*. Little, Brown, 2021.

Holzman, Jac, and Gavan Daws. *Follow the Music: The Life and High Times of Elektra Records in the Great Years of American Pop Culture*. First Media, 1998.

Hortis, C. Alexander. *The Mob and the City: The Hidden History of How the Mafia Captured New York*. Prometheus, 2020.

Jarnow, Jesse, *Wasn't That a Time: The Weavers, the Blacklist and the Battle for the Soul of America*. Da Capo, 2018.

Johnson, Ellen, *Jazz Child: A Portrait of Sheila Jordan*. Rowman & Littlefield, 2014.

Katz, Steve. *Blood, Sweat and My Rock 'n' Roll Years*. Lyons, 2015.

Kelley, Robin D. G. *Thelonious Monk: The Life and Times of an American Original*. Free Press, 2009.

Klein, Joe. *Woody Guthrie: A Life*. Knopf, 1980.

Kooper, Al. *Backstage Passes & Backstabbing Bastards: Memoirs of a Rock 'n' Roll Survivor*. Hal Leonard, 2008.

Lavin, Christine. *Cold Pizza for Breakfast: A Mem-Wha??* Tell Me, 2010.

Lawrence, Tim. *Love Saves the Day: A History of American Dance Music Culture, 1970–1979.* Duke University Press, 2003.

Levy, Aidan. *Saxophone Colossus: The Life and Music of Sonny Rollins.* Hachette, 2022.

Neff, Peter Lee. *That's the Bag I'm In: The Life, Music and Mystery of Fred Neil.* Blue Ceiling, 2019.

Nisenson, Eric. *Open Sky: Sonny Rollins and His World of Improvisation.* St. Martin's, 2000.

Ouellette, Dan. *Ron Carter: Finding the Right Notes.* ArtistShare, 2008.

Pertz, Timothy Josiah Morris. *The Jewgrass Boys: Bluegrass Music's Emergence in New York City's Washington Square Park, 1946–1961.* Harvard University, 2004.

Petrus, Stephen, and Ronald D. Cohen. *Folk City: New York and the American Folk Music Revival.* Oxford University Press, 2015.

Pollock, Bruce. *The Bleecker Street Tapes: Echoes of Greenwich Village.* Trouser, 2023.

Reaven, Marci, and Steve Zeitlin. *Hidden New York: A Guide to Places That Matter.* Rivergate, 2006.

Roby, Steven, and Brad Schreiber. *Becoming Jimi Hendrix.* Da Capo, 2010.

Roche, Terre. *Blabbermouth.* Self-published, 2013.

Rotolo, Suze. *A Freewheelin' Time: A Memoir of Greenwich Village in the Sixties.* Broadway, 2008.

Roxon, Lillian. *Lillian Roxon's Rock Encyclopedia.* Grosset & Dunlap, 1971.

Santoro, Gene. *Myself When I Am Real: The Life and Music of Charles Mingus.* Oxford University Press, 2000.

Scaduto, Anthony. *Dylan.* Signet, 1973.

Scaduto, Anthony. *The Dylan Tapes.* University of Minnesota Press, 2022.

Shelton, Robert. *No Direction Home: The Life & Music of Bob Dylan*, revised and updated by Elizabeth Thomson and Patrick Humphries. Omnibus, 2011.

Strausbaugh, John. *The Village: A History of Greenwich Village.* Ecco, 2013.

Thal, Terri. *My Greenwich Village: Dave, Bob and Me.* McNidder and Grace, 2023.

Van Ronk, Dave, with Elijah Wald. *The Mayor of MacDougal Street: A Memoir.* Da Capo, 2005.

The Village Voice Map & Guide to Greenwich Village and the East Village. Village Voice, 1969.

Wainwright, Loudon III. *Liner Notes.* Blue Rider, 2017.

Ward, Geoffrey C., and Ken Burns. *Jazz: A History of America's Music.* Knopf, 2005.

Warner, Andrea. *Buffy Sainte-Marie: The Authorized Biography.* Greystone, 2021.

Wetzsteon, Ross. *Republic of Dreams: Greenwich Village, the American Bohemia, 1910–1960.* Simon & Schuster, 2002.

Wolfe, Charles, and Kip Lornell. *The Life & Legend of Leadbelly.* HarperCollins, 1992.

Woliver, Robbie. *Bringing It All Back Home.* Pantheon, 1986.

Woodward, Bob. *Wired.* Simon and Schuster, 1984.

NEWSPAPER, MAGAZINE, AND ONLINE ARTICLES

CHAPTER ONE: 1957

Author interviews: David Amram, Ramblin' Jack Elliott, Aaron Kilberg, Barry Kornfeld, Christine Lavin, Bob Porco, Jack Prelutsky, Sonny Rollins, Peter Stampfel, Terri Thal, Happy Traum, Elijah Wald.

Asbury, Edith Evans. "Slum Fight Boils in Washington Sq." *New York Times*, January 29, 1954.

Bennett, Charles G. "2-Lane Roadway in 'Village' Gains." *New York Times*, July 17, 1958.

"Could Sing and Dance." *Brooklyn Daily Eagle*, August 2, 1891.

Fine, Arnold. "A Fight for Survival—New York Coffeehouses." *Brooklyn Daily*, November 17, 1961.

Freeman, Ira Henry. "New Projects Will Change the Fact—and the Character—of the Washington Square Area." *New York Times*, December 8, 1957.

Gatewood, Worth. "Bulldozers in Bohemia." *Daily News*, February 14, 1954.

Grutzner, Charles. "NYU Wins Right to Evict Tenants." *New York Times*, December 31, 1957.

Grutzner, Charles. "Six-Block Project to Rise in Village." *New York Times*, July 15, 1957.

Hoefer, George. "Cafe Society Downtown and Uptown—The Wrong Place for the Right People." *DownBeat '67, 12th Yearbook*, 1967.

"Home Ownership Up, Census Report Shows." *Spokesman-Review* (Spokane, WA), April 14, 1957.

Kelly, Frank A. "Art of Minstrelsy Lives Again in Cellar." World Wide News (syndicated), September 24, 1942.

Kornfeld, Barry. "Folksinging in Washington Square." *Caravan* 18 (August-September, 1959).

Les. "Stardust Beat." *New York Age*, November 23, 1957.

"Letters to the Times." *New York Times*, October 22, 1953.

"Local Laws of the City of New York." Municipal Reference Library, New York, 1931.

McGlinchy, James. "Bumps in Bohemia: Village Suffering a Split Personality." New York *Daily News*, April 16, 1954.

"Minstrel Using a Washtub Bass." *New York Times*, May 16, 1955.

"One Liquor Seller to Jail." *New York Times*, November 2, 1919.

Pegler, Westbrook. "H-T Gives Free Plug to Cafe Society." *Knoxville (TN) Journal*, June 14, 1948.

"Report on the Committee of Local Laws in Favor of Adjusting a Local Law to Regulate Dance Halls and Cabarets and Providing for Licensing the Same." Municipal Assembly of the City of New York, 1926.

Runyon, Damon. "The Brighter Side." New York *Daily Mirror*, June 22, 1939.

Stolls, Jerry. "Folk Songs Go Round and Round at 'Circle.'" New York *Daily News*, September 1, 1957.

Sullivan, Robert. "20 Years in a Cellar." New York *Daily News*, December 5, 1954.

Trent, George. "'Kentucky Ballads' Are Laying the Sophisticated in the Aisles." *Courier-Journal* (Louisville, KY), April 11, 1948.

"Washington Square Plan Wins." *New York Times*, May 11, 1935.

Wilcock, John. "Music-Makers Quit the Scene (but Only for the Wintertime)." *Village Voice*, October 26, 1955.

"Work Starts Soon on Washington Square." *New York Times*, October 3, 1939.

Zapol, Lisa. "David Amram—Oral History Interview." Greenwich Village Society for Historic Preservation, 2014.

CHAPTER TWO: 1958–1960

Author interviews: Judy Collins, John Conley, Christina Mitchell Diamente, Delores Dixon, Sharon D'Lugoff, Ramblin' Jack Elliott, Carolyn Hester, Erik Jacobsen, Sheila Jordan, Danny Kalb, Jonathan Kalb, Steve Katz, Barry Kornfeld, Julia Ann Mitchell-Conley, Tom Paxton, Peter Stampfel, Noel Paul Stookey, Steve Swallow, Terri Thal, Happy Traum, Dick Weissman, Tim Ziegler.

Alden, Robert. "'Village' Tension Upsets Residents." *New York Times*, September 29, 1959.
"Around Town." New York *Daily News*, November 1, 1959.
"Beatnik Café Sues in 'Hazard' Closing." *New York Times*, June 25, 1960.
Bennett, Charles G. "Washington Square Traffic to Halt While Road Issue Is Decided." *New York Times*, October 4, 1958.
"Cabaret Bureau Hit; Action Against Village Gate Put Off." *Village Voice*, October 27, 1960.
Davis, Francis. "Ornette's Permanent Revolution." *Atlantic*, September 1985.
Duncan, Val. "What Is the Beat Generation?" *Newsday*, August 5, 1959.
"50 Speak Up on Park Road, 39 to Say No." New York *Daily News*, May 15, 1958.
"4 Coffee Shops Are Guilty of Entertainment." New York *Daily News*, October 15, 1960.
Frishberg, Dave. "How History Almost Happened at the Page Three." artsjournal.com, 2006.
Gelb, Arthur. "Voice of the Beatnik Is Stilled in the 'Village.'" *New York Times*, October 20, 1960.
Goddard, J. R. "Van Ronk Fills Minetta with Passionate Wail." *Village Voice*, August 4, 1960.
Isaacs, Stan. "Meet the Impresario of Off-Beat Talent." *Newsday*, January 31, 1962.
Kenny, Jack. "Modern Eve Adams Driven from Eden." New York *Daily News*, December 7, 1927.
Klein, Edward. "The Beat Generation in the Village." New York *Daily News*, February 19, 1958.
Klein, Edward. "So This Is Liberty?" New York *Daily News*, October 18, 1959.
Knowles, Clayton. "Moses Hints at Advance to Rear in Battle of Washington Square." *New York Times*, May 19, 1958.
Laarhoven, Kasper Van. "The Story of the Gaslight Cafe." bedfordandbowery.com, December 28, 2016.
Millstein, Gilbert. "New Battle of Our Washington Square." *New York Times Magazine*, May 4, 1958.
"OPA Court Orders Hit 65 Restaurants." *New York Times*, October 21, 1944.
"Planners Urge 36-Foot Road for Washington Square." New York *Daily News*, October 22, 1958.
"Queer Doings Net Suspension for Vill. Clubs." *Billboard*, November 25, 1944.
Savage, Tom. "On Broadway Adventures." *Tuskegee (AL) Herald*, December 18, 1956.
Sharbutt, Jay. "'Good Joint in the (Greenwich) Village' Is Now a Hallmark." Associated Press, December 7, 1980.
Shelton, Robert. "Folk Music Makes Mark on City's Night Life." *New York Times*, November 17, 1960.

Shelton, Robert. "Folk-Song and Singers." *New York Times*, October 12, 1958.

Solomon, Linda. "New York on a Shoestring." *Kings Courier* (Brooklyn, NY), December 3, 1960.

Stearn, Jess. "Coffee Brews Up Some Rare Beans." New York *Daily News*, March 8, 1959.

Stearn, Jess. "The V Girl Boom." New York *Daily News*, November 14, 1954.

Sylvester, Robert. "Dream Street." New York *Daily News*, March 6, 1958.

Talese, Gay. "Court Backs Bach with Café Au Lait." *New York Times*, October 23, 1959.

"Tension Boils Up in Square, but Major Riot Averted." *Village Voice*, July 28, 1960.

Wetzig, Mina. "Beatniks vs. Copniks." New York *Daily News*, June 28, 1959.

Wilson, John S. "Extremes of Jazz Meet Nightly in 'Village.'" *New York Times*, November 3, 1960.

CHAPTER THREE: 1961–1962

Author interviews: Judy Collins, Delores Dixon, Bonnie Dobson, Daniel Drasin, Ramblin' Jack Elliott, Carolyn Hester, Erik Jacobsen, Billy James, Danny Kalb, Steve Katz, Barry Kornfeld, Tom Paxton, Ron Radosh, Marc Silber, Peter Stampfel, Noel Paul Stookey, Steve Swallow, Terri Thal, Happy Traum, Dick Weissman, Peter Yarrow.

"Art D'Lugoff." NYPR Archive Collections, WNYC, March 6, 1960.

Benjamin, Philip. "Mayor Backs Ban on Park Singing." *New York Times*, April 12, 1961.

Cassidy, Joseph, and Jack Smee. "Park Songfest in Village Boils into Slugfest." New York *Daily News*, April 10, 1961.

Clendenin, Michael. "Gaslight Boss in Row with Cop, Jailed." New York *Daily News*, April 29, 1961.

"Coffee Shop Man Charges Cops Milked Him." New York *Daily News*, February 8, 1962.

"Elektra's 15th Anny: From Dormitory to Big Share of Indie Dollar." *Cashbox*, January 18, 1966.

Federici, William. "Coffee House Issue Is Poured into Magistrate's Percolator." New York *Daily News*, April 13, 1961.

Federici, William, and Sidney Kline. "Coffee House Quiz Sizzles with a Lot of Self-Expresso." New York *Daily News*, August 8, 1961.

"Gaslight Cafe Beats Fire-Law Violation by a Technicality." *New York Times*, March 10, 1961.

Hofman, Paul. "Folk Singers Riot in Washington Square." *New York Times*, April 10, 1961.

Kleiner, Dick. "Two Bears, Gal—Road to Stardom." *Sunday Home News* (New Brunswick, NJ), July 22, 1962.

"Making the Village Scene." *New York Times*, February 12, 1961.

Nelsen, Don. "Special Trane Pulls into VV." New York *Daily News*, October 29, 1961.

"Police Probe Café Owner's Bribe Charge." New York *Daily News*, April 6, 1961.

"Resolution to Investigate Certain Statements Allegedly Made by Policemen in Regard to Negroes Patronizing Night Clubs in Greenwich Village." Council of the City of New York Collection, 1961, box 052723, LaGuardia and Wagner Archives, LaGuardia Community College, New York City.

"Revolt in Washington Square." *New York Times*, April 11, 1961.

Richards, Steve. "Two Cops Face Charges of Bribery in Village." New York *Daily News*, May 28, 1961.
Robertson, Nan. "Folk-Song Rally Mocks Parks Ban." *New York Times*, April 24, 1961.
"South Village Historic District Designation Report." NYC Landmarks Preservation Commission, December 17, 2013.
"Truce Plan Works a Second Sunday in Washington Square." *New York Times*, May 22, 1961.

CHAPTER FOUR: 1963–1964

Author interviews: Eric Andersen, Joan Baez, Judy Collins, James Cromwell, Ramblin' Jack Elliott, Jim Glover, Arlo Guthrie, Herbie Hancock, Danny Kalb, Barry Kornfeld, Bruce Langhorne, Sonny Ochs, Tom Paxton, Susan Martin Robbins, Buffy Sainte-Marie, John Sebastian, Peter Stampfel, Noel Paul Stookey, Happy Traum, Ian Tyson, Sylvia Tyson.

Abramson, Martin. "'Sonic Boom' Fading in Folk Music." Memphis *Commercial-Appeal*, August 24, 1964.
"Anti-Beatnik, 73, Kills Owner of Coffee Shop." New York *Daily News*, April 1, 1963.
Asbury, Edith Evans. "Greenwich Village Argues New Way of Life." *New York Times*, August 4, 1963.
"City Cracks Down on Coffeehouses." *New York Times*, November 3, 1964.
Gansberg, Martin. "15 'Village' Shops Ordered to Close." *New York Times*, March 25, 1964.
Henshaw, Tom. "Folk Singing Sweeps Land." Associated Press, November 17, 1963.
Iachetta, Michael. "Music with a Message." New York *Daily News*, October 20, 1963.
Kirk, Christina. "Strings Are the Thing." New York *Daily News*, April 19, 1964.
Krebs, Albin. "Bruce's Act 'Obscene.'" Herald Tribune News Service, November 6, 1964.
Lamb, Bob. "The Journeymen Discover a New Musical Innovation." *Macon (GA) Telegraph and News*, October 20, 1963.
Shelton, Robert. "Folk Music Rings Out Vividly in Hootenanny at Carnegie Hall." *New York Times*, September 23, 1963.
Shelton, Robert. "Guitarist, 18, Charms Audiences." *New York Times*, July 13, 1963.
Shelton, Robert. "Old Music Taking on New Color." *New York Times*, August 17, 1963.
Shelton, Robert. "This Long-Haired Singer Is No Beatle." *New York Times*, February 21, 1964.
Strand, Alf. "Goateed Singer Uses 'Beat' Idioms Though He's Thoughtful Musician." *Leader-Post* (Regina, SK), April 25, 1963.
Wilson, John S. "Cabaret Business Nears Low Point." *New York Times*, March 12, 1964.
Wolfe, Paul. "The 'New' Bob Dylan." *Broadside*, December 20, 1964.
Zitrin, Richard. "He's a Changed Man." *Akron (OH) Beacon-Journal*, January 18, 1976.

CHAPTER FIVE: 1965–1967

Author interviews: Eric Andersen, Roy Blumenfeld, David Bromberg, Peppy Castro, Judy Collins, Noam Dworman, Eric Eisner, Gary Giddins, Arthur Gorson, Arlo Guthrie, John Hammond, Erik Jacobsen, Danny Kalb, Jonathan Kalb, Lucy Brown Karwoski, Steve Katz, Lenny Kaye, Peter Kogan, Al Kooper, Barry Kornfeld, Lowell Levinger, Arthur Levy, Phillip

Namanworth, Jack Prelutsky, John Sebastian, Mark Sebastian, Marc Silber, Jason Solomon, Terri Thal, Happy Traum, Jesse Colin Young.

"Blues Project Is Complete Band." *Times Tribune Sun* (Scranton, PA), June 18, 1967.

Glover, Bob. "'Teeny Boppers' Invade the Village." *Daily Register*, October 11, 1966.

Larratt, Pamela. "Folk-Rock Sounds at Bushnell." *Hartford Courant*, October 28, 1966.

Larson, John. "Wild New 'Blues Project' Plays Electronic Folk-Rock." *Daily Sun* (San Bernardino, CA), July 9, 1966.

Lax, Eric. "Why Do Young People Love 'Lemmings'?" *New York Times*, May 27, 1973.

Lloyd, Jack. "'Lemmings' Is a Put Down That Only Youth Can Serve." *Philadelphia Inquirer*, November 4, 1973.

Marra, Joe. "The Desperate Days of the Lovin' Spoonful." *Sixteen*, December 1965.

McCurdy, Glen A. "The Making of a Folk-Rock Legend 1967." *Chicago Tribune*, May 14, 1967.

Nachman, Gerald. "Close Up: Folk Singer." *New York Post*, June 17, 1965.

O'Neill, Edward. "City Will Pack in Cabaret Cards." New York *Daily News*, August 9, 1967.

Scott, Vernon. "Being Alive, Young and 'With It.'" United Press International, July 25, 1967.

Shelton, Robert. "Phil Ochs Returns with Own Songs." *New York Times*, November 25, 1966.

"A Symposium: Is Folk Rock Really 'White Rock?'" *New York Times*, February 20, 1966.

"Tyrone Youths." *Tyrone (PA) Daily Herald*, June 16, 1973.

Von Hoffman, Nicholas. "The Exodus from the Village." *Chicago Daily News*, February 21, 1966.

Wilson, John S. "The Two Faces of Nina Simone." *New York Times*, December 31, 1967.

CHAPTER SIX: 1968–1975

Author interviews: Peter Aaron, Bruce Alterman, Eric Andersen, Scott Barretta, John Berenzy, Roy Blumenfeld, David Bromberg, Denny Brown, Chevy Chase, Sharon D'Lugoff, Erik Frandsen, Debbie Goodman, Arthur Gorson, Christopher Guest, Kristian Hoffman, David Hood, Janis Ian, David Johansen, Danny Kalb, Lenny Kaye, Carol Klenfner, Rod MacDonald, Phillip Namanworth, Sonny Ochs, Allan Pepper, Binky Philips, Ron Radosh, Susan Martin Robbins, Suzzy Roche, Terre Roche, Arlen Roth, Paul Samwell-Smith, Marc Silber, Jason Solomon, Rob Stoner, Michael Tannen, Terri Thal, Catherine Todd, Happy Traum, Jane Traum, Loudon Wainwright III.

"All That Jazz." New York *Daily News*, October 29, 1971.

Bottel, Helen. "Your Port in a Storm: Helen Help Us!" *Daily Item* (Sunbury, PA), August 31, 1968.

Braudy, Susan. "James Taylor, a New Troubadour." *New York Times*, February 21, 1971.

Burnham, David. "A Wide Disparity Is Found in Crime Throughout City." *New York Times*, February 14, 1972.

Campbell, Mary. "Blues Project Together Again for Three Concerts." Associated Press, July 12, 1973.

Canby, Vincent. "Talent Scouts for College Cafes Are Convened at the Bitter End." *New York Times*, June 25, 1968.

Carmody, Deirdre. "Woman, 28, Slain in the 'Village.'" *New York Times*, August 9, 1973.

Corwin, R. David, Jerome Krase, and Paula Hudis. "Greenwich Village: Statistical Trends and Observations." New York University, October 1969.

Elwood, Philip. "Rollicking 'Wonders' Back Again." *San Francisco Chronicle*, May 28, 1971.

Feather, Leonard. "Situation in New York Depicts Struggle of Jazz in Club Scene." *Los Angeles Times*, June 23, 1968.

Fields, Sidney. "Young-Old Mind of Janis Ian Bridges Communication Gap." *Buffalo Evening News*, December 1, 1967.

"Folk Singers to Perform Monday at Student Center." *Daily Advertiser* (Fayette, LA), October 31, 1970.

Gillin, Beth. "Van Ronk Gone Wrong?" *Courier-Post* (Camden, NJ), April 13, 1968.

Greenhouse, Linda. "At the Precincts: Asking for Blood and Decrying It." *New York Times*, August 26, 1973.

"Hotel Collapse Forces Relocation of Four Plays." *New York Times*, August 9, 1973.

"Irate Village Demands City Move Addicts." New York *Daily News*, April 11, 1971.

Jahn, Mike. "Lament for the Village." *Baltimore Sun*, January 21, 1973.

Johnson, Pete. "Len Chandler—Man Who Makes the News Musical." *Los Angeles Times*, November 3, 1968.

Kahn, Joseph. "Hotel Wall Blamed in Collapse." *New York Post*, October 5, 1973.

Kifner, John. "Cafe Figaro Shuts Doors in 'Village.'" *New York Times*, January 1, 1969.

Lee, Vincent, Philip McCarthy, Robert Crane, and John Murphy. "Old Village Hotel Collapses." New York *Daily News*, August 4, 1973.

Leogrande, Ernest. "The Cream Cheese Incident." New York *Daily News*, November 1, 1975.

Leogrande, Ernest. "The $155-an-Hour Ego Trip." New York *Daily News*, September 4, 1970.

Leogrande, Ernest. "New Beginning for End." New York *Daily News*, May 24, 1975.

"Letter to the Editor: Jude Roche." *Sunday Record Call* (Hackensack, NJ), June 1, 1969.

Lloyd, Jack. "Pure Folk Music Is Alive at the Lair." *Philadelphia Inquirer*, December 14, 1974.

Marsh, Dave. "Bottom Line Ascending as Max's Tries to Hang On." *Newsday*, September 16, 1974.

"Mercer Arts Center Is Undamaged, Mostly." *New York Times*, August 4, 1973.

Mills, Josh. "Keeping on Top at the Bottom Line." New York *Daily News*, February 9, 1975.

Montgomery, Paul L. "Hotel Had Been Fined Before Collapse." *New York Times*, August 5, 1973.

O'Haire, Patricia. "Dylan Misses Big-30 Bash." New York *Daily News*, May 24, 1971.

"Panhandlers Stalk Streets and Shops in the Village." *Buffalo Evening News*, August 30, 1968.

Parker, Jerry. "Clubs: Birthday Jam." *Newsday*, May 16, 1972.

Phillips, McCandlish. "Mercer Stages Are a Supermarket." *New York Times*, November 2, 1971.

"Rock & Roll Offed at Cafe Au Go Go." *Rolling Stone*, December 27, 1969.

Rockwell, John. "Music Clubs Resist Perils of Overkill." *New York Times*, August 4, 1974.

Rockwell, John. "The Pop Life." *New York Times*, August 2, 1974.

Rudis, Al. "Loudon Wainwright III—Fabulous Songs and Unique Style." *Chicago Sun-Times*, November 29, 1970.

Schumach, Murray. "Broadway Central Hotel Collapses." *New York Times*, August 4, 1973.

Seligsohn, Leo. "They're Putting It to the Rock Generation." *Newsday*, September 6, 1973.

Shepard, Richard F. "Janis Ian, 16, Sings Well for Her Age." *New York Times*, August 7, 1967.

Stone, Marilyn M. "Songs Are Because of Things That Happen to You." *Poughkeepsie (NY) Journal*, August 23, 1970.

Truscott IV, Lucian K. "Bob Dylan: Freewheelin' Through the Village." *Rolling Stone*, August 28, 1975.

Truscott IV, Lucian K. "Gay Power Comes to Sheridan Square." *Village Voice*, July 3, 1969.

Walker, Gerald. "The Rock Road Leads to the Bottom Line." *New York Times*, May 4, 1975.

Watt, Douglas. "'Lemmings' Is a Wow at the Village Gate." New York *Daily News*, January 27, 1973.

Whitbread, Jane. "Runaways." *Look*, July 25, 1967.

CHAPTER SEVEN: 1976–1980

Author interviews: Lili Añel, John Berenzy, Mort Cooperman, Peter Cunningham, Peggy Duncan-Garner, Steve Forbert, Robert Fripp, Kate Greenfield, Michael Hill, Robin Hirsch, Phil Hurtt, Lucy Kaplansky, Joe Lauro, Maria Kenny, D. C. LaRue, Christine Lavin, Rod MacDonald, Carolyne Mas, David Massengill, Ira Mayer, Paul Mills, Willie Nile, Allan Pepper, Roger Probert, Ron Radosh, Suzzy Roche, Terre Roche, John Rockwell, Brian Rose, Bridget St. John, Cristy St. John, Larry Sloman, Michael Tannen, Loudon Wainwright III, Elijah Wald, Lucinda Williams, Robbie Woliver.

Brady, Shaun. "Sex, Drugs and Jazz." *Jazz Times*, July-August, 2016.

Cruickshank, Ken. "Ex-Student Editor Wins New Trial in Libel Case." *Hartford Courant*, September 28, 1973.

Emerson, Ken. "The Village People: America's Male Ideal?" *Rolling Stone*, October 5, 1978.

Finkelstein, Mel. "The Monster of Fifth Avenue." New York *Daily News*, October 14, 1979.

King, Bill. "Carolyne Mas Part of New Village Wave?" *Atlanta Constitution*, October 12, 1979.

Lawson, Terry. "Dave Van Ronk: 'I'm Bored' by Most of What Passes as Pop Music These Days." *Journal Herald* (Dayton, OH), July 22, 1978.

Lee, Vincent, and Harry Stathos. "Nab 10 in Village Attack; Say It Was over Pot." New York *Daily News*, September 11, 1976.

McGavin, Jack. "As a Folksinger, Dave Van Ronk Has Been Around." *Morning Call* (Allentown, PA), November 2, 1978.

Meier, Andrew. "'The Only People They Hit Were Black': When a Race Riot Roiled New York." *New York Times*, December 10, 2022.

Musto, Michael. "Village People Go Macho." *New York Times*, June 15, 1979.

"Neighborhood Changes in New York City During the 1970s: Are the 'Gentry' Returning?" *Federal Reserve Bank of New York Quarterly Review*, Winter, 1983-1984.

Nelsen, Don. "Horn of Plenty—Jazz in New York." New York *Daily News*, November 4, 1977.

Nelsen, Don. "Variety Is Name of Game at Brecker Bros. Place." New York *Daily News*, March 1, 1979.

"Nixon Cartoon in Student Paper Brings Three Arrests." United Press International, November 23, 1968.

Palmer, Robert. "Willie Nile Sings Rock and Folk." *New York Times*, July 29, 1978.

Peck, Abe. "The Village People—The Cartoon That Conquered the World." *Rolling Stone*, April 19, 1979.

Rockwell, John. "After Politics, There's Rock, Disco or Pop Clubs to Visit." *New York Times*, August 8, 1980.

Rockwell, John. "'Cornelia Street' Evokes Mood of Folk-Music Scene." *New York Times*, July 3, 1980.

Rockwell, John. "Folk Music Is Back with a Twang." *New York Times*, April 30, 1978.

Rockwell, John. "Roche Sisters Are Now a Trio." *New York Times*, March 21, 1978.

Rockwell, John. "The Roches—A Highly Promising Folk Trio." *New York Times*, April 1, 1979.

Rockwell, John. "Steve Forbert, New Folk Singer." *New York Times*, December 3, 1977.

Rockwell, John. "The Three Roches." *New York Times*, May 17, 1979.

Tomasson, Robert E. "Man, 22, Dies of Injuries Suffered in Washington Square Gang Rampage." *New York Times*, September 14, 1976.

Treaster, Joseph B. "White Youths Attack Blacks in Washington Square." *New York Times*, September 9, 1976.

Zapol, Liza. "Oral History Interview: Maria Kenny." Greenwich Village Society for Historic Preservation, South Village, 2015.

CHAPTER EIGHT: 1981–1986

Author interviews: Steve Addabbo, Eric Andersen, Danny Bensusan, Steven Bensusan, Shawn Colvin, James Cromwell, Mark Dann, Dennis Diken, Donna Diken, Ron Fierstein, Erik Frandsen, Michael Hill, Nancy Jeffries, Lucy Kaplansky, Joe Lauro, Christine Lavin, Rod MacDonald, Carolyne Mas, David Massengill, Paul Mills, Angela Page, Allan Pepper, Suzzy Roche, Terre Roche, Brian Rose, Jay Rosen, Suzanne Vega, Vincent T. Vok, Andrea Vuocolo, Robbie Woliver.

Carlton, Bill. "Dylan Sound-Alikes to Sing." New York *Daily News*, July 19, 1982.

"Folk City Ends 25-Year West Village Stand." *New York Times*, March 28, 1986.

Gaiter, Dorothy J. "A Tame Trip to the 'Village.'" *New York Times*, May 26, 1982.

Hinckley, David. "Folk Music Finds Outlet." New York *Daily News*, March 14, 1984.

McLaughlin, Jeff. "Trying to Make a Go at It." *Boston Globe*, March 4, 1985.

Siskel, Gene. "Most Frightening Horror of 'I Spit on Your Grave' Is Its Mainstream America Audience." *Chicago Tribune*, July 14, 1980.

Stokes, Geoffrey. "Just Like a Dylan." *Village Voice*, August 3, 1982.

"Students to Visit Village Despite 'Raw Lifestyles' Fears." *Post-Star* (Glen Falls, NY), May 22, 1982.

Vega, Suzanne. "The Songwriters Exchange." *CooP: The Fast Folk Musical Magazine*, March, 1982.

Weiss, Murray. "Won't Tighten Security at Dancin' Ron's Building." New York *Daily News*, February 23, 1981.

Wilson, Earl. "It Happened Last Night." Syndicated, December 24, 1980.
White, Joyce. "The Village Cop." New York *Daily News*, September 23, 1982.

EPILOGUE: 2002–2004

Author interviews: Lili Añel, Shawn Colvin, Mort Cooperman, Sharon D'Lugoff, Kate Greenfield, Mitch Greenhill, Christine Lavin, David Massengill, Terre Roche, Eve Silber, Suzanne Vega, Andrea Vuocolo.

Anderson, John. "Success—From a Distance." *Newsday*, December 2, 1990.
Bowles, Pete, and Rafer Guzmán. "Bottom Line: It's Over." New York *Daily News*, January 24, 2004.
Breslin, Jimmy. "Imperiled Village Gate Opened Way to Genius." *Newsday*, June 1, 1983.
McShane, Larry. "Famous N.Y. Club Falls to Bottom Line." Associated Press, September 20, 2003.
Singleton, Don. "Owner Asks Stars to Save Bitter End." New York *Daily News*, May 17, 1992.

ARCHIVES AND COLLECTIONS

Cafe Society and Five Spot memorabilia, Ivan Black Collection (JPB 06-20), New York Public Library for the Performing Arts.
Back issues of *Caravan*, *Gardyloo*, and *Chooog 2-5*, the Southwest Collection/Special Collections Library, Texas Tech University, Lubbock, Texas.
David Hajdu, interviews with Mary Travers and Sam Charters, 1997–1998.
Newbold Morris memos, March 1961; Department of Parks memo, March 19, 1961; Borough President memo, March 19, 1961; letter to Israel (Izzy) Young, March 28, 1961; letter from Executive Officer, April 3, 1961; letters to Morris, April 13 and April 14, 1961; letter to Wagner from Socialist Workers Party, May 6, 1961; letters from Morris, April 24, May 10, May 11, May 16, and May 23, 1961; letter to Theodore Bikel, June 15, 1961; New York City Department of Parks General Files, Manhattan, Washington Square Park, NYC Municipal Archives.
"Suze Rotolo." FBI file for Suze Rotolo, document 100-HQ-435482.
"Robert Shelton Folk Rock Feud," "Izzy Young/the Bronx," "Folklore Center Ca. 1958," Richard A. Reuss papers, Collection C6, Indiana University Archives, Bloomington, Indiana.
"Dave Van Ronk." FBI file for Dave Van Ronk, documents 100-440146, 100-136446, courtesy Aaron J. Leonard.
Elijah Wald, interviews with Sam Hood, Hugh Romney (Wavy Gravy), and Len Chandler (some conducted with Dave Van Ronk), in the Elijah Wald Collection #20522, Southern Folklife Collection, Wilson Library, University of North Carolina at Chapel Hill.
Israel (Izzy) Young interview conducted by Richard A. Reuss, transcript, in the Ronald D. Cohen Collection #20239, Southern Folklife Collection, Wilson Library, University of North Carolina at Chapel Hill.
Israel (Izzy) Young, Washington Square Park "beatnik riot" scrapbook, compiled and organized by Mitch Blank. Izzy Young collection (AFC 2015/040), box 23, Library of Congress, American Folklife Center.

VIDEOS AND AUDIO

Randy Brecker interview, "Seventh Avenue South and the Loft Scene," Facebook.

Kevin Burke, *Your Hometown* podcast, Museum of the City of New York, episode 11, "Suzanne Vega—East Harlem and the Upper West Side, Manhattan," 2021.

Art D'Lugoff interviews (parts 1A to 1G), 2020, Rafi DL channel, YouTube.

John Gilliland, "Pop Chronicles Interviews #40—José Feliciano," audio recording, 1969, University of North Texas Libraries, UNT Digital and UNT Music Library.

Elijah Wald, "Old Friends: A Songobiography," www.elijahwald.com/songblog.

index